Sanctity and Pilgrimage in Medieval Southern Italy, 1000–1200

Southern Italy's strategic location at the crossroads of the Mediterranean gave it a unique position as a frontier for the major religious faiths of the medieval world, where Latin Christian, Greek Christian and Muslim communities coexisted. In this study, the first to offer a comprehensive analysis of sanctity and pilgrimage in southern Italy between 1000 and 1200, Paul Oldfield presents a fascinating picture of a politically and culturally fragmented land which, as well as hosting its own important relics as significant pilgrimage centres, was a transit point for pilgrims and commercial traffic. Drawing on a diverse range of sources from hagiographical material to calendars, martyrologies, charters and pilgrim travel guides, the book examines how sanctity functioned at this key cultural crossroads and, by integrating the analysis of sanctity with that of pilgrimage, offers important new insights into society, cross-cultural interaction and faith in the region and across the medieval world.

Paul Oldfield is Lecturer in Medieval History at the University of Manchester. His previous publications include *City and Community in Norman Italy* (Cambridge, 2009).

D1452483

Abstract

This monograph represents the first comprehensive study of sanctity and pilgrimage in medieval southern Italy in the period 1000 to 1200, and contributes to a deeper understanding of both the region as it moved through profound transitions and the medieval-wide development of sanctity and pilgrimage. As the region was highly unusual in sheltering Greek Christian, Latin Christian and Muslim communities, this study represents a chance, through the examination of sanctity and pilgrimage, to offer a new perspective on a politically and culturally fragmented land which acted as a Mediterranean frontier for the major religious faiths of the medieval world, and to analyse how sanctity functioned at such a key cultural crossroads. It also offers the opportunity to compare sanctity in a liminal zone with other forms throughout Europe, addressing the extent to which southern Italy was marginalized. Thus the monograph explores the impact of high-level political transitions, Church reform and urbanization on South Italian saints' cults; it examines the interface between Latins and Greeks through the prism of South Italian–Greek saints; and it tracks the revival of sanctity on the island of Sicily as it moved from Muslim to Christian control. At the same time, the analysis of external and internal pilgrimage patterns evidences the nature of southern Italy's connections to the wider world, its role in the topography of international pilgrimage and the existence of internal frontiers within the region itself. One consequence of increasing pilgrim traffic to southern Italy seems to have been the dissemination throughout Europe of classical, folkloric and pagan legends which gave the region a sense of otherness and the sinister overlaid with the romantic and mystical. When contrasted with the region's strategic location as a bridge between the two main Christian pilgrimage centres of Rome and Jerusalem, and its integration into the Crusading movement, southern Italy was indeed enveloped in a raft of contradictions which appear to have left an enduring legacy.

This work is supported by

Arts & Humanities
Research Council

Sanctity and Pilgrimage in Medieval Southern Italy, 1000–1200

Paul Oldfield

University of Manchester

CAMBRIDGE
UNIVERSITY PRESS

University Printing House, Cambridge CB2 8BS, United Kingdom

One Liberty Plaza, 20th Floor, New York, NY 10006, USA

477 Williamstown Road, Port Melbourne, VIC 3207, Australia

4843/24, 2nd Floor, Ansari Road, Daryaganj, Delhi - 110002, India

79 Anson Road, #06-04/06, Singapore 079906

Cambridge University Press is part of the University of Cambridge.

It furthers the University's mission by disseminating knowledge in the pursuit of education, learning and research at the highest international levels of excellence.

www.cambridge.org
Information on this title: www.cambridge.org/9781316648902

© Paul Oldfield 2014

First published 2014
First paperback edition 2017

A catalogue record for this publication is available from the British Library

Library of Congress Cataloging in Publication data
Oldfield, Paul (Lecturer in medieval history)
Sanctity and pilgrimage in medieval southern Italy, 1000–1200 / Paul Oldfield, Manchester Metropolitan University.
     pages   cm
Includes bibliographical references.
ISBN 978-1-107-00028-5
1. Italy – Church history – 476–1400.   I. Title.
BR874.O43   2014
284.5′804–dc23   2013044464

ISBN 978-1-107-00028-5 Hardback
ISBN 978-1-316-64890-2 Paperback

To Kate, Finlay and Sebastian – smiles, mischief and adventures

Contents

Acknowledgements

Innumerable individuals deserve my sincerest gratitude for their invaluable assistance during the gestation and completion of this book. The Department of History and Economic History, Manchester Metropolitan University, provided generous teaching remission during the early stages of the project. Latterly, the support of the Department of History at the University of Manchester and its T. F. Tout fund, and the award of an Early Career Fellowship from the Arts and Humanities Research Council, along with valuable feedback from its anonymous reviewers, enabled me to draw the work together during its final challenging phases. The team at Cambridge University Press were also incredibly supportive; I am particularly grateful for the insightful comments of the anonymous reviewers, and for the guidance of my editorial team. I would also like to thank the editors of the *Journal of Ecclesiastical History* (volume 62, 2011) and of the *BBC History Magazine* (July 2012 edition) for granting me permission to reutilize parts of works published therein. Thanks are also due to Nick Scarle for producing the maps. Countless colleagues and peers have offered their assistance in far greater ways than I could have hoped. Drafts were read, articles and books dispatched to me, and queries of all types were repeatedly answered by Corinna Bottiglieri, Sulamith Brodbeck, Edoardo D'Angelo, Amalia Galdi, Ármann Jakobsson, Kathryn Jasper, Andrew Jotischky, Christopher MacEvitt, Alex Metcalfe, Maureen Miller, Rosemary Morris, Annliese Nef, Francesco Panarelli, Amy Remensnyder, Jonathan Shepard, Melanie Tebbutt, Elisabeth Van Houts, Carl Watkins, Chris Wickham, Ian Wood and none more so than Graham Loud, who continues to guide and inspire in equal measure. I also reserve a special debt of gratitude to Ian Moxon for meticulously proofreading the entire manuscript and offering innumerable suggestions for improvement. My research was also greatly enriched by feedback offered on papers delivered at the University of Manchester; at Queen's University, Belfast; and at All Souls College, Oxford. All errors and inaccuracies that remain within are mine, and mine alone.

I am also incredibly grateful for the support of friends and family; particularly my father (for his confidence in me) and my parents-in-law Sally (perhaps the historical novel next?) and John (who has now earned two exclamation marks!!). My mother passed away during the very early stages of this book but the years of her care and encouragement continue to live with me. This book was almost entirely written in an attic, up to which regularly filtered the wonderfully varied sounds of my two young boys and my wife all doing the sorts of things young families do. Cycles of laughter, tears, play, quarrels and even the silence of sleep accompanied the tapping on my keyboard. Occasionally also, those two small boys would pay the most welcome of visits, their fingers straying to delete buttons and light switches, leaving me smiling and renewed. I have the great pleasure in knowing that every time I reread this book I encounter those sounds and sights again, and to know that my family are truly part of this work. For when the idea for this book was born so too was my first son, Finlay, and by the time it was well on its way to completion my second, Sebastian, had arrived. And the one irreplaceable constant throughout has been my wife, Kate, who has accepted, supported, protected and nurtured in the fullest meaning of every one of those words. If pilgrimage is ultimately about the search for inner peace, I have been truly fortunate to not have to travel to find it. This book and my family have grown together, it is theirs, and I dedicate it to them with a gratitude that knows no bounds.

Abbreviations

AB	*Analecta Bollandiana*
Al. Tel.	*Alexandri Telesini Abbatis Ystoria Rogerii Regis Sicilie Calabrie atque Apulie*, ed. L. De Nava, FSI 112 (Rome, 1991).
Amatus	*Aimé du Mont-Cassin, Ystoire de li Normant*, ed. M. Guéret-Laferté (Paris, 2011).
AS	Acta Sanctorum
ASCL	*Archivio storico per la Calabria e la Lucania*
BISIME	*Bullettino dell'istituto storico italiano per il medio evo*
CDBI	*Le pergamene del duomo di Bari (952–1264)*, ed. G. B. Nitto de Rossi and F. Nitti di Vito, Codice diplomatico barese I (Bari, 1867).
CDBV	*Le pergamene di S. Nicola di Bari. Periodo normanno (1075–1194)*, ed. F. Nitti di Vito, Codice diplomatico barese V (Bari, 1902).
CDBVI	*Le pergamene di S. Nicola di Bari. Periodo svevo (1195–1266)*, ed. F. Nitti di Vito, Codice diplomatico barese VI (Bari, 1906).
Chron. Cas.	*Chronica Monasterii Casinensis*, ed. H. Hoffmann, MGH SS xxxiv (Hanover, 1980).
Falco	*Falcone di Benevento, Chronicon Beneventanum*, ed. E. D'Angelo (Florence, 1998).
FSI	Fonti per la storia d'Italia.
Historia S. Cataldi	*Historia Inventionis et Translationis S. Cataldi*, AS May, ii (Paris, 1866), 569–74.
Liber de Regno	*La Historia o Liber de Regno Sicilie e la Epistola ad Petrum Panormitane Ecclesie Thesaurium di Ugo Falcando*, ed. G. B. Siragusa, FSI 22 (Rome, 1897).
Malaterra	*De Rebus Gestis Rogerii Calabriae et Siciliae Comitis, Auctore Gaufredo Malaterra*, ed. E. Pontieri, RIS 5 (Bologna 1927–8).

MEFRM	*Mélanges de l'ecole française de Rome. Moyen âge*
MGH	Monumenta Germaniae Historica [SS = Scriptores; SRLI = Scriptores Rerum Langobardicarum et Italicarum]
RIS	*Rerum Italicarum Scriptores.*
Romuald	*Romualdi Salernitani Chronicon*, ed. C. A. Garufi, RIS 7 (i) (Città di Castello, 1935).
RS	Rolls Series
SM	*Studi medievali*
Trani	*Le carte che si conservano nell'archivio dello capitolo metropolitano della città di Trani (dal IX secolo fino all'anno 1266)*, ed. A. Prologo (Barletta, 1877).
Tyrants	*The History of the Tyrants of Sicily by 'Hugo Falcandus', 1154–1169*, trans. G. A. Loud and T. Wiedemann (Manchester, 1998).
VQPAC	*Vitae Quatuor Priorum Abbatum Cavensium*, ed. L. Mattei-Cerasoli, RIS 6 (v) (Bologna, 1941).
Wil. Apulia	*Guillaume de Pouille, La Geste de Robert Guiscard*, ed. and trans. M. Mathieu (Palermo, 1961).

Map 1. Southern Italy and Sicily

Map 2. The major routeways in southern Italy and Sicily

Introduction

Saints, pilgrimage and southern Italy

The day after the chest carrying the most holy Nicholas was transported by Abbot Elias [...] into the church of San Benedetto [of Bari], the rumour of an event so great and glorious spread with extraordinary speed beyond the walls of Bari. First it reached the settlements and villages in the territory of Bari, scattering this most happy news through the ears of everyone. And immediately, as if they were in a race, from all parts men and women of all ages rushed [to Bari]. What more can I say? Because of the dense ranks of men and women, of old and young, of the sick of all types, the widest streets and paths were extremely crowded; from here and there echoed hymns of praises sung with the highest voice. And in truth everyone together competed to praise, bless, and glorify Almighty God, who had deigned to enrich this region with so great a treasure, to have rendered it famous with such a great brilliance, to have visited upon it such great consolation and blessing.[1]

Thus John the Archdeacon of Bari described the ecstatic reception of the relics of St Nicholas at Bari in 1087, and the foundation in southern Italy of one of medieval Europe's most celebrated cults. Over recent decades scholars have significantly deepened our understanding of the sentiments, interrelationships, and cultural, religious and political exchanges which intersect in events such as those described by John.[2] As a result, we are able more than ever to appreciate how saints' cults, the practice of pilgrimage and the accompanying hagiographical texts, open new perspectives on all manner of fundamental features of medieval society. The region of southern Italy and Sicily, boasting an extensive body of hagiographical works, is no exception. It experienced profound transitions in the period

---

[1] P. Corsi, *La traslazione di San Nicola: le fonti* (Bari, 1988), 67.

[2] General studies include: P. Brown, *The Cult of the Saints. Its Rise and Function in Latin Christianity* (Chicago, 1981); A. Vauchez, *La Sainteté en Occident aux derniers siècles du moyen âge: d'après les procès de canonisation et les documents hagiographiques*, revised edn (Rome, 1988); P. J. Geary, *Furta Sacra. Thefts of Relics in the Central Middle Ages* (Princeton, 1978); V. Turner and E. Turner, *Image and Pilgrimage in Christian Culture. Anthropological Perspectives* (New York, 1978); specialist studies include: P. Golinelli, *Città e culto dei santi nel Medioevo Italiano*, new edn (Bologna, 1996); T. Head, *Hagiography and the Cult of Saints. The Diocese of Orleans 800–1200* (Cambridge, 1990).

running from 1000 to 1200, moving from a politically, ethnically and religiously diverse entity, with Muslim, Greek and Latin communities, to a unified monarchy (from 1130) ruled by descendants of Norman infiltrators, which was increasingly Latinized and subject to papal influence. During the same time span, southern Italy also experienced a renewed flourishing of saints' cults and pilgrimage, which functioned on a number of levels: the devotional, the psychological, the individual, the communal, the economic and the political. An investigation of saints' cults and pilgrimage in southern Italy offers new contributions towards a holistic understanding of both the diversity and uniformity present in a fragmented and complex region as it moved through deep changes. Fundamentally, it can focus our understanding of how the region functioned at the frontier of the Muslim, Greek and Latin worlds, and how sanctity itself developed in a liminal zone.

Saints' cults thrived and pilgrimage remained ever popular because of their multi-faceted value. Saints were divine intercessors; having walked on earth they thereafter mediated between the terrestrial and celestial. Their relics were deemed to have supernatural qualities, which increased in potency the nearer one was to them. The Central Middle Ages were a golden era of pilgrimage as more and more people of all backgrounds sought cures and spiritual assistance at the tombs of saints. In all manner of ways, saints and their shrines offered protection, legitimacy and support in an unstable and rapidly transforming world. Holy relics would especially reappear at times of insecurity and political turmoil. In the political landscape of southern Italy in which parvenu powers were a recurrent feature, whether they were Norman dukes, kings or emergent urban communities, sources of legitimacy were highly prized and carried great weight. Many power-holders and communities sought associations with a saint; their choice revealed much about their self-identity and conception of authority. Saints' acceptance could often signify important socio-political transitions, as when members of the Norman elite began to be treated favourably by South Italian saints in hagiographical works and historical narratives.[3] Conversely, a saint's disapproval of a ruler or a community served as a powerful rebuke generated by an opposing party. So significant was the role of saints, and the need to obtain their favour and their relics, that violence and crime often occurred and were justified in their name, as Patrick Geary has demonstrated so clearly.[4] Consequently, as well as being home to one of the most celebrated of *furta sacra*

---

[3] A. Galdi, *Santi, territori, potere e uomini nella Campania medievale (secc. XI–XII)* (Salerno, 2004), 61–6.
[4] Geary, *Furta Sacra*.

(St Nicholas at Bari) southern Italy and Sicily witnessed a series of other translations and relic thefts during the Central Middle Ages. Because of the qualities attached to them saints were often able to fuse fractious communities together and saints rapidly became symbols of cross-cultural interaction and unity for many, especially in Europe's expanding cities, and even (as we shall see in southern Italy) between Latin and Greek Christians. But these very virtues in turn created tension and, paradoxically, violent rivalries within and between communities. This assortment of qualities ensured that shrine centres remained at the core of communities, and that innumerable individuals opted to visit them, thus rendering the act of pilgrimage a conspicuous feature of the medieval landscape.

More widely still, in southern Italy in the Central Middle Ages sanctity and pilgrimage operated within, and reflected the collision of, diverse worlds: the meeting of different faiths, and ancient and contemporary forms of worship; the simultaneous flourishing of eremitism and urbanization; and the continued centrality of the local, while horizons were broadening and cross-cultural communication increasing. The fact that southern Italy could also boast possession of the relics of a series of 'A-list' universal saints meant that their shrines became important pilgrimage centres. The symbiosis between sanctity and pilgrimage was accentuated in southern Italy through its strategic position at the crossroads of the Mediterranean. It operated as a constant transit point for pilgrims and other commercial traffic, much of it moving to Rome and the eastern Mediterranean, and the evolution of international pilgrimage and the crusading movement would have a profound effect on South Italian sanctity.

In exploring sanctity and pilgrimage one must acknowledge and identify the limitations inherent in using hagiographical works. Myth, embellishment and plagiarism abound within the hagiographical text. Awareness of the hagiographer's aims is vital; his task was to place his saintly subject on a par with other, usually ancient, holy men and to do so required the use of a common set of exemplary motifs. John Howe called this 'hagiographic light' which reduced 'earthly events to silhouettes against a golden backdrop'.[5] Indeed, simply put, the hagiographical text was not designed to assist historical enquiry. But literary patterns contained within the texts carry important messages as does the seemingly incidental material included within these works. The historiography of relic cults has also long attempted to identify the varying influences upon

---

[5] J. Howe, *Church Reform and Social Change in Eleventh-Century Italy. Dominic of Sora and his Patrons* (Philadelphia, 1997), 66.

their construction.[6] Recent studies by scholars such as Simon Yarrow and Samantha Herrick have shown that both clerical and secular inputs into cults and their associated representations were crucial and often convergent. It would be misleading, for instance, to suggest that churchmen manipulated a submissive lay community. Recurrent evidence in miracle collections and other sources for lay dissent and unbelief indicates that churchmen could not simply ignore secular opinion and needed to structure its responses and messages in a manner which would resonate with the laity.[7] Certainly, the hagiographer often wrote for an audience that was not solely ecclesiastical or elite, for many of these texts formed the basis of sermons for feast celebrations, were thus read out publicly, often shaped to engage and entertain, and could be transmitted and transformed in oral exchanges within the wider lay community.[8] As saints' cults often functioned in a shared space and culture, the approval of both laity and clergy was integral. Thus hagiographical works can reasonably be viewed as constructions of a variety of communities, creating different traditions, and thus reflecting a mosaic of interests and beliefs.

As is the case for most regions of medieval Europe, hagiographical works are among the most abundant sources available to the historian of medieval southern Italy. *Vitae* (accounts of saints' lives), *miracula* (collections of, usually, posthumous saintly miracle-working) and records of translations of relics survive for many of southern Italy's saints, some produced almost contemporaneously, others decades or centuries after the saint's death. In many instances a number of overlapping local hagiographical traditions developed, some of which were wholly spurious. Those produced much later, and even the suspiciously inauthentic, still retain their value but in different ways – they elucidate how memory and truth functioned, how the past was understood and could be manipulated, and they show the splicing of contemporary concerns onto older subject matter. For example, wandering/eremetical saints were often founders of religious houses which subsequently developed into monastic orders, which then retrospectively composed *vitae* within a predominantly monastic framework.[9] Southern Italy in the period 1000 to 1200 could

---

[6] Most famously in the work of Brown, *Cult of the Saints*.
[7] Chapter 6 explores some of the challenges of using miracle collections to discern pilgrimage patterns.
[8] S. Yarrow, *Saints and their Communities. Miracle Stories in Twelfth-Century England* (Oxford, 2006), 16–120. See also B. De Gaiffier, 'L'Hagiographie et son public au Xi siècle', in his *Études critiques d'hagiographie et d'iconologie* (Brussels, 1967), 475–507; S. K. Herrick, *Imagining the Sacred Past. Hagiography and Power in Early Normandy* (Cambridge, Mass., 2007), 6–10.
[9] Galdi, *Santi*, 35–6, 80–1.

boast a prodigious production of hagiographical material, both textual and visual.[10] With its rich library, the renowned abbey of Montecassino led the way, especially in the eleventh century.[11] In the early to mid-twelfth century, the abbey's librarian Peter the Deacon also proved to be a prolific hagiographer, historian and forger.[12] Elsewhere, bishops and abbots composed or sponsored hagiographical works. Alfanus of Montecassino (d. 1085) continued to produce hagiographical material as archbishop of Salerno. Amandus, bishop of Bisceglie, compiled a hagiographical dossier on the discovery in 1168 of saints at Bisceglie, and earlier as a deacon of Trani wrote an account of the translation of St Nicholas the Pilgrim. The *vita* of St Gerard, bishop of Potenza, was composed by his successor Manfred, and *The History of the Translation of the Body of St Agatha from Constantinople to Catania* was the work of Maurice, bishop of Catania. In the late twelfth century the *bios* of the Greek-Italian saint, Vitalis of Castronuovo, was translated into Latin at the instigation of the bishop of Tricarico. Other hagiographers of medieval southern Italy tended to be part of the lower echelons of the Church, or were often simply anonymous: Nicephorus and John, who wrote competing accounts of the translation of St Nicholas to Bari, were a Benedictine monk and archdeacon respectively; John of Nusco, author of at least some sections of the *vita* of St William of Vercelli, was apparently a monk of Monte Goleto. However, as these works almost exclusively related to saints connected to their particular sees or monasteries, it remains difficult to identify any of these hagiographies as emerging from *scriptoria* which could be defined as centres of broader hagiographic production akin to Montecassino. Significantly, the important monasteries of Cava and Montevergine, both boasting saintly founders, as well as the city of Benevento where so many saints were translated in the Early Middle Ages, never developed into established centres for hagiographic output.[13] Likewise, in the Early Middle Ages Naples arguably created the most significant body of

---

[10] O. Limone, 'Italia meridionale (950–1220)', *Hagiographies II*, ed. G. Philippart, Corpus Christianorum (Turnhout, 1996), 11–60.

[11] See F. Newton, *The Scriptorium and Library at Monte Cassino, 1058–1105* (Cambridge, 1999).

[12] See *Petri Diaconi Ortus et Vita Iustorum Cenobii Castrensis*, ed. R. H. Rodgers (Berkeley, 1972); H. Bloch, *The Atina Dossier of Peter the Deacon of Montecassino. A Hagiographical Romance of the Twelfth Century* (Vatican City, 1998).

[13] 'The Lives of the First Four Abbots of Cava' appears not even to have been produced within Cava but at the abbey of SS Trinità di Venosa, probably by abbot Peter II (1141–56): H. Houben, 'L'autore delle "*Vitae Quatuor Priorum Abbatum Cavensium*"', *SM* 26 (1985), 871–9; a Beneventan exception could be the abbey of S. Sophia, which was reasonably productive in the hagiographic field: Galdi, *Santi*, 56, 271; A. Vuolo, 'Agiografia beneventana', *Longobardia e longobardi nell'Italia meridionale. Le istituzioni ecclesiastiche*, eds. G. Andenna and G. Picasso (Milan, 1996), 199–237.

hagiographical works anywhere in Europe, and yet after 1000 production diminished dramatically.

Nevertheless, collectively a huge body of hagiographical works was still produced in southern Italy between 1000 and 1200. In addition, the historian of South Italian sanctity and pilgrimage can also utilize a much wider base of material: calendars, martyrologies, necrologies, exultet rolls, charters (particularly those on urban privileges), narrative chronicles (Falco of Benevento's chronicle represents a valuable lay perspective on sanctity), pilgrim travel guides and onomastic patterns.[14] To these can be added evidence from coin dies, church dedications and, as art historians have long acknowledged, iconographic decoration in religious buildings, most famously from the royally sponsored Cappella Palatina and the Cathedral of Monreale.[15]

Despite, or perhaps because of, the existence of such a diverse range of source material pertaining to an equally diverse and fragmented region, a comprehensive analysis of the salient features of sanctity and pilgrimage in southern Italy in the Central Middle Ages has, to my mind, yet to be achieved. This is the principal aim of the present study. Of course, several superb works have been produced on particular elements of South Italian sanctity and pilgrimage by, among others, Thomas Head, Amalia Galdi, Oronzo Limone, Jean-Marie Martin and Antonio Vuolo. Yet, these tend to fall into three main categories: (1) works on sanctity and pilgrimage within particular regions;[16] (2) works on particular saints' typologies, or on individual saints;[17] (3) broader works on religion, belief and interfaith

---

[14] For excellent examples of South Italian necrologies and martyrologies see C. Hilken, *Memory and Community in Medieval Southern Italy. The History, Chapter Book, and Necrology of Santa Maria del Gualdo Mazzocca* (Toronto, 2008); for exultet rolls see T. F. Kelly, *The Exultet in Southern Italy* (Oxford, 1996); for naming evidence see M. Villani, 'Il contributo dell'onomastica e della toponomastica alla storia delle devozioni', *Pellegrinaggi e itinerari*, ed. G. Vitolo (Naples, 1999), 249–66.

[15] For coinage see L. Travaini, *La monetazione nell'Italia normanna* (Rome, 1995); for church decoration see S. Brodbeck, *Les Saints de la cathédrale de Monreale en Sicile* (Rome, 2010); O. Demus, *The Mosaics of Norman Sicily* (London, 1950); W. Tronzo, *The Cultures of his Kingdom: Roger II and the Cappella Palatina in Palermo* (Princeton, 1997); E. Borsook, *Messages in Mosaic. The Royal Programmes of Norman Sicily (1130–1187)* (Oxford, 1990).

[16] For example: T. Head, 'Discontinuity and discovery in the cult of saints: Apulia from late Antiquity to the High Middle Ages', *Hagiographica* 6 (1999), 171–211; Galdi, *Santi*; Vuolo, 'Agiografia beneventana', 199–237; J.-M. Martin, 'Les Modèles paléochrétiens dans l'hagiographie apulienne', *Bulletin de la société nationale des antiquaires de France* (1990), 67–86.

[17] For example: A. Vuolo, 'Monachesimo riformato e predicazione: la "vita" di San Giovanni da Matera (sec. XII)', *SM* 27 (1986), 69–121; O. Limone, *Santi monaci e santi eremeti; alla ricerca di un modello di perfezione nella letteratura agiografica dell'Apulia normanna* (Galatina, 1988); Howe, *Church Reform*.

relations in medieval southern Italy.[18] The present study thus aims to combine all these separate strands into one work, in a blended approach which spans two centuries, which does not exclude any region of southern Italy, which engages with an array of diverse source material, and which integrates an analysis of sanctity with that of pilgrimage in order to deepen our knowledge of society, cross-cultural interaction and faith in the region.

It is important here to establish some points of qualification and classification. First, unless specified, the label 'southern Italy' is used to cover the entire southern zone of modern-day Italy, stretching from the Abruzzi and the Campanian zones just south of Lazio to, and including, the island of Sicily. Second, the definition of 'saint' is of course a contested issue, and I opt for a more holistic interpretation. In other words, formal canonization, a surprisingly rare phenomenon in the Middle Ages, or the existence of contemporary forms of 'official' hagiographical and other evidence to affirm a cult are not here deemed the sole measures. A number of South Italian saints were either not officially approved by Rome, or their associated *vitae* or *miracula* were produced much later than their alleged lifetimes. Nevertheless, it is clear that contemporaries still deemed these figures to have saintly qualities, and that many of the later *vitae* or *miracula* were likely based on more contemporary accounts. Indeed, Aviad Kleinberg has shown that medieval perceptions of sanctity were extremely fluid and should be understood on a case-by-case basis. Beyond this, the attributions of 'supernatural spiritual power' and 'moral excellence' were the only loose criteria within which various hazy typologies of sainthood could function.[19] In short, if attempts were made in the period 1000 to 1200 to promote devotion for an individual as a saint, whether they were contemporary or ancient, or if a cult arose only after 1200 for an individual living between 1000 and 1200, these will all be considered. I have similarly aimed at a more inclusive interpretation of how to identify pilgrimage, as revealed in Chapters 5 and 6, which I hope brings new evidence into play. In both cases I am convinced that considering the widest spectrum offers the richest outcome. Of course, it must be understood that a work of this scope can make no claims to cover all aspects of all saints' cults and

---

[18] G. A. Loud, *The Latin Church in Norman Italy* (Cambridge, 2007); V. Ramseyer, *The Transformation of a Religious Landscape. Medieval Southern Italy 850–1150* (Ithaca, 2006); A. Metcalfe, *Muslims and Christians in Norman Italy. Arabic Speakers and the End of Islam* (London, 2003). The collected essays found in *Pellegrinaggi e itinerari dei santi nel Mezzogiorno medievale*, ed. G. Vitolo (Naples, 1999) and *Tra Roma e Gerusalemme nel Medioevo. Paessagi umani ed ambientali del pellegrinaggio meridionale*, ed. M. Oldoni, 3 vols (Salerno, 2005) cover elements across the three categories.

[19] A. M. Kleinberg, *Prophets in Their Own Country. Living Saints and the Making of Sainthood in the Later Middle Ages* (Chicago, 1997), 4–8.

patterns of pilgrimage which functioned in the years 1000 to 1200. Inevitably, I have not been able to explore certain themes and sources as deeply as they deserve – much more could be said, for example, on theological discourses on sanctity, on toponymic sources, or on the typology of miracles performed by specific saints. In most cases, cults enjoyed brief surges of activity before settling down to longer periods of seeming dormancy. I have mostly aimed to identify these surges and explore them thematically in order to highlight the main patterns in the evolution of sanctity and pilgrimage in southern Italy.

Thus, the present study is divided into the following sections. The second part of this introductory chapter offers a brief overview of the socio-political history of southern Italy from the Early Middle Ages until 1200 in order to assist readers in contextualizing what then follows. Chapter 1 provides an examination of South Italian sanctity in early medieval Italy in order to understand the legacies and models, and the continuities and disruptions, which shaped the evolution of sanctity after 1000. Geographically it covers the whole of southern Italy, exploring how sanctity in Campania functioned under the Lombards, created conflicts and aided the creation of embryonic civic identities; how saints' cults in Apulia were marked by instability; and how Siculo-Calabrian sanctity was forged within a triangular relationship between Rome, Byzantium and Islam. Thereafter, Chapters 2, 3 and 4 examine sanctity between 1000 and 1200, doing so along both geographic and thematic lines. Chapter 2 focuses primarily on saints and their cults in the Latin zones of mainland southern Italy and assesses the impact on them of some key forces – the Normans, Church reform and urbanization. Chapter 3 addresses evidence for cross-cultural interaction between Latins and Greeks by analysing Greek–Italian saints and cults, and locates its findings within the wider relationships that evolved between eastern and western Christianity. Chapter 4 examines the role of sanctity in the island of Sicily as it was re-Christianized under Norman rule, tracing the extent to which old cults were revived and new saints found to augment Sicily's sacred map. As Palermo also became the centre of the new Kingdom of Sicily after 1130, the chapter also considers the role of saints in the 'capital', and the promotion of cults by the monarchy. The second part of the book, composed of Chapters 5 and 6, focuses directly on pilgrimage. Chapter 5 examines southern Italy's fundamental role in the topography of international pilgrimage. Its strategic location, its emerging infrastructures and its own renowned shrines attracted streams of pilgrims on their path to salvation. At the same time, southern Italy's classical and folkloric traditions, and its challenging landscapes, conferred upon it a sinister and dangerous quality which many pilgrims could not have avoided.

Chapter 6 considers more directly pilgrimage activity at South Italian shrines, and tracks the origins, identities and destinations of the pilgrims found there. In addition the chapter addresses the extent to which these patterns might have eroded internal frontiers within southern Italy, and also examines the presence of southern Italians at shrines beyond the region.

Throughout this study South Italian sanctity and pilgrimage will be consistently located within their wider context, and contrasts and comparisons made where appropriate. Indeed, Chapters 3 and 5 are implicitly based on the region's connectivity with other territories. To be able to identify any defining patterns within sanctity and pilgrimage in medieval southern Italy would allow fruitful comparison with other regions of Europe, and further pursuit of the age-old question of southern Italy's perceived marginality. Indeed, it seems in fact that southern Italy should be placed more to the centre rather than on the periphery of many core medieval developments, as a result of its location in the Mediterranean, and of its simultaneous and intimate interfaces with the Latin, Greek and Islamic worlds. In the context of sanctity and pilgrimage, these factors undoubtedly made the region a holy crossroads, one which played a pivotal role in the growing internationalism of sanctity. At the same time, its unique location at a crossroads heavily shaped South Italian forms of sanctity and pilgrimage, opening them to a myriad of external influences.

Religion, society and politics: the South Italian background

(i)   Late Antiquity and the Early Middle Ages

The development of saints' cults in southern Italy before 1000 was set against the backdrop of some of the great socio-religious and political transitions which took place in the Mediterranean: the metamorphosis of structures inherited from the Roman world, cycles of invasion and changes in rulership, and the increased interaction of different religious faiths.[20] Unified control of southern Italy and Sicily, achieved in the Roman period, and briefly reasserted by the Byzantines during the Gothic War (536–54), proved thereafter to be a chimera which would not rematerialize in any substantive form until the twelfth century.[21] The region suffered recurrent invasions and the establishment of various, competing

---

[20] For a masterful account of these transitions see C. Wickham, *The Inheritance of Rome. A History of Europe from 400 to 1000* (London, 2009).

[21] Excellent overviews of the pre-Norman period can be found in G. A. Loud, *The Age of Robert Guiscard. Southern Italy and the Norman Conquest* (Harlow, 2000), 12–59; Loud,

regimes. The Ostrogothic invasion was followed by the Gothic War, and Justinian's efforts to reintegrate southern Italy and Sicily into the 'Roman Empire'. However, the arrival of the Lombards in 568 set the pattern for centuries of fluctuating zones of influence. The establishment of a Lombard duchy at Benevento, elevated to a principality in 774, increasingly confined Byzantine control to Sicily and to restricted parts of Apulia, Lucania and Calabria by the mid-eighth century. By this point, the settlement patterns of parts of southern Italy had been fundamentally altered through warfare and plague. In Apulia, for example, a number of urban centres had collapsed, and episcopal sees had been rendered defunct; by the ninth century there were only six bishoprics whereas there had been fifteen three centuries earlier.[22] The political landscape of southern Italy was dramatically transformed further in the ninth century with the beginning of the Muslim conquest of Sicily in 827, an extended process which was not complete until the fall of the last Byzantine stronghold at Taormina in 902. The repercussions of the rise of Muslim power and naval dominance in the Mediterranean also impacted on the South Italian mainland.[23] In Apulia intervention took on a semi-permanent manifestation when the major cities of Taranto (846–80) and Bari (847–71) fell under Muslim rule and were established as emirates.[24] Elsewhere, the Muslim presence was characterized by raiding and the establishment of short-term bases. Muslim raids on Calabria and coastal Campania were frequent and devastating. In the 880s the great Northern Campanian monasteries of S. Vincenzo al Volturno and Montecassino were destroyed and their monks forced into exile, while a Muslim base was established at the mouth of the Garigliano River (c.880–915). Muslim bands on the mainland forged ad hoc alliances with local Christian powers, most notably with the Neapolitans in the mid-ninth century. Some were hired as mercenaries by Lombard rulers and played an influential role in the civil war that engulfed the Beneventan principality in the mid-ninth century.

This civil war splintered South Italian Lombard power into separate principalities based on Benevento, Capua and Salerno; the three would never again simultaneously fall under the rule of one dynasty. The rivalries of the cities on the coast of the Tyrrhenian Sea – Naples, Gaeta and

Latin Church, 10–59; A. Metcalfe, *The Muslims of Medieval Italy* (Edinburgh, 2009), 4–87; B. Kreutz, *Before the Normans. Southern Italy in the Ninth and Tenth Centuries* (Philadelphia, 1991).

[22] J.-M. Martin, *La Pouille du VI au XII siècle* (Rome, 1993), 146–60, 248–50; Loud, *Latin Church*, 17–19.

[23] Metcalfe, *Muslims of Medieval Italy*, 4–32; C. D. Stanton, *Norman Naval Operations in the Mediterranean* (Woodbridge, 2011), 9–24.

[24] G. Musca, *L'emirato di Bari, 847–71* (Bari, 1964); Metcalfe, *Muslims of Medieval Italy*, 16–22.

Amalfi – only added further disunity. In the meantime, despite losing Sicily, Byzantine power on the mainland revived from the late-ninth century. A series of campaigns restored large parts of Apulia, especially Bari, northern Calabria and Lucania, to Byzantine control, and saw the creation of new Byzantine provinces (*themata*), indicative of greater stability.[25] The Byzantine resurgence continued steadily throughout the tenth century, pushing into the zone of northern Apulia, where the majority population was Latin-rite, briefly intervening in Campania, and sparking a further series of inconclusive campaigns against the Lombard powers, who from the 960s were able to counter with sporadic support from the Ottonian emperors. By the end of the tenth century Ottonian intervention had proved to be of limited success, and a more fixed border emerged between the Lombard and Byzantine zones. But southern Italy was far from stable. With the partial exception of Salerno, the Lombard principalities were becoming decentralized and vulnerable; the increasing appearance of fortified settlements (*castella*), a process termed *incastellamento*, created minor centres of aristocratic power which fragmented princely prerogatives.[26] In Byzantine territories rebellions among the Lombard populations of Apulia were causing acute challenges, and Muslim raids increased in intensity. A Muslim attack, for instance, was recorded on Oria in 977, which left the city in flames and apparently saw the entire community deported to Sicily, while in 988 a raid on Bari resulted in the enslavement of men and women.[27] Even in Islamic Sicily internal factionalism was creating a volatile climate as this 'frontier' island was split by cycles of civil strife.[28]

Another complex entity overlaid the mosaic of political, cultural and religious forces: the Christian Church. As the cultural and doctrinal divide began to widen between western and eastern Christendom, some of the early manifestations of a pending religious schism between the two could be detected in southern Italy where both forms of the Christian faith converged. Both the papacy and the patriarch of Constantinople competed for jurisdictional ascendancy over southern Italy, each hoping that this would ensure the region's loyalties. In many ways this competition was motivated as much by politics as it was by religion. During the reign of Emperor Leo III (717–41), and the Iconoclast dispute, the ecclesiastical jurisdiction of Calabria and Sicily was transferred to Constantinople from

---

[25] For Byzantine southern Italy more generally see V. Von Falkenhausen, *Untersuchungen über die byzantinische Herrschaft in Süditalien vom 9. bis ins 11. Jahrhundert* (Wiesbaden, 1967).
[26] Loud, *Age of Robert Guiscard*, 44–7.
[27] *Lupus Protospatharius, Annales*, ed. G. H. Pertz, MGH SS v (Hanover, 1844), 55, 56.
[28] Metcalfe, *Muslims of Medieval Italy*, 36, 47–8, 53–4, 69–79.

Rome. This situation prevailed broadly until the Norman conquest of Calabria and Sicily, although in the latter region it appears that diocesan structures had collapsed under Islamic rule. Especially in the second half of the tenth century, both the papacy, aiming to recover its lost jurisdiction in southern Italy and influenced equally by Ottonian policies, and Byzantium attempted to create new episcopal structures in southern Italy to safeguard intervention from the other side, or as a tool to advance further jurisdictional claims. The papacy promoted Capua (966), Benevento (969) and Salerno (c.983) to archiepiscopal status. Some were given suffragan sees in areas located in Lombard–Byzantine borderlands, as well as within Byzantine Italy itself: Benevento was given suffragan sees in Byzantine Capitanata, and Salerno in Byzantine Lucania and Calabria.[29] In response Byzantium, hoping to affirm local loyalties to the empire, raised a number of sees to archbishoprics, particularly in the Lombard areas of Byzantine Apulia (these included Trani, Brindisi and Siponto). For both parties these represented potentially incendiary redrawings of the South Italian ecclesiastical map.

It was also apparent that by the later tenth century the papacy was aiming to establish a more ordered Church organization in southern Italy. The roots of the great eleventh-century Church reform movement were visible, but still, as one eminent scholar noted, the Church in southern Italy remained distinctly disorganized by 1000. Effective archiepiscopal authority was embryonic at best; some areas of the ecclesiastical map remained merely as blueprints whereas others were riddled by competing claims, and lay influence on the Church was marked.[30] By c.1000, the main feature of both the secular and monastic churches in southern Italy was their fluid and amorphous character. South Italian monasticism had suffered from a combination of invasions, raids and aristocratic usurpations in the Early Middle Ages, which was only partially offset by the Christianization of the Lombards and patronage from their elites. In Sicily, under Islamic rule, some important fragments of a monastic network survived, and the Christian faith may have been more robust there than traditionally considered, but it was still in a highly disordered state, and the secular church fared worse still.[31] Only in the second half of the tenth century is it possible to detect early signs of recovery throughout mainland southern Italy in the form of new monastic foundations and

---

[29] Loud, *Latin Church*, 33–5.
[30] Loud, *Latin Church*, 36–44; Ramseyer, *Transformation*, 7–110.
[31] Metcalfe, *Muslims and Christians*, 13–18; Metcalfe, *Muslims of Medieval Italy*, 35; see also generally L. T. White Jr's classic study, *Latin Monasticism in Norman Sicily* (Cambridge Mass., 1938).

restructuring programmes. Monasticism was also peculiarly varied in southern Italy where it was heavily influenced by Greek forms emanating from Sicily, Calabria and Lucania. Eremitic, lavriotic and cenobitic forms of Greek monasticism coexisted alongside Latin forms, among which the Benedictine rule was not even the most common.

Inevitably, such fundamental political and jurisdictional upheavals were mirrored by equally fundamental transitions in the socio-religious make-up of the populations of southern Italy. By around 1000, on the mainland, a Latinized Lombard population was spread across Campania, large parts of Apulia and some zones in Lucania and northern Calabria. On the other hand, Greek Christian communities were most evident in the traditional strongholds of mainland Byzantine Italy: southern and central Calabria, southern Lucania, the Salento peninsula in southern Apulia, and even Sicily under Islamic rule. However, the Byzantine revival of the tenth century generated a concomitant process of Hellenization, while Muslim raids in southern Calabria, and instability in Sicily, may also have displaced Greek Christians further north on the mainland. Consequently, zones in northern Calabria, Lucania and central Apulia which were reintegrated into Byzantine control also experienced demographic shifts, and the increasing establishment of immigrant Greek communities. These zones also acted as springboards for Greek migration further north, into regions such as the Cilento and areas around Salerno, which had never been under Byzantine control. On the island of Sicily, Muslim rule led to a gradual, but incomplete, Islamicization of the island's population. The south and west evolved into areas populated primarily by Muslims, a mixture of converted Sicilians or immigrants from other regions of the Islamic world. Nevertheless, as Alex Metcalfe has demonstrated, varying shades of socio-ethnic ambiguity operated on the island.[32] Acculturation created groups whose faith and cultural background were difficult to distinguish and who fused traditional Islamic and Christian identities. Indeed, since the late seventh century Sicily had been classed as a distinct administrative province (*theme*) in the Byzantine empire, and Greek cultural and religious influences increasingly spread across the island, enhanced further when Sicily passed under the ecclesiastical jurisdiction of Constantinople in the mid-eighth century. The Greek Christian rite thus gradually predominated in Sicily, and even after the Muslim conquest a sizeable Greek Christian population remained on the island, increasingly concentrated in the north-eastern Val Demone region. The extent to which the Greek Christian communities moved

---

[32] Metcalfe, *Muslims and Christians*, 22–4, 86–8, 93–6.

between Sicily and Calabria, and the reasons why, have been hotly debated.[33] The idea of an apparently large-scale exodus of Greek Christians from Sicily now no longer seems sustainable, and although significant movement did take place, it is questionable how much was driven by direct maltreatment by the island's Muslim communities. It is, above all, most apparent that early medieval southern Italy's 'shifting political frontiers were often quite distinct from the linguistic and cultural ones', which thus created a fluid landscape of interface and assimilation between different communities.[34] Hostilities and rivalries played out at the highest political levels were not always matched in localized contexts. Clearly, southern Italy was a frontier zone, but one which acted more as a gateway than a barrier.

(ii)   Norman infiltration and monarchy (1000–1200)

Contact and exchange clearly occurred across the numerous political, religious and socio-cultural frontiers of early medieval southern Italy. Nevertheless, on a broad scale, by 1000 southern Italy remained a culturally and religiously divided landscape, politically unstable and fragmented. It could offer opportunities for aspiring newcomers, and the Normans fitted the bill perfectly.[35] Over the first decades of the eleventh century an assortment of Norman warriors arrived in southern Italy where they mostly took up employment as mercenaries for the warring Lombard rulers in Campania. Some were also hired to assist Apulian rebels in uprisings against Byzantine rule. The Normans gradually received more wealth and land, and soon saw from the inside how weak and divided were the region's rulers. By the 1030s and 1040s groups of Normans began to operate independently from any superior power in establishing their own power bases at Aversa and Melfi amidst growing anarchy in the south. Norman exploits became more ruthless and disruptive, and by the 1050s two leading Normans had come to the fore: Robert Guiscard of the Hauteville family, a lesser-noble kin group from Normandy, and Richard Quarrel. The formation of a coalition force led by Pope Leo IX to oust the

---

[33] Key works include: L.-R. Ménager, 'La Byzantinisation religieuse de l'Italie méridionale (IXe–XIIe siècles) et la politique monastique des Normands d'Italie', *Revue d'histoire ecclésiastique* 53 (1958), 747–74; *Les Actes grecs de S. Maria di Messina*, ed. A. Guillou (Palermo, 1963), 19–33; Metcalfe, *Muslims and Christians*, 13–15.

[34] Loud, *Latin Church*, 13.

[35] Of the many excellent overviews of the Norman period see: M. Caravale, *Il regno normanno di Sicilia* (Rome, 1966); Loud, *Age of Robert Guiscard*; Metcalfe, *Muslims of Medieval Italy*; H. Houben, *Roger II of Sicily. A Ruler between East and West*, trans. G. A. Loud and D. Milburn (Cambridge, 2002); D. Matthew, *The Norman Kingdom of Sicily* (Cambridge, 1992).

disparate groups of Normans resulted in the latter unifying for the first time and defeating the papal force at the battle of Civitate in 1053. The papacy promptly reversed its previous hostility, aware that the Normans were now a permanent fixture in the south, and hopeful that they might provide the military backing to forward the Church-reform movement in the face of opposition from the Salian emperors of Germany. Consequently, in 1059, a papal–Norman rapprochement was achieved which legitimized the territorial acquisitions of Guiscard and Quarrel. The former was invested with the new title of Duke of Apulia, Calabria and in the future Sicily, and the latter was confirmed as Prince of Capua, having ousted the Lombard dynasty there in 1058. Thereafter, the papal–Norman alliance was full of friction, but managed to hold together.

Subsequent Norman advances continued at a rapid pace, particularly by Robert Guiscard who pushed deep into Byzantine territories; Calabria was almost entirely subdued in the 1060s and large parts of Apulia, with some major urban centres, began to acknowledge Guiscard's rule. The 1070s saw the Normans extinguish regimes which had been established in southern Italy in some form or other for centuries. Guiscard's capture of Bari brought to a close the Byzantine presence in the south, his conquest of Salerno (1076/7) ended the Lombard principality, and general Norman pressure forced the Lombard prince of Benevento to bequeath rule of the city to the papacy after his death (in 1077). Benevento would remain a papal enclave in southern Italy until the nineteenth century. All the while, Guiscard had to contend with rebellious Norman nobles who refused to defer to him, as well as periods of conflict with the Normans at Capua. By the 1080s Robert Guiscard had reached the apogee of his power, ruling parts of Campania and most of Calabria, Apulia and (as we shall see) Sicily. He was also a player on the international scene. In this decade Guiscard undertook an ultimately unsuccessful invasion of Byzantium and demonstrated to the outside world the force of his alliance with the papacy by rescuing Pope Gregory VII at Rome in 1084 from the threat of the German emperor Henry IV. At the same time, the Norman conquest of Muslim Sicily was entering its final stage.[36] It had been a protracted affair, begun in 1060 and directed primarily by Guiscard's younger brother Roger I who would eventually take the title Count of Sicily although he remained theoretically subordinate to his elder sibling. Guiscard only intermittently assisted in the campaign, and Roger had to rely on the prowess of his small number of Normans, the support of native Sicilian Christians and the disunity among the Muslims on the island. Key battles

---

[36] Metcalfe, *Muslims of Medieval Italy*, 88–111.

were fought at Cerami (1063) and Misilmeri (1068), and the fall of Palermo (1072) and Syracuse (1085) proved pivotal events. In 1091, Roger mopped up the final remnants of resistance.

As the twelfth century dawned, the main phase of the Norman military conquests had come to an end. Its three protagonists had also passed away: Richard Quarrel (d. 1078), Robert Guiscard (d.1085) and Roger I (d. 1101). At no point had any one Norman ruler unified the peninsula: the Quarrel dynasty at Capua remained outside Hauteville control, the Count of Sicily was effectively free from interference from the mainland, and Naples and Benevento were still independent city-states. In the absence of Richard Quarrel and Guiscard, political power on the mainland fragmented. The power of the Norman princes of Capua contracted dramatically, and Guiscard's successors could not command the same authority. In the increasing power vacuum, urban communities and their leaders were forced to act more autonomously, and some nobles took an increasingly independent stance.[37] The period stretching from the first arrival of the Normans up to the fateful year of 1127 had generated significant transitions, but also allowed for much underlying continuity. At the risk of making sweeping generalizations, the transitions involved the expulsion of established regimes, the creation of new secular and ecclesiastical lordships, and the growing influence of Latin Christianity, most notably in Sicily. On the other hand, the Normans were always a minority group, numbering perhaps only some 2,500 immigrants in total. As a result, they adopted pragmatic policies which encouraged continuity. There were no mass expulsions of native populations, and urban communities were allowed forms of de facto autonomy. Some Frankish customs were imported, but the Normans maintained many of the existing traditions, laws, administrative structures and the officials who operated them. Greek Christians (for more see Chapter 3) were not subject to a Latinization programme and, more notably, the Muslims of Sicily, in return for payment of a head tax, were broadly given lenient surrender pacts which allowed for indirect rule (the *dhimmī* system) and the retention of their religion and customs, albeit restrictions and significant inequalities were inherent in the arrangement. Moreover, evidence suggests that by the first decades of the twelfth century Norman identity in the south was weakening, and that Normans and natives were assimilating.[38]

---

[37] P. Oldfield, *City and Community in Norman Italy* (Cambridge, 2009), 29–54.

[38] G. A. Loud, 'The *Gens Normannorum*. Myth or reality?', *Proceedings of the Fourth Battle Conference on Norman Studies 1981*, ed. R. A. Brown (Woodbridge, 1982), 104–16 (reprinted in his *Conquerors and Churchmen in Norman Italy* (Aldershot, 1999)); J. Drell, 'Cultural syncretism and ethnic identity: the Norman conquest of southern Italy and Sicily', *Journal of Medieval History* 25 (1999), 187–202.

When Duke William of Apulia, the grandson of Robert Guiscard, died in 1127 without an heir, a succession crisis emerged which would carry huge repercussions. The duchy of Apulia was claimed by Roger II of Sicily (the son of Count Roger I), who was William's closest relative and controlled an increasingly powerful island, which had not fragmented as the mainland had done. Roger II faced opposition from the papacy, the Prince of Capua and other mainland groups. However, in 1128 Roger II's superior force enabled him to acquire the duchy, and then in 1130 he controversially raised the status of his territories to that of a kingdom: a novel creation with no historic precedent.[39] Civil war ensued, with opposition from mainland cities and nobles, and it also took on international dimensions which saw the kingdom's legitimacy embroiled in a papal schism which ultimately drew the intervention of the German emperor. Nevertheless, Roger's superior resources and tenacity prevailed, and by 1139 he finally subdued mainland southern Italy, absorbing Naples and Capua, and earned papal recognition. The Kingdom of Sicily, stretching from the island of Sicily to the Abruzzi on the mainland, was a unique creation. It was a multi-ethnic, multi-faith, pariah state, for internally it was populated by a mosaic of communities, and externally it was shunned by most of the rulers of Christendom, especially the Byzantine and German emperors, and the papacy too. The Norman kings of Sicily responded to these challenges by constructing a highly efficient administrative state, based on a combination of Lombard, Byzantine and Arab–Islamic models, but which delegated flexible autonomy to a number of entities and regions within the kingdom.[40] Their control was not tyrannical, as their detractors claimed; rather it was effectively pragmatic. The kings themselves were increasingly able to rule from Palermo, and only sporadically visited the mainland. Despite the existence of tensions between some of the kingdom's Greek, Latin and Muslim communities, and the eruption of serious revolts in 1155–6 and 1160–2, the kingdom gradually stabilized and flourished. Its pivotal setting at the heart of the Mediterranean allowed it to control a great deal of trade and commerce, and the monarchy accrued enormous wealth. Its public image exuded power, affluence and exoticism, reflected in the celebrated Palermitan royal palaces and parks, in the sumptuous decoration in the royal chapel (Cappella Palatina) and the royal cathedral at Monreale, and in the royal ceremonial. To some external observers (see Chapter 5) this was interpreted as a dangerous deviance, but gradually the Kingdom of Sicily was

---

[39] Houben, *Roger II*, 30–75.

[40] H. Takayama, *The Administration of the Norman Kingdom of Sicily* (New York, 1993); J. Johns, *Arabic Administration in Norman Sicily. The Royal Dīwān* (Cambridge, 2002).

rehabilitated and reintegrated into the international community. The Treaty of Benevento (1156) created a lasting peace with the papacy, the Peace of Venice (1177) ended hostilities with the German Empire, and members of the Norman dynasty forged marriage alliances with other royal houses. Furthermore, it was apparent that the kingdom was central to the geopolitical balance of the Mediterranean, to its commerce and to events in the Levant, where Byzantium and the crusader states loomed large in the mind of western Europe. Its integral importance undoubtedly aided friendly ties with western Europe, as perhaps did the general trend towards Latin dominance within the kingdom. From the 1150s the government was increasingly Latinized, with Greek officials and the Palace Saracens being gradually marginalized in favour of Latin churchmen. Sicily was opened up to more Latin immigration, and while Greek Christian communities remained relatively secure, Greek elements within the kingdom were played down. The construction of the royal cathedral at Monreale (c.1174–c.1183) articulated a more assertive Latin-Christian outlook, and King William II (1166–89) was the first Sicilian monarch to show a keen interest in Crusading. William II's death without an heir was followed by the short reign of Tancred and his son William III (1190–4); the last of the Norman Hauteville kings was defeated by the German Staufen emperor Henry VI who had claimed the throne on William II's death through his own Sicilian wife Constance. In 1194, the Kingdom of Sicily passed to the rule of the Staufens, who inherited a uniquely powerful, alluring, yet challenging agglomeration of territories.

Part I

Sanctity

1   Sanctity in early Medieval Southern Italy

Many saints trace their roots back to the formative period of early Christianity, either through having lived in that distant period in which their cults originated, or having utilized templates of sanctity which functioned in that era. It is essential, therefore, before proceeding to our analysis of the Central Middle Ages, to step back and survey South Italian sanctity prior to 1000. Crucial elements of the historical traditions, legacies, continuities and discontinuities which were absorbed into saints' cults in southern Italy in the period 1000 to 1200 were inherited from developments which occurred in the Early Middle Ages. What follows, therefore, is a synthesis of the complex transitions and characteristics of South Italian sanctity prior to 1000, spread over a number of centuries and stretching across the mainland and the island of Sicily.

A high-level framework of political and ecclesiastical division, fragility and rivalry encasing a vibrant low-level core of cross-cultural contact characterized early medieval southern Italy, and the history of sanctity in the same region must be understood within this climate. One common feature of early medieval sanctity is the limited source material. Southern Italy is no exception, although in some regions the evidence is quite rich. The extant manuscripts of many of the hagiographies covering early medieval South Italian cults are often anonymous and/or date to the eleventh and twelfth centuries, although it would appear that a number of these were based on earlier copies or traditions. Also, the inclusion of post-mortem miracles in many of these early hagiographies is fairly restricted, and limits one potential avenue for tracking pilgrimage and the development of a cult. Certainly many works acknowledged the miracle working associated with holy relics; both the *vita* of St Elias the Troglodyte and the translation of St Bartholomew included some twenty examples. But this sort of quantity was unusual, and larger, more formalized *miracula* collections did not appear in southern Italy until c.1100.[1]

---

[1] *Vita S. Eliae Spelacotae*, AS September, iii (Paris, 1868), 881–7; Anastasius Bibliothecarius, *Sermo Theodori Studitae de Sancto Bartolomeo Apostolo*, ed. U. Westerbergh (Stockholm, 1963), 14–17.

There are hints at scriptoria producing hagiographical works at Capua, Salerno and more clearly at Benevento, but it is only at Naples and the great monastery of Montecassino where fully functioning hagiographical 'schools' can be detected. Edoardo D'Angelo's comprehensive survey of early medieval mainland South Italian hagiography has shown that the motives behind the creation of a range of texts included the simple need to record defining events such as translations and relic discoveries, the commemoration of the construction of buildings to house shrines, the expression of supremacy over alternative forms of faith and political/communal rivalries.[2] In many cases, cults focused on local saints, often bishops or martyrs of the early Christian Church, many arriving by sea from Africa or the Levant. One prominent topos of the region's hagiographical output, in Campania particularly, was the 'ships of the saints' in which saints or their relics – including Saints Priscus, Erasmus, Canius and Trophimina – underwent a divine ordeal at sea before reaching the region.[3] The sea as a means of exchange and instability looms large in early medieval South Italian hagiography. Elsewhere, a distinctive group of eremitical/monk saints emerged in Sicily, Calabria and Lucania as those regions slipped in and out of Byzantine rule. Early medieval southern Italy also developed cults with universal appeal. As we shall see, the apostles Bartholomew and Matthew were relocated to Benevento and Salerno respectively. The Sicilian martyr saints, Agatha and Lucy, were soon venerated across Christendom. The famous monastery of Montecassino represented another hot spot on the landscape of early medieval sanctity in the Latin regions of southern Italy, as did the even more renowned sanctuary of the Archangel St Michael at Monte Gargano. Both established a reputation as leading shrine centres throughout the Christian world.

Campania: Lombards, conflicts and civic identities

In the Latin zones of early medieval southern Italy the greatest evidence for saints' cults and hagiographic production is concentrated around the main urban settlements in Campania where they also expressed ongoing political conflicts and contributed to the formative development of civic consciousness. Benevento and Salerno, centres of Lombard dynasties, as well as the important coastal city of Naples, were at the forefront of these developments. The Lombard rulers of Benevento initiated an extraordinary programme of relic collection and patronage of saints' cults, which

[2] E. D'Angelo, 'Agiografia latina del mezzogiorno continentale d' Italia (750–1000)', *Hagiographies IV*, ed. G. Philippart, Corpus Christianorum (Turnhout, 2006), 105–6.
[3] A. Vuolo, 'Le nave dei santi', *Pellegrinaggi e itinerari*, ed. G. Vitolo (Naples, 1999), 57–66.

attempted to establish the city as a Lombard sanctuary, sacralizing the dynasty, so important to a people with a recent pagan past, and asserting its independence from Carolingian and Byzantine control.[4] It has been calculated that in the century between 750 and 850 the bodies of 145 saints were deposited in the city cathedral, with an additional 81 in the urban monastery of Santa Sofia.[5] They arrived from other regions of southern Italy, from Rome and from Byzantium. Among the most significant translations were the African martyrs, the 'Twelve Brothers', in 760 and the Byzantine military saint, Mercurius, in 768.[6] As the Beneventan principality expanded further in the first half of the ninth century more relics arrived. Some of these included: St Sabinus, bishop of Canosa; St Leucius, bishop of Trani; St Ianuarius, a Beneventan bishop who had become a famed patron saint of Naples; the virgin St Trophimina from Minori; and, most prestigious of all, the Apostle St Bartholomew from the Lipari islands.[7] With the arrival of St Bartholomew, Benevento joined an elite group of shrine centres claiming primary possession of apostolic relics. Although a small number of additional relics were transferred to Benevento after St Bartholomew's arrival, the great phase of Beneventan translation activity slowed in tandem with the declining political fortunes of the principality. From the later ninth century Benevento even faced a contest over the possession of its elite apostle saint. Emperor Otto II requested ownership of the relics of St Bartholomew, and although the Beneventans claimed to have duped the emperor by giving him the relics of another saint, uncertainty over their true location dominated thereafter.[8]

The significance of Lombard Benevento's intensive movement of relics should not be overlooked. As Thomas Head concluded, it represented 'a

---

[4] See especially Vuolo, 'Agiografia beneventana', 199–237.

[5] G. Luongo, 'Alla ricerca del sacro. Le traslazioni dei santi in epoca altomedioevale', *Il ritorno di Paolino*, ed. A. Ruggiero (Naples and Rome, 1990), 35 n. 76.

[6] (The Twelve Brothers) *Translatio Corporum SS duodecim fratrum*, AS September, i (Paris, 1868), 142–55; (St Mercurius) *Translatio S. Mercurii*, ed. G. Waitz, MGH SRLI (Hanover, 1878), 576–80; H. Delehaye, 'La Translatio s. Mercurii Beneventum', *Mélanges Godefroid Kurth*, vol. i (Liège, 1908), 17–24, argues that this St Mercurius was actually a forgotten Apulian saint of the same name.

[7] (St Sabinus) *Vita Inventio et Translatio S. Sabini*, AS February, ii (Paris, 1864), 328; (St Leucius) *De Translationibus S. Leucii*, AS January, i (Paris, 1863), 673; (St Ianuarius) *Translatio SS Ianuarii, Festi, et Desideri*, AS September, vi (Paris, 1867), 888–91; *Chronicon Salernitanum*, ed. U. Westerbergh (Stockholm, 1956), ch. 60 p. 60 and ch. 68 p. 65; (St Trophimena) *Historia et Inventionis et Translationis S. Trophimenae*, AS July, ii (Paris, 1867), 233–40; M. Oldoni, 'Agiografia longobardo secolo ix e x: la leggenda di Trofimena', *SM* 12 (1971), 583–636; (St Bartholomew) for the sources on the translation see Anastasius Bibliothecarius, especially 8–17.

[8] *Chron. Cas.*, Bk II.24, pp. 208–9. One tradition claimed Bartholomew's body rested at Rome and his skin at Benevento: *Roberti de Monte Cronica*, ed. L. C. Bethmann, MGH SS vi (Hanover, 1844), 505.

graphic indication of the displacement of power' from other South Italian settlements to Benevento, and was used to counter the emerging development of cults in Benevento's main rival city of Naples.[9] The Lombard rulers of Benevento bolstered their authority further through ties with the shrine of St Michael on Monte Gargano in northern Apulia. There is no need to give more than a brief outline here of the origins and early development of this eminent cult, it being one of the few in southern Italy that has rightly received much scholarly attention.[10] If the date of the apparition of St Michael the Archangel in a grotto on Monte Gargano remains unclear, it is certain that the sanctuary was established in the decades either side of 500, that from the seventh century it was frequently receiving visitors and by the eighth and ninth centuries, as a leading pilgrimage centre, it was attracting visitors from across Christendom. Subterranean chapels and churches dedicated to the saint spread across southern Italy in the Early Middle Ages, and famous centres of the cult were established across Europe. It should be no surprise then that the rulers of Benevento attempted to appropriate as the special Lombard patron a military saint centred on an internationally recognized sanctuary. Varying forms of media were used to express these ambitions. Prince Grimoald IV had coins minted bearing St Michael's effigy, while the *Liber de apparitione sancti Michaelis in Monte Gargano* framed the early Beneventan relationship with St Michael in the context of conflict with Naples.[11] Of Lombard origin, the *Liber de apparitione* was composed at the end of the eighth or the start of the ninth century. The text located Siponto, the episcopal see with jurisdiction over Monte Gargano, not in northern Apulia but in the Beneventan sphere of Campania, and depicted the Neapolitans as still persisting in pagan rites ('pagani adhuc ritibus oberrantes') when they attacked St Michael's shrine. The Beneventans appealed to St Michael and he appeared to the bishop of Siponto to announce the victory which was subsequently achieved over the Neapolitans who consequently converted to Christianity.

Other features of Beneventan sanctity reveal the process of Christianization and the rise of the secular Church. Both themes converge in the *vita* of St Barbatus, which was, according to Vuolo, the most renowned hagiographical text from Benevento, composed at some point

[9] Head, 'Discontinuity', 183.
[10] See the essays collected in *Culte et pèlerinages à Saint Michel en occident: les trois monts dédiés à l'archange*, ed. P. Bouet et al. (Rome, 2003).
[11] *Liber de Apparitione Sancti Michaelis in Monte Gargano*, ed. G. Waitz, MGH SRLI (Hanover 1878), 540–3; B. Vetere, 'Il "Liber de Apparitione" e il culto di San Michele sul Gargano nella documentazione liturgica altomedievale', *Vetera Christianorum* 18 (1981), 423–42.

between the early ninth and early tenth centuries.[12] The *vita* presents Barbatus as a missionary of the mid-seventh century, who confronted the remnants of pagan practices among the Lombards of Benevento. Barbatus successfully establishes the Catholic faith and is elected as Benevento's first bishop. In light of the importance of the shrine at Monte Gargano it is also significant that in the text Barbatus is given ecclesiastical jurisdiction over Siponto. The *vita* evidences the rising profile of Benevento's episcopate in the early ninth century and its role as protector of the city, aided further by the arrival of the relics of St Ianuarius, another famous former bishop, and the increasing transfer of holy relics into and around the city's cathedral precinct.[13] The shift towards housing relics in the cathedral rather than at Santa Sofia signalled both a transition away from the Lombard court's dominance of the sacred landscape of the city, and the growth of episcopal ties with Rome.[14]

In comparison to Benevento, the other main Lombard centres experienced much less intense development of saints' cults.[15] Conspicuous evidence at Salerno for the cultivation of its own shrine centres is only apparent from the mid-ninth century, the period in which the city was establishing its own breakaway principality. The city's bishop, Berard I (d. 860), oversaw the translations of the African martyrs Fortunatus, Gaius and Ante, and of the bishops Quirino and Quingesio.[16] If these moves were intended to promote Salernitan prestige, they were on a small scale compared with the translation in 954 of the Apostle St Matthew from Lucania, which placed the city firmly on the map of Christian sanctity. The translation account, composed probably in the second half of the tenth century, also reveals the religious, diplomatic and political interactions between the Latin and Greek worlds.[17] St Matthew's relics were allegedly discovered in western Lucania, a border zone contested between Salerno and the Byzantines, by two individuals with Greek names, one of whom, Atanasio the monk, was portrayed as motivated more by lucre than piety. Atanasio attempted to transfer the relics to Constantinople but was thwarted by a divinely inspired storm which prevented him from leaving the port at Amalfi. If the hagiographer displays evidently anti-Byzantine

---

[12] *Vita Barbati Episcopi Beneventani*, ed. G. Waitz, MGH SRLI (Hanover, 1878), 556–63; Vuolo, 'Agiografia beneventana', 217.

[13] Vuolo, 'Agiografia beneventana', 223–6.

[14] These ties were apparent in the shift away from a local Beneventan liturgy to the Roman Gregorian style: T. F. Kelly, *The Beneventan Chant* (Cambridge, 1989), 29.

[15] For the more limited cultic activity at Capua see Galdi, *Santi*, 197–203 and D'Angelo, 'Agiografia latina', 58–60.

[16] *Chronicon Salernitanum*, ch. 97 p. 98; D'Angelo, 'Agiografia latina', 61–3.

[17] *Chronicon Salernitanum*, ch. 165 p. 170; see also A. Galdi, 'Il santo e la città: il culto di S. Matteo a Salerno tra X e XVI secolo', *Rassegna storica salernitana* 13 (1996), 22–55.

views, it must be said that Atanasio later reappears at the Salernitan princely court to advise on the successful use of a relic of St Matthew in an exorcism. There was a further important diplomatic footnote to the translation of 954: Landulf, prince of Benevento, requested and received an arm of St Matthew, and the relic worked miracles on arrival at Benevento. This episode symbolized the rapprochement between the princely dynasties of Salerno and Benevento, which had recently been in conflict. Although Prince Gisulf of Salerno played a role in the translation of 954, and one of the miracles which occurred shortly afterwards took place in the princely household, St Matthew's cult was not subsequently associated directly with Lombard princely power, unlike a number of cults at Benevento. Thereafter, until c.1000 the cult of St Matthew developed steadily at Salerno, but not spectacularly. Church dedications to the saint, the creation of a confraternity of the cathedral of St Matthew and the payment of tithes on the saint's feast day show how the cult increasingly entered daily life. However, it was not until the arrival of the Normans, and transitions occurring in the late eleventh century, that St Matthew's began to form into a shrine centre with the renown worthy of an apostle.

The main centres of Lombard power were not the only areas in Campania to promote saints' cults and hagiographic output at such a level. Outside the orbit of Lombard power, early medieval Naples developed into a prodigious centre of hagiographical production, with bilingual Greek–Latin translators, and became the home of several local cults. Some scholars believe the quality and quantity of hagiographical output in Naples to be unrivalled anywhere in early medieval Europe.[18] Among the ranks of the many skilled Neapolitan hagiographers were Paul the Deacon, Athanasius II bishop of Naples and Peter the Subdeacon. This hagiographic and cultic activity was partly a product of the city's precocious development of its own civic identity, fostered by progressively dissolving links with Byzantium and an enduring acknowledgement of difference from Lombard southern Italy. Neapolitan hagiography certainly focused on traditional saints of the early Christian Church but it also found its own local exemplars. A number of texts were dedicated to Neapolitan saints, mostly city bishops, who entered the city's sanctorale. These included Aspren (the first bishop of Naples, d. 69, who was said to be selected by St Peter); Agrippinus (sixth bishop of Naples in the third century and the first to be claimed as a saint); Ianuarius (the Beneventan bishop martyred at nearby Pozzuoli in the early fourth century); Severus

---

[18] D' Angelo, 'Agiografia latina', 69–84; F. Dolbeau, 'Le Rôle des interprètes dans les traductions hagiographiques d'Italie du sud', *Traduction et traducteurs au moyen âge*, Actes du colloque international du CNRS, 26–28 Mai 1986 (Paris, 1989), 145–62.

(twelfth bishop of Naples, who lived between 363 and 409); and Athanasius I (bishop of Naples 850–72).[19] The *Gesta episcoporum Neapolitanorum*, a narrative of the city's episcopal history which was completed by c.900, also portrayed many of these Neapolitan bishops in a quasi-hagiographical light.[20] More vividly, the 'Marble Calendar' of the mid-ninth century, so called because the feast days of a range of saints were inscribed on marble slabs, portrays a sanctorale composed of a distinctively Neapolitan core (including names such as St Ianuarius, St Severus and St Agnellus), accompanied by other South Italian saints (such as St Lucy of Syracuse and St Rufus of Capua) and finally adding in saints from Byzantine calendars.[21] By the ninth century, from the ranks of the various Neapolitan saints, St Ianuarius and St Agrippinus had emerged as the most prominent holy protectors of the city. In the late ninth-century *Vita Athanasii Episcopi Neapolitani*, St Agrippinus is singled out as 'patronus et defensor' of Naples, and St Ianuarius presented as the city's 'tutor'.[22] Similarly, in the ninth-century account of St Agrippinus' post-mortem miracles both saints are seen to work in tandem, preventing the betrayal of Naples to the Lombards and seeing off a Muslim naval attack.[23] Like Benevento, relic translations also occurred at Naples: St Ianuarius arrived from Pozzuoli c.400, St Severinus of Noricum arrived in the Bay of Naples also in the fifth century (and was retranslated into the city in 902) and Sossius (martyr and companion of Ianuarius) arrived in 906.[24]

It is no coincidence that all these developments at Naples were mirrored at Benevento. Beneventan city bishops were venerated as saints, hagiographic output increased and relic translations intensified, all of which converged in the figure of St Ianuarius who epitomized the rivalries between the two cities. During a period of open war between Naples and Benevento, the latter obtained the relics of St Ianuarius in 831 and translated them back to the city where he had once been bishop. In view of the disgrace of losing a key patron saint, it is no surprise that the *Translatio sanctorum Ianuarii, Festi et Desiderii* (the last two were Ianuarius' companions) was subsequently produced in Benevento.[25] The Neapolitans reciprocally refused to acknowledge the relic theft, and

[19] Galdi, *Santi*, 288–95.

[20] *Gesta Episcoporum Neapolitanorum*, ed. G. Waitz, MGH SRLI (Hanover, 1878), 402–36.

[21] H. Delehaye, 'Hagiographie napolitaine', *AB* 57 (1939), 5–64.

[22] *Vita et Translatio S. Athanasii Neapolitani Episcopi (BHL 735 e 737)*, ed. A. Vuolo (Rome, 2001), 118.

[23] *Ex Miraculis Sancti Agrippini*, ed. G. Waitz, MGH SRLI (Hanover, 1878), 463–5.

[24] In the early tenth century translation accounts were composed by John the Deacon (both edited by G. Waitz in MGH SRLI (Hanover, 1878): *Translatio Sancti Severini*, 452–9; *Translatio Sancti Sosii*, 459–63).

[25] *Translatio SS Ianuarii, Festi, et Desideri*, 888–91; *Chronicon Salernitanum*, ch. 57 pp. 57–8.

his cult continued to thrive in the city centred on the catacombs where the saint's body had been located.[26] As Thomas Granier made clear, urban, religious and political rivalries in this part of Campania could be enacted through a 'War of the Saints', involving localized saint–bishops or universally recognized archangels. However, the incendiary movement of relics, and the competitive desire to emulate patterns of veneration, were actually generated by channels of peaceful interaction and exchange working in the background, and this too should not be overlooked.[27]

At the nexus of a great deal of the political, cultural and spiritual exchanges in Campania stood the great monastery of Montecassino; its scholars produced many of the region's hagiographical works, and its monks contributed to the development of local cults. However, like the sanctuary of St Michael on Monte Gargano, by the end of the Early Middle Ages, the monastery was also reputed as one of Christendom's leading shrine centres, housing the relics of its founder St Benedict whose Rule had given birth to Benedictine monasticism.[28] The life of St Benedict and his holy virtues are well known, thanks in large part to Gregory the Great's account in his *Dialogues*. Born at Nursia in Umbria around 480, Benedict became a hermit and withdrew to Subiaco around the year 500.[29] Having established a following and a number of minor monasteries, Benedict founded Montecassino in c.529 as the centre for his new monastic template, where he composed his famous Rule before dying in c.550. Soon afterwards Benedict's relics and those of his sister St Scholastica were deposited in the monastery's oratory and a cult rapidly developed. Unfortunately, thereafter until the mid-eighth century Montecassino's history was fractured. The monastery was destroyed in 581 by the Lombards, and no monks inhabited it until c.718 when it was restored by a new abbot, Petronax, and entered a phase of renewal. However, the community of Montecassino was forced to leave the monastery again in 883 by Muslim raids, which resulted in the death of Abbot Bertharius and a number of monks. The community did not return until

[26] St Januarius' relics were housed in the city's Capodimonte catacombs from the early fifth century, where St Agrippinus' relics had also been placed in the third century: G. Otranto, *Italia meridionale e Puglia paleocristiana. Saggi storici* (Bari, 1991), 30–3.

[27] T. Granier, 'Napolitains et Lombards aux VIIIe–XIe siècles. De la guerre des peuples à "la guerre des saints" en Italie du sud', *MEFRM* 108 (1996), 435–50.

[28] H. Bloch, *Monte Cassino in the Middle Ages*, 3 vols (Cambridge, Mass., 1986) and A. O. Citerella and H. M. Willard, *The Ninth-Century Treasure of Monte Cassino in the Context of Political and Economic Developments in South Italy*, Miscellanea Cassinese 50 (Montecassino, 1983), offer the best overviews of the early history of the monastery.

[29] Gregory the Great, *Dialogues*, ed. A. de Vogue, 3 vols (Sources Chretiennes 251) (Paris, 1978–80), Bk II 126–249; J. M. Petersen, *The Dialogues of Gregory the Great in their Late Antique Cultural Background* (Toronto, 1984), 27–31, 36–54, 165–7.

949 under Abbot Aligernus. Significantly, during the first hiatus in Montecassino's history, the relics of both Benedict and Scholastica were allegedly translated in c.672 to the French monastery of Fleury-sur-Loire. After the first restoration by Abbot Petronax, Montecassino claimed that, in 751, some or all of the relics of St Benedict and his sister had been returned, events which have created an unresolved legacy of dispute between Fleury and Montecassino. In a masterful piece of detective work, Paul Meyvaert demonstrated that by the end of the ninth century the monastery refused to acknowledge that St Benedict's relics had ever been removed to Fleury.[30]

How far this impacted on external perceptions of Montecassino as a shrine centre is hard to measure, but it seems that the monastery was always deemed a special holy place by virtue of its shared history with St Benedict. Moreover, as the monastery flourished as a centre of Christian faith and learning it established high-level political, cultural and religious networks spreading beyond Italy, and attracted individuals noted for their virtues and achievements, some welcomed permanently into the community, others as temporary visitors/pilgrims. In 747–8 the founding abbot of Fulda, St Sturmi (abbot 747–79), visited Montecassino on the advice of his 'mentor' St Boniface (d. 755), the renowned historian and grammarian Paul the Deacon enjoyed two spells at the monastery in the later eighth century, and Charlemagne famously halted there in 787.[31] Many of these visitors and members of the Cassinese community also attained the aura of sanctity and thus enhanced the reputation of Montecassino as a sacred centre. Towards the later tenth century, St John of Gorze, the monastic reformer, St Adalbert of Prague and the Calabrian Greek St Nilus of Rossano spent time at the monastery. Many of the early abbots of Montecassino, and those running the monastery at key junctures in its history, were subsequently venerated as saints. The first four successors of Benedict, Constantine (d. c.565), Simplicius (d. c.575), Vitalis (d. c.579) and Bonitus (d. post-582), were all deemed to be saints.[32] Later saints included the abbot Petronax (d. 762) and the abbot Bertharius (d. c. 884). Admittedly, many of these 'Montecassino saints' were considered as such primarily by Montecassino itself, with little external evidence for veneration of particular cults. Peter the Deacon's *Ortus et vita*, compiled in the 1130s, is one famous example of this

---

[30] P. Meyvaert, 'Peter the Deacon and the tomb of St Benedict: a re-examination of the Cassinese tradition', *Revue bénédictine* 65 (1955), 3–70 (reprinted in his *Benedict, Gregory, Bede and Others* (London, 1977)).

[31] *Vita S. Sturmi*, ed. G. H. Pertz, MGH SS ii (Berlin, 1829), 366–77; Citarella and Willard, *Ninth-Century Treasure of Monte Cassino*, 11.

[32] Meyvaert, 'Peter the Deacon', 52–6.

Cassinese perspective. It catalogues some thirty individuals associated with Montecassino from its foundation in c.529 up to c.1000 who appear to have been deemed saints, a veritable conveyor belt of holy men, but it is often unclear by how long some of these traditions pre-date Peter's work.[33] Nevertheless, through its founder, its reputation at the heart of Benedictine monasticism, and the spiritual vibrancy cultivated within, by c.1000 Montecassino was immersed in an aura of sanctity which spread across Christendom.

Apulia: sanctity disrupted

Although the region of Campania supplies a relative abundance of hagiographical works and proof of local cults, Apulia has left only traces of both in the early medieval period. The disparity between the two regions is difficult to understand in its entirety. Certainly the peculiar conditions at Naples and Benevento, described previously, aided the promotion and survival of cults there. Admirable studies by Jean-Marie Martin and Thomas Head have, on the other hand, demonstrated how plague, warfare and recurrent instability in Apulia saw urban centres and episcopal sees collapse and disappear, creating a legacy of discontinuity in the history of many Apulian cults.[34] Only minimal traces of cults survive before the eleventh century, at which point many were 'rediscovered' and provided with new hagiographical texts to present mythical streams of continuity with late antiquity.[35] The process of revival post-1000 will be explored in Chapter 2, but it is sufficient here to agree with Head's view that the starting point for a number of these early medieval cults (such as St Secundinus at Troia and St Cataldus at Taranto) should be dated to the later period. Of course, we have already discussed one renowned case of an Apulian shrine centre with remarkable continuity: St Michael's on Monte Gargano. The remote and non-urban location on the Gargano promontory seems to have played a role in its survival, and the peculiar dynamics of this particular cult rapidly moved its influence beyond the confines of Apulia.

The restricted material, the problems inherent in a number of saintly legends and the challenges in distinguishing between many early Christian saints with the same name (fourteen saints carried the name Eleuterius for example) make it difficult to understand much about sanctity in the region at this stage. The scraps of early medieval evidence,

---

[33] *Petri Diaconi Ortus et Vita*, 1.
[34] Martin, 'Modèles', 67–86; Head, 'Discontinuity', 171–211.
[35] C. Colomba, 'Repertorio agiografico pugliese', *Hagiographica* 16 (2009), 1–54.

combined with information presented when saints' cults were 'revived' after 1000, suggest that the saint–bishop was the most popular template for sanctity in early medieval Apulia. The following figures were among those who by the eleventh century were claimed in some traditions, of varying degrees of authenticity, to have been saint–bishops in early medieval Apulian sees: Eleutherius of Aecae (second century); Mark of Aecae (third/fourth century), Leucius of Brindisi (third/fourth century), Secundinus of Aecae (fifth century?), Lawrence of Siponto (c.500) and Cataldus of Taranto (seventh century). In truth, for most there is considerable uncertainty over their real identities and dates, while at the same time the memory of many other local saints may simply have been erased permanently during the disruptions of the Early Middle Ages. The various legends of Eleutherius, for example, make him a martyr at Rome, or a bishop at Aecae or Canne, and his relics were translated either to Illyricum, or to Rieti or to Aecae. However, the initial root of the traditions stems from Latin and Greek texts which seem to date from somewhere between the sixth and ninth centuries, and his name was entered in the *Hieronymianum* martyrology, dating probably to the fifth century and the first Western Christian universal martyrology, as well as on the Marble Calendar of Naples.[36] At the least, we can say there was an early medieval cult of a St Eleutherius which had some links to central and southern Italy.

The cult of Saint Sabinus, bishop of Canosa (514–66), offers a rare exception of an Apulian cult which can be firmly attested in the early medieval period. Indeed, the account of Sabinus' life, including the later discovery of his relics and their translation, appears to be one of the oldest surviving hagiographical texts dedicated to a saint based in Apulia. It was composed around 800 but certainly built upon an older text, and Sabinus' miracle working, his prophetic gifts and ability to combat poison, had already been recorded in the *Dialogues*.[37] Sabinus certainly operated in the highest political and ecclesiastical circles of his day. He was a friend of St Benedict and spent time at Montecassino, he acted as a papal envoy to Constantinople and proved a formidable opponent for the Ostrogothic king Totila. After his death Sabinus' relics were translated to the cathedral

---

[36] For Eleutherius see *De S. Eleutherio*, AS April, ii (Paris, 1865), 525–39; A. Galdi, 'Troia, Montecassino e i Normanni: la traslazione di S. Eleuterio tra identità cittadina e dinamiche di potere', *Vetera Christianorum* 47 (2010), 65–6, 68–72; *Martyrologium Hieronymianum*, AS November, ii(ii), ed. H. Quentin (Brussels, 1931), 197, 663; Delehaye, 'Hagiographie Napolitaine', 18, 42: Gregory the Great's *Dialogues* records a St Eleutherius connected to Spoleto, Bk III.33 pp. 392–401.

[37] *Vita Inventio et Translatio S. Sabini*, 324–9; Martin, *Pouille*, 248–9; A. Campione, 'Note sulla vita di Sabino di Canosa: inventio et translatio', *Vetera Christianorum* 25 (1988), 617–39; Gregory the Great, *Dialogues*, Bk III.5 pp. 272–7; Petersen, *Dialogues*, 45, 47, 65, 167.

at Canosa, and later, in the ninth century, part of these appear to have been moved to Bari and Benevento, traditions which would cause some controversy in the later eleventh century. Post-mortem miracles attest the presence of pilgrims at Sabinus' shrine, one even arriving from Spain having first visited the shrine of his namesake Saint Sabinus, bishop of Spoleto, who in a vision directed the pilgrim to the shrine in Apulia; early evidence perhaps of Sabinus' growing fame, and of the emerging rivalry with other comparable shrine centres.[38] The cult of St Leucius is also reasonably well documented. His relics were located by Gregory the Great at Brindisi and near Rome, while a church dedicated to the saint (dating possibly to the fifth century) has been discovered at Canosa.[39] Between the seventh and ninth centuries, St Leucius' relics were subjected to a series of translations which reveal a network of interrelationships between some of southern Italy's urban centres. St Leucius' relics were apparently transferred from Brindisi to Trani; subsequently they were moved to Benevento after Trani had suffered a Muslim raid. Later negotiations arranged for the return of half of the relics to Trani, and some eventually found their way back to Brindisi through the local bishop's friendship with the prince of Benevento. The information on the translations, entirely plausible, is however supplied only in John of Trani's eleventh-century work, which built on earlier traditions.[40] In summary, not only is much of our knowledge on early medieval sanctity in Apulia reflected through the works of eleventh-century authors with varying agendas, but it is also striking that the only surviving pre-1000 hagiographical works which relate to saints who are unambiguously associated with Apulia are concerned with those who had their relics transferred to Benevento.[41] If we add to this the Beneventan promotion of the shrine at Monte Gargano, it is clear that some of our main channels of information on early medieval sanctity in Apulia are both spatially external and temporally distant from the region and era in question.

The Siculo-Calabrian saints: cults between Rome, Byzantium and Islam

Within southern Italy, the regions with the closest historical, political, cultural and religious connections to the Byzantine world were Sicily and

---

[38] *Vita Inventio et Translatio*, 327.
[39] Head, 'Discontinuity', 180; M. Castelfranchi Falla, 'Continuità dall'antico: la basilica di San Leucio a Canosa. Nuove acquisizioni', *Vetera Christianorum* 22 (1985), 387–94.
[40] *De Translationibus S. Leucii*, 672–3; G. Cioffari et al., *Agiografia in Puglia. I santi tra critica storica e devozione popolare* (Bari, 1991), 130–2.
[41] Head, 'Discontinuity', 183.

Calabria, where the history of sanctity in the Early Middle Ages demonstrates the multiple interchanges that operated between the South Italian peninsula and the Eastern Mediterranean. It is possible to identify in Sicily and Calabria two broad categories of sanctity. The first was formed around the more traditional model of early medieval saint: martyrs, confessors and early Church officials. They were almost exclusively based on the island of Sicily before the beginning of the Muslim invasion in 827. The second category was shaped by a distinctive group of saints who moved between Sicily and the mainland in the ninth and tenth centuries, and thus a time when the former was under Islamic rule and open to Arab–Islamic colonization. The saints broadly adopted an ascetic and eremitical lifestyle, based on Eastern Orthodox practices, which espoused movement and withdrawal from the world.

For both groups of saints, the evidence for them and the later development of their cults carries several challenges. A great debt of gratitude is owed to the founder of Sicilian hagiographical studies, the Jesuit Ottavio Gaetani (d. 1620), who drew together the lives of various Sicilian saints in his ambitious *Vitae Sanctorum Siculorum* (published 1657). Yet, Gaetani's magnum opus poses several problems of its own, through overlooking other important material and rephrasing some of the language found in the manuscripts.[42] In many of the cases of saints alive prior to the Muslim arrival, hagiographical dossiers survive primarily in Greek texts; however, there are a number – Agatha of Catania, Lucy of Syracuse, Pancratius of Taormina, Marcianus of Syracuse, Leo of Catania – for which Latin and Greek versions survive. Unfortunately, it is largely impossible to ascertain conclusively whether the Latin or the Greek text was the original, and therefore to trace an important signpost in a cult's dissemination, although we do know that St Agatha's *passio* was originally in Latin and St Lucy's in Greek.[43] Many Sicilian saints from late antiquity and the Early Middle Ages remain ephemeral figures whose historicity is questionable. This is compounded by the fact that many failed to establish a wider presence beyond the island.[44] As is the case for many saints across Europe in this early period, several Sicilian saints are difficult to identify

[42] S. Costanza, 'Per una nuova edizione delle "Vitae Sanctorum Siculorum"', *Schede medievali* 5 (1983), 313–25.

[43] G. Philippart, 'L'Hagiographie sicilienne dans le cadre de l'hagiographie de l'occident', in *La Sicilia nella tarda antichità e nell'alto medioevo*, ed. R. Barcellona and S. Pricoco (Catania, 1999), 179–83; S. Pricoco, 'Un esempio di agiografia regionale: la Sicilia', *Santi e demoni nell'alto medioevo occidentale (secoli V–XI)*, Settimane di studio del centro italiano di studi sull'alto medioevo 36 (Spoleto, 1989), 321.

[44] Alongside Agatha and Lucy, the only other saints to appear in the *Martyrologium Hieronymianum* who were certainly based in Sicily were Euplus of Catania, Marcianus of Syracuse and Pancratius of Taormina, 78, 329, 359, 436, 647.

and biographical data are disconcertingly obscure. For example, a hermit saint of the fifth century, Calogerus, was venerated at Fragalà, but may in fact have been the same figure as a St Calogero of Sciacca; and in all there are up to seven possible identities for saints called Calogero in Sicily. Traces of a cult of a St Olivia of Palermo do not allow us to locate her martyrdom firmly either in the Vandal era or during the time of Muslim rule in Sicily. Moreover, while some early Christian saints in Sicily had African associations, many having fled persecution, others have been erroneously credited with African origins.[45]

In the cases of some Siculo-Calabrian saints and their cults, the period of Muslim rule inevitably impacted on them, their continuity and their survival in historical record, much as occurred, through different factors, in early medieval Apulia. The collapse of Sicily's diocesan structures during the Islamic period signalled the loss of repositories of a range of potentially valuable liturgical sources, and of centres which traditionally might have promoted cults. Relics were moved to the mainland to safeguard them, or so at least the justification ran: the relics of the saint–bishop Marcianus of Syracuse were allegedly transferred to Gaeta in the ninth century.[46] There is also no surviving Sicilian calendar or martyrology dating from the Early Middle Ages, nothing approaching the Carthaginian martyrology or the Neapolitan Marble Calendar. Significantly, none of the *vitae* of the wandering Siculo-Calabrian saints of the ninth and tenth centuries dealt with figures who resided solely in Sicily, and consequently these texts were actually produced on the mainland. For other saints' cults the period of Muslim rule may well have been of little consequence, and these particular cults naturally had short life-spans and limited reach regardless of other external forces. Certainly, we must often rely on evidence for a cult's development which exists from outside of Sicily, such as church dedications in Rome, the *Hieronymianum* martyrology and the Constantinopolitan synaxarium, but these reveal little about its evolution on the island itself. In some instances, as we shall see in later chapters, evidence for some level of continuity only materializes during the Christian revival of the late eleventh and twelfth centuries through the production of new martyrologies, sacramentaries and other hagiographical texts, and the dedication of new or revived religious houses. Evidence from the early twelfth-century *vita* of St Lucas di Isola di Capo Rizzuto shows that the memory of St Elias the

[45] F. Scorza Barcellona, 'Santi africani in Sicilia (e siciliani in Africa) secondo Francesco Lanzoni', *Storia della Sicilia*, ed. S. Pricoco (Catania, 1988), 37–55.
[46] G. Kaftal, *Saints in Italian Art. Iconography of the Saints in Central and South Italian Schools of Painting*, vol. 2 (Florence, 1965), 717.

Troglodyte's cult was still alive in Calabria.[47] Likewise, St Filaretus of Seminara modelled his life on St Elias of Enna, entered the latter's monastery, which was still functioning in the eleventh century, and an apparition of St Elias directed a pilgrim to Filaretus' tomb.[48] The manuscript transmission for a number of these ninth- and tenth-century *vitae* is late and some survive only in Latin translations, erecting further barriers, but again this suggests tangible cultic continuities.

On the other hand, most of the *vitae* of the ninth- and tenth-century Siculo-Calabrian saints were originally composed by contemporaries who were either disciples of the deceased saint, or who had access to acquaintances of the saint. They offer unusual access into the world of these saints as they lived, and some include post-mortem miracles too. The *vita* of St Elias the Troglodyte, for example, concludes with some twenty miracles associated with his tomb and various contact relics (including a monk whose toothache was healed by touching his teeth with the saint's table knife).[49] However, being written so soon after the saint's death can restrict our understanding of a cult's subsequent development; we must search for other corroborative evidence, which is often minimal, much later or located in different regions, and we may suspect that the silence surrounding some of the cult's later evolution indicates only short and intense periods of vibrancy, perhaps while those who had experienced contact with the saint still lived. Indeed, because many of these cults were associated with isolated landscapes and monasteries they were not as accessible as the urban ones often associated with martyrs and bishops, and thus they relied on more restricted and fragile bonds of personalized devotion.

On the whole, the evidence we do have on sanctity in Sicily prior to the Muslim invasion appears to conform to patterns recognizable across the early medieval world. Indeed, Sicily's most famous saints, dating from the very early period of Christianity on the island, were martyrs.[50] Two of these were the virgin martyrs St Agatha of Catania (d. 251) and St Lucy of Syracuse (d. 304). Both were interconnected from an early stage. Lucy's *passio* records her pilgrimage to Agatha's tomb and suggests

---

[47] *Vita di S. Luca, vescovo di Isola Capo Rizzuto*, ed. and trans. G. Schirò (Palermo, 1954), 89.

[48] *Vita S. Philareti Monachi*, AS April, i (Paris, 1866), 607–8, 614.

[49] *Vita S. Eliae Spelacotae*, 881–7.

[50] Another prominent martyr with connections to Sicily was St Vitus. His traditions placed his death during the reign of Diocletian, but fused legends with another Vitus of Lucania. His relics were translated to the German monastery of Corvey in the ninth century: *Historia Translationis S. Viti*, ed. G. H. Pertz, MGH SS ii (Berlin, 1829), 576–85.

a relationship of dependence.[51] Their cults must have been successful on a local level to act as the base for their rapid development into universal cults. The two saints were incorporated into the famous *Hieronymianum* martyrology, had numerous churches and place names dedicated to them, particularly on mainland Italy, and appeared in several prominent frescoes.[52] Their cults certainly flourished in Ravenna and Rome, where Pope Gregory the Great was an important agent in their development. He dedicated a Roman monastery and a basilica to the two Sicilian saints and introduced them into the liturgy of the Roman Church.[53] The cults of Agatha and Lucy were also popular in the Byzantine world. Given that Sicily was ruled from Byzantium and that the Sicilian Church passed under the jurisdiction of the patriarch of Constantinople in the eighth century, it should be little surprise that this occurred, particularly as Syracuse was the main Byzantine administrative and cultural centre on the island. Both cults were absorbed into many of the Byzantine synaxaria, and Greek versions of both Agatha's and of Lucy's *passiones* were produced alongside Latin ones. The continued appearance of Agatha and/or Lucy in renowned historical and liturgical sources, such as Bede's *Ecclesiastical History*, the Marble Calendar of Naples and Usuard of St-Germain-des-Pres' ninth-century martyrology, testifies to the growing dissemination of their fame.[54] South Italian sources claim that the relics of both Agatha and Lucy remained in Sicily until they were translated to Constantinople in c. 1040; however, other sources offer a counter-tradition which suggests that the relics had already been removed from Catania long before this date.[55] What does seem clear, however, is that both cults had experienced contraction in Muslim Sicily to such an extent that in the early eleventh century such universally venerated saints appear to have been almost forgotten in their native island, or at best withdrawn into more private spheres of devotion.[56]

---

[51] *Martirio di Santa Lucia: Vita di Santa Marina*, ed. and trans. G. Rossi Taibbi (Palermo, 1959), 50–1; M. Stelladoro, *Agata, la martire* (Milan, 2005), 96–102; V. Milazzo and F. Rizzo Nervo, 'Lucia tra Sicilia, Roma e Bisanzio; itinerario di un culto (IV–IX secolo)', *Storia della Sicilia*, ed. S. Pricoco (Catania, 1988), 95–135.

[52] *Martyrologium Hieronymianum*, 78, 647. St Agatha also appeared in the Carthaginian calendar of the sixth century: Kaftal, *Saints*, 5.

[53] Milazzo and Rizzo Nervo, 'Lucia', 115–21; St Nilus of Rossano died in 1005 at the monastery of St Agatha near Tusculum, c.20km from Rome: *Vita S. Nili*, AS September, vii (Paris, 1867), 317.

[54] *Bede's Ecclesiastical History of the English People*, ed. and trans. B. Colgrave and R. A. B. Mynors (Oxford 1969), iv. 20, 398; *Usuardi Martyrologium*, Patrolgia Latina 213–14 (Paris, 1852), 733–4; 797–8; Delehaye, 'Hagiographie Napolitaine', 12, 42.

[55] *The Letters of Pope Gregory the Great*, trans. J. R. C. Martyn, 3 vols (Toronto, 2004), vol. 1 Bk 1.52 p. 175 indicates that attempts were made to transfer some of Agatha's relics to the island of Capri before 591.

[56] For more see Chapter 4.

Alongside these renowned martyrs, Sicily produced a number of saint–bishops prior to the arrival of the Muslims. The legends of two – St Marcianus of Syracuse and St Pancratius of Taormina – were by the ninth century underpinned by an association with apostolic mission. Amy Remensnyder revealed a similar tendency in southern France, commencing in works of the ninth century, to convert local patron saints like St Martial of Limoges into apostolic figures. In this way an intimate association with 'the primordial layer of Christianity' could be asserted.[57] St Marcianus of Syracuse was reputedly appointed by St Peter, and the church of Syracuse was thus deemed to be the second founded after Antioch. Indeed, one of the earliest Christian communities in Italy has been discovered at Syracuse, with its impressive catacombs and rich collection of early Christian epigraphs.[58] Likewise, St Pancratius of Taormina's legend claims he was born in Antioch, was also sent on an apostolic mission to the island by St Peter to become Taormina's first bishop and was subsequently martyred by pagans.[59] Cults of both of the saints were apparent by the sixth century when they were entered into the *Hieronymianum* martyrology.[60] Later, Pope Gregory the Great's intervention in Sicily revealed the emergence of more saint–bishops. The pope elected his close associate, Maximianus (d. 594), who had been abbot of Gregory's monastery of St Andrew's in Rome and a papal ambassador, to be bishop of Syracuse and chief legate for the entire Church of Sicily.[61] He was later included by Gregory in his *Dialogues* where he recounted how Maximianus was miraculously saved from shipwreck when returning to Rome from Constantinople.[62] In his correspondence, Gregory also acquitted a Bishop Gregory of Agrigento (d. 638), who was almost certainly the St Gregory of Agrigento whose *vita*, composed probably in the seventh century by the hegumen of the monastery of St Sabas at Rome, depicts him as a key figure in the Western Church.[63]

It is apparent that the papacy briefly played an important role in the lives of Sicily's earliest saints, and in the promotion of their cults, arguably

---

[57] A. G. Remensnyder, *Remembering Kings Past. Monastic Foundation Legends in Medieval Southern France* (Ithaca, 1995), 93–9, quotation at 98.

[58] Otranto, *Italia meridionale*, 35–6.

[59] Pricoco, 'Un esempio di agiografia regionale', 334, 347–8.

[60] *Martyrologium Hieronymianum*, 329, 359. Pancratius' cult was still active in the ninth century and his shrine was visited by the Siculo-Calabrian St Elias of Enna: C. J. Stallman-Pacitti, 'The encomium of St Pancratius of Taormina by Gregory the Pagurite', *Byzantion* 60 (1990), 334–65.

[61] *Letters of Gregory the Great*, vol. 1 p. 99 and Bk II.5 p. 196, vol. 2 Bk V.20 p. 398.

[62] Gregory the Great, *Dialogues*, vol. 2 Bk III.36, pp. 408–41.

[63] *A Translation of Abbot Leontios' Life of Saint Gregory, Bishop of Agrigento*, trans. J. R. C. Martyn (Lampeter, 2004).

more so than anywhere else in southern Italy in the Early Middle Ages. Pope Gregory the Great's efforts to forge closer devotional bonds with the Sicilian Church were channelled through the island's saints. His frequent interventions in the island were driven by the papacy's and his own family's claims over vast Sicilian estates and by the fear that Byzantine political control might pull Sicily out of Rome's orbit.[64] Territorial, jurisdictional and liturgical struggles converged in a highly contested space. It should, for example, be no surprise that Gregory's close friend St Maximianus was dispatched to Syracuse, the political and cultural heart of Byzantine Sicily. Evelyne Patlagean also isolated, among the hagiographies of the early Sicilian saints, a series of *vitae* in which the primacy of Rome and its apostles emerged as the central narrative scheme.[65] These *vitae* date mostly to the eighth and ninth centuries; all were produced in Greek, quite probably by Greek monks resident at Rome, and include the lives of St Pancratius of Taormina, St Marcianus of Syracuse, St Gregory of Agrigento (probably composed in the seventh century) and St Philip of Agira, founder of the famous monastery on the slopes of Etna, whose life is dated in one legend to the fifth century. All pre-date the more renowned hagiographical cycle of the Siculo-Calabrian saints, which is discussed later in this chapter and which commences with the *vita* of St Elias of Enna. In each *vita*, Rome plays a pivotal role in the formation of the saint. Pancratius and Marcianus were given apostolic missions, and the former was invested at Rome. Rome is also the setting for the central drama of Gregory of Agrigento's *vita* where his demonstration of miraculous powers and an apostolic apparition led to the saint's acquittal from false charges and enabled his episcopal investiture.[66] The *vita* of St Philip of Agira included an episode at Rome in which Philip miraculously speaks in Latin, having hitherto only spoken Syrian, and thereafter is dispatched to Agira in the name of St Peter to engage in battle with demons.[67] Consequently, the Sicily that emerges in these *vitae* is one constructed from a Roman perspective.

This series of *vitae* appears to have been produced by Graeco-Roman monks and reveals another point of interface between the Eastern and Western branches of Christianity which continued even after the Iconoclast controversy and well into the Central Middle Ages

[64] J. Richards, *Consul of God. The Life and Times of Gregory the Great* (London, 1989), 140–61.
[65] E. Patlagean, 'Les Moines grecs d'Italie et l'apologie des thèses pontificales (VIIe–IXe siècles)', *SM* 5 (1964), 579–602.
[66] *Translation of Abbot Leontios' Life of Saint Gregory*, 167–68, 173–75, 189–92, 201–2, 217, 218.
[67] Patlagean, 'Les Moines grecs', 583.

(see Chapter 3).[68] Moreover, although the underlying message in these texts is Roman primacy, Constantinople and Eastern Christianity are also depicted respectfully. Both Pancratius and Marcianus were easterners whose missions were formed at Antioch. Throughout the *vita* of Gregory of Agrigento, the saint appears as a prominent theologian highly regarded at Constantinople, where he attended an important Church council and confounded some heretics. Indeed, that Gregory was imprisoned at one point in Rome on false accusations may reveal critiques of the machinery of papal government. When Gregory was released and eventually assigned the bishopric of Agrigento, the pope and the emperor of Constantinople cooperated to ensure Gregory was able to establish himself in the city.[69]

In this context, the two *vitae* of St Leo, bishop of Catania, offer further evidence in early medieval Sicily for the fluctuating balance of influence between Rome and Constantinople.[70] Serious doubts remain over Leo as a historical figure, and of his two *vitae* one places him in the reigns of Constantine IV and Justinian II (681–5), the other in those of Leo IV and Constantine VI (775–80). The texts themselves were almost certainly composed between c.730 and c.850, and therefore most likely after the Iconoclast dispute and Sicily's jurisdictional transfer to the patriarchate of Constantinople. Byzantium features more heavily in Leo's *vitae* than in those considered previously. Leo was born at Ravenna and was eventually appointed bishop of Catania.[71] The texts present him as a protector of vulnerable communities in Sicily, and a tireless combatant of paganism and heresy. In fact, much of Leo's *vitae* is concerned with his struggles with a sorcerer called Heliodorus who terrified the Sicilians and vexed the hierarchy at Constantinople. Byzantine officials repeatedly failed to bring Heliodorus to justice; he managed to escape arrest in Constantinople whose inhabitants pleaded for Leo of Catania to intervene, the latter's reputation apparently having reached the Byzantine capital. Leo finally defeated the sorcerer when both entered a fire and Leo emerged unscathed. Consequently, St Leo of Catania is found in Byzantine synaxaria, which also inform us that Leo was believed to have built a church in

---

[68] Also, in the ninth century an encomium of St Pancratius of Taormina was produced by a Greek author who appears to have migrated to Sicily from Constantinople: Stallman-Pacitti, 'Encomium', 334–65.

[69] *Translation of Abbot Leontios' Life of Saint Gregory*, 41–48, 162–6, 235–6 and n. 340.

[70] The shorter version of these two *vitae* has been edited by A. Acconcia Longo, 'La vita di s. Leone vescovo di Catania e gli incantesimi del mago Eliodoro', *Rivista di studi bizantini e neoellenici* 26 (1989), 3–98.

[71] G. Da Costa-Louillet, 'Saints de Sicile et d'Italie meridionale aux VIIIe, IXe et Xe siècles', *Byzantion* 29–30 (1959–60), 89–95.

Catania dedicated to St Lucy and containing some of her relics; further evidence of the interconnections between Catania and St Agatha on the one hand, and Syracuse and St Lucy on the other.[72] Thus Byzantium begins to emerge ever more clearly alongside Rome in the history of Sicilian sanctity, an imprint which would have lasting legacies. As Sicily's political and religious links with Byzantium evolved, its saints were absorbed into Byzantine liturgical and hagiographical texts. We have already seen that this was the case for Saints Agatha and Lucy, and others to feature included St Pancratius of Taormina and St Gregory of Agrigento; thus Rome was not able to monopolize these Sicilian saints.[73]

Significantly, the distinctive group of Siculo-Calabrian saints of the ninth and tenth centuries did not appear in the universal Byzantine liturgical texts, aside from occasional insertion in the margins. If to some extent this reflected the island's detachment from the East during Muslim rule, it also arose from the fact that by this later period the content of most of the synaxaria had been finalized and did not easily allow for new additions. Thus, the cults of the ninth- and tenth-century Siculo-Calabrian saints remained localized in the South Italian landscape. However, the saints of the ninth and tenth centuries developed distinguishing features familiar to Eastern Orthodox spiritual practices.[74] The impact of Byzantine political and ecclesiastical control of Sicily, as well as direct cultural links established with the East, was primarily responsible for the development. Most from this group rejected the concept of *stabilitas loci*, opting instead for lives of almost perpetual migration founded on the principle of separation from one's kin, friends and homeland. For many, these objectives were realized through combined phases of cenobitic, lavriotic and eremitic living. Most also lived in extreme abstinence, enduring intense forms of fasting and rigorous mortification. The harsh landscapes of Sicily, Calabria and Lucania contributed. Large parts were mountainous, forested and remote, others were full of subterranean caves which offered ideal spaces for meditation and withdrawal. The *vitae* of this group of Siculo-Calabrian saints display numerous similarities. Some of these arise from the employment of common hagiographic topoi, but others are representative of a shared geographic, political and spiritual climate.

The wanderings of some of the early medieval Siculo-Calabrian saints took them far from their *patria*; a physical reinforcement of the

---

[72] Da Costa-Louillet, 'Saints', 95.
[73] A. Luzzi, *Studi sul sinassario di Constantinopoli* (Rome, 1995), especially chapters 3 and 5.
[74] Da Costa-Louillet, 'Saints', 89–173 offers an excellent overview of these saints and has been invaluable for the following sections. See also generally M. Scaduto, *Il monachesimo basiliano nella Sicilia medievale: rinascita e decadenza sec. XI–XIV* (Rome 1947).

psychological separation from kin and community, and a search for locations which could intensify devotion and communication with God. Some moved from Sicily to Calabria and beyond. St Leo–Lucas of Corleone (810–910) moved from Corleone to Calabria and journeyed to the shrines at Rome.[75] St Vitalis of Castronuovo (d. c.990) travelled back and forth between Sicily and Calabria, visited Rome and Bari, and eventually ended his life in Lucania near Rapolla.[76] St Sabas the Young (d. 990–1) moved from Calabria to the Mercurion, a remote zone on the Lucania–Calabria frontier populated by hermits and small monastic communities. From there, Sabas visited Syracuse, Atrani (near Amalfi) and Rome where he died. Sabas was accompanied by his father, St Christopher, and brother, St Macarius, who thus followed similar paths to the Mercurion and Rome.[77] St Lucas of Armento (d. 993) also travelled from Sicily, via Reggio, to Lucania, where Greek Orthodox colonization from Calabria had been growing in the tenth century in line with the Byzantine reconquest of the region, and settled first at Noa and then Armento.[78] By contrast, St Elias the Troglodyte (860/70–960) travelled in the opposite direction from Reggio to Sicily. He eventually moved to Patras in Greece and finally returned to Calabria where he had spells in monastic communities and in isolated grottos.[79] More prominent examples of this wandering ethos can be found in the cases of St Nilus of Rossano (910–1005) and St Elias of Enna (823–903). Nilus ultimately moved permanently beyond the Greek zones of mainland southern Italy to establish himself, with his followers, in Campania, spending time at Capua, Montecassino, Gaeta and Tusculum near Rome.[80] Finally, the life of St Elias of Enna offers a remarkable account of movement and interconnections across the Eastern Mediterranean: captured in his youth in Sicily by Muslims, he served as a slave to Christian masters in Africa, purchased his freedom and travelled to Palestine, visited the Holy Sepulchre at Jerusalem, where he adopted the monastic habit, and visited the Jordan, Mount Tabor, Mount Sinai, Alexandria and even some shrines in Persia, before returning to Sicily. Subsequently Elias moved from Palermo to Taormina, then to the Peloponnese in Greece, before undertaking a pilgrimage to Rome (between 885 and 891) via Corfu. Later he moved to Calabria to establish a monastery near Reggio, and

---

[75] *Vita S. Leonis Lucae Corilionensis Abbatis*, AS March, i (Paris, 1865), 98–102.
[76] *Vita S. Vitalis Abbatis*, AS March, ii (Paris, 1865), 26–35.
[77] Da Costa-Louillet, 'Saints', 130–42.
[78] *Vita S. Lucae Abbatis Armenti*, AS October, vi (Paris, 1868), 337–41.
[79] *Vita S. Eliae Spelacotae*, 848–87.
[80] *Vita S. Nili*, 262–320.

finally travelled to Constantinople for a meeting with the emperor, but died en route near Thessalonika.[81]

The forms of movement were driven by key staging-posts and pulses of activity which saw these saints enter monasteries or establish new ones, and then usually withdraw to a more remote location to avoid the community and 'fame' that had consequently built up around them. St Vitalis is a prime example of the life path of the early medieval Siculo-Calabrian saint which fluctuated between the cenobitic and eremitic templates. His first experience of a monastic house was at San Filippo, Agira, on the slopes of Mount Etna. This renowned monastery was at the hub of the Christian religious network on the island, much as Montecassino was, on a far more prominent level, in Campania. Indeed, Saints Leo–Lucas, Sabas, Christopher, Macarius and Lucas of Armento all spent time in the monastery. Vitalis later spent twelve years in solitude on the slopes of Mount Etna, then moved to Calabria where he met a hermit and lived in remote wilderness; however, he subsequently founded a monastery and built a church near Turris (in Lucania).[82] Similarly, Lucas of Armento entered San Filippo, Agira, spent some time in the grotto of St Elias the Troglodyte to further his spiritual education, and restored a monastery in Lucania before withdrawing from it. Others founded religious houses too: St Elias of Enna at Saline near Reggio and Leo–Lucas co-founded two monasteries. Most famously, St Nilus of Rossano entered the monasteries of Mount Mercurion and San Nazaro in his early life, and died at the monastery of Sant'Agata near Tusculum. In between he also founded the monasteries of San Michele in Valleluce (on Montecassino lands), Serperi (near Gaeta) and, most famously, Grottaferrata (near Rome).[83]

In most cases, the actions of the saints were consistently shaped by spiritual ordeals and ascetic ideals, framed by the wilderness around them. St Vitalis spent his nights submerged to the neck in water, battled with demons in cavernous retreats and tamed wild animals. St Elias the Troglodyte's epithet was a result of his time spent in caves, and St Nilus lived periodically in the wilderness surviving on a diet restricted to basic foodstuffs such as acorns, bread and roots. Often, the saint's spiritual evolution was enhanced by encounters with other holy men. Some of these may have been hagiographical inventions, yet it is abundantly clear

---

[81] *Vita S. Eliae Junioris*, AS August, iii (Paris, 1867), 489–509; Da Costa-Louillet, 'Saints', 95–109. There has not been space here to consider other contemporary Siculo-Calabrian saints in the same depth, such as St Fantinus the Younger (c.927–c.1000) who was born in Calabria and died in Thessalonika: *La vita di San Fantino il Giovane*, ed. E. Follieri (Brussels, 1993).

[82] *Vita S. Vitalis*, 26–35.

[83] Da Costa-Louillet, 'Saints', 89–173.

that Calabria and Lucania in the ninth and tenth centuries were home to a remarkable network of Greek-rite hermits and monks, many of whom were deemed saintly, and whose lives would undoubtedly have intersected.[84] The *vitae* of these saints offer glimpses of a landscape full of holy men and exchanges between them. St Elias the Troglodyte's early spiritual development was aided by the company of a monk named Arsenius, a man considered to be a saint of whom we know little more; he also had contacts with a St Nicodemus who was born at Saline.[85] St Nilus encountered St Fantinus the Younger, a contemporary hermit and abbot, who healed Nilus and offered him spiritual guidance.[86] Spiritual supervision and understanding were conspicuously transmitted across generations. The *vita* of St Elias the Troglodyte claimed he met his elder namesake St Elias of Enna and his disciple Daniel, who tested his credentials at their monastery at Saline and decided that the younger Elias should govern their disciples. Towards the end of his life, St Elias the Troglodyte visited Elias of Enna's relics at Melicucca, and fell ill on his feast day.[87] St Vitalis' fame led to a meeting with St Lucas of Armento, who was even cured by Vitalis.[88] Such bonds continued in the afterlife. Following his death, Vitalis' body was eventually translated from Turris to Armento; subsequently the saint appeared to the lamenting inhabitants of Turris to comfort them and inform them of his desire to rest with St Lucas of Armento.[89] Evidence for this cross-generational guidance also continued into the later Norman period (see Chapter 3). As part of their spiritual journey most of these Siculo-Calabrian saints also undertook a pilgrimage to Rome; St Lucas of Armento was the only one of those thus far considered who did not. It seems that Rome's spiritual and political power exerted a strong pull for this group of saintly men, no doubt also enhanced by its proximity in contrast to other major spiritual centres at Constantinople and the Holy Land. The Eastern Mediterranean enabled travel and contact, but until the mid-eleventh century its seas were host to pirates and dominated by Muslim powers, not an auspicious combination for unarmed Christian saints. While some of our saints (St Fantinus the Younger and Elias the Troglodyte) did travel to the Greek islands and the

---

[84] A. Peters-Custot, *Les Grecs de l'Italie méridionale post-byzantine. Une acculturation en douceur (IXe–XIVe siècles)* (Rome, 2009), 607, offers a useful summary diagram of these connections.

[85] *Vita S. Eliae Spelacotae*, 853; S. Borsari, *Il monachesimo bizantino nella Sicilia e nell'Italia meridionale prenormanne* (Naples, 1963), 46.

[86] *Vita S. Nili*, 275–7; *Vita di San Fantino*, 433–5.

[87] *Vita S. Eliae Spelacotae*, 879.

[88] *Vita S. Vitalis*, 29.

[89] *Vita S. Vitalis*, 35.

Peloponnesian peninsula, St Elias of Enna appears to offer a rarer case by visiting the Holy Sepulchre and by attempting (unsuccessfully) to visit Constantinople.[90]

The spiritual virtues of these saints were laid out unambiguously by their hagiographers, many of whom had known their subjects personally. All performed miracles which were drawn from the standard stock, but which singled them out as protectors of their local communities: miraculous cures, escapes, the ending of droughts and the vanquishing of enemies ranging from Muslims to demons. Some were also known for their gift of prophecy: St Elias of Enna was particularly expert at prophesying deaths and the outcome of battles, at one point correctly predicting a Byzantine naval victory at Reggio.[91] Collectively, these attributes made these wandering saints, who were so well connected to a variety of networks, attractive as 'spiritual fathers', advisors and informants. Almost all had been born into the middling ranks of society, with affluent parents who had ensured an education for them. Consequently these saints had some intellectual and cultural capital, and were likely to be adept communicators and mediators. Their services were in demand from those in the elite social and political strata, adding further complication to the saint's desire for solitude, and mirroring Rosemary Morris's views on the 'Byzantine saint' as 'an active participant in the affairs of the world'.[92] St Elias of Enna's ability to prophesy on battles resulted in a Byzantine admiral consulting him on how to defeat a Muslim force, and his fame earned him an invitation to the imperial court at Constantinople and great patronage for his monastery at Saline. Indeed, after Elias' death, Emperor Leo VI tried unsuccessfully to transfer his relics to the Byzantine capital.[93] St Vitalis' reputation was known to the governor (catapan) of Bari who arranged for a meeting with him in the city. After a consultation St Vitalis saved the catapan from a destructive thunderstorm.[94] It would also seem that the pilgrimage to Rome of a number of Siculo-Calabrian saints had disseminated their reputation northwards across the Italian peninsula. According to the *vita* of St Sabas, the saint was known to the Byzantine administrative elite, to members of the ruling classes in Campania, and to Otto II and his imperial circle. Sabas was 'headhunted' by both the prince of Salerno and the *patricius* of Amalfi to negotiate in Rome the release of their respective sons who were hostages at the Ottonian court. Both were

---

[90] *Vita S. Eliae Junioris*, 492, 505–6.
[91] *Vita S. Eliae Junioris*, 494.
[92] R. Morris, 'The political saint of the eleventh century', *The Byzantine Saint*, ed. S. Hackel (London, 1981), 43.
[93] *Vita S. Eliae Junioris*, 507.
[94] *Vita S. Vitalis*, 29–30.

eventually liberated, and St Sabas died in Rome in the company of Otto II's Byzantine wife Theophanu. If there are potential anachronisms in the dating of some of these events, the message remains clear: St Sabas was arbitrator and counsellor at the very highest level.[95] St Nilus of Rossano was similarly in wide demand. He received visits from high Byzantine functionaries, who sought advice and even discussion on the Holy Scriptures; he took on the role of protector of the people of Rossano; he was treated favourably by the prince of Capua who encouraged the abbot of Montecassino to donate land to St Nilus for a monastic community; he was warmly welcomed at Montecassino for a brief stay; and he had consultations with Emperor Otto III who was returning from pilgrimage to Monte Gargano.[96]

Finally, the *vitae* of these Siculo-Calabrian saints reveal significant interactions with Muslims. It is a relationship which has attracted much historiographical debate, for historians have applied evidence from these texts to address issues such as the survival of Christianity in Muslim-ruled Sicily, Muslim religious toleration and the nature of migration and settlement between island and mainland.[97] First, it is certain that the Muslim presence and acts of aggression serve as a useful literary tool for the hagiographers of the Siculo-Calabrian saints. The Muslim can be packaged as the metaphorical counterfoil to the holy man – unbelieving, greedy and punitive. Muslim actions were presented as both indiscriminate and targeted persecution, in order to construct a physical and emotional climate which compelled the saint to separate himself from all that was dear to him, and to provide a framework for the saint's miraculous interventions: powerful imagery which was simultaneously didactic and entertaining. If we negotiate our way through these considerations it appears that the hagiographies actually offer a reasonably balanced picture on Muslim interaction with both the saints and the local Christian communities.

Through the prism of the saints' personal experiences it is clear that Christian communities suffered violence and displacement as a result of the Muslim campaigns on Sicily, and this is amply supported by Arabic and Greek sources.[98] St Elias of Enna was enslaved by Muslims who had raided Enna, St Leo–Lucas chose to leave the monastery of San Filippo, Agira, and move to Calabria to avoid Muslim forces, and St Elias the Troglodyte's companion was killed by Muslims when they moved to

---

[95] Da Costa-Louillet, 'Saints', 130–9.
[96] *Vita S. Nili*, 281, 289–90, 302–5, 313–14.
[97] See Ménager, 'La Byzantinisation', 747–74; *Les Actes grecs*, ed. Guillou, 19–33; Metcalfe, *Muslims and Christians*, 13–15.
[98] Metcalfe, *Muslims and Christians*, 14.

Sicily from Calabria.[99] St Sabas, his father St Christopher, his brother St Macarius and other family members all took refuge in Calabria from Muslim incursions, and some of their movements thereafter were dictated by this continuing menace.[100] In the decades around 1000, St John Terista's father was killed by Muslim raiders in Calabria, and his mother taken into slavery in Palermo with her young son.[101] Many of these saints were also able to demonstrate their miraculous virtues vis-à-vis the Muslims, suggesting on the one hand that the infidel 'threat' was so entrenched as to forge common experiences across a large region and across a variety of communities. On the other hand, some of these encounters may well have originated out of hagiographical topoi, constructed or intensified to create resonant messages about sin and correct Christian worship. The *vita* of St Vitalis described a devastating attack on Lucania by Sicilian Muslims who had arrived 'propter peccata populi', and in many of the *vitae* the Muslims are portrayed as divine punishment for lax Christianity.[102] The threat was to be countered not by the sword but by obtaining God's grace. St Elias of Enna received a vision of torrents of blood which enabled him to foresee successfully the Muslim capture of Taormina. His subsequent prayers and fasting contributed to the defeat of the Muslim army as it moved through Calabria to Cosenza.[103] St Elias the Troglodyte's life was punctuated by short spells in refuge in the mountains as Muslim raids passed by. On one occasion, the saint sheltered in a *castellum* with his monks and averted a Muslim strike by urging them all to repent their sins; on another, a huge abyss opened before Elias' monastery and forced the terrified Muslims to retreat.[104] Sometimes the saint did more than withstand the Muslims, instead entering into dialogue with them, aiming at a lasting peace or conversion. On his travels St Elias of Enna healed, preached to and even baptized Muslims.[105] St Vitalis, on one occasion, defended his monastery alone and was about to be decapitated when a bolt of lightning struck down his Muslim executioner. Vitalis healed the stricken man and delivered a sermon to the remainder of the Muslim party, warning them to 'cease shedding Christian blood' and threatening their destruction if they continued to do so; in response the Muslims promised no longer to attack Christians.[106]

---

[99] *Vita S. Eliae Junioris*, 490; *Vita S. Eliae Spelacotae*, 850–1; *Vita S. Leonis Lucae*, 99.
[100] Da Costa-Louillet, 'Saints', 134.
[101] S. Borsari, 'Vita di S. Giovanni Terista. Testi greci inediti', *ASCL* 22 (1953), 136–7.
[102] *Vita S. Vitalis*, 34.
[103] *Vita S. Eliae Junioris*, 501.
[104] *Vita S. Eliae Spelacotae*, 876; Da Costa-Louillet, 'Saints', 121.
[105] *Vita S. Eliae Junioris*, 492, 494.
[106] *Vita S. Vitalis*, 31.

If we consider the entire texts of these *vitae*, it would seem that, while the Muslim threat might frame many of the events within, it was, in actual fact, often relegated to the background. When the Muslims are brought to the foreground it is usually to illustrate the saint's miraculous virtues in a way that is intended to transmit powerful and emotive imagery, all the easier to digest when set against a recognizable foe. St Vitalis' escape from decapitation and St Lucas of Armento's defeat of a Muslim force while riding a white horse surrounded by flames are striking examples.[107] But alongside these climactic episodes, and the background of ongoing raids, it has to be recognized that the saints also displayed their powers in other arenas – averting famine, combating demons, protecting communities from overbearing Christian lay rulers (Byzantine or Lombard). The enemy was not solely the Muslim (or *barbari* or *agareni* as the *vitae* usually labelled them). The language of our sources is too evasive to determine whether some or any of these Muslim raids were primarily motivated by religious animus. In the *vitae* we find plenty of episodes of attacks on monks, monasteries and churches, but equally as many on all manner of lay communities. There are few unambiguous examples of a deliberate attempt by Muslim forces to target a religious site simply because it was Christian. In the *vita* of St Elias the Troglodyte, Muslims disinterred the body of the holy man Arsenius because they thought they would find treasure, and then attempted to burn the body afterwards.[108] However, such a literally and metaphorically inflammatory act is more suggestive of a literary attempt to shock the audience, and if it did actually occur would seem to be the type of opportunistic plundering that regularly takes place in frontier zones where opposing sides either do not share norms of conduct, or deliberately reject them in order to damage an opponent psychologically. We might also ask if the attempt to decapitate St Vitalis was because he was a Christian monk, or because he was an obstacle to a store of booty. Indeed, because Greek-rite monks were respected figures and were integrated into the lay world around them, many would have acted as mediators; and we see some of our saints in this capacity, negotiating with Muslim parties. St Nilus famously requested the emir of Palermo to release three captive monks, and he respectfully complied. However, if negotiations had failed these monks were also likely to have been victims caught in the crossfire.[109]

---

[107] *Vita S. Lucae*, 340; S. Caruso, 'Crucisque signo munitus. Luca da Dèmena e l'epopea anti-saracena italo-greca', *Byzantion* 73 (2003), 319–38.

[108] *Vita S. Eliae Spelacotae*, 862.

[109] *Vita S. Nili*, 301–2; R. Morris, *Monks and Laymen in Byzantium, 843–1118* (Cambridge, 1995), 90–119.

In the picture of Muslim–Christian relationships emerging from these *vitae*, the spiritual vocation of our saints should not be overlooked. The spiritual and mental orientation of some of the saints encouraged movement, refuge and separation, and thus the Muslim threat was not always intrinsically responsible for these aspects of the saint's life. Some of the saints were clearly predisposed to migrate and, more importantly, were able to do so; many came from the middle ranks of society and were unburdened by ties and responsibilities in their native lands. St John Terista (d. late eleventh century?) was encouraged to leave for Calabria to become a true Christian, but he also actually migrated in order to reclaim his family's patrimony there.[110] Moreover, hagiographers were likely to fit movement into a divinely inspired narrative in which the Muslims could play an important didactic role. In contrast, the outlook and circumstance of a rural peasant were more likely to compel him to remain *in situ*, endure the Muslim threat and find accommodation with it. In addition, we must not see movement from Sicily to the mainland in polarized terms of a transition from danger to security; Calabria, Lucania, Apulia and Campania all suffered from Muslim military intervention. The Muslim threat is apparent particularly in several early medieval Campanian hagiographies.[111] The Muslim presence and perceived threat did not dissolve on the mainland. In short, we must acknowledge the limitations in the hagiographies of these Siculo-Calabrian saints for revealing patterns of larger-scale emigration from Sicily or for identifying Muslim religious persecution. Clearly, the *vitae* show destruction caused by Muslim forces, and some displacement as a result, but it would be problematic to take that evidence further. What we find in the *vitae* is evidence of the often indiscriminate collateral damage caused by warfare in a contested frontier zone, and much of the conflict appears to operate on the level of military and economic, rather than religious, dimensions. That there is definitely a discontinuity in the history of Sicilian sanctity associated with the period of Muslim rule is undoubted and inevitable, and extending the evidence from the *vitae* of the Siculo-Calabrian saints would suggest that Christian worship, including cults, was vulnerable in a Muslim-controlled territory. However, it also suggests that this was the by-product of large and prolonged transitions effected by Arab–Islamic immigration, the economic and political marginalization of Christian communities, and the fallout from frontier conflict, rather than by targeted attacks on forms of Christian worship, such as shrines and cults.

---

[110] Borsari, 'Vita', 137–8.
[111] *Ex Miraculis Sancti Agrippini*, 463–4, depicted St Agrippinus of Naples warding off Muslim naval attacks; and see also *Translatio Sancti Sosii*, 460–1.

Corroborating evidence might be found in the fact that during the entire period of Muslim rule on Sicily there are scarce examples of Christian victims who were considered to be martyrs. There is reference in the Constantinopolitan synaxarium to four martyrs of Syracuse, and other hints of martyrs in the ninth and tenth centuries, but the low numbers are revealing as is the Church's apparent reluctance to promote them.[112] L. T. White argues convincingly that there was no systematic persecution of Sicily's Christian population.[113] St Elias of Enna appears to have been able to move freely across Sicily when he returned to the island, while St Elias the Troglodyte actually moved from Calabria to Sicily. St Vitalis, St Filaretus of Seminara (who left Sicily in c.1040) and many of the saints considered here were also able to receive a Christian education in Sicily, sometimes in settlements directly under Muslim control.[114] We should resist drawing too straight a line between the Muslims and other challenges and suffering that Sicily's Christian population endured. Some migration to the mainland was forced by famine, another indirect result of the war zone that Sicily often was. The *vita* of St Sabas speaks of migration induced by terrible famine and even cannibalism on the island as a deleterious by-product of the Muslim raids.[115] The collapse of an organized diocesan network on Sicily appears to have been the result of its marginalization from Christian Europe during the Muslim period, lack of patronage, and indirect socio-cultural pressure to assimilate, rather than of a sustained assault by Muslim parties. Monasticism certainly suffered, and even San Filippo, Agira, appears to have collapsed in the later tenth century, but a number of houses survived to preserve Christian worship and the traditions of the island saints.

The first century and a half of Muslim rule in Sicily had been a fractious period with fluctuating zones of power, encouraging opportunistic raids and a booty economy. However, as we move into the second half of the tenth century, signs suggest that Muslim Sicily was stabilizing, even if it did not endure long into the eleventh century. Its rulers began to establish a more structured central administration, assimilation between Christian and Muslim was increasing, and so-called 'internal jihads' against Christian communities were driven as much by political and strategic agendas as by religious ones.[116] For a more complete understanding of the functioning of Christianity in Sicily during this period, and more

---

[112] F. Scorza Barcellona, 'Note sui martiri dell'invasione saracena', *La Sicilia nella tarda antichità e nell'alto medioevo*, ed. R. Barcellona and S. Pricoco (Catania, 1999), 219.

[113] White, *Latin Monasticism*, 30–5.

[114] *Vita S. Philareti*, 605.

[115] Da Costa-Louillet, 'Saints', 135.

[116] Metcalfe, *Muslims of Medieval Italy*, 44–66, 79.

especially of the fortunes of its Christian cults, we must also turn to developments following the Norman arrival in the eleventh century (in Chapter 4). Evidence from the later period does at least indicate that while saints' cults were in a state of decay on the island, some still commanded a sufficient level of veneration among the Christian communities in Sicily and elsewhere in the Christian world to serve as a base point for their later revival after the end of Muslim rule.

2 The Latin mainland: South Italian saints, Normans, Church reform and urbanization

The evolution of South Italian sanctity in the Central Middle Ages was a complex process which developed in varied forms, some conflicting and distinct, some colliding and overlapping. Ancient saints, representing a past world, were venerated alongside contemporary saints, some rather different from their forerunners in origin and status, others displaying evident commonalities. Most of the early medieval cults examined in Chapter 1 continued into the Central Middle Ages, but many tended to fade into the background after an initial period of intense cultic activity, their continued presence usually attested in feast days, church dedications and liturgical materials. Some older cults were given a new life, rebranded through new hagiographies and relic translations. Medieval southern Italy was not inherently conservative in its veneration of saints, and our period witnessed the emergence of new cults, some native, some imported. The Latin zones of the mainland produced a group of new saints for the first time since the fifth to seventh centuries, excepting isolated cases at Naples and Montecassino. At the same time, many saints' cults orbited around two seemingly contrasting worlds, one urban and populous (southern Italy experienced profound urban expansion and the restructuring of urban episcopal sees in the years 1000 to 1200), the other remote and isolated (the Church reform, which promoted separation from the secular world, and new waves of monasticism and eremitism). Finally, overlaying all these developments was the arrival of the Normans, bringing a new ruling elite, different connections to a wider world and, ultimately, unification of the south. Cults developed uneven rhythms of expansion and contraction. Many experienced brief surges or pulses of increased activity which resulted in new hagiographies, relic translations or building works at shrines. These pulses often correlated with wider transitions: changes in lay rulership, accelerated change within the ecclesiastical world, and significant demographic shifts. This chapter will thus examine the salient features of South Italian sanctity between 1000 and 1200 via a thematic investigation shaped by those major transitions. No claims are made here to cover every dimension of every South Italian saint's cult, and indeed this chapter focuses on the Latin areas of the mainland – primarily Campania, central and northern Apulia and the Abruzzi – where many of those themes are especially apparent. Evidence from Sicily and from the zones of Greek settlement on the mainland will be incorporated, but Chapters 3 and 4 are devoted specifically to sanctity in these regions.

The Normans and South Italian sanctity

The traditions surrounding the Normans' arrival in southern Italy are varied. Nevertheless, the common thread of pilgrimage binds at least two accounts offered by chroniclers of eleventh-century southern Italy. According to Amatus of Montecassino, in c.1000 some forty Norman pilgrims returning from the Holy Sepulchre rescued Salerno from a Muslim siege and were beseeched by the Salernitans to return with more Normans to defend them in the future.[1] Around a decade or so later, William of Apulia depicted the Normans as pilgrims at the shrine of St Michael on Monte Gargano, where they encountered the Lombard rebel Melus who recruited their military prowess for his anti-Byzantine uprising.[2] However, the pious traits exhibited in these earliest Norman visitors were not immediately reflected in those who followed in the subsequent decades. The state of conflict in which the Norman mercenaries immersed themselves allowed little space to promote cults or show devotion to saints. Indeed, relationships with the local church were strained; it was often targeted by Normans or caught in the crossfire of conflicts associated with them. The idea of the pious Norman would have seemed a fallacy to many native South Italians in the first half of the eleventh century, and few Norman churchmen arrived in the peninsula to offer an alternative face to early Norman activity. Consequently, the main narrators of the early Norman infiltration focus on their military valour, but also implicitly on the damage they wrought.

Some hagiographical and monastic accounts go further and indicate that the Normans were considered to be the enemies of saints in the early period of their infiltration. One of the traditions of the rediscovery of the relics of St Cataldus depicts the citizens of Taranto anxiously transferring them from the countryside to within the city, amidst fears that a band of Normans camped on a nearby mountain might steal the relics in transit. The account is set in 1094 but seems to preserve memories of Norman

---

[1] Amatus, Bk I.17–19, pp. 249–51.
[2] Wil. Apulia, Bk I, pp. 98–100 lines 11–27.

lawlessness earlier in the eleventh century.[3] More prominent was the opposition from the patron saints of monasteries which suffered from the insecurity generated by the Norman presence.[4] Two closely connected works, the *Dialogues* of Desiderius, abbot of Montecassino (1058–87), and the *Montecassino Chronicle*, signal St Benedict's displeasure towards the Normans in the first half of the eleventh century. Campania, in which lay the vast territories of Montecassino (*Terra Sancti Benedicti*), was often a battleground in the 1020s to 1040s on which the Normans were conspicuous players.[5] The *Dialogues* (completed c.1076–9) was Desiderius' attempt to record the miracles performed by St Benedict. While the style and some of the themes of Desiderius' *Dialogues* imitated the earlier famed work of the same name by Pope Gregory the Great, which also contained material on St Benedict, nevertheless Desiderius' piece was firmly situated in the climate of eleventh-century Montecassino, both in its content and its purpose.[6] One of the *Dialogues'* key messages revolved around St Benedict's protection of his monastery. Two miracles recorded therein present the Normans as an aggressive foe. In one, a Norman who pillaged fishermen of Montecassino was drowned by a large divinely inspired wave.[7] In the other, a band of Normans who had actually been hired to defend Montecassino started pillaging its lands instead like a 'crawling crab'. As a result, St Benedict appeared to a peasant informing him that the Normans 'who had invaded his belongings' would be expelled from them. An ensuing battle (dated to 1045) was subsequently recounted by the *Dialogues* in which the Norman 'infestation' was rooted out of the *Terra Sancti Benedicti*.[8] The *Montecassino Chronicle* (continued up to the 1120s), generally more neutral in tone, concurred that the Norman expulsion was achieved 'with the help of Father Benedict', and also recorded a vision by a peasant in which St Benedict beat the Normans with a staff, thus foretelling the recovery of a fortified site on Montecassino's lands. Indeed, a monk, understood to be St Benedict, even appeared alongside the men of Montecassino as they fought to recover the fortification from Norman occupation.[9] Other

---

[3] A. Hofmeister, 'Sermo de Inventione Sancti Kataldi', *Münchener Museum für Philologie des Mittelalters und der Renaissance* 4 (1924), 101–14.

[4] See G. A. Loud, 'Monastic miracles in southern Italy, c.1040–1140', *Studies in Church History* 41 (2005), 115–19.

[5] H. E. J. Cowdrey, *The Age of Abbot Desiderius. Montecassino, the Papacy, and the Normans in the Eleventh and Early-Twelfth Centuries* (Oxford, 1983), 108–17.

[6] Desiderius, *Dialogi de Miraculis Sancti Benedicti*, ed. G. Schwarz and A. Hofmeister, MGH SS xxx (2) (Leipzig, 1934); Loud, 'Monastic miracles', 111–12.

[7] Desiderius, Bk I.11, p. 1124.

[8] Desiderius, Bk I.22, pp. 1138–9.

[9] Chron. Cas., Bk II.70–2, pp. 308–14; Loud, 'Monastic miracles', 116–7.

monastic saints protected their monasteries from the Normans with equal vigour.[10] The monastery of S. Clemente a Casauria in the Abruzzi suffered great instability later on in the period from c. 1090 to c.1100. St Clement acted with severity against those despoiling his abbey: Normans Hugh Mamouzet and Richard, count of Manopello, incurred St Clement's displeasure and both consequently perished.[11]

However, as Graham Loud makes clear, the presentation in these monastic sources of the Normans as 'conscienceless predators' was undoubtedly misleading.[12] These great monasteries were wealthy but also vulnerable. Conflicts and controversies were inevitable in periods of insecurity, and, importantly, leading monastic houses could respond by harnessing high-profile saints and a stock of highly educated monks to articulate their own position. Therefore, vivid, but not necessarily representative, portrayals of the plundering Norman, enemy of saints, emerge from some monastic houses. When taken in their entirety, it is also clear that these monastic sources show that members of the native community also preyed on monastic lands and earned the wrath of their patron saints. Montecassino was especially hostile to the Lombard prince of Capua, Pandulf IV, and various Lombard nobles caused trouble on monastic lands.[13] Elsewhere, lesser religious centres and urban communities were not able to construct opposition to the Normans through their local saints, or did not see the need to, opting instead for accommodation and collaboration with the newcomers.

In any case, the Norman presence in southern Italy soon experienced a positive transformation which increasingly discouraged opposition. The 1050s and 1060s, the era of papal–Norman rapprochement and the beginning of the conquest of Sicily, saw the rehabilitation of the Normans. The narrative sources, particularly Amatus' chronicle, enact a shift which transmuted the Normans into God's warriors, their actions legitimized by divine favour, and their earlier misdemeanours now set in a grander divine scheme. As the eleventh century progressed the Normans began to control more territories, conditions stabilized, and more Normans were able to patronize religious houses and develop more positive relationships with local saints. Montecasssino performed a notable volte-face under the abbacy of Desiderius, becoming a firm ally of the Quarrels at Capua and of the Hautevilles.[14] However, there is limited evidence of

---

[10] Loud, 'Monastic miracles', 117–8.
[11] *Chronicon Casauriense*, ed. L. A. Muratori, RIS 2 (ii) (Milan, 1726), 869–70, 871, 872–4.
[12] Loud, *Latin Church*, 76.
[13] Desiderius, Bk I.10, p. 1124; 13, pp. 1125–6; Loud, *Latin Church*, 71–6.
[14] Cowdrey, *Age of Abbot Desiderius*, 107–76.

direct connections between the Normans and sanctity in southern Italy. The Normans tended to support cults from a distance, financing the building of new cathedrals and religious houses, rather than to control and shape them openly. As we shall see in Chapter 4, the interrelationship between Normans and saints in Sicily was similar. Saints featured barely at all in the record of the Norman conquest of Sicily, an enterprise that had potentially charged religious dimensions, and thereafter the Normans primarily engaged with cults indirectly through supporting the revival of a church network and the production of liturgical works on the island. On the mainland, the chief chronicles and charter documentation offer little on Norman influence on South Italian sanctity, suggesting that the Norman attitude towards sanctity in southern Italy was neither contentious nor unconventional, and certainly did not provoke much comment. In southern Italy there was none of the controversy aroused in England following 1066, when the influx of Norman churchmen brought some new Normanno-French cults and instances of initial uncertainty about Anglo-Saxon saints. Accommodation was reached in Norman England, and Anglo-Saxon cults rehabilitated by the twelfth century, but for a period sanctity in England had been a contested issue.[15]

In southern Italy, neither the episcopate nor monastic houses were filled with many Normans, even when accounting for the problems inherent in associating ethnic identity with anthroponyms. Some zones, such as the principality of Salerno, appear to have received almost none at all. On the other hand, some Frenchmen were appointed to episcopal sees or entered monasteries from the second half of the eleventh century. Aversa, Melfi, Mileto, Troia and Venosa appear to have had a series of Normanno-French bishops, but they were all centres of Norman activity and were notable exceptions.[16] As a result, new saints from northern Europe did make some impression in southern Italy, finding their way into local liturgical works. The monasteries at Sant'Eufemia in Calabria and SS Trinità di Venosa in Lucania were staffed with a larger body of Normanno-French monks, who brought with them the liturgy and monastic customs of St Evroult in Normandy.[17] The sanctorale associated with Rouen and Le Mans infiltrated some South Italian liturgical works, most prominently in Sicily, while a number of the magnificent South Italian exultet rolls show Norman

[15] S. J. Ridyard, 'Condigna Veneratio: post-conquest attitudes to the saints of the Anglo-Saxons', *Anglo-Norman Studies* 9 (1987), 179–206; P. A. Hayward, 'Translation narratives in post-conquest hagiography and English resistance to the Norman conquest', *Anglo-Norman Studies* 21 (1999), 67–93.

[16] Loud, *Latin Church*, 119–27.

[17] See H. Houben, *Die Abtei Venosa und das Mönchtum im normannisch-staufischen Süditalien* (Tübingen, 1995).

influence.[18] While insertion into the liturgy should not be underestimated, since it established a saint as a conduit for expressing authority, and communal memory and identity, it remains the case that new Normanno-French saints' cults rarely transcended the liturgical sphere and thus never displaced their native counterparts.[19] Positive evidence for more direct imposition of Norman cults (relic transfers, new shrine centres or church dedications) is largely absent.[20] The scarcity of Normans within the South Italian church, and the overall low number of Norman immigrants, necessitated a muted veneration of 'Norman' saints.

Moreover, the few examples of possible Normanno-French churchmen playing a direct role in saints' cults show that they identified with and promoted local South Italian saints. According to one tradition, the rediscovery of the relics of St Cataldus at Taranto occurred under the episcopate of Drogo (attested c.1071), a Norman-named bishop who had started renovating the old cathedral.[21] An alternative tradition, the *Sermon on the discovery of St Cataldus*, claimed the relics were rediscovered outside the city in 1094, and emphasized the tension felt by the citizens of Taranto in moving the relics into the city without alerting a band of predatory Normans based nearby.[22] The bishop of Taranto at the time was said to be (an otherwise unattested) Gilbert who, the account tells us, was a Norman. The citizens of Taranto feared he might betray news of the translation to his fellow Normans, but also realized they needed his skill and input to develop the cult. Gilbert duly assisted the Tarentini and was central to the final stages of the translation thereafter, although popular pressure forced Gilbert to deposit the relics in the church of S. Biagio and not in the cathedral. The two traditions clearly contradict, but the *Sermon* may at least preserve a rare glimpse of the tension created by the presence of a Norman bishop and the clashes this could generate with the local lay and clerical communities. Nevertheless, the binding force of a local cult offered the space for collaboration between the opposing parties, and showed where most bishops' loyalties ultimately lay.

In the city of Troia, which fell under the rule of Robert Guiscard in around 1060 and thereafter became a key centre of ducal power, Normanno-French bishops promoted the development of local cults.

[18] T. F. Kelly, *The Exultet*, 74–6, 211; Manchester, John Rylands Library, MS 1 offers a fine example of an Italian exultet roll.
[19] For the importance of the liturgy see S. Boynton, *Shaping of a Monastic Identity. Liturgy and History at the Imperial Abbey of Farfa, 1000–1125* (Ithaca, 2006), 184–229.
[20] With the possible exception of the late twelfth-century mosaic images of northern European saints at Monreale: see Chapter 4.
[21] *Historia S. Cataldi*, 569.
[22] Hofmeister, 'Sermo', 107–110.

Stephen *normannus*, bishop of Troia from 1059 to 1080, took an interest in St Secundinus who was alleged to be an early bishop of Aecae, an ancient settlement to which Troia claimed to be heir. His relics had apparently been rediscovered in the period between 1022 and 1034, during which an anonymous author wrote the *Historia inventionis corporis S. Secundini*. Stephen built on these past traditions and requested that Montecassino rewrite an *Inventio Secundini*, which was produced in c.1067, along with a poem and a hymn, by the accomplished Montecassino monk and hagiographer Guaiferius.[23] The promotion of a local cult advertised Stephen's efforts to effect a reconciliation between the urban community and its new Norman overlords, and to deepen his see's Christian heritage.[24] Later, other relics, of Saints Eleutherius, Pontianus and Anastasius, were translated to Troia from Tivera (near Velletri) in 1104 during the episcopacy of Bishop William I (1102–6), a Frenchman.[25] The cults of these saints were consolidated by his compatriot and successor, William II (1106–41), to whom the translation account was dedicated; he presided thereafter over the continued renovation of the city's cathedral, which incorporated on its main bronze doors images of the three saints, alongside Secundinus.[26] There is some further evidence for Norman churchmen commissioning the production of hagiographical texts dedicated to South Italian saints, even Greek Orthodox ones. A Latin translation of the life of St Elias the Troglodyte (d. c.960) was produced, probably in the 1080s, by a Benedictine monk from the Latin monastery of Sant'Eufemia in Calabria. If the dates are correct, Sant'Eufemia's Norman abbot Robert de Grandmesnil almost certainly initiated the translation, and indeed some of the language and concepts of the *Life* were 'Normannized'. While this hagiographical work may show genuine devotion to a native, Greek Christian saint, and a Latin attempt to acculturate with the surrounding Greek Christian community, it is also notable that Sant'Eufemia claimed ownership of the Calabrian monastery that was dedicated to St Elias.[27]

---

[23] E. D'Angelo, 'Inventio Corporis et Miracula Sancti Secundini Troiani Episcopi', *Scripturus Vitam: lateinische Biographie von der Antike bis in die Gegenwart – Festgabe für Walter Berschin zum 65. Geburtstag*, ed. D. Walz (Heidelberg, 2002), 841–54 and *Historia inventionis corporis S. Secundini*, AS February, ii (Paris, 1864), 530–5.

[24] As discussed by C. Bottiglieri, 'Literary themes and genres in southern Italy during the Norman age: the return of the saints', *Norman Tradition and Transcultural Heritage*, ed. S. Burckhardt and T. Foerster (Farnham, 2013), 97–124.

[25] A. Poncelet, 'La Translation des SS. Éleuthère, Pontien et Anastase', *AB* 29 (1910), 09–26, at 416.

[26] Galdi, 'Troia, Montecassino e i Normanni', 63–83; Bloch, *Monte Cassino*, i. 560.

[27] M. V. Strazzeri, 'Una traduzione dal Greco ad uso dei normanni: la vita Latina di Sant'Elia lo Speleota', *ASCL* 59 (1992), 1–108 (includes the Latin edition of the *Life* at 42–86).

The South Italian Normans, both churchmen and secular rulers, were fortunate enough to have established their positions in the second half of the eleventh century when southern Italy began to experience the effects of Church reform, urbanization and the growing popularity of pilgrimage, all of which shaped the profound expansion of South Italian cults. This was strikingly apparent in the period between c.1070 and c.1125 which saw several new saints' cults established and old ones revived.[28] During this period, southern Italy was a far from stable landscape; disorder, uprisings and social upheaval occurred, but the main era of military conflict and power shifts had largely passed. Now Norman lords consolidated their control over a vast swathe of territories, with the Hautevilles at the top of the pyramid. Certainly, many native lords retained their positions, and some cities (Naples and Benevento) escaped Norman dominance; generally speaking, however, many of those revived or newly emerging saints' cults were located in lands under Norman lordship. It is true that other forces – those mentioned earlier – drove this broad growth of cults and that in a number of cities in the late eleventh and early twelfth centuries Norman rule was nominal at best. Nevertheless, it is striking that, in many cases, the emergence or re-emergence of a cult took place after a Norman takeover and must have required the tacit assent or cooperation of Norman lords or churchmen. As we have seen, the translation of the relics to Troia in 1104 was driven primarily by the city's Normanno-French bishop at a time when the city was largely self-governing. Nevertheless, the translation account describes Duke Roger Borsa as 'the most noble supporter of churches and saints', and makes clear that his permission was behind the enterprise.[29] The cooperation of the Norman elite was particularly important when shrines were housed in new cathedrals and churches. This period saw a large wave of magnificent cathedral and church reconstructions particularly in Apulia, where over twenty building programmes commenced at this time (including the cathedrals at Brindisi, Canosa, Taranto and Troia). In some cases this was facilitated by the patronage of Norman lords, which enabled religious institutions to form their own temporal bases from which construction could be financed.[30]

Most famously, the relics of St Nicholas were translated from Myra to Bari in 1087. The initiative came from the Barese citizenry, but they were under the lordship of Robert Guiscard's son and successor Roger Borsa

---

[28] Just some of these include: St Matthew at Salerno, St Nicholas and St Sabinus at Bari, St Mennas at Caiazzo, St Cataldus at Taranto, St Canius at Acerenza, Saints Secundinus, Eleuterius, Pontianus and Anastasius at Troia, St Nicholas the Pilgrim at Trani.

[29] Poncelet, 'Translation', 424.

[30] Martin, *Pouille*, 618–19; T. Garton, *Early Romanesque Sculpture in Apulia* (New York, 1984), 130–5.

when it took place. Later, in 1089, Roger handed Bari over to his famous elder half-brother Bohemond, who governed the city from a distance with pragmatism and sensitivity.[31] The church of S. Nicola, where the saint's shrine was housed, and its first two governors (Elias and Eustasius) thereafter engaged in several territorial and financial transactions with Bohemond's officials and vassals which suggest an atmosphere of collaboration.[32] A charter of 1101, for example, reveals that Bohemond had already donated three-quarters of an olive plantation to the hospital of St Nicholas of Bari.[33] Indeed, Urban II visited Bari and dedicated the new church of St Nicholas in 1089 at both Roger's and Bohemond's request.[34] Elsewhere, various Norman lords, most prominently the Quarrels and later the Hautevilles, were conspicuous benefactors of Montecassino and, by extension, of St Benedict.[35] Amatus framed the interrelationship between patronage of a religious house and its officials, on the one hand, and devotion to its patron saint, on the other, when he presented Prince Richard of Capua's desire to give Montecassino lordship over the city of Aquino because of victories he had gained through 'the glorious merit of St. Benedict and of the brothers who were in the holy monastery and through their prayers'.[36] Therefore, Norman rulers must be positioned, if only in an indirect supporting role, in the striking development of saints' cults in the late eleventh and early twelfth centuries.

The Norman relationship with saints' cults was eminently effective. It articulated Norman piety, and legitimated their presence, while creating space for collaboration with local communities by allowing them to channel their devotion into cults which enhanced their own sense of identity and heritage. Often, this collaboration is difficult to detect openly, as at Bari, and Normans rarely feature in the hagiographical works of the eleventh century. An obvious opportunity to create a relationship with a saint could occur when a city fell, articulating divine approval for a change in rulership, but with the exception of Salerno (as we shall shortly see) this potential collaboration was rarely promoted. Certainly there is very little evidence that the Normans as a group nurtured any collective devotion for specific saints within southern Italy. The Normans might well have felt an

---

[31] Oldfield, *City and Community*, 33–6.
[32] CDBV, nos. 14, 15, 18–20, 32, 57; a grandson of one of Robert Guiscard's elder brothers was buried in the cemetery of the church of St Nicholas, and suggests continuing bonds between the shrine and the Hautevilles: CDBV, no. 50.
[33] CDBV, no. 34; in 1111 Robert, count of Conversano, the son of the previous Norman count Geoffrey, donated a church near Frassineto to St Nicholas of Bari: CDBV, no. 56.
[34] CDBI, no. 33.
[35] H. Dormeier, *Montecassino und die Laien im 11. und 12. Jahrhundert* (Stuttgart, 1979), 28–52, 114–21, 155–6.
[36] Amatus, Bk VI.24–25, pp. 435–7.

affinity for the cults of eastern warrior saints, like St George and St Demetrius, but their popularity in southern Italy was based far more on their pre-established universal popularity, on eastern Mediterranean roots and local South Italian devotions, rather than through Norman promotion.[37] It is certainly quite perplexing that the Normans did not cultivate stronger ties with the cult of St Michael on Monte Gargano. Indeed, according to William of Apulia, the Norman story in the south began with pilgrimage to the shrine. Although the shrine continued to grow during the Central Middle Ages, and the security of Norman rule helped, there is no direct evidence that the Normans found a common identity with, or promoted, the cult. The Norman lords of Monte Sant'Angelo, under whose dominion Monte Gargano fell, did not even adopt an image of the saint on their seals. The shrine had strong pre-existing Lombard and Byzantine associations, but this might have made it, if anything, more appealing to the Normans as another mechanism to stress continuity and legitimacy.[38]

Occasionally we catch glimpses of more direct intervention from Norman churchmen, as we have seen, and also from secular rulers. The Norman Count Robert of Caiazzo, son of a younger brother of Prince Richard I of Capua, instigated two translations of the relics of St Mennas, thus reviving the cult of a putative sixth-century hermit.[39] The first translation moved the relics in 1094 from Mount Taburno, in the Beneventan archdiocese, to Caiazzo, located in the Capuan archdiocese. The second movement (influenced partly by Montecassino) of the relics occurred between 1102 and 1107 when they were transferred to the new church of St Mennas at S. Agata dei Goti, a location apparently more secure from claims made on the saint's remains by the Beneventan archbishop.[40] Not only did Robert build this new church at S. Agata dei Goti but he also commissioned an associated dossier of hagiographical works, including an expanded *vita* and two translation accounts.[41] Furthermore, Robert requested Montecassino to produce these texts, and the task fell to Leo of

---

[37] Imagery of these military saints appeared in Palermitan royal buildings, and Nicetas Choniates referred to Sicilian devotion to St Demetrius. But these all date from the mid- to late twelfth century, at which point Norman identities in the south had effectively disappeared.

[38] J.-M. Martin, 'Les Normands et le culte de Saint-Michel en Italie du sud', *Culte et pèlerinages*, ed. P. Bouet et al. (Rome, 2003), 31–64, at 341–3.

[39] Cowdrey, *Age of Abbot Desiderius*, 39–41.

[40] Bottiglieri, 'Literary themes'.

[41] H. Hoffmann, 'Die Translationes et Miracula Sancti Mennatis des Leo Marsicanus', *Deutsches Archiv für Erforschung des Mittelalters* 60 (2004), 441–81. The life is edited by G. Orlandi, 'Vita Sancti Mennatis. Opera inedita di Leone Marsicanus', *Istituto lombardo, Accademia di scienze e lettere, Rendiconti, Classe di lettere* 97 (1963), 467–90.

Ostia, the celebrated author of part of the *Montecassino Chronicle*, who wrote them in stages between 1094 and his death in 1115.[42] Robert, a generous benefactor of Montecassino, turned to the monastery to gain access to an authoritative tradition of hagiographical writing and to gain legitimacy from an esteemed South Italian monastery.[43] He was clearly eager to present his piety in wider circles; the first translation account depicts Robert ruminating on how to adorn his new church at Caiazzo with relics, while one of the *miracula* added after the second translation shows him being healed through his devotion to St Mennas, and subsequently attending a celebratory ceremony for the saint's feast day.

However, Robert's devotion to St Mennas was not the most conspicuous example of a connection between a Norman and a South Italian saint. Duke Robert Guiscard demonstrated an eagerness to advertise ties to St Matthew and to promote his cult at Salerno.[44] The earliest indication of this relationship appears in Amatus' chronicle, composed c.1078–80. In the section just prior to his description of the Battle of Civitate (1053), Amatus portrays St Matthew's pro-Norman inclinations unequivocally and at an early stage in the Norman infiltration. Archbishop John of Salerno (1047–57) had fallen ill, and had been carried before the relics of St Matthew. During his sleep, St Matthew appeared to the archbishop and prophesied the papal defeat at Civitate with the ringing warning:

for whoever will attempt to expel the Normans will either die or suffer great affliction, because this land was given to the Normans by God. On account of the perversity of those who held it and the marriages which they made with the Normans, the just will of God has conveyed the land to them.[45]

Thus Amatus begins to construct the Norman transition away from predatory plunderers to pious warriors. Thereafter, St Matthew appears in Amatus' work as a tool to contrast the depravity and duplicity of Prince Gisulf II of Salerno with the piety and virtue of Robert Guiscard, and so to justify the Lombard prince's eventual downfall at the hands of the Norman duke.[46] On one occasion, some wealthy Pisan merchants visited

---

[42] Hoffmann, 'Translationes', 458–9.

[43] Bottiglieri, 'Literary themes'; G. A. Loud, 'The Norman counts of Caiazzo and the abbey of Montecassino', *Monastica I. Scritti raccolti in memoria del XV centenario della nascita di San Benedetto (480–1980)*, Miscellanea Cassinese, 44 (Montecassino, 1981), 199–217 (reprinted in his *Montecassino and Benevento in the Middle Ages* (Aldershot, 2000)).

[44] On the cult see the excellent works of Amalia Galdi: 'Il santo e la città', 21–92; 'La diffusione del culto del santo patrono: l'esempio di S. Matteo di Salerno', *Pellegrinaggi e itinerari*, ed. G. Vitolo (Naples, 1999), 181–91.

[45] Amatus, Bk III.38, pp. 332–3.

[46] The author of the *Lives of the First Four Abbots of Cava* (composed c.1141–56) also fitted the Norman conquest into a divine plan, and depicted one of Cava's saintly abbots, Leo (d. 1079), prophesying the fall of Gisulf's sinful rule, VQPAC, 13.

St Matthew's shrine after they believed the saint's intervention had saved them from shipwreck.[47] Having offered gifts at the shrine, the Pisan merchants discovered that their ships had been looted on Gisulf's orders, and they themselves were subsequently imprisoned, tortured and held for ransom. Gisulf's treachery was thus given a sacrilegious edge by exploiting devotion to St Matthew, a message particularly distasteful to the Salernitans. Maintaining the same theme, we find the desperate prince, shortly before his defeat, molesting 'God and the saints', breaking into St Matthew's vault and destroying the sacred vessels found there.[48] Finally, Amatus brought Guiscard, in the aftermath of Salerno's capitulation, into a direct relationship with St Matthew. The Lombard prince had stolen a tooth of St Matthew, and Guiscard requested its return because he 'did not want the city to lose that relic'.[49] In response Gisulf deceitfully sent the tooth of a Jew. Guiscard soon discovered the ruse and threatened violent retribution if the genuine relic was not handed over. Consequently, St Matthew's tooth was hastily dispatched 'to the devout Duke Robert'. Amatus' construction of the triangular relationship – Guiscard, St Matthew, Gisulf – was composed for the purpose of justifying and explaining Guiscard's conquests and his capture of Salerno. The framework was straightforward and, conversely, Norman reversals could be explained through the resistance of native saints. When Prince Richard of Capua attempted to capture Naples in 1078 he noticed a contingent of armed men dressed in white aiding the defenders. Richard, believing one of them to be the city's archbishop, asked him why he was helping the resistance, to which the prelate replied that one of the armed men was none other than St Ianuarius who 'protects and defends this city'. Richard refused to believe this and continued the siege, only for it to fail and the prince to die shortly afterwards.[50]

How far Amatus' use of St Matthew to encourage sympathy for the Norman cause was disseminated within Salerno is impossible to know. But other evidence indicates that Amatus accurately reflected Robert's relationship with St Matthew, for the Norman was fully conscious of the importance of the cult, and expressed this to the Salernitans. Guiscard forged an alliance with Archbishop Alfanus I of Salerno (1058–85) which was articulated most visibly through St Matthew. Alfanus was highly educated and a celebrated poet, composing various hymns in honour of St Matthew (and other lesser Salernitan saints), and cultivated the bond

---

[47] Amatus, Bk VIII.4, pp. 483–4.
[48] Amatus, Bk VIII.18, p. 494.
[49] Amatus, Bk VIII.29, p. 506.
[50] Chron. Cas., Bk III.45, p. 423.

between the Salernitan *cives* and their patron saint.[51] Both Norman duke and Lombard prelate collaborated in the renovation of the city cathedral in 1080, which led to the rediscovery and translation of the relics of St Matthew into a grand new shrine. Guiscard's name appears above the cathedral's main portal as well as on the lintel above its bronze doors, where it states in verse: 'A church has been given to thee, O Apostle, by Duke Robert. In return for his merits, may he too be granted the gift of the kingdom of heaven.'[52] Salernitan coinage displayed the effigy of St Matthew, and Guiscard was alleged to have taken a relic of the saint's arm with him on his expedition to Byzantium in 1081.[53] It appears that, alongside any personal devotion to the saint, Guiscard sensed an opportunity to play down the Norman takeover and to enhance the cultural splendour of Salerno. After 1080, under Norman rule, the cult's prominence in Salerno rose significantly (see more later in this chapter) and showed how little it had been cultivated previously by the Lombard ruling elite. Key dynamics which enabled Norman domination intersected through the cult: the nurturing of civic loyalty towards the new rulers, alliances with native churchmen which allowed positive depictions of the Normans to be encapsulated both visually and ideologically, and the approval of institutions such as Montecassino and the papacy, which conferred legitimacy. The often fractious relationship between Guiscard and Montecassino could only have been improved through collaboration with Archbishop Alfanus, a former Montecassino monk, and by enabling Abbot Desiderius to transfer some relics of St Matthew to Montecassino; Pope Gregory VII personally congratulated Alfanus on the discovery of St Matthew's relics, which were later (in 1085) buried in the city's cathedral.[54] The cult also shaped the devotional attitudes and the secular exchanges of other Normans of the same generation. For example, in 1090, Robert, count of the Principate (d.1099), the son of Guiscard's brother William (d.1080), confirmed the archbishopric of Salerno's rights over lands at Licinano and Eboli, doing so on account of his devotion to St Matthew 'through whose prayers to God we are daily assisted'.[55] The

---

[51] P. Delogu, *Mito di una città meridionale (Salerno, secoli VIII–XI)* (Naples, 1977), 181–90; *I carmi di Alfano I, arcivescovo di Salerno*, ed. A. Lentini and F. Avagliano, Miscellanea Cassinese 38 (Montecassino, 1974), nos. 7–9 pp. 84–9, nos. 58–60 pp. 225–8; B. Vetere, 'Cattedrale, santo patrono e cives', *Salerno nel Medioevo*, ed. H. Taviani-Carozzi et al. (Galatina, 2000), 55–95.

[52] Bloch, *Monte Cassino*, i. 83 n. 2.

[53] Travaini, *La monetazione*, 262, 271–5; Chron. Cas., Bk III.45, 57, pp. 423, 437–8; IV.73, p. 539.

[54] Bloch, *Monte Cassino*, i. 82–4; *The Register of Pope Gregory VII – 1073–1085*, trans. H. E. J. Cowdrey (Oxford, 2002), no. 8 pp. 373–4.

[55] *Pergamene salernitane (1008–1784)*, ed. L. E. Pennacchini (Naples, 1941), no. 10 p. 52.

cult of St Matthew was thus a set piece statement of the Norman strategy of rule, and it was undoubtedly replicated in various other cases of Norman–native collaboration at lower levels.

It should, however, be noted that by the first quarter of the twelfth century it is more problematic to speak of Norman identity in the south.[56] First-generation Normans had virtually all died out, and assimilation and intermarriage had blurred the boundaries between native and newcomer. Robert of Caiazzo was a second-generation Norman. He and others of later generations may have been aware of their Norman descent, but how far this shaped their actions and ideologies is open to question, and this remains true in the context of saints and their cults; and of course the genealogical links became weaker with every passing generation. I have thus restricted discussion of the Normans here for the most part to the period before c.1100, and from this perspective it should also be noted that when cults began to revive, notably on Sicily, it was mostly in the twelfth century when the 'Normannitas' of its ruling elite was far more difficult to identify. Nevertheless, it is important to remember that some twelfth-century kin groups, most notably the 'Hauteville' kings, are still widely labelled 'Norman' by scholars. For more on the latter and their relationship with saints, see the section on 'Palermo, the monarchy and national saints' in Chapter 4.

Ecclesiastical revival

It is evident that the Normans engaged with South Italian saints' cults in various ways which enhanced their own integration into southern Italy as well as their control over it. As territorial lords and benefactors of local religious houses, the Normans contributed towards the development of several new and revived cults in the second half of the eleventh century. The history of South Italian sanctity on the mainland was thus shaped by the Norman takeover. However, an even deeper influence on the region's saints' cults was exercised by the momentous transitions occurring both in the Western Church and in the intrinsic nature of medieval spirituality and faith. Many South Italian saints and their cults either contributed on some level to these transitions or were a product of them.[57] Moreover, many of these transitions within the medieval Church seemed to conflict

---

[56] N. Webber, *The Evolution of Norman Identity, 911–1154* (Woodbridge, 2005), 71–84, 177–8; Loud, '*Gens Normannorum*', 104–16.

[57] For a wider understanding of these transitions in a South Italian context a great debt is owed to the magisterial study by Loud, *Latin Church*. Also important is Ramseyer, *Transformation*.

notably with the very presence of the Normans, and yet ultimately these seemingly contrasting worlds found points of connection, very often in the form of saints' cults.

From the early to mid-tenth century a wide-reaching reform movement in the Western Church began to materialize. Initially it seems to have been based in some key monastic centres (such as Cluny in Burgundy and Gorze in Lorraine) but gradually by the eleventh century it had permeated the wider Church and sections of lay society. From the mid-eleventh century the papacy increasingly tried to guide the reform movement, and to some scholars the Fourth Lateran Council of 1215, directed by Pope Innocent III, concluded its natural cycle. The reform movement was in truth an amorphous phenomenon with varied objectives which were endowed with greater significance at different times by different groups.[58] It intersected with an evident upsurge in lay piety, evidenced particularly in the Truce and Peace of God movements and the rising popularity of pilgrimage, with socio-demographic changes, with increasing levels of education and literacy, with the revived prominence of western eremitism, and with a more assertive papacy to generate a potent energy. If, however, the movement is reduced to its common fundamentals, the reformers aimed for greater separation between the religious and secular spheres, demanding freedom from lay interference in Church affairs. They campaigned too for a moral reform within the Church, eradicating simony and nicolaitism, emphasizing pastoral duties and espousing the ideals of the *vita apostolica* which rejected excessive wealth; ideals which were absorbed by a wave of new monastic orders. While demanding religious independence and freedom, to be successful the reform movement also implicitly required more organized ecclesiastical networks, both monastic and diocesan. Of course, such ambitious objectives created widespread conflict, most notably the infamous Investiture Contest (c.1072–c.1122) between the papal reforming party and the German emperors. At this time of crisis for the papacy southern Italy served as a useful refuge for embattled popes – particularly Urban II – and it also provided them with Norman military support.

(i)   *Papal influence and the secular Church reorganized*

Geographical proximity to Rome and its political alliances ensured that southern Italy and its saints' cults experienced the considerable impact

---

[58] The literature on the Church reform is extensive. See the excellent overview provided by M. C. Miller, 'New religious movements and reform', *A Companion to the Medieval World*, ed. C. Lansing and E. D. English (Oxford, 2009), 211–30.

of the reform movement, increasingly directed as it was by the papacy. The main impact on the region, as Graham Loud has extensively demonstrated, was to trigger a reorganization of the diocesan map, standardizing it and integrating it more firmly with Rome. Prior to the mid-eleventh century, ecclesiastical provinces had been merely embryonic in the Lombard zones and decidedly chaotic in Apulia and Calabria.[59] From the mid-eleventh through to the first decades of the twelfth century, across the mainland many South Italian bishoprics were established, revived or revitalized in close cooperation with the papacy and their new Norman allies. In the former Byzantine zones, the jurisdiction of sees also passed into Rome's orbit. By the twelfth century their internal structures, parish networks, dependent churches and revenues were organized more efficiently. Overall, the reform movement generated an extensive material renewal within many dioceses. This process necessitated the construction of a series of new or refurbished churches and cathedrals, which in turn was mirrored by a wave of new, restored or expanded cults with associated hagiographical works. Collectively they articulated the status and permanency of these episcopal sees. Indeed, c.1070–c.1120 witnessed one of the most intense periods of cultic activity in southern Italy since the promotion of cults in ninth-century Benevento. Apulia was a particular hot spot for the construction of new religious houses, and consequently for a host of redefined saints' cults and relic translations. A notable pattern saw the 'rediscovery' of saints, for which pre-existing evidence of cults in the same location was extremely tenuous. Together they reveal the historical discontinuities and fractures in memory that afflicted various South Italian religious institutions in the Central Middle Ages at exactly the point when new reforming forces urged greater engagement with an untarnished earlier era of Christian history and the need for models to encapsulate the new zeitgeist in which the Church was more stridently self-confident. It is notable that in Sicily, as Chapter 4 makes clear, the revival of old cults was far more muted during the same period. The discontinuity with its Christian heritage was far greater, and the reorganization and revival of the Christian Church on the island was at a far more embryonic stage in the late eleventh and early twelfth centuries. Advancing saints' cults via any concerted programme was not yet possible, and would only begin to occur well into the twelfth century at St Agatha's shrine at Catania. The papacy and the Church reform movement at this point were far less influential forces on the Sicilian Church and its cults, while

---

[59] Loud, *Latin Church*, 181–254.

Roger I of Sicily's acquisition of papal legatine powers in 1098 represented an additional barrier to external intervention.

Building programmes reconstructed cathedrals at Taranto (from c.1070) and Troia (c.1090–c.1125), and soon saints were rediscovered (often during the renovation works) and interred within them to honour the greater pretensions of these sees, and to affirm their 'ancient' legacies. In reality the cults of St Cataldus at Taranto and SS Secundinus and Eleutherius at Troia show no certain sign of existence in these cities before their so-called rediscoveries or return. The establishment of cults was promoted by bishops who clearly hoped to sacralize their present episcopal sees through linkage to a holy past. At Taranto two conflicting traditions on Cataldus' rediscovery exist. One, dating from the mid-twelfth century, states that the saint's relics were found during renovation of the cathedral by Bishop Drogo, whose only known date is 1071. The saint was found with a gold pendant cross carrying his name, and his sanctity was authenticated by some miraculous cures.[60] Subsequently, Cataldus was interred in a new altar in the refurbished cathedral, although his relics were later moved by Archbishop Rainaldus (1106–19), and again in 1151 when Archbishop Gerald arranged a formal translation in which the relics were displayed publicly before being placed in a new reliquary. Berlengarius, the hagiographer of *The Invention and Translation of St Cataldus*, ended his account with a list of miracles performed by the saint (for more see Chapter 6).[61] The second tradition, also of the twelfth century, appears in the already discussed *Sermon on the discovery of St Cataldus*, an anonymous work which placed the rediscovery outside Taranto in the year 1094, indicated the central role of the city's Norman bishop and added a few additional miracles.[62] Significantly, the *Sermon* claimed the relics were deposited not in the cathedral but in the church of S. Biagio. These competing traditions suggest factions within the Church of Taranto during a period of revival and reform following its transfer to the jurisdiction of the Latin Church in the second half of the eleventh century.

Similarly, the episcopal see at Troia, a city founded by the Byzantines only in 1019 near the abandoned ancient site of Aecae, was directly subordinate to Rome by c.1060.[63] We have already seen that its Norman bishop Stephen consolidated the cult of St Secundinus. The

---

[60] Historia S. Cataldi, 569.
[61] Historia S. Cataldi, 570–4.
[62] Hofmeister, 'Sermo', 107–14.
[63] And also temporarily as early as 1030: *Les Chartes de Troia. Édition et étude critique des plus anciens documents conservés à l'archivio capitolare, 1 (1024–1266)*, ed. J.-M. Martin, Codice diplomatico pugliese 21 (Bari, 1976), no. 2.

relics of Secundinus, a putative former bishop of Aecae, were allegedly rediscovered in the period between 1022 and 1034, and the hagiographical text produced at that time was later reworked at Stephen's request into the *Inventio Secundini* by the Montecassino hagiographer Guaiferius in c.1067. Simply put, Secundinus' presence conferred a foundation legend on a new episcopal see desperately in need of one.[64] The subsequent translation of the relics of SS Eleutherius, Pontianus and Anastasius from Tivera in 1104 also occurred while the cathedral was still being reconstructed, and formed part of the wider articulation of the episcopacy's identity. In Chapter 1 we noted that, while a St Eleutherius was venerated in southern Italy in the Middle Ages, he appears to have had multiple identities, none of which was explicitly associated with Troia's ancient forerunner, Aecae. The formal ceremony associated with the arrival of the relics in 1104 also allowed the city's bishop to stand visibly as the leader of the urban community, and stimulated the creation of a text which would preserve that memory, while images of Troia's saints would soon adorn the cathedral's main doors.[65] It should not be surprising that Troia's neighbouring diocese, Bovino, discovered in 1090 the relics of a St Mark, apparently another early bishop of Aecae, and clearly a response to Troia's efforts to appropriate the region's early Christian heritage.[66]

Similar 'rediscoveries' of local saints occurred elsewhere as episcopal sees experienced revival and reorganization from the later eleventh century. In 1080 Archbishop Arnold of Acerenza found the body of St Canius, martyred at Atella in the third or fourth century. Apart from the saint's alleged translation to Acerenza in 799 little suggests a thriving cult before the eleventh century. The annals of Lupus Protospatharius make clear the interconnection between 'rediscovery' and the reconstruction of the episcopacy, for they record that Arnold immediately commenced construction of a new cathedral after the relics were found.[67] St Mennas, as we have seen, was 'rediscovered' at Caiazzo and initially placed in the city cathedral in c.1094, and again veneration of this saint had previously been markedly limited. When his relics were transferred to S. Agata dei Goti in 1110 the cult received papal endorsement, for Pope Paschal II consecrated the church.[68] Perhaps the most notable example of papal influence in this trend of 'rediscoveries' occurs in the case of St Lawrence, bishop of Siponto. With papal approval, the archbishopric of Siponto finally

---

[64] Head, 'Discontinuity', 192.
[65] Poncelet, 'Translation', 422–4.
[66] Martin, *Pouille*, 620.
[67] *Lupus Protospatharius*, 60.
[68] Galdi, *Santi*, 229–47.

achieved autonomy from the archbishopric of Benevento in 1066, and from this era date two *vitae* of St Lawrence of Siponto. Both texts claim St Lawrence to have been bishop of Siponto around the fifth or sixth century, and equate him with the anonymous bishop whose vision of St Michael was so central to the *Liber de apparitione*.[69] Nevertheless, no historical evidence survives for a Bishop Lawrence, and all signs of his cult date from the mid-eleventh century onwards, as the revived archiepiscopal see asserted its independence in alliance with the papal reform movement.[70] The two *vitae* date very likely to the mid-eleventh century and to c.1100 respectively: a settlement named S. Lorenzo in Carminiano appeared on the nearby Tavoliere Plain in 1092, while during excavations in 1099 Lawrence's relics were allegedly discovered and transferred to a new cathedral which was consecrated by Pope Paschal II in 1102. Indeed, the later of the two *vitae* emphasizes the role of Pope Gelasius I in Lawrence's consecration as bishop, a papal prerogative deemed a key principle of the eleventh-century reform movement.

In some cases cults were revived which had clearly existed in the Early Middle Ages but which had subsequently suffered a period of contraction. Once again these revivals were set firmly in their current climate of rivalries and reorganization within regional ecclesiastical hierarchies. Prior to 1063, the archbishop of Trani commissioned a new hagiographical work on the invention of the ancient bishop, St Leucius. This was at a time when the jurisdictional map of Apulia was in flux, and ecclesiastical rivalries were evident between the Churches of Trani and Bari.[71] At Bari, efforts were made by the archiepiscopacy in the later eleventh century to reconnect with its distant past through saints' relics in order to assert current ascendancy within both the city and Apulia more widely. Of course, in 1087 Archbishop Urso (1080–9) had to look on as a group of citizens and local clergy brought the famed relics of St Nicholas of Myra to Bari; Urso's attempt to claim the relics for the cathedral failed, and they were installed instead in the newly constructed basilica of S. Nicola.[72] The translation of St Nicholas caused friction among both

---

[69] See Chapter 1.

[70] T. Catallo, 'Sulla datazione delle "vitae" di Lorenzo vescovo di Siponto', *SM* 32 (1991), 129–57; Martin, 'Modèles', 81–3.

[71] *De Translationibus S. Leucii*; Martin, *Pouille*, 620; A. Pratesi, 'Alcune diocesi di Puglia nell'età di Roberto il Guiscardo: Trani, Bari e Canosa tra Greci e Normanni', *Roberto Guiscardo e il suo tempo*, Atti delle prime giornate normanno-sveve, Bari, 28–29 maggio 1973 (Bari, 1991), 225–42.

[72] For the main translation accounts, the most accessible editions (although they contain some inaccuracies) are in F. Nitti di Vito, 'La traslazione delle reliquie di San Nicola', *Iapigia* 8 (1937), 295–11, at 336–66, 388–96. Italian translations can be found in Corsi, *La traslazione*.

the secular and lay communities within Bari, and it is in this context that we might also understand the efforts made to 'rediscover' relics within the cathedral. The *Inventio of S. Sabini*, composed by the same John the Archdeacon who produced a (pro-archiepiscopal) version of the translation of St Nicholas, presents Urso's efforts to relocate the relics of the confessors St Memorus and St Ruffinus, early bishops of Canosa.[73] Urso died before the task could be accomplished but significantly it was taken up by his successor Archbishop Elias (1089–1105). Elias was also the first rector of the basilica of S. Nicola, where St Nicholas's relics lay, and he continued to hold this office whilst also archbishop. In him the two main poles of ecclesiastical power within the city were united, and Elias' desire to continue Urso's search for the relics articulates the ongoing reconciliation. However, St Memorus and St Ruffinus were not discovered. Unexpectedly, in 1091, Elias' team unearthed the relics of St Sabinus of Canosa, and this shift in the account signals another pressing concern at Bari. Canosa had been the pre-eminent archiepiscopal see in early medieval Apulia, and Sabinus the pre-eminent holy bishop. By the eleventh century Bari's demographic expansion and importance as the governmental centre of Byzantine Italy had contributed to the creation of the dual-titled archiepiscopal see of Canosa–Bari. Through the *Inventio S. Sabini* the Barese church clearly expresses its claims to Canosa's ancient ascendancy. Not only were St Memorus and St Ruffinus said to be earlier bishops of Canosa, but Sabinus' body was allegedly found at Bari covered with a cloth which stated it had been moved there 240 years previously (that is in 852) by a Bishop Angelarius. The body was exhumed, placed in a new marble tomb and returned to its original location, while Bari's suffragan bishops and its delighted *populus* observed the ceremony. St Sabinus' cult did not eclipse St Nicholas's in Bari, but it quite likely never intended to. St Sabinus was a local saint with a distinguished Apulian past who complemented rather than competed with the high-profile Nicholas who, as a South Italian parvenu, was notably different. More importantly, for the Church of Bari the cult of St Sabinus marked its superiority vis-à-vis the ancient see of Canosa and established its jurisdictional pretensions in Apulia. Both Trani and Bari were vying with each other in the eleventh century to use the archiepiscopal title, and at times Bari claimed Trani as its suffragan.[74] To appropriate Canosa's past status and heritage was to assert a current ascendancy. As we shall see shortly, part of Trani's response was to create

---

[73] *Inventio S. Sabini*, in *Antiche cronache di terra di Bari*, ed. G. Cioffari and R. Lupoli Tateo (Bari, 1991), 279–81.

[74] Pratesi, 'Alcune diocesi', 225–42.

its own St Nicholas, labelled the Pilgrim, a Greek youth who had died in the city in 1094.

Fortunately, cults at some South Italian shrine centres had been of sufficiently high standing to maintain greater continuity with preceding generations, and consequently their revival aroused far less controversy. Hagiographies and established traditions could be reutilized. Nevertheless, the impetus of Church reform (combined with the role of the Normans and, as we shall see, urbanization) saw a number re-emerge after years of apparent stagnation. Most conspicuously, the cult of St Matthew at Salerno was revived in 1080. By c.1000 (see Chapter 1) the cult had been consolidated in Salerno, but during the subsequent decades there was little evident expansion. With the archiepiscopate of Alfanus I, and his ties to Rome and Montecassino, the archdiocese of Salerno was reorganized and its structures standardized, as Valerie Ramseyer has recently demonstrated.[75] Robert Guiscard was a driving force in propelling St Matthew's cult firmly into the limelight, but once again in the backdrop we find papal influence and the renovation of the cathedral, the symbolic heart of a newly ordered archiepiscopacy. Pope Gregory VII personally congratulated Alfanus on the rediscovery of the saint's relics, which were translated to a grandiose refurbished cathedral in 1080, and the pope famously died in exile in the city.[76] Alfanus, part of Rome's reforming circle, produced poems on St Matthew which also cemented the triangular association between prelate, saint and citizen. In doing so, he expounded a central tenet of his own ecclesiology which chimed with the reform movement, namely that the bishop should care for the health of his flock, in this case through the agency of St Matthew.[77] On these foundations, the cult generated a wider presence, both in the city and across Christendom, and attracted greater streams of patronage.

In the face of a number of jurisdictional amendments to its archdiocese, the circling of predatory Norman and Lombard nobles, a marked increase in urban violence and factionalism, and Benevento's direct submission to papal authority, the Beneventan Church also rearticulated its relationship with a number of its long-established saints' cults in the period from c.1090 to c.1125. With the ending of the Beneventan Lombard princely dynasty in 1077, the archbishopric and the city's old saints were needed to stress continuity in a rapidly changing world. What emerged was the most

---

[75] Ramseyer, *Transformation*.

[76] *Register*, no. 8 pp. 373–4,

[77] V. Ramseyer, 'Pastoral care as military action: the ecclesiology of Archbishop Alfanus I of Salerno (1058–85)', *The Bishop Reformed. Studies in Episcopal Power and Culture in the Central Middle Ages*, ed. J. S. Ott and A. Trumbore Jones (Aldershot, 2007), 189–208.

intensive programme of hagiographical output and cultic activity in the city since the golden era of the ninth century. Given the city's sacred heritage, old cults associated with the Lombard era were the focus of a revival driven by the archbishops Roffred I (1076–1107) and Landulf II (1108–19). Among the many new hagiographical works was a *passio* of St Modestus, composed by the famed rhetorician Alberic of Montecassino and dedicated to Roffred, who also encouraged a Beneventan monk named Martin to compose a *Translatio S. Bartholomei* which built on an earlier account.[78] Roffred's successor Landulf was a hagiographer in his own right, composing a hymn for St Mercurius and, it seems, a sermon dedicated to the Twelve Holy Brothers.[79] During Roffred's episcopate the *Adventus S. Nycolai* was also produced by an anonymous author. Claiming that St Nicholas's patronage had been transferred from Bari to Benevento, its polemic was self-evidently a response to the growing prestige that St Nicholas's shrine conferred on the Church of Bari to the detriment of Benevento's historic claims to ecclesiastical primacy in the south. Another way to reassert Benevento's status was through the special relationship with the city's papal overlord. An anonymous *vita* of Pope St Leo IX (d.1054), who spent time in Benevento, was produced in the city. Within fifteen years of the pope's death, Benevento also boasted a church dedicated to him where he was believed to work miracles.[80]

Hagiographical renewal was accompanied by efforts to create a more conspicuous presence for Benevento's saints within the city. In 1112, Landulf began construction of a new basilica dedicated to the Apostle St Bartholomew, one of Benevento's leading cults.[81] Later, two separate episodes demonstrate that several local cults had been neglected and that their renewal was connected to the archbishop's understanding of their potential value to the urban community as well as to his own status. In 1119, with the archdiocese ravaged by petty conflict, Landulf II, 'searching for ways to save his people', showed in public the bodies of the Saints Marcianus, Dorus, Potitus and Prosperus, Felix, Cervolus, Stephen the Levite and John the twenty-first archbishop of Benevento, all of which had

---

[78] A. Lentini, 'Sulla "passio S, Modesti" di Alberico Cassinese', *Benedictina* 6 (1952), 231–5; Galdi, *Santi*, 265–9.

[79] Vuolo, 'Agiografia beneventana', 230–7.

[80] For the Beneventan *vita* of St Leo IX see S. Borgia, *Memorie istoriche della pontificia città di Benevento dal secolo VIII al secolo XVIII*, 3 vols (Rome, 1763–9), i. 299–348; Vuolo, 'Agiografia beneventana', 236–7; Galdi, *Santi*, 274. Leo IX was also commemorated in Beneventan marytrologies: see the twelfth-century example in London, British Library, Add MS 23776, 11v.

[81] Falco, 4; by 1179 a confraternity of St Bartholomew also existed in the city: Oldfield, *City and Community*, 235.

been deposited in an unworthy tomb.[82] The urban community's response was ecstatic, and we will discuss it further shortly, but for now it is important to note that the bodies were reinterred in a great public ceremony which expressed the archbishop's centrality within his city and his archdiocese. For the ceremony took place in the presence of the suffragan bishops of Frigento, Montemarano and Ariano, and Landulf II thereafter remitted a quarter of the sins of everyone who attended the ceremony, or who visited the shrine up to eight days after the feast of the Apostles Peter and Paul. Five years later, Archbishop Roffred II (1120–30) oversaw the invention and translation of St Barbatus, another of Benevento's most esteemed saints.[83] Once again the tomb even of this saint had, according to Falco of Benevento, 'in truth not been well conserved', and Roffred's plans to enlarge the cathedral required it to be repositioned. After Barbatus' relics were displayed publicly, joyous candllit processions occurred throughout the city for the next eight days, and Falco of Benevento recorded some miracles performed on local laypeople.[84] The concentrated period of hagiographic and cultic activity was driven by the city's archbishops and replicated the strategies of their ninth-century predecessors. It was a programme that was never repeated again in medieval Benevento with the same intensity, perhaps because of its success: the city's saints, and the archbishop, were firmly repositioned as a force for stability at the heart of the community. Visceral confirmation came in the response to the huge earthquake which struck Benevento in 1125, compelling the terrified citizens to rush to the cathedral and to the monastery of S. Sofia, staying 'in the places of the saints, groaning and weeping'.[85]

Not all cults associated with the secular Church during the great phase of activity between c.1070 and c.1125 were rooted in southern Italy's distant past. In a few cases, brand new shrine centres were established with no claims to appropriate earlier local traditions. Again, these shrines assisted in repositioning the secular Church at the heart of South Italian communities and once more attracted papal intervention. On the Amalfitan coast, the bishopric of Ravello was established in 1086–7, and became subject directly to the papacy in 1090.[86] Within the following decades its bishop Constantine Rogadeo (1094–1150) appears to have

---

[82] Falco, 46–52.
[83] Falco, 74–82.
[84] Roffred oversaw another invention and translation of the saints Ianuarius, Festus and Desiderius in 1129, whose relics Falco again claimed had not been duly revered: Falco, 104–6.
[85] Falco, 82.
[86] *Italia Pontificia*, ed. P. F. Kehr, 10 vols (Berlin, 1905–75): viii. *Regnum Normannorum – Campania*, ed. P. F. Kehr (1961), 402, nos. 1, 2.

established a collection of relics in the cathedral.[87] These included a relic of the blood of St Pantaleon, a Greek martyred at Nicomedia in 303, who was already popular in the Amalfitan zone, and to whom Ravello's cathedral was dedicated. Commercial links to the eastern Mediterranean explain the channel for this veneration, if not the specific reasons, and various local families used the Pantaleon forename. Therefore the Church of Ravello did not, as at Troia, attempt to appropriate a saint from the South Italian past, but instead further developed the cult of an already popular foreign saint into a defined shrine centre sponsored by the episcopacy. Similarly, at Bari, devotion for St Nicholas was evident well before the famous translation of the saint's relics from Myra to Bari in 1087, which led to the establishment of a renowned shrine centre.[88] It was located in a newly built church which was staffed by secular canons, independent from the city's archbishop despite the latter's best efforts. Some scholars have read into the conflict that arose in Bari over possession of the relics a clash between an aristocratic party led by a pro-Guibertine archbishop and a party inspired by Church reform and led by the Barese mercantile classes. Indeed, the papal reformers were certainly keen to show their approval of the new cult centre and Urban II personally dedicated the new church in October 1089.[89] However, as Agostino Pertusi has convincingly argued, this is too simple a delineation of various interwoven dynamics that converged around the translation in the city in 1087, and the conflicts appear linked more to efforts among sections of the laity and regular clergy to redefine the boundaries of archiepiscopal authority, as well as to renewed and emotive forms of lay piety.[90]

Further north on the Apulian coastline the city of Trani also nurtured its own novel Nicholaitan cult, this time of a certain St Nicholas the Pilgrim. More will be said on Nicholas later in this chapter in the context of eremitism, but again the papacy was involved alongside the city's archbishop. St Nicholas the Pilgrim was born in Greece, had entered a monastic house in his youth, and then undertook an eremitic life of solitude and perpetual wandering. After numerous challenges and tribulations he crossed the Adriatic and eventually arrived at Trani. Many of Trani's inhabitants were convinced he was insane, but one of the saint's hagiographers, Adelferius, recorded the city's Archbishop Bisantius

---

[87] A. Galdi, 'La diffusione del culto di San Pantaleone in Campania e in Puglia nei secoli xi–xv', *Pantaleone da Nicomedia: santo e taumaturgo tra oriente occidente*, Atti del convegno, Ravello, 24–26 luglio 2004, ed. C. Caserta and M. Talalay (Naples, 2006), 65–8.

[88] See A. Pertusi, 'Ai confini tra religione e politica. La contesa per le reliquie di S. Nicola tra Bari, Venezia e Genova', *Quaderni medievali* 5 (1978), 9–16.

[89] CDBI, no. 33.

[90] Pertusi, 'Ai confini tra religione', 26–48.

interviewing Nicholas and approving his vocation.[91] Thus the archbishop was a pivotal figure in Nicholas's eventual acceptance, which paved the way for his post-mortem cult. After St Nicholas the Pilgrim's death in 1094, Bisantius began rebuilding the city cathedral in 1097, which was dedicated to the saint and housed his shrine, and he also commissioned a hagiographical dossier to encourage papal approval of the cult. In c.1099 Pope Urban II tacitly approved a formal cult of St Nicholas, one of the earliest recorded papal interventions in this arena, when he referred the final decision back to Trani's archbishop.[92]

It is clear then that during an intense phase of rebuilding, reorganization and revival in the South Italian secular Church, relics and cults acquired an integral role. They were both a cause and an effect of the transition, a stimulus to change as well as being indicative of it. Cults were often made most visible at points of transformation in order to justify the status quo or to articulate a new religious or political landscape. They were conduits for advertising local ecclesiastical hierarchies of power and jurisdiction and for expressing cooperation or antagonism within them. As these cults were 'rediscovered', revived or newly established, great processions and cere-monies accompanied the formal dedication of their shrine centres or translations. Such ceremonies were opportunities for large religious and lay gatherings to congregate, exchange information and establish their respective interrelationships.[93] On St Matthew's annual feast day a formal procession involved the bishops of the Salernitan province, symbolically articulating their subordination to the archbishop of Salerno.[94] In the week after the arrival of St Nicholas at Bari, the cult was recognized by a number of local religious dignitaries including the bishops of Bitonto and Conversano – both suffragans of Bari – as well as the archbishop of the neighbouring metropolitan see of Brindisi.[95] Similarly, in 1119 the sub-ordinate bishops of Frigento, Montemarano and Ariano witnessed the reburial of a set of relics in the Beneventan cathedral.[96] When the relics of

---

[91] *Vita S. Nicolai Peregrini*, AS June, i (Paris, 1867), 239 (Limone, *Santi*, 135–68, also provides an edition of St Nicholas's hagiographical dossier, which I have consulted, although references in this study are to the more readily available Acta Sanctorum edition); P. Oldfield, 'St Nicholas the Pilgrim and the city of Trani between Greeks and Normans, c. 1090–c.1140', *Anglo-Norman Studies* 30 (2008), 168–81.

[92] *Vita S. Nicolai Peregrini*, 243; Trani, no. 25.

[93] L. I. Hamilton, *A Sacred City. Consecrating Churches and Reforming Society in Eleventh-Century Italy* (Manchester, 2010), 56–88.

[94] G. Vitolo, 'Città e chiesa nel mezzogiorno medievale: la processione del santo patrono a Salerno (sec. XII)', *Salerno nel XII secolo. Istituzioni, società, cultura*, Atti del convegno internazionale, giugno 1999, ed. P. Delogu and P. Peduto (Salerno, 2004), 134–45, at 138–9.

[95] Nitti di Vito, 'La traslazione', 352.

[96] Falco, 50.

Saints Eleutherius, Pontianus and Anastasius arrived at Troia in 1104, the translation account recorded that the city's bishop invited his neighbouring counterparts from Tertiveri and Bovino to witness their arrival.[97] These episodes reveal rare but valuable glimpses of the operation of metropolitan organization and interdiocesan relationships, such prominent features of the late eleventh-century renewal coursing through the South Italian Church. Moreover, papal presence at the consecration of several of these new shrine centres might be read as a strategy to bind these cults and their supporters to the reforming papacy.[98]

The secular Church continued to undergo reform and reorganization throughout the remainder of the twelfth century, but the process was far more incremental, and it is notable that thereafter surges of cultic activity in mainland southern Italy were more muted. Occasionally relics were retranslated into refurbished shrines: St Nicholas the Pilgrim at Trani in 1142 and St Cataldus at Taranto in 1151, both events performed with great ceremony before large crowds.[99] Also, relics continued to be 'rediscovered' in ways that illuminated the previous neglect of some local cults. An obscure saint, Priscus, was discovered between 1138 and 1143 in the small Apennine settlement of Quintodecimo, a see subordinated to the archdiocese of Benevento until in 1058 its episcopal status was transferred to nearby Frigento.[100] The process of the discovery revealed the functioning of the diocesan structures, for the local archpriest informed his superior, the bishop of Frigento, who then passed on the news up the hierarchy to the archbishop of Benevento. The bishop of Frigento and the archbishop of Benevento both subsequently approved the authenticity of the relics. The latter then travelled to Mirabella, where the relics were finally interred, but having got lost on the route he was aided by a divine sign which signalled both the location of the saint's new resting place, and the broader spirit of intradiocesan collaboration which seemed to prevail. In addition, the relics of three other rather obscure saints, Maurus, Pantaleon and Sergius, were discovered near Bisceglie and eventually transferred, again in a great ceremony attended by many of the neighbouring bishops, to a location in or near the city cathedral in 1167. In both cases, at Quintodecimo and Bisceglie, the hagiographers struggled to overcome the almost complete absence of earlier local traditions for

---

[97] Poncelet, 'Translation', 423–4.
[98] L. I. Hamilton, 'Desecration and consecration in Norman Capua, 1066–1122: contesting sacred space during the Gregorian reforms', *Haskins Society Journal* 14 (2003), 137–50, at 142.
[99] *Vita S. Nicolai Peregrini*, 244; Historia S. Cataldi, 570.
[100] *Historia inventionis S. Prisci*, AS September, i (Paris, 1868), 216–18; Head, 'Discontinuity', 197–203.

these cults, and resorted to evasive summaries of their earlier disjointed cultic histories.[101]

(ii) Bishop-saints

In the late eleventh and early twelfth centuries many bishoprics in southern Italy were engaged intensively in justifying their recent foundation or their newly expanded jurisdictions. Patrimonies and revenues had to be claimed or reclaimed. As we have seen, an excellent way to stabilize the present was to anchor it in the distant past, which often stimulated the revival or fabrication of local saints from the palaeo-Christian era. Thus, bishop-saints re-emerged – Leucius at Trani, Sabinus at Bari – or were effectively created – Lawrence at Siponto, Cataldus at Taranto. As these bishop-saints were located in what now appears a utopian era of Christian purity diligently guided by the papacy, they embodied, by their very nature, elements of the new Church-reform movement. However, these ideals were not explicitly expressed in the eleventh- and twelfth-century hagiographical works associated with these saints, and their antiquity inevitably detached them from contemporary developments. Reforming ideals were more likely to be reflected thus in modern saints. In this period of transition in the South Italian Church a few contemporary bishops did attain the status of sanctity, and, as Amalia Galdi has rightly noted, some of them displayed signs of the influence of the reforming movement.[102]

Southern Italy's bishop-saints shared some common features. They were (with a few exceptions) bishops of small, fledgling dioceses – most were seemingly either the first or second recorded bishops of their sees.[103] With one exception they occupied their sees in the important phase between 1070 and 1125. Thus St Amatus of Nusco (d. 1093?) was probably the first bishop of Nusco, which had achieved episcopal status as a suffragan of the archbishopric of Salerno in 1070–80.[104] St John of Montemarano was the first recorded bishop of the see of Montemarano in the Beneventan province, which seems to have achieved its new status when (according to John's *vita*) Pope Gregory VII, staying at Salerno (most likely in 1084–5) ordered

---

[101] The cult of St Maurus had links to Gallipoli, but not directly to the region around Bisceglie: Martin, 'Modèles', 76–7.

[102] For a superb treatment of the hagiographies of South Italian bishop-saints see Galdi, *Santi*, 100–82, to which the following discussion is indebted.

[103] The case of St Lucas, bishop of the small Calabrian see of Isola di Capo Rizzuto, will be covered in Chapter 3.

[104] *Italia Pontificia*, viii. 341.

John's consecration.[105] Another new diocese, subordinate to Benevento, was created at Montecorvino, a settlement which had been founded only in the early eleventh century in the Capitanata region. Consequently, one of its earliest bishops (probably the second), Albert of Montecorvino (c.1081–1137?), was reputed to be a saint. St Gerard of Piacenza (d.1119) was believed to be the first bishop of Potenza in Lucania (subject to the arch-bishopric of Acerenza).[106] Question marks remain over the historicity of some of the bishop-saints, their *vitae* often representing the only evidence for their existence, while for those who can be identified through other sources, proof of their cults is either late or limited. For St Amatus of Nusco we must rely on two conflicting hagiographical traditions dating to the fifteenth and sixteenth centuries, but they do at least suggest that Amatus' cult was acknowledged in the twelfth century with two separate translations effected by bishops of Nusco in 1143 and c.1200 respectively, and record a set of post-mortem miracles situated in the 1120s and 1150s.[107] Albert of Montecorvino's *vita* was reputed to have been composed by his episcopal successor but it survives only in a copy dated to 1499.[108] The surviving version of the *vita* of St John of Montemarano does at least appear to have been an original written shortly after John's death (c.1090s?), and a fresco in the crypt of the church of Montemarano dating to the eleventh/twelfth century is reputed to depict the bishop-saint, and evidence the early pro-motion of his cult.[109] However, in truth this is the only evidence we have for the saint. Similarly, almost the only information on St Gerard of Potenza comes from his laconic *vita*, allegedly composed by his successor Manfred, who claimed to have presented the text at Rome and achieved a viva voce canonization for Gerard from Pope Calixtus II in 1122–3.[110] Two further examples of contemporary bishop-saints from Apulia are even more prob-lematic. Roger of Canne (attested from 1100 to 1117) and Richard of Andria (bishop from 1158 to 1196) are both attested in contemporary charters and historical documents, but their cults are not in evidence before 1275 and the fifteenth century respectively.[111]

From the patchy surviving evidence it is possible to conclude that these bishop-saints were largely products of the wide ecclesiastical reordering in

---

[105] *De S. Joanne Episcopo Confessore Civitatis Montis Marani*, AS August, iii (Paris, 1867), 510.
[106] Other bishop-saints like St Bernard of Carinola (c.1100) and St Roger of Canne (1100–17) also appear to have been bishops of sees of relatively new foundation; see Galdi, *Santi*, 153–75.
[107] Galdi, *Santi*, 117–32.
[108] *Vita S. Alberti Episcopi Montis Corvini*, AS April, i (Paris, 1866), 434–6.
[109] Galdi, *Santi*, 113–14.
[110] *De S. Gerardo Episcopo et Confessore Potentiae in Italia*, AS October, xiii (Paris, 1883), 469.
[111] Martin, 'Modèles', 80–1.

southern Italy. In some aspects their lives, at least as portrayed in their *vitae*, were attuned to some of the current reforming principles. Monastic models – eremitism, abstinence, asceticism – were evident in the lives of Albert of Montecorvino, who was a monk before reluctantly assuming his episcopal office, in Amatus of Nusco and in John of Montemarano. Admittedly, in the south the prevailing influence of Greek Orthodox monasticism should not be overlooked, but its key components also framed much of the reformers' approach. The theme of physical labour, another re-emerging monastic ideal, was apparent in St John of Montemarano's *vita* when he worked in the fields to assist the poor.[112] The reform's aims to inculcate monastic ideals into the secular Church and to root out clerical immorality are here evident. St John of Montemarano at one point tackled a sinful priest whose church was full of worms by praying to God, and beseeching the people and clergy to encourage him to confess and undergo penitence.[113] St Albert of Montecorvino in his later life was burdened by a wicked priest who sought to kill him and succeed to the episcopal throne.[114] Another important feature of the Church reform, pastoral care, also featured in some of these bishop-saints' lives. St Gerard of Potenza was an active preacher, while he, Amatus of Nusco and John of Montemarano all performed the biblical miracle of turning water to wine and thus were presented as offering sustenance to the lay community.[115] We may assume that most of these South Italian bishop-saints, pioneers within their dioceses, also achieved the material revival of their sees, another broad objective of the reform. John of Montemarano's hagiographer was keen to emphasize that he cared for both the spiritual and terrestrial wealth of his see.[116] Finally, it is notable too that lay/political influence within these *vitae* is almost entirely absent, ecclesiastical freedom from lay control being a key component of the reform movement.[117] An unnamed duke of Apulia is referred to in the life of St Albert of Montecorvino, for instance, but only as a devotee drawn to visit the saint when his fame spread across the region.[118]

Whether intentionally or not, these hagiographers fitted their subjects into the framework of reform and revival. However, one bishop-saint, thus far not discussed, displays more overt connections with the papacy and enacted a concerted programme of reform in his diocese. St Berard of

[112] *De S. Joanne*, 511.
[113] *De S. Joanne*, 511.
[114] *Vita S. Alberti*, 433.
[115] *De S. Gerardo*, 468.
[116] *De S. Joanne*, 511.
[117] Galdi, *Santi*, 182.
[118] *Vita S. Alberti*, 433.

Marsia in the Abruzzi (bishop of the see from 1110 to 1130) was in some senses an ideal Gregorian bishop. Certainly, some of the components of his *vita* parallel the 'model' episcopal hagiographies of nearby Latium which were undoubtedly shaped by the reform.[119] Descended from the lineage of the counts of Marsia, he was a monk at Montecassino before Paschal II called him to Rome and appointed him first as a papal official, and then later as a cardinal deacon and cardinal priest. In 1110 the same pope consecrated Berard as bishop of Marsia at the young age of thirty, replacing a bishop who was associated with the anti-pope Guibert. Thereafter the *Vita Berardi* (composed by Bishop John of Segni between 1138 and 1153) details how he reformed clerical standards in his diocese.[120] He campaigned against simony, clerical marriage and improper clerical customs. He also mediated in secular disputes, promoted moral reform among the laity and conducted charitable enterprises. Berard was thus a curial bishop, given various papal commissions during his career, and was an active reformer. However, John Howe has demonstrated that most of Berard's actions were primarily dictated by local and not papal needs, and that his hagiography and miracle collections did not conform to papal standards nearly as much as one would expect.[121] Berard's actions and miracles were firmly set in a local context, and indeed he hailed from the local nobility. Furthermore, his post-mortem cult was promoted not by the papacy (which did not acknowledge Berard's sanctity until the nineteenth century), but by local popular devotion and also it seems by the desperate canons of the diocesan cathedral, which was increasingly being challenged for local ascendancy by the collegiate church of San Giovanni at Celano.

None of the South Italian bishop-saints, even St Berard of Marsia, could be defined as reforming bishops in a fuller sense, as could an Anselm of Lucca (d. 1086), who was situated at the geographical heart of the reform movement and whose *vita* was framed by the reform cause.[122] This might evidence the strong local variations of reform in southern Italy and indeed across Europe; variations which rarely conformed to the ideals developed at the reform's papal centre. Equally, none

[119] P. Toubert, *Les Structures du Latium médiéval*, 2 vols (Rome, 1973), ii. 789–933, for figures such as St Peter of Anagni and St Bruno of Segni.

[120] *Vita Berardi*, AS November, ii (i) (Brussels, 1894), 128–34.

[121] See J. Howe, 'St Berardus of Marsica (d. 1130) "model Gregorian bishop"', *Journal of Ecclesiastical History* 58 (2007), 400–16; Loud, *Latin Church*, 217–18.

[122] K. G. Cushing, 'Events that led to sainthood: sanctity and the reformers in the eleventh century', *Belief and Culture in the Middle Ages. Studies Presented to Henry Mayr-Harting*, ed. R. Gameson and H. Leyser (Oxford, 2001), 187–96; Howe, 'St Berardus', 401–2, notes 2–8 contain a comprehensive bibliography of research on bishops and the reform across medieval Europe.

of the cults of these South Italian saints attained prominence beyond a local orbit. For some reason later officials of their sees believed that the identification of such bishop-saints offered a better chance to fill the void in cults attached to their (often) new churches rather than an attempt to appropriate ancient ones. But these dioceses were small and economically fragile; they did not have the essential components to establish their cults more thoroughly. Contemporary prelates of great metropolitan sees, such as Alfanus I at Salerno and Landulf II at Benevento, had all the credentials for successful episcopal cults, but their churches already had an ancient heritage to draw on alongside high-profile urban cults.[123] Comparisons with other regions are illuminating. Only a few bishops who were in office in England between 1066 and c.1200 attained sanctity. These included Wulfstan of Worcester (d. 1095), Anselm of Canterbury (d. 1109), William of York (d. 1154), Hugh of Lincoln (d.1200) and, most famously, Thomas Becket of Canterbury (d. 1170), who became the embodiment of the moral reform of the Church.[124] Despite the small number of English bishop-saints, they were drawn from a considerably smaller number of episcopal sees (21 sees in England and Wales in the twelfth century, compared with 144 in the Kingdom of Sicily), which were economically and politically powerful and could promote these cults far more extensively. In central and northern Italy, on the other hand, rapid urban growth, and the continued political and economic power of episcopal sees, stimulated the promotion of a plethora of bishop-saints, men like Ubaldus of Gubbio (d. 1160), Galdino of Milan (d. 1176) and Lanfranc of Pavia (d. 1194).[125] Overall, the contemporary bishop-saint was still a relatively rare phenomenon in the Central Middle Ages, and in some cases *vitae* might be better understood as guides to the office than as advertisements of sanctity.[126] Nevertheless, in southern Italy it should not be overlooked that the bishop-saints were a distinct group of new saints who emerged in the Latin zones for the first time in centuries. Though problems with historicity and evidence prevail, it cannot however be coincidence that a group of independent works focus on bishop-saints from a key period of reorganization and reform.

[123] It might be noted that Sicily in the Norman period only produced one bishop-saint, Gerlandus; see Chapter 4.

[124] See R. Bartlett, *England under the Norman and Angevin Kings, 1075–1225* (Oxford, 2000), 461–3.

[125] M. C. Miller, *The Bishop's Palace. Architecture and Authority in Medieval Italy* (Ithaca, 2000), 133–7; D. Webb, *Patrons and Defenders. The Saints in the Italian City States* (London, 1996), 33–92.

[126] T. Head, 'Postscript: the ambiguous bishop', *The Bishop Reformed. Studies in Episcopal Power and Culture in the Central Middle Ages*, ed. J. S. Ott and A. Trumbore Jones (Aldershot, 2007), 250–64.

In this context it is also pertinent to note evidence for South Italian devotion to St Thomas Becket, the martyred archbishop of Canterbury and symbol of Church freedom. The dissemination of Becket's cult in the decades following his murder in 1170 represents one of the most spectacular medieval examples of the rapid and wide movement of a saint's influence beyond his shrine. It was aided by Angevin family connections, Becket's diverse appeal as a saint who represented both Church and State, while a phenomenal quantity of visual imagery associated with the saint was dispersed across Europe, literally making him an iconic figure.[127] The earliest extant image of the saint following his canonization in 1173 is considered to have been found in the decorative programme at Monreale.[128] Wider evidence exists of Becket's cult in southern Italy. He was included in sanctorales and calendars, and churches were dedicated in his name, as was the case at Catania in the 1170s and Bari by 1190, while in 1179 the monks of S. Sofia of Benevento were allowed an additional dish on Becket's feast day.[129] Relic fragments were found in various places: in the nunnery of S. Cecilia at Foggia, in the city of Gravina in Apulia and in a pendant owned by Margaret of Navarre, William II's mother.[130] Clearly, St Thomas Becket offered a compelling template to further frame South Italian familiarity with the model of the reform-minded bishop-saint.

(iii)   Monastic and eremitical saints

Another distinctive feature of the religious revival in the Western Church was the novel forms of Latin monasticism and eremitism, influenced by the *vita apostolica*, which contributed to the emergence of several new saints in medieval southern Italy. Of course, such influences had long prevailed in southern Italy and Sicily, particularly in the areas of Greek Christian settlement. These zones produced a wave of Greek Christian eremitical saints, and continued to do so in the period between 1000 and 1200 in line with the revival of Greek monasticism after the arrival of the

---

[127] R. Gameson, 'The early imagery of Thomas Becket', *Pilgrimage. The English Experience from Becket to Bunyan*, ed. C. Morris and P. Roberts (Cambridge, 2002), 46–89.

[128] Brodbeck, *Saints*, 738–9.

[129] For example, his commemoration was added in a later hand to a twelfth-century Beneventan martyrology: London, British Library Add MS 23776, 33r; CDBV, no. 155; Martin, *Pouille*, 620 n. 398; Benevento, Museo del Sannio, Fondo S. Sofia, vol. 28, no. 9, edited in G. A. Loud, 'A Lombard abbey in a Norman world. St. Sophia, Benevento, 1050–1200', *Anglo-Norman Studies 19* (1997), 303–4 (reprinted in his *Montecassino and Benevento in the Middle Ages* (Aldershot, 2000)).

[130] *Martyrologium Pulsanensis Cenobii Sancte Cecilie de Fogia (Sec. XII)*, ed. G. De Troia (Brindisi, 1988), 40–1; CDBV, no. 147; Gameson, 'Early imagery', 51; *I Normanni, popolo d'Europa, 1030–1200*, ed. M. D'Onofrio (Rome, 1994), 518, no. 329.

Normans (see Chapters 3 and 4). The Latin regions of the mainland also witnessed the establishment of influential new, reformed monastic orders, which in most cases boasted founders who were soon venerated as saints. These founding fathers were heavily influenced by eremitism and the *vita apostolica*, but almost all died in ordered cenobitic houses. Furthermore, their cults were gradually subsumed into Benedictine monastic networks which produced *vitae* which retrospectively enhanced more conventional monastic features in order to normalize their subjects' more unorthodox religious practices.[131] Nonetheless, this paradoxical systematizing of the unorthodox was a notable aspect in the evolution of western monasticism in the Central Middle Ages.

However, before considering this group of saints we must first note the presence in southern Italy of two particular hermit monks – Bruno of Cologne and Joachim of Fiore – who were considered saints in some circles after their deaths. Both were Latin but ended their lives in the Greek-influenced zone of Calabria, and both evidenced a more radical interpretation of the new reforming currents. Moreover, both were renowned figures in the wider Western Church, and were counsellors to the ecclesiastical and political elites of their day. On the one hand, their universal fame beyond southern Italy and their more extreme views made them atypical models of South Italian sanctity; on the other, their reform-ing inspiration and willingness to combine eremitism and cenobitism without completely excluding the surrounding lay world was a template found in other new eremitical saints on the South Italian mainland.

It could rightly be said that one of the Western Church's most prom-inent reforming saints was active in southern Italy at the end of the eleventh century: St Bruno of Cologne (d.1101).[132] Bruno founded the Carthusian order, a radical new religious order based on a solitary lifestyle in which the monks lived in individual cells but within an eremitical community guided by a prior. The community was almost entirely detached from worldly contact, and devoted to meditation and a strict interpretation of the Benedictine Rule. Already a key figure in the Western Church, Bruno had been called to Rome in 1090 from his eremitic retreat at La Chartreuse in the lower Alps to assist Urban II (Bruno's former pupil) in furthering the papal reform agenda. Bruno eventually retreated with some companions to the 'desert' of Calabria where in 1091 Roger I and the Greek bishop of Squillace aided Bruno in founding S. Maria della Torre, an isolated eremitic house some twenty kilometres from Mileto.

---

[131] Galdi, *Santi*, 35–6, 80–1.
[132] For more on St Bruno, see the essays in *San Bruno di Colonia: un eremite tra oriente occidente*, ed. P. De Leo (Catanzaro, 2004).

Indeed, one of the legends of St Bruno claimed he often spent time with Roger I. It was at S. Maria della Torre that Bruno spent most of the remainder of his life, following an eremitic model which fused naturally with local Greek Orthodox monastic ideals, mortifying his body, meditating and displaying a particular devotion for the Marian cult which became so popular in the Central Middle Ages. It was at S. Maria that Bruno died in 1101. Two additional Carthusian houses were also founded in Calabria around 1100. Subsequently the eremitical features of the religious life of these Calabrian Carthusian houses were gradually substituted for a more conventional Benedictine model, at least in the two later foundations, and this would be a pattern repeated in other southern Italian monastic orders of the twelfth century.[133] It is clear that Bruno's disciples considered him in saintly terms, but Carthusian ideals of humility prevented them from directly promoting Bruno's sanctity, and he was included in the Roman calendar of saints only in the seventeenth century.

Joachim of Fiore (d. 1202), a Calabrian by birth, also became a hermit, withdrawing to the slopes of Mount Etna and also the vicinity of Cosenza in Calabria. Like many other South Italian eremitical saints his vocation intersected with cenobitism for he was also attracted to the ideals of the Cistercians, one of the twelfth century's most successful reforming orders. Consequently Joachim established associations with some of the few Cistercian houses in Calabria, at the abbey of Sambucina, at Corazzo (where he became abbot), and then Casamari by 1183. Struggling to balance his conflicting desires for solitude and community, and to create what he considered to be a more original model of the religious life than even the Cistercians could offer, Joachim retreated to the mountainous wilderness of Calabria's Sila plateau where in 1188 he founded the small community of San Giovanni in Fiore. At the time of Joachim's death, Fiore was gradually constructing its own monastic order. However, Joachim was also a gifted, but controversial, writer and exegete who promoted challenging apocalyptical and mystical philosophies. His insights were sought by some of the leading figures of the late twelfth century, and he was often found at the papal court in Rome or the royal court at Palermo. Joachim's monastic foundations received support from King Tancred of Sicily and Henry VI of Germany, and he was even allegedly interviewed by Richard I of England when the king resided at Messina in 1190–1.[134] Following his death, contemporaries moved

---

[133] Loud, *Latin Church*, 484–5.
[134] *Gesta Regis Henrici Secundi Benedicti Abbatis*, ed. W. Stubbs, 2 vols, RS 49 (London, 1867), ii. 151–5 and also in *Chronica Magistri Rogeri de Houedene*, ed. W. Stubbs, 4 vols, RS 51 (London, 1868–71), iii. 75–9.

quickly to establish his sanctity. Two *vitae* were produced, one before 1209 by an anonymous author, the other by Joachim's friend Luke, archbishop of Cosenza from 1202 to 1224, and his body was ceremonially translated to San Giovanni in Fiore in 1240.[135]

In several ways, Bruno and Joachim were similar to other hermit saints from central and northern Italy; men like St Romuald of Ravenna (951–1027), a pioneering figure who founded the Camaldolese order of hermits, or St Peter Damian (d. 1072), who promoted a comparable mixed eremitic–cenobitic model within the congregation of Fonte Avellana.[136] Parallels could also be made with several other lower-profile South Italian eremitical/monastic saints who were also evidently influenced by reforming ideals. Indicative of these trends was St Alferius, the first abbot of the great monastic order of SS Trinità di Cava, situated a few kilometres west of Salerno. Indeed, Cava's first four abbots – Alferius (d. 1050), Leo (1050–79), Peter (1079–1123) and Constable (1123–4) – were all venerated within the abbey as saints, and by the time the *Lives of the First Four Abbots of Cava* had been composed (c.1141–56), the monastery had created a vast and powerful network spreading across southern Italy.[137] However, Cava's founder, Alferius, had led an eremitical existence having left the princely court at Salerno in c. 1020. He dwelled in a cave at Metiliano near Salerno, from where his fame gradually attracted a monastic community around him (and indeed a visit from Desiderius, future abbot of Montecassino).[138] Although Alferius also stayed briefly at the famous monastery of Cluny in Burgundy, Cava did not develop into a Cluniac-influenced house, and only appears to have evolved into a true Benedictine house during the abbacy of St Leo.[139] If Alferius' saintly successors conformed to a more conventional portrait of the monastic abbot, Leo still personally distributed bread to *pauperes* in Salerno, and Peter was known for his practice of mortification and refusal to drink wine.[140]

Other eremitical founders of monastic orders on whom we are far better informed were St John of Matera and St William of Montevergine. In both cases their monastic orders eventually followed the conventional

---

[135] The *vitae* are edited in H. Grundmann, 'Zur Biographie Joachims von Fiore und Rainiers von Ponza', *Deutsches Archiv für Erforschung des Mittelalters* 19 (1960), 528–44. Joachim, however, never received official Roman canonization.

[136] K. L. Jasper, 'Reforming the monastic landscape: Peter Damian's design for personal and communal devotion', *Rural Space in the Middle Ages and Early Modern Age. The Spatial Turn in Premodern Studies*, ed. A. Classen (Berlin, 2012), 193–208.

[137] VQPAC; see also Houben, 'L'autore delle "Vitae"', 871–9.

[138] VQPAC, 5–7.

[139] VQPAC, 5–6; Loud, *Latin Church*, 53.

[140] VQPAC, 12, 19–20.

Benedictine Rule, but they continued to exhibit signs of the reforming and eremitical ethos which inspired their founders.[141] St John of Matera (c.1084–c.1139) founded the monastery of S. Maria di Pulsano in c. 1129 on the Gargano peninsula, which eventually became the centre of the Pulsano monastic congregation. It is evident that John's *vita* uses several exemplars from the New Testament and employs the template of Gregory the Great's *Dialogues*, retrospectively fitting John's actions into the traditions of Benedictine monasticism which for large parts of his life might have been alien to him. On the other hand, the *vita*'s derivative features are balanced by the fact that it seems to have been mostly written in the 1140s by an anonymous monk, undoubtedly from Pulsano, who offers a close perspective.[142] Born of affluent parents, John soon rejected worldly affairs and followed an extreme form of the ascetic life, travelling throughout Apulia, Lucania, Calabria, Sicily and Campania. In his formative years he stayed in a Greek Orthodox monastery in Taranto, where his intense austerity brought maltreatment from the monks. John opted to leave the monastery for greater solitude and abstinence. He spent over two years in Sicily, practising mortification, withdrawn from the world, combating the devil and following the exemplars set by St Anthony and St Paul. A vision from St Peter inspired John to return to Apulia where he passed a further two-and-a-half years in solitude before restoring a church dedicated to the Apostle at Ginosa. Here, John attracted some followers, and here too he reconnected with the world, inspired now to imitate the apostolic preachers.[143] John's new path often led to trying experiences. Accused of concealing some treasure, he was imprisoned by the count of Ginosa but miraculously managed to escape. Soon after, he visited Bari where he preached against simony and feud, urging 'temperance to the greedy, chastity to the lustful, and charity to those in discord'.[144] Such preaching to the laity brought accusations of heresy from the local clergy and John was condemned to the stake. Fortunately, the ruler of the city (apparently Prince Grimoald) recognized John's piety, liberated him, and allowed him to continue preaching.[145]

---

[141] Loud, *Latin Church*, 470–82.

[142] *Vita S. Iohannis a Mathera*, AS June, v (Paris, 1867), 37–8; see also F. Panarelli, *Dal Gargano alla Toscana: il monachesimo riformato latino dei pulsanesi (secoli xii–xiv)* (Rome, 1997). It is, however, possible that the work was written by multiple authors, with the sections on miracles added as late as 1177. The original *vita* has not survived and the manuscript tradition is problematic; see Limone, *Santi*, 48–51, 59–60; Vuolo, 'Monachesimo', 69–121.

[143] *Vita S. Iohannis*, 37–8; Vuolo, 'Monachesimo', 94.

[144] *Vita S. Iohannis*, 38.

[145] *Vita S. Iohannis*, 39.

Thereafter, John moved to the sanctuary of St Michael on Monte Gargano, commencing the last phase of his life on the Gargano peninsula. John stayed at the shrine for over a year, and while there he was supplicated by the local inhabitants to help end a drought. John's response demonstrated his conviction of the need for moral reform, for he revealed that the corruption of the people and the sins of one particular canon of the shrine of St Michael were responsible; following a collective display of penitence by the local inhabitants the drought ended.[146] In c.1129, inspired by a vision of the Virgin Mary, John founded the church at Pulsano, on a remote hill in the region of Monte Sant'Angelo.[147] The small community of six expanded within six months to fifty, and the remainder of John's life was devoted to his abbacy. John founded and reformed a number of subordinate houses, and performed miracles which took place mainly in the locality of the Gargano peninsula.[148] Most of John's miracles focused on Pulsano monks, but his healing of the son of the lord of Siponto, and his role in preventing a nobleman from possessing a church and living with a nun, showed that he continued to maintain contact with the lay elite at the same time as promoting reforming ideals, while some of his miracles also aided the poor.[149] John's *vita* reveals how his cult was utilized following his death in June 1139 to assert internal Pulsano power relationships as well as to protect the congregation's status externally. John had died at the dependent house of S. Giacomo at Foggia, and one miracle prevented the transferral of his body to the main house at Pulsano (which seems to have finally occurred in 1177). Post-mortem apparitions of John also aimed at protecting Pulsano's position within Roger II's newly established monarchy. John appeared to both his abbatial successor Jordan (1139–45) and to Roger II to steer them towards agreement about, and royal approval of, the election of the new abbot.[150] The *vita* concludes thus with the assurance of royal protection.

John's life was framed by the rejection of wealth, by stringent ascetic ideals and dietary abstinence, and increasingly by the importance of manual labour, so favoured by new monastic orders such as the Cistercians.[151] It is clear that John's independent form of eremitism was influenced by the Greek Orthodox model, nurtured in Taranto, Calabria

---

[146] *Vita S. Iohannis*, 39.
[147] *Vita S. Iohannis*, 40.
[148] *Vita S. Iohannis*, 42–8.
[149] *Vita S. Iohannis*, 42–4; Limone, *Santi*, 58.
[150] *Vita S. Iohannis*, 49–50.
[151] A number of John's miracles occurred in the context of the monks working in the woods and collecting timber: *Vita S. Iohannis*, 44–6. Loud, *Latin Church*, 474–7; Limone, *Santi*, 51–63.

and Sicily; but once at Pulsano he took the title of abbot, and the monastic order he created eventually adopted conventional Benedictine infrastructures and, by 1177, the Benedictine Rule.[152] John thus played his part in the wider renewal of traditional Benedictine cenobitism. Indeed, the Pulsano order prospered in the decades immediately after John's death. By 1177 it had fourteen dependencies, with most in northern Apulia but some too in Rome and Tuscany. Although the speed of the expansion created some disorder already by the 1170s and clear difficulties by the early thirteenth century, it remained the only religious establishment besides Montecassino to push beyond the borders of the Kingdom of Sicily.[153] Moreover, the establishment of a series of dependencies dispersed the cult of St John and other later Pulsanese saints, as well as generating nodes for other forms of localized devotions. For instance, the nunnery of S. Cecilia of Foggia, incorporated into the Pulsano congregation by 1177, had produced at the end of the twelfth century a rich martyrology which commemorated St John of Matera and his two successors, abbots Jordan and Joel (1145–77), who were both deemed as saints in the martyrology.[154] Indeed, the text records that Joel's translation was responsible for liberating Apulia from a two-year-long drought.[155] The martyrology also consolidated devotion for local Apulian saints, inserting record of the translations of SS Eleutherius, Pontianus and Anastasius to Troia, and of St Nicholas to Bari, mention of the feast day of St Lawrence of Siponto, and notice of the *depositio* of St Sabinus at Canosa.[156]

The parallels between St John of Matera and his contemporary St William of Montevergine (c.1085–1142) are striking, although it might be argued that William followed a more western model of eremitism. William's *vita*, like John's, poses several challenges. It was composed and possibly rewritten in stages from the mid-twelfth to the mid-thirteenth century by multiple authors, undoubtedly with different agendas.[157] However, again like John of Matera's *vita*, the work was initially commenced soon after William's death by an author who knew his subject

[152] Martin, *Pouille*, 683.
[153] Panarelli, *Dal Gargano alla Toscana*, 137–236; Martin, *Pouille*, 685; Loud, *Latin Church*, 480.
[154] *Martyrologium Pulsanensis*, 12–13, 15, 41–2.
[155] *Martyrologium Pulsanensis*, 41.
[156] *Martyrologium Pulsanensis*, 40–2.
[157] The authors were John (possibly a monk of S. Salvatore di Goleto), a monk from Montevergine who utilized information from a John of Nusco, and an anonymous author who added post-mortem miracles dated to 1185 and 1257–8. For a comprehensive analysis of the *Vita et Obitus Sancti Guilielmi* and its composition see F. Panarelli, *Scrittura agiografica nel mezzogiorno normanno. La vita di San Guglielmo da Vercelli* (Lecce, 2004) ix–l with an edition of the *vita* at 3–52. See also Limone, *Santi*, 31–45.

personally, and it is therefore a rich source. A North Italian, from Vercelli, William undertook a pilgrimage to Compostela at the age of fourteen and while there began wearing two iron rings around his stomach and chest, the sign of a penitent pilgrim.[158] William first encountered southern Italy when he halted in Apulia before the year 1130, postponing an intended pilgrimage to Jerusalem in order to undertake the *vita eremitica* for over two years in the region of Melfi. Here he performed his first miracle on a blind man and acquired a fame for holiness which convinced him to continue his journey to Jerusalem.[159] The first of apparently three encounters with St John of Matera altered his plans, for John beseeched William to remain in southern Italy and work for the salvation of its people. William remained, but embarked on a search for an isolated mountainous retreat to continue his eremitic vocation, although in the process he acquired a companion. Thereafter he intensified his asceticism. He began wearing a breastplate and bonnet, both made of iron, survived on a meagre diet primarily consisting of beans and chestnuts, slept on a rock and spent nights standing on one leg reciting Holy Scripture before a cross.[160]

As William attracted more followers he eventually established an isolated eremitic community at *Virgilianus mons* (Montevergine, near Avellino in the Apennines), where, with the support of members of the local nobility, he built a church in c.1124. Henceforth, William was constrained to maintain a balance between community and solitude. Some of the priests in the group advocated a more organized framework to guide their vocation than William was willing to concede. William was seemingly opposed to taking the title of abbot and disputes arose over how to dispose of the monetary gifts received by the community: some of the priests believed it was vital to invest them in the running of the monastery, while William insisted on donating these revenues to the *pauperes* and challenged the priests to renounce secular goods, 'for you have chosen God as your inheritance'.[161] The solution, in c.1128–9, saw William withdraw from Montevergine, appointing a deputy in his place, and immersing himself once again in an eremitical and penitential existence on Monte Laceno.[162] Eventually, after a further meeting with St John of Matera, William founded another monastery, S. Salvatore di Goleto, thirty kilometres east of Avellino. Significantly it was originally established

---

[158] *Vita et Obitus Sancti Guilielmi*, 4–7.
[159] *Vita et Obitus Sancti Guilielmi*, 8–9.
[160] *Vita et Obitus Sancti Guilielmi*, 11–14.
[161] *Vita et Obitus Sancti Guilielmi*, 17–18.
[162] *Vita et Obitus Sancti Guilielmi*, 18.

as a double cloister for men and women, an idea firmly in line with the pioneers of monastic reform of the twelfth century. It was in this monastery that William died in 1142, and where his relics were retained.

Thus, like John of Matera, extreme asceticism, mortification, charitable work and solitude dominated William's spiritual make-up. Also, like John, William interacted with both the elites and the poor through his miracle working and founding of religious houses.[163] William's legacy remained strong in the monastic order that subsequently developed with its centre at Montevergine. His earliest prescriptions for the nuns' religious life at S. Salvatore di Goleto were certainly stricter than normal Benedictine standards, and yet, gradually, religious life at Montevergine and its dependent houses became increasingly conventional: between 1161 and 1172 it began observing the Benedictine Rule, and from the later twelfth century greatly expanded its patrimony to become one of southern Italy's wealthiest monastic orders.[164] Ultimately, the hagiographers of both John and William had a difficult task, for the monastic orders they founded boasted neither older traditions to draw upon nor established scriptoria to take advantage of. As we have noted, the authors of these *vitae* tried to fit their subjects into a more conventional monastic framework that perhaps represented more current developments. Thus, St John of Matera received the aid of St Benedict when curing a possessed monk, while a change in authorship in William's *vita* also signalled a shift in its tone, which saw focus move away from the saint's personal attributes – love of God, simplicity, charity – towards his relationships with the political elite and particularly Roger II.[165] Indeed, both *vitae* ultimately appeal for royal protection as both saints were posthumously drawn into the mainstream, while William's *vita* appears also to have been employed to communicate the delineation of the respective spheres of influence of the expanding monastic orders of Montevergine and Pulsano. In one of the encounters between William and John, the two saints established their zones of action: John 'in oriente' (Apulia) and William 'in occidente' (Campania).[166] In short, these saints as presented in their *vitae* had multiple identities. They were eremitical and monastic and reforming and conventional all at the same time, and this quite likely reflected the reality of the ongoing tensions within the reforming monastic climate of the twelfth century.

Unfortunately space permits only brief reference to some of the other eremitical/monastic saints of southern Italy who were associated with the

---

163 For examples of these varied interactions see *Vita et Obitus Sancti Guilielmi*, 20–2, 26.
164 *Vita et Obitus Sancti Guilielmi*, 25; Loud, *Latin Church*, 478–9.
165 *Vita S. Iohannis*, 46–7; Limone, *Santi*, 38–45.
166 *Vita et Obitus Sancti Guilielmi*, 21.

reform movement in all its varying guises, but in doing so we can at least appreciate how broadly new spiritual ideals intersected with sanctity in the region. The life of St John of Tufara (d. 1170) bore similarities with those of St William of Montevergine and St John of Matera: he was a hermit who in 1156 founded the monastery of Santa Maria del Gualdo Mazzocca in northern Apulia which eventually became the centre of a new monastic congregation. Although the initial monastery was a joint community of hermits and secular priests, it appears to have immediately adopted the Benedictine Rule, unlike at Montevergine and Pulsano. A *vita* of St John was produced between 1197 and 1203 and was subsequently used in an application for papal canonization.[167] At the other extreme of our period, and on the northern frontiers of the region, the hermit St Dominic of Sora (d. 1032) had already promoted many of the ideals which would be inherent in the later Gregorian Reform. A tireless founder of monasteries loosely tied together across the Apennines from the Abruzzi to southern Latium, Dominic combined cenobitic and eremitic ideals which were broadly based on a Benedictine model. The most comprehensive *vita* of the saint was produced by the Montecassino hagiographer Alberic in c.1067–70, which showed Dominic's path to sanctity via a series of miracles performed throughout his life. But the initial patronage of this great monastic centre failed to prevent Dominic's own monastic confederation from collapsing soon after his death. As John Howe has shown, Dominic's reforming approach was too disorganized and informal to survive the more assertive reform agendas produced in the later eleventh century.[168] It is equally important to emphasize that not all eremitical saints who were active in the Latin zone of southern Italy inevitably operated within an institutional or communal framework. Some, like the Greek wandering hermit St Nicholas the Pilgrim of Trani, were characterized by a combination of eremitism and pilgrimage through which they aspired to the newly popular spiritual ideals of absolute poverty, purity and penitence, exemplified through their preaching and miracle working. Indeed, St Nicholas the Pilgrim's earliest miracles were largely anti-monastic in tone, enabling him to escape from the oppressive Greek monks of Hosios Loukas and cross the Adriatic, and were indicative of the positive force of eremitism (taming nature and combating the devil), while his post-mortem miracles emphasized his affinity with pilgrims and laypeople.[169]

---

[167] The petition was successful, and John was formally acknowledged as a local saint in 1221, even though the papacy did not actually officially recognize his sanctity until 2005: Hilken, *Memory and Community*, 37–8. Galdi, *Santi*, 42–3, 54.

[168] For comprehensive treatment of St Dominic see Howe, *Church Reform*.

[169] *Vita S. Nicolai Peregrini*, 231–46.

The new reforming and monastic ideals inspired and created a number of new South Italian saints in the eleventh and twelfth centuries. However, long-established monasteries which adhered more rigorously to the traditional Benedictine ethos of *stabilitas loci* also continued to promote their own monastic saints. As was the case for all types of cult, this promotion was characterized by surges of activity which often coincided with key transitions in the history of the centre which oversaw the cult. For instance, the monastery of S. Clemente a Casauria, founded in c.873 by the Carolingian emperor Louis II and the most influential religious house in the Abruzzi, rearticulated its relationship with its patron saint (alleged to have been St Peter's immediate successor at Rome) in the late eleventh century when the Norman influx created disorder in the region.[170] Thus in the last two decades of the eleventh century St Clement firmly (re)appears as protector of the monks of Casauria, his relics were 'rediscovered' in 1104 and the monastery was rededicated at a public event in 1105.[171] The monastery's chronicle, completed shortly after 1182, also conferred on St Clement a pivotal role in its history in the late eleventh and twelfth centuries, in which he performed a series of miracles to protect the monastery, some of which were distinctly punitive.[172] The monastery also expressed its alliance with the new Sicilian monarchy through its patron saint; the monastery's chronicle recorded Roger II's interest in St Clement, and recounted the saint's apparition in c.1140 in order to assure the abbot about the king's favourable attitude to the monastery.[173]

The redevelopment of the cult of a patron saint of an ancient Benedictine monastery was even more apparent at Montecassino. As the monastery entered its so-called 'golden era' under Abbot Desiderius (1058–87), coterminously with the Norman takeover and a crucial phase of the wider Church reform, so too did it promote anew the cult of St Benedict. There is no need to revisit the long-running contest between Montecassino and Fleury over the ownership of Benedict's relics, but in 1068, while the main church at Montecassino was being renovated, the body of St Benedict was (allegedly) unexpectedly discovered.[174] Indeed, almost certainly in response, new efforts were made at Fleury in the eleventh century to reaffirm its possession of the relics; a short collection of miracles composed at Fleury contained one in which St Benedict

[170] G. A. Loud, 'Monastic chronicles in the twelfth-century Abruzzi', *Anglo-Norman Studies* 27 (2005), 101–31.
[171] There is surprisingly little certain evidence for devotion of St Clement at Casauria prior to the late eleventh century.
[172] See for example the following miracles: *Chronicon Casauriense*, 870, 873–4.
[173] *Chronicon Casauriense*, 888–9.
[174] Chron. Cas., Bk III.26, p. 395.

appeared to the abbot of Montecassino to assure him that he had volun-
tarily transferred to the French abbey.[175] In any case, Montecassino
promoted its rediscovery to the widest possible audience when the new
basilica was consecrated in 1071 in the presence of Pope Alexander II,
Archdeacon Hildebrand (the future Pope Gregory VII), three Roman
cardinal bishops, at least three cardinal priests, and various South Italian
churchmen, dukes and princes.[176] In the monastery's scriptorium the
production of various texts, which achieved wide fame during Desiderius's
abbacy, also formed part of the same programme. It connected the
present-day monastery to the pristine time of Benedict's life, and thus
was attuned to eleventh-century reforming aspirations. The magnificent
Codex Benedictus was produced during Desiderius' era; it contained the
lives of Benedict, his sister Scholastica and his disciple Maurus, and
resonated with contemporary reforming themes, such as St Benedict
preaching to the laity and his struggles with enemies of the Church.[177]
The composition of Desiderius' *Dialogues* in the 1070s resembled Gregory
the Great's work on St Benedict, and extolled the miracle workings of
St Benedict. The reworking in c.1100 of the *Montecassino Chronicle* by Leo
Marsicanus incorporated many of the miracles recorded in the *Dialogues*,
and added some of its own. Notably, Leo's account of St Benedict's
healing of the emperor Henry II in 1022 was overtly intended to demonstrate St Benedict's presence at Montecassino. Following his recovery
from bladder stones Henry II asserted that 'no living person should
henceforth doubt that Father Benedict lies here alongside his sister', and
promptly offered several precious gifts to the monastery.[178] Amatus' earlier
account of this event, written in c.1080, showed that Montecassino's
monks had previously been aware of doubts over their possession of
Benedict's body, for the saint apparently said to the emperor, 'Do you
think that I want to leave the place where I was brought by the angels, where
I wrote the rule of monks and where most of my body was buried?'.[179] By
1100, Montecassino's position on possession of St Benedict's relics was
unequivocal; a response to continued counterclaims at Fleury, and the
twelfth-century continuation of the *Montecassino Chronicle*, alleged that in
1107 the pope affirmed the Fleury translation to be false.[180]

---

[175] Head, *Hagiography*, 153, 56–7.
[176] Chron. Cas., Bk II.29, pp. 398–400.
[177] *The Codex Benedictus. An Eleventh-Century Lexionary from Monte Cassino, Vat Lat 1202*,
ed. P. Meyvaert, 2 vols (New York, 1982); for insightful discussion see Hamilton, *Sacred
City*, 66–8.
[178] Chron. Cas., Bk II.43, p. 248; for the full episode 43–4, pp. 247–52.
[179] Amatus, I.28, pp. 257–8; Loud, 'Monastic miracles', 121–2.
[180] Chron. Cas., Bk IV.29, pp. 494–5.

It has been commented with some justification that, beyond devotion to its own chief patron saint, Montecassino in the Central Middle Ages was largely conservative and restrained in the promotion of other saints from within its own ranks.[181] A cult never materialized around Desiderius, for example, as it did for some of the abbots of Cava, and more famously of Cluny in Burgundy. However, there is sufficient evidence to revise this picture to some extent. Peter the Deacon, Montecassino's librarian, archivist and part-time forger, produced in the mid-twelfth century the *Ortus et Vita Iustorum Cenobii Casinensis*, a directory of his monastery's saintly residents, some thirty-five of whom seem to have lived after 1000.[182] Men such as the Amalfitan Leo, the Venetian John Gradenigo, the Germans Theodamar and Gebizo, and the Iberians Fortunatus and Guinizo were all associated with the Montecassino community and considered to have displayed saintly virtues.[183] Some of these qualities were standard hagiographic fare; in many cases, miracles attendant on their deaths, often columns of fire reaching to the heavens, were the first certain sign of sanctity. However, the works of Peter and, to a lesser extent, Desiderius suggest that Montecassino was not so conservative as to overlook the virtues of its own eremitic saints and the renewed prominence of the eremitical life in contemporary spirituality. Jean-Marie Sansterre has demonstrated how Montecassino's brand of Benedictine monasticism left space for eremitism and that a notable minority of its monks followed the eremitical life.[184] The presence of the Calabrian Greek hermit St Nilus in the region of Montecassino in the 990s undoubtedly influenced some members of the community.[185] A number of the individuals listed in Peter the Deacon's work – including John Gradenigo, Fortunatus and Guinizo – were hermits who installed themselves on the lands of Montecassino and were incorporated into its community. Certainly, Montecassino's promotion of this saintly type was modest, and Peter, Desiderius and other Montecassino hagiographers tended to subsume eremitism within the framework of cenobitism. Nevertheless, through the channel of its eremitical saints, Montecassino demonstrated its support of the reform movement, and a surprisingly eclectic belief that solitude and community were not incompatible.

Furthermore, Montecassino's promotion of saints was not purely inward-looking, for this period was one of prolific hagiographical output

---

[181] Cowdrey, *Age of Abbot Desiderius*, 30–1.
[182] Some of these figures were also recorded in Desiderius' *Dialogues*.
[183] *Petri Diaconi Ortus et Vita*, 52–64, 71–6.
[184] J.-M. Sansterre, 'Recherches sur les érémites du Mont-Cassin et l'érémitisme dans l'hagiographie cassinienne', *Hagiographica* 2 (1995), 57–92.
[185] For Nilus see Chapters 1 and 3.

by its monks on behalf of various South Italian cults.[186] A number of these texts have been encountered elsewhere in this study. We have already seen that Alberic of Montecassino wrote a *vita* of St Dominic of Sora in the 1060s; and among his other works he composed a *vita* of St Aspren, the first bishop of Naples, for Archbishop Peter of Naples (c.1094–1100) and a *Passio sancti Modesti* for Roffred, archbishop of Benevento (1076–1108). The monk Guaiferius produced in the 1060s an expanded work on St Secundinus for the bishop of Troia, and John of Gaeta, the future Pope Gelasius II (1118–19), wrote between 1078 and 1088 a *vita* of St Erasmus, patron saint of Gaeta. This pattern was continued into the twelfth century with the Montecassino chronicler Leo Marsicanus being responsible for an account of the translation of St Mennas for Count Robert of Caiazzo, and Peter the Deacon who produced an imaginative fictitious hagiography of a St Mark of Atina in gratitude for time spent in exile at Atina between 1128 and 1131.[187] Thus, Montecassino was central to the wider renewal of South Italian sanctity in the eleventh and twelfth centuries.

Urbanization and civic devotions

It is true that many of southern Italy's monastic and eremitical saints attracted devotion primarily from a restricted ecclesiastical circle, despite some evidence for lay interaction with these saints or pilgrimage to their shrines. Furthermore, the reforming ethos, evident in some South Italian cults, stressed the chasm between the ecclesiastical and the secular. Nevertheless, it also imbued the urban classes with a new ideal of piety, and a number of southern Italy's cults in the Central Middle Ages were undoubtedly 'popular' in the sense that they received extensive support from the laity. In the most conspicuous cases these cults were based in cities which were experiencing rapid physical expansion and social transition in the eleventh and twelfth centuries. The growing size of urban communities, the evolution of civic consciousness, and aspirations for urban independence were all evident in southern Italy's urban communities during the Norman era.[188] In this climate, local saints' cults were employed to articulate emergent urban power and civic identities and to balance tensions within expanded communities – often they were rare neutral poles around which fractious solidarities could find commonalities. This process occurred in many urban centres across Europe. It was

---

[186] Cowdrey, *Age of Abbot Desiderius*, 39–42.
[187] Bloch, *Atina Dossier*; Peter also constructed an elaborate, fictitious *passio* of a St Placidus, whom he presented as a Sicilian disciple of St Benedict.
[188] See generally Oldfield, *City and Community*.

particularly notable in the rising communal cities of northern Italy, but many urban cults in England, especially in the decades either side of 1200 (such as St William's at York and St Frideswide's at Oxford), built on phases of pastoral reform to unify fractious communities by expressing potent civic ideals which circumnavigated increasing royal intervention.[189] The growing urbanization of mainland southern Italy in the Central Middle Ages thus played its own part in the development of South Italian sanctity.

Large urban crowds were regularly attested at the interring or translation of relics. At the burial of St Nicholas the Pilgrim at Trani in 1094 apparently the 'entire city eagerly flocked together', while the saint's retranslation in 1142 saw 'such an assembly of people that the space of the city could hardly contain them'.[190] The relics of St Eleutherius and his companions were allegedly welcomed outside Troia in 1104 by almost ten thousand citizens.[191] If we are encountering the embellishments of a hagiographical topos, it was one sufficiently in line with other evidence for civic devotion to suggest that it was grounded in reality, and the urban laity were active participants. Indeed, urban cults in three of the mainland's largest cities –Salerno, Bari and Benevento – indicate the cultivation of close bonds between saint and citizen. At Salerno, civic pride was increasingly channelled into devotion for the cult of St Matthew, diverting attention from the collapse of the Lombard ruling dynasty in 1076–7, and driven by Robert Guiscard and the city's archbishop, Alfanus I. A cathedral confraternity dedicated to St Matthew, which attracted civic devotion, had been established in Salerno in c.1000, but the rediscovery of the saint's relics in 1080 and the rebuilding of the cathedral provided a new nexus for civic pride and piety. We have already seen how Amatus of Montecassino's account of Guiscard's capture of Salerno stressed the bonds between the citizens and their patron saint. So too did the works of Archbishop Alfanus who composed eight poems to St Matthew, one typical verse reading, 'the body of the apostle has come for the salvation of the faithful clergy and citizens of Salerno, praise be to the son of God'.[192] Significantly, parts of these works were absorbed into the Salernitan

---

[189] See S. Rees-Jones, 'Cities and their saints in England, circa 1150–1300: the development of bourgeois values in the cults of Saint William of York and Saint Kenelm of Winchcombe', *Cities, Texts and Social Networks, 400–1500. Experiences and Perceptions of Medieval Urban Space*, ed. C. Goodson et al. (Farnham, 2010), 193–213.

[190] *Vita S. Nicolai Peregrini*, 240, 244.

[191] Poncelet, 'Translation', 422.

[192] *Carmi*, nos. 7–9 pp. 84–9, nos. 58–62 pp. 225–32; Galdi, 'Il santo', 72–3; B. Vetere, 'Cattedrale', 55–95. At the same time Alfanus I helped to reinvigorate the cults of other local Salernitan saints – such as Fortunatus, Caius and Ante – through relic translations, and the production of liturgical works and hymns: *Carmi*, nos. 10–11 pp. 90–3, no. 58 p. 225.

liturgy and used on the feast of the translation (6 May), an important civic event with processions throughout the city's parishes.[193] In the twelfth century local church dedications to the saint increased as does onomastic evidence for the popularity of Matthew as a personal name in both the Salernitan region and throughout southern Italy.[194] The increased use of St Matthew's effigy on Salernitan coinage further deepened the saint's urban omnipresence, and the civic elites were keen to announce their devotion.[195] In c.1100, Landulf Butrumiles, from an influential Salernitan family, donated bronze doors to the cathedral on which were depicted his wife and himself in a panel alongside St Matthew.[196] The most intense phase of urban activity surrounding St Matthew's cult occurred again in those critical decades around 1100, and while there is a notable paucity of miracles worked by the saint for individual Salernitans, by the mid-twelfth century Matthew was intrinsically acknowledged as the city's patron saint. In 1162, according to the chronicle attributed to Romuald II, archbishop of Salerno (1153–81), as King William I prepared to punish Salerno for its role in a rebellion the royal camp was destroyed by a storm brewed up by St Matthew, 'who has been given by God to the city of Salerno as patron and defender'.[197]

It is possible to witness clearly at Bari the emotional intensity and political tensions which urban cults generated within a city. The arrival of the relics of St Nicholas of Myra in 1087 was the result of a civic enterprise conceived almost entirely through lay initiative. Nicephorus' account of the translation credits 'some wise and illustrious' merchants of Bari for the plan to steal the relics whilst trading at Antioch.[198] John the Archdeacon added that the Barese translators were driven by 'divine inspiration', but that more worldly motives – economic gain and civic pride – were also apparent: John noted that the Baresi were desperate to acquire the relics before the Venetians in order to avoid dishonour and infamy.[199] The magnetism of the holy relics of St Nicholas, who was a

---

[193] Galdi, 'La diffusione del culto del santo patrono', 182–6.

[194] Galdi, 'Il santo', 65–7, 75 n. 157 gives charter references for individuals called Matthew; see other examples in Cava dei Tirreni, Archivio della badia di S. Trinità, *Arca* xxiv no. 30, xxxiii no. 38; *Codice diplomatico salernitano del secolo XIII*, vol. 1 (1201–1281), ed. C. Carucci (Subiaco, 1931), no. 1 pp. 43–4, pp. 50–2, and all the Matthews in the *Necrologio del Liber Confratrum di S. Matteo di Salerno*, ed. C. A. Garufi, FSI 56 (Rome, 1922), 353–6, 410–11; Villani, 'Il contributo dell'onomastico', 262–6.

[195] Travaini, *La monetazione*, 262, 271–5.

[196] D. F. Glass, *Romanesque Sculpture in Campania. Patrons, Programs and Style* (Pennsylvania, 1991), 66–7.

[197] Romuald, 251.

[198] Nitti di Vito, 'La traslazione', 337.

[199] Nitti di Vito, 'La traslazione', 359–60.

patron of sailors and travellers, could offer an alternative route to channel traffic and pilgrims through its port, and to rival Venice's commercial expansion. Both John's and Nicephorus' works capture the significance of the translation for the Barese community's evolving sense of civic consciousness. Nicephorus celebrated the luminous splendour that the relics would bestow on Bari and all of Apulia:

> Rejoice, o Bari, for you welcome within you a new inheritance of salvation! Rejoice, that you should be considered the most worthy of praise amongst all the cities of Apulia. Rejoice, that you should be crowned by a triumphal victory. Indeed, Nicholas in Greek means 'victory of the people'; and he indeed has won, when he has welcomed under his protection the Baresi and all the Pugliesi, freeing them from slavery to maladies.[200]

John believed that Bari's act had been fulfilled for the salvation of all Europe and that:

> even if the cities and provinces of all the West have rightly rejoiced at so marvellous a gift, nevertheless we shall see Bari shine through an extraordinary, exceptional and almost exclusive supremacy.[201]

Indeed, Nicephorus' work was commissioned by the Barese judge Curcorio as well as other leading citizens of Bari and the priests of its holy churches.[202] Both main accounts of the translation express the widespread joy which erupted among the Baresi at the news of the arrival of the relics:

> almost all the men and women, old and young, children and babies waited [at the port] with attentive looks and exultant souls for the arrival of the ships which brought a joy so great to Bari and to all Italy.[203]

Unfortunately, such a great prize sparked tensions and conflict. Archbishop Urso claimed the relics for his cathedral, while the translators insisted on placing them under the guardianship of Elias, abbot of the Barese monastery of S. Benedetto, until a new church could be built to house a shrine. As discussed already, perhaps this was a clash over the extent of archiepiscopal authority and conflicting views on the urban laity's input into the cult; all we can say for sure is that opposing factions within the city were reluctant to relinquish control over such a valuable asset.[204] Indeed, so reluctant were they that violence and bloodshed ensued. John the Archdeacon, writing in favour of the archbishop, refused

---

[200] Nitti di Vito, 'La traslazione', 346; Corsi, *La traslazione*, 64.
[201] Corsi, *La traslazione*, 64.
[202] Nitti di Vito, 'La traslazione', 336.
[203] Nitti di Vito, 'La traslazione', 365.
[204] See the brief analysis, in Geary, *Furta Sacra*, 94–103; CDBV, no. 164, provides a twelfth-century list of the translators, which suggests that they were a mixed social group.

to speak of what he called 'an internal struggle' which divided the city into two factions, preferring instead that the episode 'should be buried in an eternal silence and swept into oblivion'.[205] Unfortunately for him, his counterpart Nicephorus was not so parsimonious with the details. Nicephorus claimed that the party who wanted the relics transferred to the cathedral was in the minority, but it clearly posed a threat as armed guards were placed around the relics' temporary shrine at the monastery of S. Benedetto.[206] Negotiations between the two factions collapsed, and the ensuing violent clashes led to the death of two youths, whose souls were believed to have found eternal bliss as a consequence. It seems that this tragedy forced reconciliation, for the relics were soon moved to where a new church was to be built, which Elias would govern with the assent of the archbishop and all the citizens. The new church, although not fully complete until the later twelfth century, was dedicated by Pope Urban II in 1089.[207] The miracles recorded by both authors in the week after St Nicholas's arrival show that the Baresi immediately flocked to the shrine, and that the rapid influx of visitors from further afield effected a dramatic change to daily life in the city.[208]

The two main translation accounts established the cult's intimate relationship with the urban community, and may partially explain why no subsequent works were produced in the twelfth century. Further miracle collections and hagiographical works produced at Bari would have also been rendered unnecessary by the legitimacy conferred by the streams of foreign pilgrims visiting the shrine (see Chapter 5) and the support of the Hauteville dynasty (see Chapter 4). Within Bari the political elite continued to bind itself to the cult. Prince Grimoald of Bari, who from c.1118 to 1131 ruled over an effectively autonomous city, styled himself as 'prince by the grace of God and St Nicholas', asserting the saint's protection over Bari.[209] The legacy of the translation, and the link between the Barese laity and St Nicholas, was given additional permanency through the establishment of a *societas* of St Nicholas, a quasi-confraternity without defined legal status, whose members were originally the sixty-two sailors who carried out the famous translation.[210] Membership conveyed a set of heritable privileges, including a seat within the church, burial next to its walls (the translators' names are inscribed on the outer archway of the church), the option to become a cleric of St Nicholas and the receipt of aid

---

[205] Nitti di Vito, 'La traslazione', 366.
[206] Nitti di Vito, 'La traslazione', 348–50.
[207] CDBI, no. 33.
[208] For more see Chapter 6.
[209] CDBV, nos. 69, 71.
[210] G. M. Monti, *Le corporazioni nell'evo antico e nell'alto medio evo* (Bari, 1934), 309–24.

to ward off poverty.[211] It should also be remembered that the church of St Nicholas was the location for the emancipation of slaves in the city, intensifying its importance to the urban underclass, while charter evidence shows that the use of Nicholas as a personal name rose rapidly after the translation to constitute nearly 10 per cent of the Barese population by 1130.[212] It is quite right then that the city's charter of privileges of 1132 prioritizes the protection of the shrine of St Nicholas, and that the Barese customs of c.1200 should name Nicholas as 'our guard and saint'.[213]

The events at Bari had parallels at other lower-profile cult centres across southern Italy, and showed not only how cults created rivalries within urban communities but also between them. The anonymous author of the *Sermo de inventione Sancti Kataldi* described a familiar cocktail of jubilation and discord on the arrival of St Cataldus' relics at Taranto. A multitude of citizens took up arms to conduct the party of translators safely into the city, and once inside the *populus* cried out their wish for physical proximity to the relics, which they wanted placed 'at the centre of the city and to be with us for the salvation of our bodies and souls'.[214] Soon after, however, the formerly unified *populus* split into factions, one favouring the deposition of the relics in the cathedral, the other in the church of S. Biagio – the latter ultimately successful. Rarely did open rivalries erupt between different shrines within the same city. Although there must have been ongoing competition among the ecclesiastical guardians of these shrines, urban communities at least seem to have been unwilling to have one of their urban saints pitched against another. The 'rediscovery' of the relics of St Sabinus in the cathedral at Bari in 1091 may be interpreted as an archiepiscopal attempt to rival the cult of St Nicholas. John the Archdeacon, the author of the *inventio S. Sabini*, claimed that on news of the discovery, 'men and women of all ages hastened full of happiness and joy, rendering thanks to Almighty God that during their life he had conceded through his generosity so great a favour'.[215] But there is no evidence to suggest that the cult of St Sabinus, having achieved popular acclamation, countered the cult of St Nicholas or split the devotional loyalties of the Baresi; rather it augmented their spiritual protection.

---

[211] A charter of 1105 (CDBV, no. 42) illuminates these privileges. They were also divisible, as revealed in a charter of 1207, CDBVI, no. 20.
[212] CDBV, no. 36; J.-M. Martin, 'Anthroponymie et onomastique à Bari (950–1250)', *MEFRM* 106 (1994), 683–701.
[213] *Rogerii II Regis Diplomata Latina*, ed. C.-R. Bruhl, Codex Diplomaticus Regni Siciliae, Ser. I.ii (1), (Cologne, 1987), pp. 54–6 no. 20; G. Petroni, *Della storia di Bari dagli antichi tempi sino all'anno 1856*, 2 vols (Naples, 1857–8), ii. 434 Rubric I.3.
[214] Hofmeister, 'Sermo', 109–10.
[215] *Inventio S. Sabini*, 281.

Interrelationships and rivalries between cities were, however, articulated through saints' cults. Certainly many cities claimed ownership of the same holy relics; the Venetians, for example, claimed possession of St Nicholas's relics in 1101.[216] Nevertheless some particular cases indicate more acute underlying inter-urban tensions. It cannot surely be coincidence that within a decade of the arrival of St Nicholas at Bari, another leading Apulian port city, Trani, promoted the cult of a St Nicholas the Pilgrim. The ecclesiastical rivalries between the two cities had been centuries in the making, and economic competition would have been increasingly important with the revival of Mediterranean commerce and travel. Trani's sponsoring of a saint, also called Nicholas, who was overtly associated with pilgrimage, undoubtedly countered Bari's Nicholaitan cult. The rivalry between the two cities appears to have been sufficiently entrenched for it to have induced in the twelfth century a distant Beneventan author to make some revealing interpolations in Nicephorus' account of the translation of St Nicholas from Myra to Bari.[217] Included in the list of sixty-two translators we suddenly encounter eight individuals with the 'tranensis' qualifier. The effect of the appearance of this new contingent from Trani was to dilute the exclusive Barese character of the 1087 mission. The Trani–Bari rivalry was used as a mechanism to weaken Bari's grip on the cult of St Nicholas. It should not be surprising that this initiative was conceived at Benevento, which had traditionally claimed an ascendant political and ecclesiastical status in southern Italy which, in turn, was being threatened by the arrival of St Nicholas's relics and Bari's rise. Thus a polemical work known as the *Adventus Sancti Nycolai in Beneventum* was produced which purported to record the transfer of the saint's patronage from Bari to Benevento at some point shortly before the text was composed around 1100. The text extolled Benevento's distinction – 'an ancient and illustrious city famous throughout the whole world' – and unashamedly aimed to entice pilgrims away from Bari.[218] The latter city was portrayed as a 'merciless land' without water, wine and bread; so bad was it that its patron saint had begun informing visiting pilgrims to head to Benevento to receive his intervention there instead.[219] Nevertheless, the Beneventan plan had no enduring success, and the miracles recorded in the *Adventus* suggest that the 'arrival' of St Nicholas attracted visitors

---

[216] It would seem that the Venetians may have obtained some genuine fragments of St Nicholas which the Barese had not removed from Myra.

[217] Nitti di Vito, 'La traslazione', 338, 380–4; for an extensive analysis see F. Babudri, 'Sinossi critica dei traslatori nicolaiani di Bari', *Archivio storico pugliese* 3 (1950), 3–94.

[218] G. Cangiano, 'L'Adventus Sancti Nycolai in Beneventum', *Atti della società storica del Sannio* 2 (1924), 151.

[219] Cangiano, 'Adventus', 147–9.

from beyond the immediate vicinity of the city of Benevento only briefly.[220]

The *Adventus* does reveal, however, aspects of the reconnection of Benevento's urban lay community with its civic saints. We have already discussed the sustained revival of cultic and hagiographic activity in the city in the later eleventh and early twelfth centuries, much of it guided by the city's archbishops. The *Adventus*, however, confers a leading role on a layman, Dacomarius, the first sole papal rector of Benevento (1077–97), who with his kin group effectively controlled the city in the late eleventh century.[221] Dacomarius promotes veneration for St Nicholas, urging the urban community to abandon vice, to reform its customs and to achieve greater spiritual devotion. He ordered that the clergy and the *populus* from each urban quarter should sing litanies and undertake nocturnal processions to the Beneventan church where St Nicholas's cult was centred, and he decreed that this church should be enlarged and improved.[222] In a later passage, the *Adventus* notes the abundance of holy protectors already resident in Benevento, naming in particular St Bartholomew, St Ianuarius, St Marcianus and St Barbatus, and suggests that St Nicholas chose not to stay with them in the cathedral because it would have created confusion and dissent over which miracles were attributed to which saint.[223]

The chronicle of Falco of Benevento builds on the re-emergence of saints in Beneventan urban life by offering some intimate accounts of the urban community's response to the rediscovery of relics, made all the more potent because the author was a layman and notary. In 1119 Archbishop Landulf II exhumed and exhibited the relics of several Beneventan saints.[224] At a challenging juncture in the city's history, threatened by factionalism and violence within its walls and by unruly lords in neighbouring territories, the response of the citizenry was euphoric: men (including Falco himself) and women rushed to the relics; in tears and carrying donations they began to kiss the holy bones. Two days later a great procession of all the priests and inhabitants of the city's urban quarters carrying torches and singing the litanies marched to the cathedral. Moved by the charged atmosphere, Falco decreed to the reader:

that you would have seen a most unusual procession and, something which had not happened for a long time, the city of Benevento bound together for the honour and veneration of the saints. Who among the citizens now living could remember

---

[220] See Chapter 6.
[221] Oldfield, *City and Community*, 41–2.
[222] Cangiano, 'Adventus', 150.
[223] Cangiano, 'Adventus', 151–2.
[224] Falco, 46–52.

when the city had been as happy at any other time? I believe that only at the arrival of St Bartholomew the Apostle, patron of the city, was Benevento so full of joy.[225]

As the celebratory procession neared its final destination it was joined by a wooden float full of candles, lamps and bells, on which young men played drums and flutes. Elsewhere in the city another huge float in the shape of a boat was constructed, carrying a giant bell, candles and an assortment of musicians. It was then transported to the cathedral, and when the streets got too narrow it was even carried the last stretch. Falco again emphasized the ecstatic atmosphere:

Oh reader, if you had been there, you would have seen what incredible exultation, what joy spread throughout the city, you would have really thought and believed that you were in another life and another type of heart, of eye and of body![226]

When the saints' bodies were redeposited in a new tomb on the following day Archbishop Landulf II thereafter remitted a quarter of the sins for everyone who visited the shrine up to eight days after the feast of the Apostles Peter and Paul.

In 1124 another comparable episode occurred in Benevento when Archbishop Roffred II ordered the invention and translation of St Barbatus.[227] Some citizens were selected to participate in the invention, and a large crowd flocked to the relics, which Falco once again was able to kiss.[228] Another citywide torchlit procession to the cathedral was organized by Benevento's ecclesiastical establishment; it was composed of 'a great crowd of the laity of both sexes and all ages; and every day for eight days each gate [urban quarter] of the city did the same'.[229] At the rededication of St Barbatus' altar the archbishop, before a huge crowd, again pardoned the sins of those who visited it. Falco later recorded three miracles which St Barbatus performed. On each occasion rumour or the ringing of bells spread news of the miracle through the city, attracting a crowd of Beneventans.[230] In the city, old cults were revived and placed in a direct relationship with an otherwise fractious laity, which identified its aspirations, salvation and communal unity with its civic saints.

Salerno, Bari and Benevento offer the best examples of lay interaction with city-based cults. But glimpses of similar relationships are evident in many other cities of southern Italy, from the sudden reappearance of St Ianuarius defending the Neapolitans in 1078 against Prince Richard

---

225 Falco, 48.
226 Falco, 50.
227 Falco, 74–82.
228 Falco, 76.
229 Falco, 76.
230 Falco, 76–82.

of Capua's siege, to the inhabitants of Bisceglie flocking to witness the discovery of three ancient saints.[231] Or at Troia, for instance, where four saints' cults were established in a small city over a period of roughly seventy years. Crowds were present at the key symbolic moments, witnessing the rediscovery or the arrival of relics, and we find a city judge with the unusual name of Secundinus (1125–69), the name of one of Troia's 'new' saints.[232] The citizens also placed their hopes in their saints' protective powers. When in 1133 King Roger II threatened to destroy the rebellious city, its bishop, clergy and citizens processed out of Troia carrying the relics of their saints before the monarch. Unfortunately for the citizens, Roger was unimpressed and ordered the destruction of the city.[233]

After 1000 a distinctive feature of most South Italian city-based cults and patron saints was their alleged antiquity. The saints concerned were overwhelmingly associated with the early Christian Church or had lived in the earlier Middle Ages. St Matthew and St Bartholomew were Apostles, St Nicholas a fourth-century bishop, the legends of Troia's 'new' saints dated to the first centuries of the Christian era, and most of the revived saints' cults which Falco celebrated at Benevento had origins earlier than the seventh century. Naples had produced an extremely rich hagiographical output in the Early Middle Ages and developed its own local sanctorale which included several Neapolitan bishops, but in the eleventh and twelfth centuries there is scant evidence of devotions for new city-based cults. Instead, we find the production of a new *vita* of St Aspren, Naples' first bishop, commissioned by Archbishop Peter of Naples (1094–1100), and production at a similar period of some records of *miracula* performed by St Severus, believed to be the twelfth bishop of Naples (d. 409), whose relics were translated to Naples in the ninth century.[234] The religious devotions of southern Italy's urban communities were not, however, inherently conservative, for a number of these ancient saints were, in effect, new arrivals within their cities – St Nicholas at Bari, St Cataldus at Taranto and the saints of Troia – or had their cults significantly redefined, as at Benevento. Nevertheless, it is striking that cases of contemporary saints whose cults were associated with urban communities remain rare. As we have seen, those new saints who did emerge on mainland southern Italy between 1000 and 1200 were either eremitical/monastic or

---

[231] Chron. Cas., Bk III.45, p. 423; *Inventio, Translationes, et Miracula SS. Mauri, Pantaleonis, et Sergii*, AS July, vi (Paris, 1868), 363, 367.
[232] D'Angelo, 'Inventio', 848–50; Poncelet, 'Translation', 422–3; Oldfield, *City and Community*, 70.
[233] Falco, 153.
[234] Galdi, *Santi*, 286–99.

episcopal. In the former case, by their vocation, men like St John of Matera, St William of Montevergine and a host of Calabrian Greek saints (see Chapter 3) were rarely city-based. In the latter case, episcopal saints like Berard of Marsia and Albert of Montecorvino occupied sees in small settlements which might barely be deemed urban. By contrast, in places like England and central and northern Italy prominent contemporary bishops were venerated as saints in larger cities, promoted no doubt through the aid of politically and financially powerful episcopal sees. It is worth reminding ourselves too that the contemporary lay saint did not feature in southern Italy, and this broadly conformed to Europewide patterns, with the obvious exception of central and northern Italy where the more extensive urban transitions created a raft of pious laymen who had recently lived within those communities. This brief trend peaked in the period from around 1200 to 1250 and included such celebrated figures as Homobonus of Cremona (d. 1197) and Raimondo Palmario of Piacenza (d. 1200).[235] The one possible South Italian exception is St Nicholas the Pilgrim who was venerated as a saint at Trani following his death there in 1094. However, there are some notable differences between Nicholas and the lay urban saints of northern Italy. Nicholas was born in Greece, and spent the majority of his short life as a wandering hermit, chanting the *Kyrie eleison*, driven by a divine calling. He only spent around two weeks in Trani before his death, and aside from his popularity amongst the city's children, who undoubtedly were attracted by Nicholas's giving out of apples and imitating the Holy Fool model of sanctity, the wider urban community were sceptical. Only after satisfying Trani's archbishop did it seem that Nicholas was acknowledged by the Tranesi, who flocked to his tomb when he died shortly afterwards. Perhaps the chance to rival Bari with its own St Nicholas proved too alluring, and soon miracles were recorded healing inhabitants of Trani. Only later did St Nicholas's miracles extend beyond the city and benefit 'outsiders'. The application to Urban II for papal approval, the production of hagiographical works in c.1098 and post-1142, and the refurbishing of a magnificent new cathedral to house the relics rooted St Nicholas within the urban community, while the saint's feast-day celebrations offered the Tranesi special masses and confession and annually reaffirmed the ties between citizens and saint.[236] Indeed, the famous Tranese sculptor Barisanus created the bronze doors of the cathedral in the later twelfth

---

[235] For translations of their *vitae* see D. Webb, *Saints and Cities in Medieval Italy* (Manchester, 2007), 46–61, 62–92. See also A. Thompson, *Cities of God. The Religion of the Italian Communes, 1125–1325* (Pennsylvania, 2005), 179–216.

[236] Trani, no. 70.

century, and advertised his own personal devotion by portraying himself in one panel kneeling before St Nicholas the Pilgrim.[237]

It is apparent that some potent and interconnected forces – the Norman takeover, Church reform, urban devotion – shaped sanctity and cults on the South Italian mainland. Different cults were affected by these to varying extents and some seemingly hardly at all. The famous shrine centre of St Michael on Monte Gargano remained rather anomalous in this respect, and demonstrated a marked continuity which seemed unaffected by wider changes in southern Italy. We have seen that the Normans did not cultivate any strong ties with the cult, and the political and military role conferred on it by the Lombards in the Early Middle Ages diminished. The shrine centre was not overtly affected by the wider reorganization of the South Italian Church and the reforming movement, apart from brief and unsuccessful attempts to raise Monte Sant'Angelo to episcopal status in the twelfth century.[238] Finally, the shrine was not located in an urban settlement, and the nearest – Monte Sant'Angelo – was small; as a consequence changes in urban devotions did not impact upon it. If anything, the cult appeared to normalize, with new churches dedicated to St Michael rarely based around the type of subterranean plan which had made Monte Gargano so distinctive. However, the shrine continued to be one of western Christendom's most popular pilgrim destinations, and an extensive service and travel infrastructure was created for it in the twelfth century (see Chapter 5). Monte Gargano thus highlights the varied paths taken by saints' cults, and the need to remember that the forces which shaped them were not common to all. Local and historic variations created subtle but innumerable differences. That this was so should be most apparent in the examinations of Greek-Italian and Sicilian sanctity which follow in Chapters 3 and 4.

---

[237] D. A. Walsh, 'The iconography of the bronze doors of Barisanus of Trani', *Gesta* 21 (1982), 91–106.

[238] Martin, 'Les Normands', 354–6.

3 Greek saints in Southern Italy: at Christendom's faultline

The frontier attributes of medieval southern Italy were never more apparent than in its role in Latin–Greek relations. The region was home to large, long-established and well-integrated Greek Christian communities which, as Byzantine and Islamic rule crumbled in the region and Norman control spread, increasingly found themselves in ever more intimate interaction with expanding Latin Christian authorities. In the eleventh century, Greek Christian communities were entrenched on the mainland, primarily in southern Calabria and in the Salento peninsula in the far south of Apulia. But communities had also settled in parts of northern Calabria, Lucania, central Apulia and even into Campania, especially around Salerno. In addition, on the island of Sicily, Greek Christians had survived under Muslim rule, and in sizeable numbers in the north-east of the island. Recent scholarship indicates that Christianity flourished on the island during the Muslim period to a far greater extent than had previously been considered. In the background of this South Italian Latin–Greek interaction loomed the increasing antagonism between the Latin Church and the Greek Orthodox Church, centred in Rome and Constantinople respectively, which accelerated in the eleventh century on a number of levels. The so-called 'schism' of 1054 may not have represented the definitive breakdown it was once held to be, but it remains a significant development, and one in which southern Italy played a key role.[1] Indeed, the status of Latin–Greek relations in southern Italy, both socio-cultural and ecclesiastical, offered a testing ground for wider relations between Rome and Constantinople for much of the subsequent medieval period.[2]

---

[1] S. Runciman, *The Eastern Schism. A Study of the Papacy and the Eastern Churches during the XIth and XIIth Centuries* (Oxford, 1955), remains important; the Norman victory over Pope Leo IX at the Battle of Civitate (1053) and a letter transmitted shortly after from the archbishop of Ochrid to the West via the archbishop of Trani formed the background to the infamous events of 1054. See also H. Chadwick, *East and West. The Making of a Rift in the Church. From Apostolic Times until the Council of Florence* (Oxford, 2003), 200–2.

[2] For the status of the Greek Church in southern Italy under Latin rule: Loud, *Latin Church*, ch. 9. It was in southern Italy at the councils of Melfi (1089) and Bari (1098), for example,

Southern Italy and the eastern Mediterranean: hagiographical transmissions and cultural interactions

Devotion to Greek or eastern saints in the region during this period provides valuable evidence for the fluctuating movement and exchanges between, and identities of, the Latin and Greek communities in southern Italy. Their saintly narratives and their posthumous veneration convey deep significance both for South Italian society and for East–West relations in the Middle Ages. As areas of southern Italy formed part of the Byzantine Empire until 1071, and contained sizeable Greek Christian communities until the end of the Middle Ages, the region was especially receptive to the circulation of eastern religious and cultural practices. Furthermore, southern Italy was central to the transmission of Greek knowledge and the spreading influence of eastern spirituality into the western world. This interaction also involved a role in the transfer of hagiographical texts, mostly from the East towards the West.[3] It is not surprising to discover that, certainly in the Greek regions of southern Italy, the sanctorale depended heavily on a Constantinopolitan model, enriched by its own local saints. Prior to the tenth century these hagiographical migrations had been more openly multidirectional. However, thereafter the great Byzantine hagiographical and liturgical collections, especially the synaxarion of Constantinople, were finalized, making it harder for new western additions to be incorporated in the East. The East's apparent resistance to accept western saints, and more pointedly the seeming ignorance in the Byzantine world of any of the new Siculo-Calabrian saints of the tenth to the twelfth centuries, should not primarily be connected to the growing schism or even decreasing interaction but should rather be viewed as the result of the formalized maturity of Constantinople's sanctoral calendar.[4] Indeed, other channels did exist thereafter for western forms of sanctity to be absorbed in the East, but in the Central Middle Ages the main impetus for hagiographical transmission came from a West that was increasingly familiar with eastern saints.

Alongside the existence of a large body of Greek-text *vitae* and *miracula* relating to local Greek–Italian saints, evidence for the diffusion of eastern

that Pope Urban II aimed to address 'differences' between the Latin and Greek Churches; see *Eadmer's Historia Novorum in Anglia*, trans. G. Bosanquet (London, 1964), 108–14 for an eyewitness account of the Bari council, and Chadwick, *East and West*, 222–5.

[3] E. Follieri, 'I rapporti fra Bisanzio e l'occidente nel campo dell'agiografia', *Proceedings of the XIIIth International Congress of Byzantine Studies (Oxford, 5–10 September 1966)*, ed. J. M. Hussey, D. Obolensky and S. Runciman (London, 1967), 355–62.

[4] E. Follieri, 'Il culto dei santi nell'Italia greca', *La chiesa greca in Italia dall' VIII al XVI secolo*, vol. 2 (Padua, 1973), 553–77. See also Luzzi, *Studi*.

hagiographical models within the Latin zones of southern Italy abounds. As we shall see, the author of the *Gesta Francorum*, almost certainly a Latin-rite South Italian, was familiar with the hagiographical traditions of Byzantine warrior saints. The hagiographer of the Greek *vita* of St Nicholas the Pilgrim of Trani, as Efthymiades recently demonstrated, also displayed a remarkable knowledge of ancient and contemporary Greek hagiography. Indeed, this saint was a Greek youth from Boeotia, who crossed the Adriatic and roamed across Apulia before his death in 1094 in Trani, the city that subsequently adopted him as its patron saint. The biography appears to be the construction of a series of oral transmissions channelled through St Nicholas's followers, particularly one disciple, Bartholomew, who accompanied him across the Adriatic.[5] A number of Latin translations were also made in the eleventh and twelfth centuries from Greek hagiographical works of Greek South Italian saints. It seems pertinent here to add in a work of Peter the Deacon, archivist and historian of Montecassino, as well as a prolific forger, who was at his most active in the 1130s. In one of Peter's works, the *Acta S. Placidi*, he created what Bloch termed a 'hagiographical-historical romance' in raising the Sicilian Placidus, a disciple of St Benedict, to sainthood. In doing so, Peter concocted a backstory to explain the manuscript transmission: the *Passio* of St Placidus was written in Constantinople, and then transferred to the Salernitan monastery of St Lawrence in 1115 by a 110-year-old Greek man named Simeon who wished to visit the site of Placidus' martyrdom in Sicily. Simeon was asked to translate the work into Latin and to transfer it to Montecassino, where it arrived at some point after 1137, but not before opposition from the abbot of St Lawrence's who deemed the Greek to be a fraud. While the subjects are fictional the framework within which Peter the Deacon placed them undoubtedly represents a familiar pattern of textual transmission.[6]

Indeed, southern Italy was more acquainted with eastern sanctity and spirituality than most other western regions as a result of a plethora of interrelationships. In the tenth and eleventh centuries a number of esteemed Italian–Greek hermits and monks, many subsequently considered saints, consolidated southern Italy's intimate relationship with Eastern Christianity and its saintly figures. Some moved seamlessly between East

---

[5] *Vita S. Nicolai Peregrini*, 231–7; S. Efthymiades, 'D'Orient en occident mais étranger aux deux mondes. Messages et renseignements tires de la vie de Saint Nicolas le Pèlerin (*BHL* 6223)', *Puer Apuliae*, ed. E. Cuozzo et al., 2 vols (Paris, 2008), i. 207–23. See also Oldfield, 'St Nicholas the Pilgrim', 168–81.

[6] H. Bloch, 'Peter the Deacon's vision of Byzantium and a rediscovered treatise in his "Acta S. Placidi"', Settimane di studio del centro italiano di studi sull'alto medioevo 34, vol. 2: *Bisanzio, Roma e l'Italia nell'alto medioevo* (Spoleto, 1988), 797–847.

and West, with their South Italian homeland functioning as a fulcrum for their activities. Key nodes within this network were Rome, Constantinople, Jerusalem, Athos, Sinai and southern Italy itself, particularly at the great Benedictine monastery of Montecassino. This movement established a climate of exchange and respect, most visibly between eastern and western monastic traditions.[7] As the eleventh century progressed this movement became more secure as Christian powers – the Normans, Venice, Genoa and Pisa – established a strong naval presence in the central Mediterranean, and restricted Muslim control of key waterways. We have already seen in Chapter 1 how in the late tenth century the Calabrian Greek St Nilus of Rossano was welcomed at Montecassino, on whose lands he established a monastery at Valleluce. He also wrote a Greek hymn honouring St Benedict, accepted a request to sing the Divine Office in Greek at Montecassino, and presided over a conference attended by the Latin monks in which divergences in Latin and Greek monastic practice were examined. He later founded, in 1004, the famous Greek monastery of S. Maria di Grotttaferrata near Rome.[8] In the following century, another Calabrian saint, Bartholomew of Simeri, founder of the monastery of S. Maria del Patir at Rossano, visited Rome in 1105 and received papal immunities for his foundation. Shortly after, he was cordially welcomed by Emperor Alexius Comnenus at Constantinople, where he received liturgical material and icons to take back to Italy, and on the same occasion a member of the imperial court gave Bartholomew power over a monastery on Mount Athos, which was in need of reform. Bartholomew thus represented a particularly direct channel through which eastern and western influences could merge at the highest levels.[9]

In the reverse direction, in the late tenth century, before becoming abbot of Montecassino, John III travelled to Jerusalem, Sinai and Athos where he stayed at the Amalfitan Benedictine monastery of S. Maria. This was a monastery, founded in the last decades of the tenth century, which in the eleventh and twelfth centuries obtained influence in the highest political circles of Constantinople, and played an important role in trans-mitting to western monasticism hagiographical traditions of both eastern and western saints. In the same period, two other monasteries were also

---

[7] A. Pertusi, 'Rapporti tra il monachesimo italo-greco ed il monachesimo bizantino nell'alto medio Evo', *La chiesa greca in Italia dall'VIII al XVI secolo*, vol. 2 (Padua, 1973), 473–520; P. McNulty and B. Hamilton, ' "*Orientale Lumen et Magistra Latinitatis*": Greek influences on western monasticism (900–1100)', *Le Millénaire du Mont Athos 963–1963, études et mélanges*, vol. 1 (Chevatogne, 1963), 181–216; Bloch, *Monte Cassino*, i. 4–14.

[8] *Vita S. Nili*, 326.

[9] G. Zaccagni, 'Il *bios* di San Bartolomeo da Simeri (*BHG* 235)', *Rivista di studi bizantini e neoellenici* 33 (1996), 205–74, especially at 256–8, 262–5.

attested at Athos which carried the South Italian epithets of 'the Calabrians' and 'the Sicilians'.[10] Relationships were also established through eastern pilgrims who visited Rome and who usually passed through southern Italy. One such figure was the Greek St Nicholas the Pilgrim, who crossed the Adriatic from Boeotia and roamed across Apulia with the intention of heading to Rome before his death in 1094 in Trani.[11]

As the twelfth century progressed the frequency and intimacy of this cross-fertilization between East and West steadily decreased, and this was reflected in southern Italy also. St Bartholomew of Simeri appears to have been the last in the line of the wandering Italo-Greek hermits to have been recorded moving between the two zones. Increasing political and military antagonism placed pressure on interaction. The Norman eviction of the Byzantines from southern Italy and Robert Guiscard's invasion of the empire in the 1080s crystallized growing tensions. The crusading movement, and Bohemond of Taranto's activities at Antioch, provided additional aggravation, while the creation of the Kingdom of Sicily in 1130 was viewed in Constantinople as a gross act of usurpation. Thereafter, brief periods of détente between the Kingdom of Sicily and the empire were punctured by episodes of open aggression: the Norman strike on Corfu (1147), the Byzantine invasion of the South Italian mainland (1155–6) and the Norman attack on Thessalonika (1185). However, in southern Italy commercial, cultural, spiritual and intellectual connections were still maintained with Byzantium.[12] Hostility mainly operated at the highest diplomatic and strategic levels, revolving around military and Mediterranean dominance, rather than being rooted in dangerous misunderstandings constructed on the back of negative stereotypes in order to portray images of religious and cultural otherness. Some of the chroniclers of the Norman conquest of southern Italy in the eleventh century – Geoffrey Malaterra, Amatus of Montecassino – repeatedly depicted the Byzantines as weak and effeminate, a standard Latin slur. However, they clearly confined this imagery to a political and military context, and seldom openly attacked the integrity of the Greek Christian rite.[13] Likewise, Byzantine literary attacks on the Sicilians, presenting them as tyrants, monkeys and sea monsters,

[10] A. Pertusi, 'Monasteri e monaci italiani all'Athos nell'alto medioevo', *Le Millénaire du Mont Athos. 963–1963, études et mélanges*, vol. 1 (Chevatogne, 1963), 217–51; see also Desiderius, Bk II.2, p. 1128.

[11] Oldfield, 'St Nicholas the Pilgrim', 168–81.

[12] On the intellectual milieu, see the activities in Sicily of Nilos Doxopatres and Henry Aristippus: Houben, *Roger II*, 98–100, 102.

[13] Indeed, one South Italian chronicler, William of Apulia, adopted a decidedly benign attitude to the Byzantines; see E. Albu, *The Normans in their Histories. Propaganda, Myth and Subversion* (Woodbridge, 2001), 106–44.

implicitly referred to the usurpation of Byzantine territories and Norman naval power, and was rarely intended to extend to a deeper level.[14] Byzantine denunciations of barbaric atrocities committed during the Norman sack of Thessalonika in 1185 represent standard revulsion for occupying forces as opposed to specific animus towards South Italians per se.[15] The pattern of increasing tension between other Latin Christian regions and Byzantium, based on greater physical detachment, tended to revolve explicitly around more exaggerated misrepresentations of each party's religious and cultural otherness. Unlike in southern Italy, they also had less chance of being corrected, which was possible when Greek-rite and Latin-rite Christians were actually able to meet on an individual and informal basis.

Southern Italy, by c.1100, had a long-established tradition of interconnections with the East stretching back to the Early Middle Ages, and these were only gradually eroded in the twelfth century. Equally important, the pattern of development of these external relationships was largely matched internally. The replacement of Byzantine political rule with that of the Normans was followed by the subordination of southern Italy's Greek churches to a Latin hierarchy, and the opening-up of the region to more Latin immigration. However, this was not an overt policy of Latinization aimed against the Greek community. Inevitably, the period of conquest created tensions between Latins and Greeks, but once this process was completed hostilities between the two parties diminished. The Norman newcomers were quick to adopt the practices of the indigenous aristocracy. This led to the patronage of existing Greek religious houses, close connections with their spiritual leaders, and a late eleventh-century revival of Greek monasticism in Calabria and Sicily. Even the Norman Bohemond of Taranto, openly hostile to the Byzantine Empire, supported Greek monasteries in southern Italy such as St Peter's of Taranto, confirming its rights in 1087.[16] Added to this, the Latin-rite takeover took place while Byzantine culture and identity retained its core

---

[14] Eustathios of Thessaloniki spoke of the 'Sicilian Skylla' and 'Charybdis', the classical sea monsters, and denounced the 'Sicilian tyrants': *The Capture of Thessaloniki by Eustathios of Thessaloniki*, trans. J. R. Melville Jones (Canberra, 1988), ch. 49 p. 59, ch. 140 p. 153; John Kinnamos repeatedly referred to Sicilian tyranny: *Deeds of John and Manuel Comnenus by John Cinnamus*, trans. C. M. Brand (New York, 1976), Bk II.4, p. 38; II.12, p. 58; III.5, p. 80; IV.3, p. 110. See also M. Gallina, 'Il mezzogiorno normanno-svevo visto da Bisanzio', *Il mezzogiorno normanno-svevo visto dall'Europa e dal mondo mediterraneo*, Atti delle XIII giornate normanno-sveve, Bari, 21–24 ottobre 1997, Centro di studi normanno-svevi, ed. G. Musca (Bari, 1999), 197–223.

[15] See generally Eustathios' *The Capture of Thessaloniki*.

[16] R. Morris, 'The Byzantine aristocracy and the monasteries', *The Byzantine Aristocracy, IX to XIII Centuries*, ed. M. Angold, British Archaeological Reports, International Series 221 (1984), 112–37, at 123–4.

integrity, allowing the Greek communities of southern Italy to feel less threatened and more open to exchange than would be the case after 1204 when that culture fragmented at its very heart. As a result, even after Latin-rite officials increasingly began to replace their Greek-rite counterparts at the Palermitan court from the 1150s onwards, Greek communities were not severely marginalized and their vibrancy and socio-religious freedoms continued until the early thirteenth century.[17]

South Italian veneration of Greek saints

Having established the wider nature of South Italian relations with Byzantium and the East, it is now possible to explore Greek sanctity in southern Italy and what it might reveal about Latin–Greek relations and identities in the region. The core collection of Greek and eastern saints venerated within southern Italy since the Early Middle Ages was composed of traditional figures connected to the biblical and early Christian era: Apostles, martyrs and confessors. Indeed, the strategic setting of southern Italy meant that, according to their *vitae* and *translationes*, a number of early eastern Christian saints sought refuge in the region, or had their relics deposited there for security in the Early Middle Ages. Furthermore, while the popularity of these saints may have spread across medieval Europe, their veneration in southern Italy always carried additional meaning given the presence of Greek Christian communities and the region's Byzantine heritage. The military saints, Mercurius, Demetrius and George, were especially venerated in Byzantium and were also popular in medieval southern Italy.[18] Mercurius' relics were actually claimed at Benevento, and he became one of the city's principal saints in the Lombard era when the Beneventan princes displayed a fascination for Byzantine military saints. The cult still thrived in twelfth-century Benevento, when a metrical *Passion* of St Mercurius was composed by the city's archbishop, Landulf II (d.1119).[19] Images of Demetrius were prominent in the royal iconographical decoration found in the Cappella Palatina in Palermo and the nearby cathedral of Monreale. In both cases, in Lombard Benevento and Norman Palermo, the Latin rulers may have hoped to convey the message that the veneration and presence of Greek warrior saints reflected the latter's approval of their territorial claims over

---

[17] Loud, *Latin Church*, ch. 9.

[18] For general discussion see C. Walter, *The Warrior Saints in Byzantine Art and Tradition* (Aldershot, 2003).

[19] A. Vuolo, 'Agiografia beneventana', 209–14, 230; the relics of the Byzantine Mercurius may actually have been confused with those of a local saint.

former Byzantine territories. However, Demetrius was not venerated solely at the political 'centre'; throughout southern Italy numerous churches, such as the one in the Salento peninsula mentioned in the *vita* of St Nicholas the Pilgrim, were dedicated to him.[20] When Sicilian soldiers captured Thessalonika, Demetrius' main cult centre, in 1185, they openly displayed their devotion to the saint in ways that suggested a crudely instinctive awareness of his powers. It was a form of devotion that distressed the locals, and which was recorded by Nicetas Choniates and Eustathios of Thessalonika. Believing the potency of the saint's unguent, the Sicilians used it for fish sauce, olive oil substitute and leather preservative, and also carried off one of Demetrius' feet as well as his golden crown.[21]

Veneration of St George in southern Italy was perhaps more widespread still. The arriving Normans absorbed a pre-existing cult of St George and developed it further. Church dedications to the saint are attested across Sicily and the mainland, and iconographical depictions located in a plethora of religious buildings including some of the most magnificent: Monreale, Trani cathedral, and the monasteries of Montevergine and Santa Sofia, Benevento.[22] St George's increased popularity in the Central Middle Ages was a result of the crusading movement and the western European nobility's evolving concept of knighthood. However, the depth of devotion to George in Norman Italy outstretched that found in Norman England, where he would only later become the national saint.[23] The cult of George, the military saint, flourished in southern Italy, building on its pre-established tradition of eastern cults, the arrival of the Normans, knights par excellence, and the region's links to the crusading movement. Literary sources confirm the connections between eastern warrior saints, crusading and southern Italy. The famous account of the capture of Antioch in 1098 provided by the *Gesta Francorum*, written shortly after the event, presented the crusading army as being aided by 'a countless host of men on white horses, whose banners were all white', a host which was led by Saints George, Mercurius and Demetrius. The anonymous author of the *Gesta* was in the retinue of

---

[20] *Vita S. Nicolai Peregrini*, 237.

[21] *O City of Byzantium. Annals of Niketas Choniates*, trans. H. J. Magoulias (Detroit, 1984), 169; Eustathios, *The Capture of Thessaloniki*, ch. 103 p. 117; evidence for the cult of Demetrius in northern France in the twelfth century may reflect interaction between the Normans of southern Italy and Normandy: see E. Lapina, 'Demetrius of Thessaloniki: patron saint of crusaders', *Viator* 40 (2009), 93–112, at 108.

[22] White, *Latin Monasticism*, 41, 318; E. D'Angelo, 'San Giorgio e i normanni', *San Giorgio e il Mediterraneo*, ed. G. de' Giovanni-Centelles (Vatican City, 2004), 198–203.

[23] J. Good, *The Cult of St George in Medieval England* (Woodbridge, 2009), shows that in Britain the cult only attained significant dimensions in the late thirteenth century.

Bohemond of Taranto, and was almost certainly from southern Italy.[24] The use of warrior saints by the author in this way hints at knowledge of early hagiographical traditions, particularly those relating to St Demetrius. As Lapina noted, the appropriation of these saints in the narrative might not only evidence South Italian devotion for them, but also demonstrate Norman efforts to assert their own political hegemony by using symbols that carried great political and religious capital among the Byzantines.[25] In Geoffrey Malaterra's account of the Norman conquest of Islamic Sicily (composed c.1100) he provides a description of the battle of Cerami (1063), which was possibly influenced by the *Gesta Francorum*. Here St George appeared before the vastly outnumbered Norman force, 'magnificently armed and mounted on a white horse, carrying a white banner with a brilliant cross fixed to the top of his lance', and guided them to victory over their Muslim foes.[26] The Normans triumphed in Sicily with the help of a Greek saint in stark contrast to the failure of the Byzantine expedition to reconquer the island in the late 1030s. Later, the author of the *Chanson d'Aspremont*, written towards the end of the twelfth century and set in Calabria, presented the Frankish warriors in combat against Muslims and receiving the aid of Saints Mercurius and George, 'the knight on that white destrier'.[27] After the commencing of the Crusades, Brindisi, a key port for crusading traffic, even claimed to house in its cathedral the arm of St George. D'Angelo has tracked the process within southern Italy through which St George was transformed from a military saint to a holy crusading knight, and its reflection of the self-identity of the Norman elite.[28]

Other eastern saints, the doctors of the Greek Church (John Chrysostom, Gregory of Nazianzus, Basil, and Athanasius of Alexandria) and St Katherine of Alexandria were venerated in medieval southern Italy, arguably earlier and with deeper resonance than elsewhere in western Europe.[29] The cult of St Katherine is indicative both of southern Italy's importance as a channel for eastern spirituality, and of its receptivity to it through its connections to Byzantium.[30] The cult's roots were based at

---

[24] *Gesta Francorum*, ed. and trans. R. Hill (Oxford, 1972), 69.

[25] Lapina, 'Demetrius', 93–112.

[26] Malaterra, Bk II.33, pp. 142–5.

[27] *The Song of Aspremont (La Chanson d'Aspremont)*, trans. M. A. Newth (New York, 1989), part 9. 424, lines 8524–7; part 9. 425, lines 8542–7 (both on p. 204); part 10. 458, lines 9391–6 (p. 224).

[28] D'Angelo, 'San Giorgio', 203–12.

[29] The eastern doctors were popular subjects in iconographic programmes, especially in Sicily in the Cappella Palatina, the Martorana and at Cefalù.

[30] C. Walsh, *The Cult of St Katherine of Alexandria in Early Medieval Europe* (Aldershot, 2007), 53–61.

Mount Sinai, but it emerged in southern Italy at Naples and the monastery of Montecassino before 1000, and a version of Katherine's *Passio* was known in the latter region by the mid-eleventh century. It may be of significance that by the eleventh century Montecassino had established a range of cordial interrelationships with Constantinople.[31] Also, Katherine was the subject of three hymns composed by Archbishop Alfanus I of Salerno (1058–85), who was himself a monk at Montecassino and who may also have encountered the cult when he visited Constantinople in 1062.[32] From southern Italy, Katherine's cult seems to have spread across Europe, significantly to other Norman centres such as Rouen, and then to England where it attained particular prominence by the Later Middle Ages.[33] There were also localized hot spots for devotion to eastern saints, often linked to a region's ties with Byzantium, or the presence of Greek Christian communities. For example, the cult of St Pantaleon of Nicomedia was popular on the Amalfitan coast. Amalfi had prosperous commercial connections in the eastern Mediterranean, and its neighbouring coastal settlement, Ravello, seems to have acquired a reliquary containing the saint's blood by c.1112.[34]

Translations and theft: Greek and eastern saints in southern Italy and perceptions of Byzantium

Relics of a number of the biblical and early Christian saints of the East were actually claimed to be present in southern Italy, further intensifying devotion to them. Some, like Mercurius at Benevento, were always associated with a Greek heritage. Others like St Matthew the Apostle, who was translated to Salerno in 954, and rehoused in a new cathedral in 1080 by Duke Robert Guiscard, seem to have had their eastern connections diluted, possibly because they were not imported into the region directly from the East. Some of the early Christian saints arrived as a result of overt relic theft from the eastern Mediterranean, and three high-profile cases are particularly illustrative of South Italian–Byzantine relations.[35] In 1087, a contingent of sailors from Bari removed the relics of the fourth-century

[31] Bloch, *Monte Cassino*, i. 4–14.
[32] *Carmi*, nos. 42–4 pp. 196–200; Amatus, Bk IV.34–37, pp. 372–5.
[33] C. Walsh, 'The role of the Normans in the development of the cult of St Katherine', *St Katherine of Alexandria. Texts and Contexts in Western Medieval Europe*, ed. J. Jenkins and K. J. Lewis (Turnhout, 2003), 19–35.
[34] Galdi, 'La diffusione del culto di San Pantaleone', 67–8.
[35] For a broader discussion see H. A. Klein, 'Eastern objects and western desires: relics and reliquaries between Byzantium and the west', *Dumbarton Oaks Papers* 58 (2004), 283–314.

eastern bishop, St Nicholas, from Myra to their city; in 1126 two Latin Christians stole the body of the virgin martyr St Agatha of Catania from a church in Constantinople and returned it to Sicily (from where it was claimed to have been originally removed by the Byzantines in c.1040); and in 1204 the Apostle St Andrew was transferred from the Byzantine capital in the aftermath of the sacking of the city during the Fourth Crusade. The transfer of St Andrew could be deemed a particularly inflammatory event. Not only was Andrew the alleged founder of the Byzantine Church, its chief patron through whom Byzantine theologians from the early thirteenth century stressed the doctrine of the equality of the pentarchy against Rome's claims to superiority, but the theft took place following the sack of Constantinople in 1204. It was the Fourth Crusade's apostolic legate Cardinal Peter Capuanus, an Amalfitan, who eventually transferred the body to Amalfi in 1208.[36] All three reveal the close interplay of South Italian–Byzantine affairs. The Baresi located the shrine at Myra because of their knowledge of the eastern Mediterranean acquired through commercial activities, particularly at Antioch, and their city's status (until 1071) as capital of Byzantine Italy. Similarly, St Andrew's body was located at Constantinople by 'honest priests and leading men of the people of Amalfi, who knew the place well, and were sufficiently learned about the body of the blessed Andrew the Apostle, and able to certify its authenticity'.[37] Indeed, the *Montecassino Chronicle* tells of an Amalfitan in the eleventh century who stole relics from the imperial palace in Constantinople and donated them to Montecassino when he became a monk of the abbey, while Amalfitan trading colonies had been present in Constantinople for centuries, and still maintained activities there despite being eclipsed by Venice, Genoa and Pisa in the twelfth century.[38] St Agatha of Catania had allegedly been translated from Sicily to Constantinople in c.1040 by the Greek commander George Maniakes during a failed Byzantine attempt to reconquer the island from Muslim control. As we shall see in Chapter 4, the various accounts of Maniakes' translation activities of c.1040 are problematic.[39] Clearly, corrupted knowledge of relic removals to Byzantium circulated in southern Italy, and later provided a basis for the

---

[36] F. Dvornik, *The Idea of Apostolicity in Byzantium and the Legend of the Apostle Andrew* (Cambridge, Mass., 1958), 289–99.

[37] P. Pirri, 'Translatio Corporis S. Andree Apostoli de Constantinopoli in Amalfiam', in his *Il duomo di Amalfi ed il chiostro di paradiso* (Rome, 1941), 144.

[38] Chron. Cas., Bk III.55, p. 436.

[39] Although St Agatha was primarily identified as a Sicilian saint, her bones resided at Constantinople for at least eighty-six years (c.1040–1126) and quite probably more (see Chapter 4), and the virgin martyr was widely venerated in the East: see Stelladoro, *Agata*, 93–101.

return translation of Agatha from Constantinople in 1126. Significantly, the translators of 1126 were two Latin Christians, a Frank who held a military office in the Constantinopolitan imperial household, and a Calabrian. Other sources confirm the presence of Latin, and particularly South Italian, mercenaries in the Byzantine capital.[40]

Interesting continuities and shifts in attitude towards the Byzantines also appear when comparing the accounts of the translations of St Nicholas, St Agatha and St Andrew. The earliest of these translations was, apparently, that of St Agatha from Catania (along with St Lucy of Syracuse) to Constantinople in c.1040. The main accounts were written between forty and ninety years later, after Byzantine rule had ended in southern Italy. Collectively they present the actions of the Byzantine commander Maniakes in a favourable light, protecting holy relics from the Muslims by transferring them to Constantinople, a bulwark of Christian faith. Bishop Maurice of Catania, who wrote an account of the 1126 translation shortly after the event, also commented on Maniakes' actions and noted that Agatha's relics were worshipped with appropriate devotion in Constantinople. However, he also suggested that the relics were originally transferred by Maniakes in order to return a failing empire 'to its former glory'; a hint that Byzantium of the eleventh century was viewed in twelfth-century southern Italy as a venerable entity, but one now in atrophy.

Similar perspectives seem to inform the two main accounts of the translation of St Nicholas to Bari in 1087, written probably within two years of the event, by the cleric Nicephorus and John the Archdeacon, both of Bari. In this case, the inhabitants of Myra in Asia Minor are presented as pitiful Christians, burdened by the devastating incursions of the Seljuk Turks. The standard medieval rationalization of relic thefts highlighted the failings of the current custodians of the holy body, and the divine will to transfer it to a more appropriate location. Although Archdeacon John suggests that the Turkish invasions were God's punishment for the sins of the inhabitants, neither he nor Nicephorus dwell further on the spiritual unworthiness of these eastern Christians. Instead they sidestep the issue, effectively sympathizing with the Christian population of Myra by focusing on the Turkish threat as the justification for the neglect of the holy body, and also on the prestigious and deserving qualities of the city of Bari (and not necessarily on any superior spiritual virtues of its people), as reason for the relic theft. Both accounts include prominent and emotional set pieces in which the people of Myra lament

---

[40] J. Shepard, 'The uses of the Franks in eleventh-century Byzantium', *Anglo-Norman Studies* 15 (1993), 275–305.

their loss. Nicephorus depicts the Barese sailors leaving the shore of Myra, few of whom 'managed to hold back tears, having compassion for their [the people of Myra's] disaster', and John encapsulated the sadness and noble anger of the Christians of Myra, portraying them 'grumbling like threatening lionesses with their cubs'.[41] As occurred in the earlier case of Agatha's removal from Catania, the theft is presented as an act for the greater welfare of Christianity, undertaken primarily as a result of Muslim pressure and not because of the inhabitants' failing Christian devotion. In both instances, the Byzantine Empire and its people are presented as good Christians burdened by increasingly insurmountable external forces. There are here obvious comparisons with the way eastern Christians were presented in the early twelfth-century western accounts of Pope Urban II's Clermont appeal of 1095 which led to the First Crusade.[42] The authors of St Nicholas's translation chose not to take the opportunity to present a wicked people, undeserving of such a famous shrine, and perhaps the explanation lies in their Barese background. The city had been until recently the Byzantine capital of the Italian theme, and also had its own sizeable Greek Christian community.

When we move into the twelfth century, Bishop Maurice of Catania's account of St Agatha's transfer back to Sicily in 1126 again presents the Byzantines in a neutral, even sympathetic, light. No reference is made to the failings of the Greeks as justification for the removal of the relics; instead the episode is seen purely as a result of God's will. In a cursory passage the inhabitants of Constantinople are portrayed informing the emperor of the theft and the 'sad portent' this represented for them all. A search party was dispatched through the city, but again Maurice describes its failure in simple terms: 'There is, said the most wise Solomon, no wisdom or counsel against the lord' (Prov. 21. 30).[43] Maurice had already suggested, in his record of Maniakes' original removal of Agatha, that her relics would buttress a crumbling empire. Here, in 1126, the bishop of Catania presents his confirmation of the decay of a once worthy empire, whose role as protector of Christendom was being transferred elsewhere. Perhaps here was a message to the large Greek Christian communities of twelfth-century eastern Sicily to look closer to home for their spiritual welfare rather than to distant Constantinople.

---

[41] Corsi, La traslazione, 26–30, 58–9.

[42] H. E. J. Cowdrey, 'Pope Urban II's preaching of the First Crusade', History 55 (1970), 177–88.

[43] Epistola Mauritii Cataniensis Episcopi de Translatione S. Agathae Virginis, AS February, i (Paris, 1863), 643–4.

The sympathetic perspectives of the Byzantines disappear in our final episode of relic theft involving St Andrew in 1204. The first brief account of the removal dates from October 1208, a few months after the saint's body had arrived at Amalfi, and is contained in a document establishing the local organization of the shrine in the city cathedral. Here the translation is presented as the manifestation of Cardinal Peter Capuanus' desire to bestow a prestigious gift on his hometown, and Constantinople is only referenced as the place where Andrew's relics had resided for a long duration.[44] However, a detailed record of the translation was provided by the Amalfitan archdeacon Matthew in the mid-thirteenth century; this may have been based on contemporary testimonies. In this account the Byzantines are afforded no sympathy for the violence they suffered in 1204 from the Latin Crusaders. For the author of St Andrew's *translatio*, the Fourth Crusade, which resulted in perhaps the greatest series of relic thefts in history, occurred because God, who was

outraged by the wicked actions of a godless people [the Greeks] which had abandoned the universal oneness and had joined [itself] in a bond of peace to the enemies of the Christian faith, decided in his profound policy, in order that there might be a single flock of Christ's sheep and a single shepherd, to overthrow the empire of the Greeks.[45]

Later, Peter Capuanus was recorded as adding that God 'wanted the Greek Church to return from error, deviation, and fault to the instructions of Catholic unity'.[46] Unlike the relic thefts of St Nicholas and St Agatha, the Greek people in the translation of St Andrew are portrayed as wicked, fully deserving of being deprived of their numerous holy relics: 'the evil of the people [...] had made them unworthy of the merits of the saints' who, 'having abandoned their pious thrones, elected to move to various places, so that they should receive fitting veneration from cultivators of the faith'.[47] The perspective encapsulates rising Latin animus towards the Byzantines in the late twelfth century, and is fully in line with changing western European attitudes. Western European sources for the Fourth Crusade denounced the Byzantines in similar fashion: the *Hystoria Constantinopolitana* of Gunther of Pairis described the Greeks as 'in rebellion against the Roman Church', while Robert of Clari recorded the attempts of the clergy in the crusader army to justify the attack by claiming that the Greeks

---

[44] The document is edited in Pirri, *Il duomo*, Appendix II, 135–9.
[45] Pirri, 'Translatio', 142.
[46] Pirri, 'Translatio', 143.
[47] Pirri, 'Translatio', 144.

were traitors and murderers and disloyal, since they had assassinated their legitimate lord, and they were worse than the Jews. And the bishops added that they would absolve, in the name of God and the Pope, all those who should attack [the Greeks. . . .] for they were the enemies of God.[48]

However, the exceptional nature of 1204 should not be overlooked. Intense moral uncertainty shrouded the sack of the city, the theft of scores of relics and the enthronement of a new Latin emperor. The response of those who were associated with these events, such as Cardinal Peter Capuanus or Gunther of Pairis' 'hero' Abbot Martin, was to construct compelling extenuating circumstances. The safest way to do this was to employ the *furta sacra* rationalization to its extreme. It required unusually severe denigration of the previous custodians of this most Christian of cities and its holy treasures, especially when the saint concerned was none other than the Apostle Andrew. Almost certainly in southern Italy, and quite probably throughout the rest of Latin Christendom, the accounts of relic translations during the Fourth Crusade may present Latin–Greek relations in a manner which may have built on, but was far from representative of, contemporary broader beliefs, and which then drew its power from reinforcement over subsequent decades.

Indeed, the messages within most translation and relic-theft accounts would eventually reach a wider audience through oral testimonies, and also through incorporation into sermons and the liturgy of the local church. Therefore, on the one hand, they needed to represent to some extent the expectations of the audience, but on the other they provided an opportunity to shape beliefs. The South Italian material reveals a mixture of attitudes towards the Byzantines. It is clear that a current of respect for the Byzantine Empire and Greek Christianity is prevalent in all three cases, even in the translation account of St Andrew.[49] Contained within them is an acknowledgement that the empire was fragile but prestigious. These beliefs in Byzantium's distinction and vulnerability coalesced to encourage and to justify the transfer of the patronage of Byzantium's powerful saints, which might also imply a transfer of imperial prerogatives. Its capital, Constantinople, is presented as an honoured Christian city, the premier storehouse of holy treasures with pedigree and authenticity. Both William of Malmesbury and Robert of Clari, who was commenting on the Fourth Crusade, digressed at length on the marvels of the city's relics and

---

[48] *The Hystoria Constantinopolitana of Gunther of Pairis*, ed. and trans. A. Andrea (Philadelphia, 1997), ch. 8 p. 84; Robert de Clari, *La Conquête de Constantinople*, ed. and trans. J. Dufournet (Paris, 2004), ch. 73 p. 157.
[49] Peter the Deacon's twelfth-century 'hagiographical–historical romance' work on St Placidus provides another South Italian example of deep fascination and respect for the Byzantine world: Bloch, 'Peter the Deacon's vision', 797–847.

other riches.[50] So did the author of the account of St Andrew's translation, who called Constantinople a 'city of innumerable saints, consecrated by relics and fortified by these bodies, whose protection earns [it] the primacy of glory among all other territories [*regna*]', before conveniently recounting how and why these saints withdrew their favour during the Fourth Crusade.[51] It is also evident that the St Nicholas and St Agatha translation accounts demonstrate South Italian empathy for the pressures faced by the Byzantines. Perhaps this was influenced by the region's Byzantine heritage, its manifold interactions with the eastern Mediterranean and its South Italian Greek communities. It is also important to remember that St Nicholas, from his new home at Bari, rapidly emerged as one of western Christendom's leading cult figures. Elsewhere in Latin Christendom similar sympathetic views continued to be held, but these tended to become more negative following the First Crusade.[52] In the translation accounts one can also identify a subconscious envy which was born from the same factors that also engendered respect, and which of course attained its most ardent South Italian manifestation in the text of St Andrew's translation. The enduring esteem of eastern saints in southern Italy was not tarnished by the growing broader unpopularity of the Byzantines, the nature and frequency of which was still inconsistent in southern Italy prior to c.1200. This pattern can also be traced in the hagiographical works concerning St Nicholas the Pilgrim of Trani, a city which acknowledged Byzantine emperors as its overlords in the late eleventh and early twelfth centuries, therefore after the initial Norman conquests.[53] Indeed, of the first two *vitae* of the saint, both composed before 1100, one was intimately concerned with Nicholas's Greek background, while the other, by the cleric Adelferius, used the Greek honorary title of *synkellus* for Trani's archbishop and called Alexius Comnenus 'the most excellent emperor', a 'cultivator of the orthodox faith'.[54] However, by the time the deacon Amandus created an additional version of the *vita* with an account of Nicholas's translation to the city's refurbished cathedral, shortly after the event around 1142, and under the reign of the new monarch Roger II of Sicily, Nicholas's Byzantine connections were overlooked.[55]

---

[50] William of Malmesbury, *Gesta Regum Anglorum*, ed. and trans. R. A. B. Mynors, R. M. Thomson and M. Winterbottom, 2 vols (Oxford, 1998–9), vol. 1, IV.355–6, pp. 625–9; Robert de Clari, *La Conquête*, chs 80–92 pp. 169–85.

[51] Pirri, 'Translatio', 144.

[52] M. Angold, 'Knowledge of Byzantine history in the west: the Norman historians (eleventh and twelfth centuries)', *Anglo-Norman Studies* 25 (2002), 19–33.

[53] Trani, nos. 23–4, 26–7, 29–30.

[54] *Vita S. Nicolai Peregrini*, 238–9.

[55] *Vita S. Nicolai Peregrini*, 246; Oldfield, 'St Nicholas the Pilgrim', 178–9.

Although this Greek saint remained as popular as ever, the new political landscape and ongoing acculturation between Latins and Greeks in the region meant that his Greek identity was of reduced significance.

Contemporary South Italian Greek saints: solitude versus society

Relationships between Latins and Greeks within southern Italy were at times unsettled, but broadly they remained cordial, and these divergences can be traced within a number of hagiographical texts for contemporary South Italian saints. It is remarkable to note that, of the contemporary South Italian saints across the period 1000 to 1200, a sizeable proportion were of the Greek rite, operating in monastic circles in Sicily and Calabria.[56] This had also been the case in the ninth and tenth centuries when a number of Greek-rite Siculo-Calabrian hermits and monks – including Elias of Enna, Leo-Lucas of Corleone, Vitalis of Castronuovo – were subsequently revered as saints.[57] This may be because the autonomy allowed to the abbots, and especially the founders, of Greek Orthodox monastic houses, and the flexibility of their monasticism, which positioned them in contact with the wider society, placed their activities more firmly in the spotlight.[58] Interestingly, during the same two centuries within the Byzantine Empire, especially during the twelfth century, contemporary holy men were becoming increasingly criticized and thus in short supply.[59] A feature common to all these South Italian Greek saints was, as Rosemary Morris identified, the synchronicity of their activities with those practised in Byzantine monastic circles across the empire; further evidence, if it were needed, of South Italian contacts with the eastern Mediterranean. Certainly, the South Italian Greek saints of the period 1000 to 1200 increasingly tended to function within the context of a more orderly and renewed cenobitic environment, more so in the twelfth than the eleventh century.[60] Nevertheless, these saints still displayed many of the characteristics of Byzantine monasticism's hybrid flexibility, which had already been in evidence in southern Italy in the *vitae* of the Siculo-Calabrian saints of the ninth and tenth centuries. Some saints combined

---

[56] See Chapter 4 for direct discussion of twelfth-century Greek–rite saints in Sicily, such as Lawrence of Frazzano and Nicholas the Hermit, and the problematic traditions associated with them.

[57] S. Borsari, *Il monachesimo bizantino nella Sicilia e nell'Italia meridionale prenormanne* (Naples, 1963), 38–72.

[58] A. Jotischky, *The Perfection of Solitude. Hermits and Monks in the Crusader States* (Pennsylvania, 1995), 97.

[59] P. Magdalino, 'The Byzantine holy man in the twelfth century', *The Byzantine Saint*, ed. S. Hackel (London, 1981), 51–66.

[60] Pertusi, 'Rapporti', 478–9.

cycles of communal and solitary living, stayed in lavrotic establishments, located their most intense spiritual experiences in mountain wildernesses, and espoused contemplation, asceticism and voluntary poverty.[61] The peculiar landscape of parts of southern Italy assisted. Calabria, southern Apulia and Sicily, all zones of notable Greek influence, were especially dotted with subterranean grottos which offered cells and chapels for the solitary holy man.[62] Parallel influences could also be traced in contemporary western Europe, where traditional distinctions between cenobitism and eremitism were being eroded, while such fluidity was especially prominent in the mixed Latin– Orthodox climate found in the crusader states.[63]

Unsurprisingly, a number of contemporary Latin Christian saints who were based in southern Italy – Dominic of Sora, Alferius of Cava, William of Vercelli, John of Matera, Bruno of Cologne, John of Tufara – fluctuated between the communal and solitary life.[64] However, the fluid interchange between cycles of cenobitic and eremitic existence was most in evidence among the South Italian saints of the Greek rite. Before establishing his own monastic congregation, St Bartholomew of Simeri (d. c.1130) lived in a near inaccessible mountain cave in Calabria, which offered little shelter and where he undertook a strict regime of fasting and abnegation, 'suffering with pleasure for God', as his biographer put it, far in excess of the norms of the solitary life.[65] St Filaretus of Seminara, having left Muslim Sicily for Calabria in the mid-eleventh century, joined the monastery of S. Elia Junior, but was allowed by his hegumen to cultivate in solitude an isolated plot of land, where the saint lived in extreme deprivation in a small hut, dressed in clothes woven with straw, and slept on a mat of branches with a stone for a pillow. St Anthony, the 'desert father' of Christian monasticism, served as an exemplar for St Filaretus, while John the Baptist, the putative first Christian hermit, was used as a model by St Bartholomew of Simeri and another saint who had migrated from Sicily to Calabria in the eleventh century, St John Terista.[66]

Many of these South Italian Greek saints sought greater spiritual enlightenment in dangerous landscapes, identifying a 'geography of

[61] R. Morris, *Monks and Laymen*, 31–63.

[62] See A. Messina, *Sicilia Rupestre* (Rome, 2008).

[63] For a thorough study see Jotischky, *Perfection of Solitude*, and H. Leyser, *Hermits and the New Monasticism. A Study of Religious Communities in Western Europe 1000–1150* (London, 1984).

[64] For more see Chapter 2.

[65] Zaccagni, 'bios', 236–41.

[66] *Vita S. Philareti*, 607–8, 610–11; Borsari, 'Vita', 142; Zaccagni, 'bios', 244, 254.

holiness' so disdained by some of the leading western monastic reformers of the day.[67] As part of such an existence, movement and physical and emotional separation from kin, community and *patria* were essential aspects of many of these saints' lives. In some cases, this may have been determined by external factors. Muslim raids and the instability of Muslim Sicily significantly shaped the formative experiences of St John Terista and St Filaretus of Seminara, detaching them both from their homelands. For St John, brought up in the Arab–Islamic culture of Palermo, the passage from Sicily to Calabria represented a rebirth (with a new baptismal name) and full communion with the Christian faith. However, the Muslim power was receding both in the wider Mediterranean and in Sicily from the mid-eleventh century. It therefore did not feature in the lives of eleventh- and twelfth-century South Italian saints in the way it had for the pre-1000 Siculo-Calabrian saints. Indeed, even in the case of St Filaretus (d. c.1070), his migration from Muslim Sicily was not the pivotal juncture; rather his full transition to a 'new' life of asceticism occurred only after he had settled in Calabria, and confirmed that the 'wandering spirit' was a fundamentally inherent state that ultimately transcended worldly events.[68] To be a *xenos* (foreigner) without roots brought spiritual objectivity and huge esteem to many of the Greek-Italian saints. The theme of 'flight' from the world was a standard motif in most of these saints' lives. It had an interconnected and tripartite functioning: flight into a monastery, flight into a wilderness and flight from fame, with the overriding objective to reveal that the individual could not escape his own sanctity.[69] A number also adopted spiritual fathers to guide their paths to divine revelation; most prominently the Calabrian St Bartholomew of Grottaferrata (d. c.1055) was the intimate disciple of St Nilus of Rossano (d.1004), continuing a pattern of cross-generational spiritual guidance established among the Siculo-Calabrian saints well before 1000.[70] Earlier Greek-Italian saints also served as more tangible, localized models for a holy life, and their cults were kept alive in the monasteries they founded by subsequent generations of Greek-rite churchmen: St Filaretus, for example, repeatedly read the *vita* of St Elias of Enna.[71]

Even figures such as St Nicholas the Pilgrim and St Lucas di Isola di Capo Rizzuto (d. c.1114), who both experienced far more sustained

[67] Jotischky, *Perfection of Solitude*, chs 1 and 7.
[68] Borsari, 'Vita', 136–45; *Vita S. Philareti*, 606–11.
[69] C. Galatariotou, *The Making of a Saint. The Life, Times and Sanctification of Neophytos the Recluse* (Cambridge, 1991), 75–80.
[70] F. Halkin, 'St Barthélemy de Grottaferrata. Notes critiques', *AB* 61 (1943), 202–10.
[71] *Vita S. Philareti*, 608.

interaction with the secular world, conformed in part to the standard models outlined above. Nicholas earned his lasting reputation for spiritual purity and innocence in the context of movement among rural and urban communities, dying in Trani where his impact was such that he was adopted as the city's patron saint. Lucas became bishop of the small Calabrian see of Isola di Capo Rizzuto, and was an untiring preacher, travelling through Calabria and Sicily, performing miracles and forming close ties with the lay world.[72] Nicholas was most thoroughly absorbed in Byzantine spiritual traditions, largely because he was actually Greek-born. He alternated between a (miserable and repressed) monastic experience at the eminent monastery of Hosios Loukas, a solitary mountainous existence amongst wild animals, and an innate 'wanderlust'. Just as for other South Italian Greek saints, St John the Baptist and St Anthony acted as guiding exemplars for Nicholas; the former appeared in a vision, while the latter seemingly encountered the saint in Greece in the guise of an old monk.[73] Nicholas's life was also characterized by separation and movement; he rejected parental authority and his miraculous crossing of the Adriatic represented a watershed between an old and new life. In Apulia, Nicholas truly was a *xenos*, an outsider. His lifestyle was broadly antisocial, but through his virtues and a divine calling he was compelled to endure what Efthymiades believes was a process of socialization, which culminated in his interaction with the lay community at Trani. In different circumstances, the other saints considered earlier experienced comparable transitions. Where Nicholas differed was in his partial adoption of the Byzantine 'paradigm of holy foolery', signalled by his apparent faux insanity and incessant chanting of the *Kyrie eleison*, and also by his complete avoidance of temporal and theological discords.[74] Lucas, despite his secular ecclesiastical office, initially embraced the monastic life, identified St Elias the Troglodyte as a model and chose his deathbed in the monastery of Vioterito.[75] He was also able to integrate successfully a passion for movement and missionary activity into his episcopal duties.

Many South Italian Greek saints practised withdrawal, but for some this was ultimately only for distinct phases, and often ended with either reception into a community of monks, or with the foundation of their own monastic house. This was partly due to the wider revival of Greek monasticism following the Norman conquest. Some eventually became

---

[72] *Vita di S. Luca.*
[73] *Vita S. Nicolai Peregrini*, 232; Efthymiades, 'D'Orient en occident', 212.
[74] S. A. Ivanov, *Holy Fools in Byzantium and Beyond* (Oxford, 2006), 196–200; Efthymiades, 'D'Orient en occident', 207, 210.
[75] *Vita di S. Luca*, 85, 109.

hegoumenos (the abbots) of monasteries; Bartholomew of Simeri and Cyprian of Reggio assumed this role in prominent monastic houses and thus became particularly visible members of the establishment from which they had often sought to escape. In both cases, their virtuous isolated existence was responsible for their later reintegration into the world. The fame of the sacrifices they made drew followers and a community around the solitary saints, no matter how reluctant they might have been. The pattern was a common one for many medieval recluses across the Christian world, from the extreme *anachoresis* (solitude) of St Nephytus the Recluse of Cyprus (d. after 1214), which was compromised when he was persuaded to govern the monastery which had formed around him, to the Durham hermit Godric of Finchale's solitude, which paradoxically created a more intense and consistent relationship with the world he had rejected.[76] Eventually, Cyprian of Reggio was 'headhunted' by the monks of S. Nicola di Calamizzi, who invited him to be their hegumen. Internal conflicts took place, but a sense of obligation ultimately outweighed personal yearning for solitude. Cyprian felt too unworthy to accept the offer, until pressure from the archbishop of Reggio encouraged his assent.[77] In Bartholomew's case, a night-time vision served as his catalyst to repudiate the solitary and contemplative life; the Virgin Mary appeared to the saint saying:

> Bartholomew, cease, for now, your impulse for the contemplative life and your desire to linger in inaccessible deserts. Indeed, it is necessary that you remain here and that you build for me in this place a school of souls, in which many, through your works, will be made worthy of salvation.[78]

Occasionally, however, this process worked in reverse, as can be seen in the case of the obscure figure of St Silvester of Troina in Sicily. Born c.1100 and deceased at some point between the 1160s and 1180s, Silvester's career initially moved along conventional lines. He entered the local Greek monastery of S. Michele at a young age, earned a reputation for charity and healing, and eventually became abbot. But Silvester soon withdrew from the post and the monastery, and built a cell nearby in which he lived.[79] Silvester's example reminds us that the saint's characteristic conflict between two different worlds could progress in a diverse order.

---

[76] Galatariotou, *The Making of a Saint*; S. J. Ridyard, 'Functions of a twelfth-century recluse revisited: the case of Godric of Finchale', *Belief and Culture in the Middle Ages. Studies Presented to Henry Mayr-Harting*, ed. R. Gameson and H. Leyser (Oxford, 2001), 187–96.

[77] G. Schirò, 'Vita inedita di S. Cipriano di Calamizzi dal cod. Sinaitico no. 552', *Bollettino della badia greca di Grottaferrata* 4 (1950), 90–1.

[78] Zaccagni, 'bios', 250.

[79] *Vita Sancti Silvestri Trainensis*, in *Vitae Sanctorum Siculorum*, vol. 2, ed. O. Gaetani (Palermo, 1657), 176–7.

Because in Greek zones monasteries traditionally undertook a great deal of the ministry of the laity, most of southern Italy's Greek saints, who usually at stages in their lives were members and leaders of Greek Orthodox monasteries, became focal points for the spiritual welfare of the surrounding lay community; and this had also been the case, in a different format, during their cycles of solitude. In other words, the Greek saints were in continual communication with the local populace, for whom they also acted as exemplars and symbols of support. Rosemary Morris summed up the Greek monk's 'flight from the world' as a mirage, and noted the quotidian nature of exchange between monastic and secular communities.[80] It is unfortunate that the hagiographers of this group of South Italian saints provide little indication of the cultural or religious identity of the recipients of their subjects' virtuous actions and miracle working. But it is clear, nonetheless, that they claimed that many people across the entire social spectrum experienced such works, and this in itself is significant. St John Terista's most famous miracle took place amongst a group of harvesters, from whom he took his epithet 'the harvester' (*Terista*). John, in *imitatio Christi*, provided bread and wine for a large group of harvesters at Robiano, the supplies of which failed to diminish. Subsequently, while the saint was praying in gratitude, a storm erupted and the harvesters fled to find shelter. When John rose from prayer he saw that all the fields had been miraculously harvested and all the bales bound, much to the amazement of the harvesters when they returned once the storm had abated. As the account then makes clear, the landholder bestowed the fields upon the saint's monastery; this gift indicates one reason why the miracle was recorded. However, the public nature of the miracle and its alleged impact were undoubtedly as important.[81] St John Terista also distributed all his family inheritance to 'the poor according to Basilian precepts', whereas St Filaretus of Seminara fed passing travellers from the produce of his allotment.[82] St Cyprian, a trained doctor, attracted great attention through his ability to heal both physical and spiritual afflictions.[83]

The hagiographers of St Nicholas the Pilgrim and St Lucas of Isola di Capo Rizzuto also attempted to demonstrate the broad social interaction engendered through their subjects' miracle workings. The underclass and the urban community of Trani were among the recipients of St Nicholas's beneficence; in one particular case a slave was released from demonic

---

[80] Morris, *Monks and Laymen*, 80–87, quote at 82.
[81] Borsari, 'Vita', 148–50.
[82] Borsari, 'Vita', 145; *Vita S. Philareti*, 612.
[83] Schirò, 'Vita', 91.

possession.[84] The saint's epithet was also earned not only by his foreign, wandering status but by his aiding of pilgrims. A number of Nicholas's post-mortem miracles involved rescuing pilgrim ships returning from the Holy Land; Trani and the Apulian ports were key transit ports for crusading and pilgrimage traffic by the twelfth century. Trani's cathedral, which has a magnificent setting overlooking the city harbour and in which Nicholas's remains were housed, served as a symbolic lighthouse which attracted passing pilgrims.[85] St Lucas too engaged with an impressive range of groups both during his lifetime missionary activities and in his post-mortem miracle working. Following Christ's example, he miraculously aided some floundering fishermen in locating a catch; he judged a dispute between two peasants; he freed the people of Squillace from the torments of a wolf by ordering three days of fasting and penance; and by similar means he assisted in ending a drought.[86] His post-mortem miracles, in contrast, were more focused on individuals who were either initially churchmen, or who adopted the monastic habit on being healed.[87]

South Italian Greek saints and the South Italian elite

It was the connection to the lower classes and the indigent which ensured these saints attained a broad appeal. But our hagiographers were equally at pains to emphasize that the spiritual virtues of these South Italian Greek-rite saints were acknowledged and respected among all echelons of South Italian society, including those at its apex. Indeed, we have already seen how some of the Siculo-Calabrian saints of the ninth and tenth centuries regularly interacted with governmental officials, princes and emperors. Noblemen and women, whose power and patronage were so important for enhancing a cult centre, were regularly attested among the recipients of saintly miracles, or shown offering their approval. St John Terista had two miraculous encounters with noblemen, one a huntsman, the other the lord of the lands on which the aforesaid 'miracle of the harvest' occurred. In both cases, the end result was the donation by these noblemen of lands to the saint's monastery.[88] Ultimately, these episodes served as exemplars to the contemporary nobility, which could in turn lead to potentially lucrative outcomes. A noble youth and a rich nobleman from France received St Nicholas the Pilgrim's aid.[89] A posthumous miracle by

[84] *Vita S. Nicolai Peregrini*, 243.
[85] *Vita S. Nicolai Peregrini*, 244–5; Oldfield, 'St Nicholas the Pilgrim', 175–6.
[86] *Vita di S. Luca*, 93–5, 99–105.
[87] *Vita di S. Luca*, 115–25.
[88] Borsari, 'Vita', 145–50.
[89] *Vita S. Nicolai Peregrini*, 241, 245,

St Lucas of Isola di Capo Rizzuto was certified by an initially reluctant governor of the settlement of Galliano.[90] Indeed, the body of evidence relating to the South Italian Greek saints shows that they also established relationships with the very highest ecclesiastical and lay authorities. In many instances these were Latin Christians, which provides a useful entry-point to explore Latin–Greek relations within this material, as in the majority of cases our hagiographers provide little indication of the cultural or religious identity of those who interacted with the saint.

As we have seen, St Nilus of Rossano was welcomed by the monks of Montecassino, while his disciple, Bartholomew of Grottaferrata, was a key influence at Rome during the embryonic phase of the papal Church reform in the 1040s and 1050s. St Nicholas the Pilgrim was interviewed by Bisantius, archbishop of Trani, and subsequently given official approval, and in the late twelfth century St Cyprian was encouraged to become hegumen of S. Nicola di Calamizzi by Archbishop Thomas of Reggio, who was almost certainly a Latin churchman.[91] Latin translations were made of the Greek *bioi* (Lives) of South Italian Greek saints. The life of St Elias the Troglodyte (d. c.960) was translated into Latin, probably in the 1080s by a Benedictine monk of the Latin monastery of Sant'Eufemia in Calabria, and most likely at the instigation of its Norman abbot Robert de Grandmesnil; while in 1194 the bishop of Tricarico commissioned the translation into Latin of the *bios* of the tenth-century Graeco-Sicilian saint, Vitalis of Castronuovo.[92] St Bartholomew of Simeri received the support of the emir Christodoulos, an Arabic-speaking Greek Christian and leading official at the Sicilian court in the early twelfth century, who was described by Bartholomew's hagiographer as his 'first collaborator and at the same time the most passionate'.[93] Christodoulos was comfortable in backing a Greek churchman before a Latin hierarchy, and it was through this high-ranking official that Roger II became acquainted with Bartholomew, and supported his monastic foundation at the Patiron, which in turn proved an important stage in the revival of Greek monasticism in southern Italy. Pope Paschal II also received Bartholomew at Rome and confirmed the independence of his monastery. The Patiron soon became the head of a network of subordinate Greek houses in North Calabria, while later Roger II seems to have entrusted the foundation of the monastery of SS Salvatore, in Messina, to Bartholomew. This monastery would become the archimandrite house for Sicily and most of

---

90   *Vita di S. Luca*, 125.
91   *Vita S. Nicolai Peregrini*, 239; Oldfield, 'St Nicholas the Pilgrim', 173; Schirò, 'Vita', 90–1.
92   Strazzeri, 'Una traduzione', 1–108; *Vita S. Vitalis*, 34.
93   Zaccagni, '*bios*', 251.

Calabria, although Bartholomew died in 1130 before this was achieved. Through its relationship with Bartholomew, the Norman elite was able to offer the fullest expression of its patronage for Greek monasticism, and also attempt to structure its hybridized format.

Bartholomew's actions, on the other hand, reveal his belief that the best path for Greek Orthodoxy in southern Italy was, as Ferrante noted, through a combination of collaboration with Latin rulers and 'spiritual and cultural union with Byzantium'.[94] While Bartholomew, or his biographer, considered Roger II as pious and rightful a ruler as the emperor of Byzantium, his spiritual loyalties evidently remained in Constantinople, as shown during his visit there. At a similar period, St Lucas of Isola di Capo Rizzuto attempted to travel to Constantinople, but was forced to turn back at Taranto for some unexplained reason. Lucas's implicit motives seem to have been the desire for a pilgrimage to a spiritual homeland.[95] In successfully visiting Constantinople, Bartholomew was, surprisingly, unusual; it would seem that none of the Siculo-Calabrian saints of the ninth and tenth centuries ever visited the great city, despite plentiful evidence of other forms of exchange. Evidence elsewhere from the peripheries of the Byzantine world demonstrates that provincial mentalities increasingly grappled with a love–hate relationship towards Constantinople, and perhaps some of our South Italian Greek saints experienced similar internal dissonance.[96] Certainly, the hagiographies of the saints Filaretus of Seminara, John Terista and Cyprian of Reggio reflect little interest, or indeed attachment, to a wider world outside Calabria and Sicily. Even St Nicholas the Pilgrim, Greek-born, preferred the option of a Roman pilgrimage over one to Constantinople, whereas St Silvester of Troina's only recorded journey outside of Sicily was to visit the pope (perhaps Adrian IV) at Rome.[97] Indeed, a number of the pre-1000 Siculo-Calabrian saints undertook a pilgrimage to Rome.

The Norman elite were patrons of Greek monasticism, and of early Greek saints (most evidently in their artistic programmes in Palermo), and this largely Graecophile portrayal is echoed in their treatment of contemporary Greek saints, as presented in the hagiographic material. As we have seen, Roger II is largely a positive force in St Bartholomew of Simeri's *bios*, with the exception of one episode which we shall discuss later in this chapter. Other South Italian Greek saints claimed connections to Norman leaders. St John Terista's hagiographer suggested that a 'Roger, son of the

[94] N. Ferrante, *Santi italogreci in Calabria* (Reggio, Calabria, 1981), 225–6.
[95] *Vita di S. Luca*, 90–1.
[96] Galatariotou, *The Making of a Saint*, 210–19.
[97] *Vita Sancti Silvestri*, 176–7.

king of the region' visited the saint to cure an ulcer on his face. Unfortunately, St John had recently died, so Roger rubbed the saint's clothing on his face, which was subsequently healed, and in gratitude gave numerous possessions to the saint's former monastery.[98] This Roger was either the son of King Roger II, who predeceased his father in 1148, or else the use of the word 'king' represents a later misunderstanding by the biographer and refers instead to Roger II, son of Count Roger I, who was born in c.1095, but who in the text had clearly entered early manhood when visiting St John. The dating of the saint's life, and indeed of his biography, remains uncertain. However, as St John lived until fourteen years of age in Muslim-ruled Palermo, he was certainly born before the city fell to the Normans in 1072, an event which is not mentioned in John's *vita*. Because in the text the saint had recently died before Roger's arrival, this could only be a plausible historical event in either of the two Rogers' lives if the saint had been born after c.1045 and lived to a venerable age. Similarly, the life of St Silvester of Troina involved a visit to Palermo where he healed the sick son of King William I, who would become the future King William II. There is, however, no other evidence to corroborate this laconic reference in this brief *vita*.[99] Whether historical events or not, the hagiographers acknowledged the power and legitimacy of the Norman leadership by representing the rulers in collaboration with these saints whose own efficacy was enhanced as a result. At the same time, patronage of these holy men and their monasteries would have been a prudent strategy for the Latin elite, achieving what Morris has termed 'spiritual insurance': protection, cures and a network of relationships which operated like an intelligence service.[100]

Further evidence on Latin–Greek relations in southern Italy

It is quite plausible that, in a number of the many cases in which recipients of the favour of South Italian Greek saints were not identified, the beneficiaries were Latin Christians. Unfortunately, however, this remains largely an argument *ex silentio* with only occasional exceptions, most notably the aforesaid Norman rulers whose exact religious orientation still remains uncertain. It would, for instance, have been useful to learn the religious identity of the nobleman from Robiano who donated lands to St John Terista's monastery. The fact that the hagiographers were not more specific may be explained on various levels; problems of memory

---

[98] Borsari, 'Vita', 150–1.
[99] *Vita Sancti Silvestri*, 176–7.
[100] Morris, 'The Byzantine aristocracy', 115–7.

connected to time lags in composing the records, the desire to not exclude any particular group from venerating the saint, and the likelihood that the socio-cultural fluidity of the South meant that Latins and Greeks may not always have been easily distinguishable, while at the same time they were comfortable in offering devotion to saints who were ostensibly attached to a different rite. We have already highlighted evidence of Latin Christian attraction to Eastern Christianity, and its influence on Latin Christian saints based in southern Italy. St John of Matera, for instance, appears to have had a dalliance with Greek Christianity during his formative years in a monastery in Taranto, and St Bruno of Cologne was attracted to eastern forms of spirituality while in Calabria, and received the support of the Greek bishop of Squillace in establishing the Carthusian order there.[101] Furthermore, some of the *bioi* of South Italian Greek saints – such as the tenth-century saints Vitalis of Castronuovo and Elias the Troglodyte, and the eleventh-century Nicholas the Pilgrim – were translated into or recorded in Latin (in the late eleventh and twelfth centuries), suggesting their use as exemplars for the Latin community. As Strazzeri has uncovered, the late eleventh-century Latin translation of the Greek life of the Calabrian St Elias the Troglodyte is an indicative example of Latin interest in the world of Greek Christianity, of how Latins attempted to shape an understanding of the Greek rite, and of the motives for this. The translator was almost certainly a Benedictine monk of the Latin monastery of Sant'Eufemia in Calabria, who had been commissioned by the monastery's Norman abbot Robert de Grandmesnil. The translation was undertaken in collaboration with a bilingual monk with the popular Greek name Elias, and faithfully replicated the narrative content of the original Greek version. However, revisions were made, the Latin version shows little interest in the philosophical underpinnings of Greek spirituality which were recorded in the original *bios*, and some of the language and concepts were 'Normanized', drawing on western notions of service and vassalage. The suspicion emerges that the translation was commissioned for pragmatic purposes: Sant'Eufemia had a patrimonial claim on the monastery, which was dedicated to St Elias, and the translation formed a wider strategy adopted by the Latin monks to integrate themselves into the rich traditions of the Greek community which surrounded them.[102]

In the case of St Nicholas the Pilgrim, we can assume that most of the 'local' support for the cult came from the large Latin Christian community in Trani. The hagiographic material, and the tacit papal confirmation of Nicholas's sanctity in c.1098, shows that many within Trani were quick to

[101] Loud, *Latin Church*, 484.
[102] Strazzeri, 'Una traduzione', 1–41.

worship him even though his Greek tongue was incomprehensible to most, while many Latin Christian pilgrims passing to or from Jerusalem experienced his miracle working.[103] It is undoubtedly significant that Nicholas's sanctity was approved by none other than Pope Urban II, quite possibly at the Church council held at Bari in 1098. Urban spent much of his pontificate forging a rapprochement between the Greek and Latin Churches: the councils at Melfi (1089) and Bari (1098), and the famous Clermont appeal (1095), all fitted into this objective. In this context, Urban appears to have identified St Nicholas the Pilgrim as a perfect manifestation of the collaboration and mutual interchange possible between East and West. Indeed, evidence on the cult of St Agatha of Catania shows the broad popular appeal of a cult across different Christian communities.[104] The cult was re-established in the twelfth century under the aegis of a Latin Benedictine cathedral chapter and via support from the Norman elite, but its Greek Christian, and in particular Constantinopolitan, heritage was of evident appeal to native Greek Christians in Sicily. Recipients of the saint's beneficence included Greek monks from Calabria and Troina; among the latter was St Silvester of Troina himself, and inhabitants from Messina, which had a large Greek Christian population in the twelfth century. It should also be noted that some of the South Italian Greek saints – ranging from St Elias of Enna in the ninth century to Bartholomew of Simeri in the twelfth century – opted to visit the shrines at Rome, and developed positive relationships with the papacy. Although there may have been a decline in East–West Church relations at the highest level in the twelfth century, saintly cults in a 'frontier' region such as southern Italy demonstrate the mutual goodwill and reciprocal relations which functioned between Latins and Greeks on a personal level in a fluid social setting.

Indeed, in the context of South Italian sanctity, there is a notable paucity of episodes of antagonism between Latins and Greeks, which mirrors broader historical patterns. Evidence of opposition from Roger II and other churchmen towards these saints can be explained by hagiographical models and other socio-political factors. In the *bios* of St Bartholomew of Simeri, Roger II did at one stage apparently believe the accusations of two monks that the saint was a fraud and a heretic. Indeed, Roger even condemned Bartholomew to burn at the stake, until two columns of fire emanating from the saint's feet as he celebrated a final mass convinced the

---

[103] St Nicholas was shown teaching the children of Trani to chant songs in Greek: *Vita S. Nicolai Peregrini*, 239.

[104] And also its potential attraction to Muslims; see more in Chapter 4.

count of Sicily of the man's righteousness.[105] Certainly this episode should be treated with caution in all its aspects: the wrongly accused saint was a hagiographical topos, so much so that in the later *vita* of William of Vercelli, a Latin Christian and founder of Montevergine, Roger II was also portrayed as harshly sceptical of that saint's virtues before being won over.[106] Roger's behaviour towards Bartholomew on this occasion is at odds with all other evidence on both his attitude towards him, and towards Greek Christianity in general. Indeed, the monks who accused Bartholomew of heresy appear to have done so only as an after-thought to their prime accusation of fraud and nepotism. No further information was supplied on the nature of the alleged heretical behaviour, and the reader is left with the impression that the monks were driven by financial motivations rather than doctrinal or cultural differences. If this was a genuine historical episode, Roger's initial condemnation of Bartholomew may have been comprehensible given the saint's imitation of 'Christ before Pilate', refusing to contest the claims and even admitting them, just as an 'authentic disciple'. Understandably, given his previous support for Bartholomew, Roger was said to be 'surprised and angry'.[107] Before St Nicholas the Pilgrim became popular in Trani, various South Italians derided the young saint, another common hagiographic tool to symbolize the struggles of saintly figures.[108] However, we do not know if these South Italians were Greek or Latin, and in any case their actions were not represented as animus towards a Greek Christian. Instead, the underlying message implies a misunderstanding of Nicholas's behaviour in combination with his youth, along with disapproval of a lay preacher transgressing episcopal authority.

More conspicuous religious antagonism, however, is evident in the *bios* of St Lucas of Isola di Capo Rizzuto, possibly as a result of this man's more confrontational and missionary approach. Lucas became involved in a dispute with some Latins in his diocese over the use of leavened and unleavened bread. He criticized the Latins' use of unleavened bread 'in the style of the Jews' and their practice of baptizing on any day, and accused them of falling 'into innumerable heresies'. The angered Latins lured the bishop into a hut they had built and then set fire to it. However, Lucas was able to celebrate mass inside with a boy who was assisting him, and both miraculously escaped unharmed.[109] The encounter suggests

---

[105] Zaccagni, '*bios*', 267–70.
[106] *Vita et Obitus Sancti Guilielmi*, 26–9, 38–43.
[107] Zaccagni, '*bios*', 268–9.
[108] *Vita S. Nicolai Peregrini*, 236, 238.
[109] *Vita di S. Luca*, 106–7.

that early twelfth-century Calabria contained pockets of tension, which could erupt if more inflexible attitudes were vented with sufficient force. In this case, labelling the Latins as Jews may have been the most damaging accusation. Indeed, Lucas demonstrated extreme commitment towards his brand of Christianity. He even visited Sicily in the decades after the Normans restored the island to Christendom. It was a land, according to his biographer, 'which was unfaithful through the atheistic enemies who lived there', and Lucas stopped in cities to ordain priests.[110] Schirò convincingly asserts that the biographer would have used clearer terminology if these enemies were Muslims, and that the ambiguous language implies that the Latins were the unbelieving foes.[111] Finally, among the entire corpus of miracles worked by the South Italian Greek saints, one of the only episodes to identify an individual as a Latin also comes from the *bios* of St Lucas. In this case, a Latin called Revetos, originally from the city of Briatico (in southern Calabria, approximately fifteen kilometres north of Mileto), had been repeatedly warned by Lucas over his behaviour towards priests. Revetos ignored these admonitions, until he was struck with illness and visited Lucas's shrine, after which he was healed. The Latin's behaviour then relapsed and he was left without speech and in a permanent state of paralysis in order to encourage his repentance.[112] Since this is the only example of a punitive miracle and the only one dealing with a miscreant, perhaps the reader is encouraged to make a negative connection with Latin Christian behaviour; if so, the text does not make this explicit. The glimpses in the text of local Greek–Latin relations are all left without further explanation amidst an air of ambiguity. Indeed, in the prologue of the *bios*, the author equates saints to shepherds because they 'chase away the wolves of heresy'.[113] The statement could be connected with Lucas's centrepiece miracle in which he saved the people of Squillace from a fearsome wolf (possibly symbolizing the devil), or it could be taken as highlighting the saint's exertions against what he considered Christian deviancy. The message remains open to interpretation.

It must be noted that the sources pertaining to Latin Christian saints in southern Italy are equally laconic on direct Latin–Greek relations. As already mentioned, St John of Matera was heavily influenced by eastern monasticism, and he spent time at the Greek monastery of Isola di S. Pietro in Taranto, where however he was treated badly.[114] This

---

[110] *Vita di S. Luca*, 90–1.
[111] *Vita di S. Luca*, 47.
[112] *Vita di S. Luca*, 121–3.
[113] *Vita di S. Luca*, 83–5.
[114] *Vita S. Iohannis*, 36–7; Bruno of Cologne and Joachim of Fiore also absorbed eastern influences; for more see Chapter 2.

suggests that Latin Christians could be accepted into Greek monasteries, but how frequent this was remains unclear, while John's difficult experience at Taranto seems to have been the product of personality clashes within the monastery. The mysterious figure of St Lucas of Bova might indicate Latin hostility to the local Greek community. Some scholars accept Lucas as a historical figure who lived between c.1050 and c.1136, and identify him as the bishop of Bova, a small settlement in the south of Calabria about twenty-five kilometres from Reggio.[115] The separate discoveries in the second half of the twentieth century of a *syntomon* (liturgical hymn) and of three pastoral letters, a discourse and a spiritual testament of a 'Lucas bishop of Bova and administrator of the great metropolitan see of Reggio', seemed to authenticate the existence of this saint.[116] From these, Lucas appears as a tireless preacher throughout Calabria and Sicily, who effectively governed the vacant archbishopric of Reggio. More importantly for the present discussion, his pastoral letters indicate that he was a Latin Christian, who spoke some Greek and who developed a mixed relationship with the local Greek communities. On the one hand, Lucas praised Calabria and the city of Reggio in general terms, but, on the other hand, he attacked some of the customs of the Greeks and Muslims which appeared to him as semi-pagan rituals. However this may be, doubts remain over the historical authenticity of St Lucas, particularly over the dubious manuscript tradition and the way it has been transmitted and translated. Even if we accept Lucas's existence, these still represent mere scraps of evidence.

Overall, the few references in the collective hagiographic material suggest that Latin–Greek interaction in southern Italy was normal enough not to arouse additional comment when it occurred. It encompassed positive, apathetic and hostile relationships, which made it no different from interaction between and within any number of other groups and communities in southern Italy. In the Central Middle Ages, the entire body of evidence connected to the veneration of Greek saints in southern Italy, contemporary natives or early Christian imports, indicates that the region's Greek communities continued to maintain their identity and security. It also suggests a real propensity for cross-cultural contact between Greeks and Latins in southern Italy, and confirms the existence of a network of cordial exchanges which had developed throughout the wider Mediterranean. In southern Italy, Latin devotion to, and appropriation of, a number of

[115] Ferrante, *Santi italogreci*, 227–34.

[116] G. Schirò, 'Quattro inni per santi calabresi dimenticati', *ASCL* 15 (1946), 17–26; P. Joannou, 'La personalità storica di Luca di Bova attraverso i suoi scritti inediti', *ASCL* 29 (1960), 179–237.

Greek saints might also have played an important role in encouraging Latins to hold positive, or at least sympathetic, views on both the indigenous Greek communities and on Byzantium itself. Interestingly, some of the above evidence suggests that, as the twelfth century progressed, Latins in southern Italy venerated Greek saints for their attractive spiritual virtues, and on occasions to communicate a political message. One could conclude that their Greek identity was gradually and subconsciously subsumed, and perhaps the same pattern existed between the region's Latin and Greek communities. Certainly, an analysis of Greek sanctity in southern Italy verifies the presence of a significant religious and cultural frontier. However, the fluid nature of this liminal zone meant that Greek sanctity in southern Italy was barely defined by the broader development of the East–West schism; instead it operated more as a force for connectivity than division.

The history of Sicilian sanctity in the Middle Ages is shaped by a conspicuous discontinuity associated with Muslim control of the island. It has already been suggested that the challenges faced by the Christian communities in Sicily during the Muslim phase often stemmed from the consequences of political, military and socio-cultural change rather than from overt religious antagonism. Any impact on Sicilian sanctity and cults should be considered in the same light. Nevertheless it is an inescapable reality that, whatever the contributing factors, for roughly two and a half centuries evidence on Sicilian saints and cults is limited, leaving, if not absolute silence, only a few mere whispers. As we have seen in Chapter 1, prior to the mid-ninth century Sicily had developed its own distinctive corpus of saints, composed most notably of proto- and virgin martyrs and holy bishops, who were linked with both Rome and Constantinople. We shall never know how the cults of these saints would have evolved in Sicily itself if there had been no Muslim invasion. It is certainly also revealing that the hagiographies of the group of Siculo-Calabrian saints of the ninth and tenth centuries were produced on the mainland, and that none of these saints remained in Sicily. It would be reasonable to imagine that contemporary saints did operate in Sicily at this time, but any forms of patronage and devotion appear to have been too fragile to emerge into view. Fortunately the reputations of some of Sicily's cults which originated before 827 had already been exported to other regions of the Christian world, while for others it would appear that devotion within Sicily was sufficiently entrenched to maintain some low-level cultic continuities. In other words, narrow internal and external channels remained available to preserve forms of sanctity which had emerged in pre-Muslim Sicily. These would, in time, be vital once the island was brought back into the Christian fold.

The challenges associated with the source material on Sicilian sanctity have already been discussed in Chapter 1, and the same issues continue into the later period too. For the earlier period these problems are offset by the greater quantity of modern historical research, and by the fact that we can at least utilize some splendid hagiographical works. After the Norman conquest, the evidence, if anything, becomes more fragmented and oblique, offering less in the way of traditional hagiographical material, but perhaps more in other ways – liturgical sources, toponymic data, church dedications, decorative cycles and so on. As a result, it is possible to track some highly significant developments in late eleventh- and twelfth-century Sicily, such as the re-emergence of an important cult centre for St Agatha at Catania, the lingering influence of Italo-Greek traditions, and how the monarchy positioned itself at the heart of a multi-ethnic and religious world.

Reviving Christianity and the Norman conquest

The narrative sources say little about sanctity during the varied phases of the Norman conquest of Sicily (1060–91), and therefore the status of saints and cults on the island when the Normans first made contact is shrouded in uncertainty. One useful channel through this obscurity is offered by accounts of the Sicilian expedition of the Byzantine commander George Maniakes, which took place from 1038 to c.1041 and which included Norman mercenaries in its ranks. Maniakes led a Byzantine effort to reconquer the island which enjoyed initial success in eastern Sicily, where Christian communities were primarily settled. However, despite controlling some key Sicilian cities (Syracuse, Messina and probably Catania), it eventually foundered owing to divisions in Maniakes' force, rebellion on the mainland of southern Italy and court intrigues at Constantinople.[1] Significantly, accounts suggest that during the military operations Maniakes also transferred some Sicilian holy relics to Constantinople. Two South Italian chroniclers are the first to record Maniakes' removal of relics: Amatus of Montecassino in his *History of the Normans* (composed c.1080) and Leo Marsicanus, in his section of the *Montecassino Chronicle* (written c.1087–1105). Both accounts mention the translation of the relics of St Lucy from Syracuse.[2] Both also offer a comparable narrative: Maniakes encountered an elderly Christian claiming to be the sole person to know the location of St Lucy's tomb, and subsequently the saint's relics were disinterred from an unidentified church. That knowledge of the sepulchre of such a renowned saint could reside only in one individual would seem unlikely and was probably a literary tool to emphasize the more likely case that saints' shrines were

---

[1] J. Shepard, 'Byzantium's last Sicilian expedition: Scylitzes' testimony', *Rivista di studi bizantini e neoellenici*, 14–16 (1977–9), 145–59; Loud, *Age of Robert Guiscard*, 78–9.

[2] Amatus, Bk II.9, p. 276; Chron. Cas., Bk II.66, p. 298.

generally in neglect; by presenting the cult in such a precarious state it could also justify the morality of Maniakes' deeds.

It is disappointing that Maniakes' removal of the relics is not mentioned in other important narratives from late eleventh-century southern Italy, and this might suggest that the cults were no longer worthy of remark. In addition, the *vita* of St Filaretus (composed after 1070, most probably in Calabria) discusses at length Maniakes' expedition and the tumults which compelled the saint to leave Sicily, and yet in this hagiographical work there is still no reference to the removal of any relics.[3] Likewise, none of the contemporary Byzantine sources records the transfer of these Sicilian relics to Constantinople. John Skylitzes' work, for instance, offers a positive narrative of Maniakes' campaign and yet fails to mention any translation activity.[4]

Fortunately, another layer is added to Maniakes' relic hunting by two further accounts dating to around ninety years after his Sicilian expedition. These both identify the relics of St Agatha of Catania among the haul dispatched to Constantinople in c. 1040.[5] The first of the two accounts is all the more significant as it is Sicilian, being the record of the translation of St Agatha's relics back to Catania from Constantinople in 1126, written soon afterwards by Maurice, bishop of Catania. We shall discuss St Agatha's return in the twelfth century later in this chapter, but for now it is important to note that Maurice included an account of the saint's earlier removal by Maniakes,

who transferred the body of God's beloved Virgin Agatha, with many other holy bodies, to Constantinople, which formerly was called Byzantium, believing the Empire of the East, which by that point was failing, would be strengthened through their prayers and virtues and returned to its former glory. Therefore the body of the most blessed Virgin and Martyr Agatha was translated from the city of Catania to Byzantium, and there was kept fittingly by certain inhabitants of the place, and most devotedly worshipped.[6]

From Normandy, the monastic chronicler Orderic Vitalis supplied another version, which he probably composed between 1127 and 1130. Orderic asserted that Maniakes removed a host of relics, including St Agatha's, 'to save them from desecration if the pagans should return'.[7]

---

[3] *Vita S. Philareti*, 605–6.

[4] John Skylitzes, *A Synopsis of Byzantine History, 811–1057*, trans. J. Wortley (Cambridge, 2010), ch. 19.16, p. 380; ch. 19.20, pp. 381–3. I am grateful to Jonathan Shepard for furnishing me with his extensive knowledge of the Byzantine material.

[5] A good overview of the medieval cult is found in Stelladoro, *Agata*.

[6] *Epistola Mauritii*, 643.

[7] *The Ecclesiastical History of Orderic Vitalis*, ed. and trans. M. Chibnall (Oxford, 1972), Vol. III, Bk. V. 86–7.

It would seem that Orderic was reasonably well informed on eleventh-century South Italian affairs through the Benedictine network linking his monastery at St-Evroult to the Calabrian monastery of Sant 'Eufemia, which had been staffed by Normanno-French monks, some of whom had transferred thence to the cathedral–monastery of Catania.[8] Consequently he acquired some information on Maniakes' relic translations, but he does not show any evidence of access to Maurice's account of the 1126 return translation.

The earliest accounts, therefore, of Maniakes' expedition record the translation of relics, but of those of St Lucy and not of St Agatha. The story of St Agatha's removal from Catania by Maniakes only emerges some ninety years after the supposed event. The silence of other important contemporary sources on the subject is disconcerting and perhaps signifi-cant. The silence of the chronicler Geoffrey Malaterra is particularly striking, for he was a monk at Catania in the 1090s and had every opportunity to be acquainted with traditions on the location of the city's patron saint. Perhaps this reflects the discomfiture of Malaterra and his monastic community at the absence of St Agatha's relics, while it must also be remembered that he was primarily composing a work focused on Norman heroism, and thus emphasizes how badly the Normans were treated by Maniakes' Byzantine commanders.[9] Evidence does suggest that St Agatha's relics were absent from the city by c.1040, for in all the extant Catanese documentation from 1040 to 1126, including some sig-nificant charters re-establishing the city's bishopric in the 1090s, there is no reference to the presence of the relics.[10] On the other hand, this does not prove conclusively that the relics were present before 1040, and the distinct possibility remains that St Agatha was removed or lost in an even earlier period. This would be in line with some earlier traditions which record St Agatha's removal from Sicily in the Early Middle Ages, and a later tradition dating to the early thirteenth century and recorded by the Venetian Andrea Dandolo (c.1307–54) which claimed the saint was removed to Constantinople some time between 976 and 1025.[11] Unfortunately, any argument *ex silentio* is problematic in light of the state of Catania's archival material. The city was struck by a shattering earthquake in 1169, while in 1197 its cathedral was burned down; much

[8] Indeed, Sant'Eufemia supplied the monastic see at Catania with its first bishop-abbot Ansger, and the chronicler Geoffrey Malaterra.

[9] Malaterra, Bk I.7–8, pp. 11–12.

[10] G. Scalia, 'La traslazione del corpo di S. Agata e il suo valore storico', *Archivio Storico per la Sicilia orientale* 23–4 (1927–9), 38–128, at 54–5.

[11] *Andreae Danduli Ducis Venetiarum: Chronica per Extensum Descripta (AD 460–1280)*, ed. E. Pastorello, RIS 12 (i) (Bologna, 1938–58), 280.

of Catania's archives was destroyed.[12] A potential solution may be found in the emphasis in the later accounts on the translation, alongside St Agatha's, of multiple relics, which remain unidentified by the authors. We may be witnessing an attempt to 'hijack' the earliest versions recording only the translation of St Lucy and to mask discontinuities in the cultic traditions of St Agatha which stretched back well before 1040. Indeed, some evidence even suggests that during the Muslim period the cult was more popular in Palermo, the city, according to one legend, where St Agatha was born. In 973, the Muslim cartographer and traveller Ibn Hawqal noted the gate of St Agatha (*Bab Shantaghathat*) as an important landmark in Palermo.[13] Nearby too was the church of Sant'Agata la Pedata, a building of uncertain date, which claimed to preserve the saint's footprint in stone and may have influenced the name of the aforesaid gate.

In any case, events after the Norman takeover suggest that St Agatha's relics were no longer located in Catania, but that her association with the city was still acknowledged. The Normans conquered Catania in 1071, but in the immediate aftermath it remained largely Muslim. The city even briefly rebelled in 1081.[14] It was not until a decade later, in 1091, that the Benedictine abbey of S. Agata was founded and attached to the re-established bishopric under its first abbot-bishop, the Breton monk Ansger. Although it is significant that the abbey was dedicated to the saint, if her relics had still been present in the city during this phase then they could have served as a powerful tool during the refounding of Catania's bishopric with some sort of translation ceremony, and could have been referenced thereafter in other contexts as a rallying point for an exposed Christian community.[15] Indeed, Geoffrey Malaterra claimed that Ansger took over the church at Catania which 'had been little supported, in so far as it had been plucked from the jaws of an unbelieving people ["incredulae gentis"]'.[16] It remains therefore uncertain when exactly St Agatha's relics were removed (and by extension also St Lucy's), but it seems that they were absent from Catania for at least most of the eleventh century and a quarter of the twelfth. Overall, the background noise from our evidence suggests that the cults of St Agatha and St Lucy clung on under Muslim rule, but

---

[12] A long debate has raged over the authenticity of some of the documents in the Catania archives; for a useful summary see Johns, *Arabic Administration*, p. 40 n. 3, and pp. 52–3.

[13] *The Book of Curiosities. A Critical Edition*, ed. E. Savage-Smith and Y. Rapoport, available at www.bodley.ox.ac.uk/bookofcuriosities (March, 2007) [accessed on 10 May, 2012], Bk. 2.12.

[14] Malaterra, Bk. IV.7, 13, pp. 88–9, 92–3; Loud, *Age of Robert Guiscard*, 162, 174–5.

[15] Not least because the new cathedral was situated near the shore while the old church of St Agatha was located on high ground further inland.

[16] Malaterra, Bk. IV.7, pp. 88–9.

only just; and it implies an even more problematic fate for lesser Sicilian saints and their cults.

In England following the events of 1066, greater evidence indicates that the Normans engaged immediately with an array of thriving native cults; following some initial scepticism Anglo-Saxon saints were gradually reintegrated into the new Anglo-Norman Church.[17] On mainland Italy, a broadly collaborative relationship between Norman newcomers and local cults took longer to develop, but had certainly emerged by the closing stages of the period of conquest. In Sicily, the Norman newcomers discovered a very different situation, conquering an island which was largely devoid of relics, and housing cults which had seemingly slipped to the peripheries of local society. Here, the Normans, few in numbers, appear to have initially deferred the articulating of any defined strategy on Sicilian cults. There were no powerful shrine centres to deal with; instead there was a collapsed ecclesiastical network to restore, and there were large Muslim communities to manage, some of which remained restless under Christian domination. At this stage, the landscape was too uncertain and volatile. Priorities lay in creating the infrastructure for military security and Christian worship, and attracting Christian colonizers; the revival and promotion of cults represented a secondary phase which could be pursued in a more settled climate. Indeed, the most detailed account of the Norman conquest of Sicily, Geoffrey Malaterra's chronicle composed in c.1100 at the end of the first phase of Norman domination, is almost entirely silent on Sicilian sanctity. Its only overt reference to a saint is found in the apparition of St George at the battle of Cerami in 1063, but he was not a Sicilian saint and it is possible to argue that Malaterra may have been drawing on similar accounts from the *Gesta Francorum* of warrior saints appearing to aid the Crusaders at Antioch in 1098.[18] We find no allusions to Saints Agatha, Lucy, Pancratius of Taormina, Gregory of Agrigento and others standing shoulder to shoulder with the Normans as they reconquered Sicily for Christianity. Furthermore, although by 1085 a Benedictine monastery was founded in honour of St Bartholomew on the island of Lipari where the saint's relics had resided until 838, no further attempts appear to have been made to establish the location as a key cult centre for this prominent universal saint.[19]

[17] On Anglo-Norman saints see the works of Ridyard, 'Condigna Veneratio', and Hayward, 'Translation narratives'.

[18] Malaterra, Bk. II.33, pp. 142–5; Bk. II.6 also refers to the aid of St Andronicus who enabled Roger I to return safely across the Straits of Messina to Reggio in 1061; but the episode did not take place on Sicilian soil and was not through the intercession of a Sicilian saint.

[19] White, *Latin Monasticism*, 77–100.

Conversely, in Normandy a series of hagiographical texts had been produced in the early eleventh century which associated current ducal authority with the early missionary activity of Normandy's apostolic saints, thus bridging the chasm opened by the period of Viking disruption.[20] In Sicily, where the chasm was even larger, no comparable efforts were overtly put in place to bolster the current Norman rulers through finding parallels in Sicily's early Christian past. The support of the Sicilian saints whose relics appear to have been removed before the Normans' appearance, and of those Siculo-Calabrian saints who had ended their peripatetic lives on the mainland, does not rematerialize during the Norman conquest. The absence of evidence may well reflect a combination of two processes: that the Normans and their commentators refused to view the conquest in religious terms, and that Sicilian sanctity had been substantially marginalized.

Reviving the old saints

From the beginning of the twelfth century increasing signs appeared that the island of Sicily was stabilizing, militarily and economically. Christian immigration was growing and an organized diocesan and monastic network was materializing. Bishoprics were founded at Palermo (1072), Troina (1079 – combined with Messina in 1096), Catania (1091), Syracuse (1092), Agrigento (1092) and Mazara (1093). Lynn Townsend White identified fifty Latin abbeys and priories built in Sicily between c.1091 and 1194. The majority were founded before 1130, a period in which the Norman rulers also encouraged the revival of numerous Greek monastic houses (around twenty-one in total).[21] A framework was erected within which saints and cults could re-emerge more vividly, initially through simple presence in toponyms or church dedications.[22] On the whole, at this early stage, it was the names of mostly non-Sicilian, universal saints that appeared: St Michael (at the monastery of Troina, 1092), St George (at the monastery of Triocala, 1097–8) and St Mary (at Palermo cathedral, 1072, and various priories: Caccamo before 1098, Tusa before 1123, Butera before 1125).[23] But houses dedicated to St Agatha were obviously founded at Catania (the cathedral abbey) in 1091, and to

[20] Herrick, *Imagining*, 112–31. See also the stimulating discussion in Remensnyder, *Remembering Kings Past*, 93–9.
[21] White, *Latin Monasticism*, 43, 53; Loud, *Latin Church*, 501–2.
[22] For instance, Amatus, Bk.V.25, p. 405, claimed Robert Guiscard built a castle called San Marco in the Val Demone owing to his devotion to the saint.
[23] White, *Latin Monasticism*, 77–103; V. von Falkenhausen, 'I monasteri greci dell'Italia meridionale e della Sicilia dopo l'avvento dei normanni: continuità e mutamenti',

St Lucy at Noto (founded c.1100) and, of course, at Syracuse (the cathedral, and by 1104 a monastery which may have been a refoundation of a sixth-century house). Roger I enabled the reconstruction of the famed Greek monastery of S. Filippo di Agira, named after the putative sixth-century saint who had established the house.[24] S. Filippo di Fragalà was also possibly dedicated to the Sicilian saint of the same name, and was refounded in 1090 with Roger's aid. Later, in 1101, his wife Adelaide made a donation to the monastery in gratitude for the cure worked on her son Roger II through the intercession of St Philip.[25] The names of saints once again began to populate clearly the spiritual map of Sicily.

Depth was also added by the production, from some of these new religious houses, of liturgical texts which slowly began to reconstruct a Sicilian sanctorale. Admittedly, some of these texts remain rather conservative, following the universal sanctorale closely, and may reflect the prime importance of reconnecting Sicily to the Latin Church. A lectionary and evangeliary found in the Biblioteca Painiana di Messina, dating probably to c.1100, reflect a universal Latin template with no discernible local variations.[26] However, other documents do show deviations. A Sicilian martyrology dating between 1101 and 1154 offers illuminating evidence.[27] Based on the template of Usuard's martyrology, it contains the standard entries for saints found in most universal Latin martyrologies, but it also adds in some South Italian mainland saints (e.g. St Barbatus of Benevento), as well as an unusually large number of French, and specifically Norman, saints (including a series of holy bishops of Rouen, two Breton saints, St Julian of Le Mans and St Gerard of Aurillac). Sicilian additions do appear too (St Calogerus and St Pancratius of Taormina), but they are strangely relegated to the margins of the manuscript.[28] The one Sicilian addition in the main body of the text is St Gregory of Agrigento and,

Il passagio dal domino bizantino allo stato normanno nell'Italia meridionale, Atti del II convegno internazionale di studi sulla civiltà rupestre medievale nel mezzogiorno d'Italia, Taranto–Mottola, 31 Ottobre–4 novembre 1973 (Taranto, 1977), 197–229, at 212; *Italia Pontificia*: x. Calabria, Insulae, ed. D. Girgensohn (Berlin, 1975), 320–1 nos. 1–3; Amatus, Bk VI.23, p. 434.

[24] White, *Latin Monasticism*, 105–17, 184–8, 202–4, 215. It was later conceded in 1126 to St Mary of the Latins in Jerusalem: *Italia Pontificia*: x. 294–5.

[25] *Byzantine Monastic Foundation Documents*, ed. and trans. J. Thomas and A. C. Hero et al., 5 vols (Washington, DC, 2000), ii. 621–36 no. 25.

[26] *Il lezionario e l'evangeliario di Messina*, ed. F. Terrizzi (Messina, 1985).

[27] F. Aricò, 'Il martirologio di Usuardo della biblioteca comunale di Palermo (sec. XII)', *Schede medievali* 43 (2005), 1–45; see also A. Nef, 'Sur les saints de la Sicile normande: à propos du martyrologe MS QQ E2 de la biblioteca comunale de Palerme', *Puer Apuliae*, ed., E. Cuozzo et al., 2 vols (Paris, 2008), ii. 477–90.

[28] Aricò, 'Il martirologio', 17, 26, 28. Equally strange, the reference in the Usuard martyrology to Saints Ruffinus and Martia of Syracuse has been omitted from this Sicilian adaptation, p. 26.

combined with other insertions for the dedication of two churches at Agrigento (the cathedral and the church of S. Nicola), it suggests that the document was produced there on the orders of its bishop.[29] It is a multi-layered text, formed around the universal sanctorale, but also shaped by the undoubted influence of the Norman rulers of Sicily and completed with the almost cautious insertion of Sicilian saints. Similarly, the codex of the *Missale Antiquum S. Panormitanae Ecclesiae*, dating to c.1130, displays signs of dependence on a Norman template with additional influence from the church of Le Mans. Its litany of saints read out on Holy Saturday included a large number from France, saints such as St Julian of Brioude (martyred during the reign of Diocletian), St Hilary, bishop of Poitiers (d. 367) and St Ouen, archbishop of Rouen (d. 684).[30]

It is apparent that the old Sicilian saints established before the Normans' arrival were revived in a modest and fairly conservative manner by a combination of Sicilian-Greek monks, Latin churchmen and Norman lay rulers. With the prominent exception of the cult of St Agatha at Catania, which we explore later in this chapter, the older Sicilian cults reappear mostly in church dedications and liturgical works, with only traces of a wider profile and veneration on the island. Indeed, if we look solely at the influx of early medieval Normanno-French saints into Sicilian liturgical sources, it would appear that they achieved equality with many of their Sicilian counterparts. This was partly a result of the increasing western European dominance of Romano-French liturgy and also partly down to the influence of the Norman newcomers. In some cases it would also seem that relics could not be recovered and thus fully functioning shrine centres could not re-emerge. This reality certainly contradicts the optimistic rhetoric in the opening paragraph of St Marina of Scanio's *bios*, written in the twelfth century, where the author claims that Sicily boasted an inexhaustible store of relics, 'a most holy assembly'.[31] Difficulties clearly arose because memory of the location of a saint's tomb had been lost, or because relics exported beyond the island could not be retrieved. St Lucy's cult in Syracuse appears to have suffered in both these respects. We have seen that local knowledge of Lucy's tomb was minimal at the time of Maniakes' expedition, and indeed other traditions claim the relics had already been removed. What is certain, however, is that there is no surviving evidence of Sicilian attempts to reclaim the body, as happened for St Agatha. In fact, the catalogue of relics compiled at Constantinople in 1204 by the Crusader and relic-hunter

---

[29] Aricò, 'Il martirologio', 36–8.
[30] *Missale Antiquum S. Panormitanae Ecclesiae*, ed. F. Terrizzi (Rome, 1970), 25–6, 34–7.
[31] The life is edited in *Martirio di Santa Lucia: Vita di Santa Marina*, 81.

Abbot Martin of Pairis records the presence of St Lucy, but at the same time it too lists St Agatha, which raises the usual problems arising out of multiple claims over relics.[32] The presence in Syracuse of the catacombs of S. Lucia, which also contained an oratory with a fresco of St Marcianus, the city's proto-bishop, may have assisted in the local maintenance of the cult.[33] However, the failure to promote St Lucy's cult on any prominent scale in Sicily is striking, especially when compared with the renewed promotion of St Agatha's cult at Catania. St Lucy's had similar potential, given the numerous associations with St Agatha, and certainly it attained universal acceptance as evidenced in liturgical sources, church dedications and toponyms found across Europe. But its dependence on St Agatha, and by extension on Catania, seems to have restricted it, and is rather odd given the ancient primacy of the Church of Syracuse in Sicily.[34] Elsewhere, important markers of veneration for St Lucy are found in the works of Siegebert of Gembloux, historian and hagiographer (d. 1112), who produced a metrical passion of St Lucy, and in those of the Byzantine poet and grammarian John Tzetzes (d. 1180), who composed an encomium for St Lucy which implicitly emphasized the saint's 'Sicilian' identity.[35] Yet, aside from church dedications in Sicily and her appearance in Sicilian martyrologies of the twelfth century, which in any case owed more to Lucy's presence in the universal templates from which they were copied, there are few signs on the island of an organized shrine centre.

Some efforts were thus clearly made from within Sicily to re-establish old cults, but the evidence suggests they were not overly ambitious. Iconographic works and liturgical documents were produced, most notably at the great cathedral at Monreale (near Palermo) in the 1180s where its elaborate mosaic cycles depicted early Sicilian saints such as Marcianus of Syracuse; however, rarely did the promotion of a cult appear to go further. St Marcianus of Syracuse's body seems never to have been fully recovered, but he at least appeared in local decorative cycles in the catacombs of Syracuse and in the mosaics at Monreale, and an arm did

---

[32] *Hystoria Constantinopolitana*, ch. 24 p. 127; William of Malmesbury's description of Constantinople in his *Gesta Regum Anglorum* (vol. 1, IV. 356.4 pp. 626–8) refers to the presence of the relics of both Lucy and Agatha. It may be that, having completed it c.1125–7, he did not have time to insert into the *Gesta* news of Agatha's return to Catania in 1126.

[33] Messina, *Sicilia Rupestre*, 50–1.

[34] Indeed, often religious houses were jointly dedicated to both saints, as was the monastery of SS Lucia and Agata at Matera, first recorded in 1208.

[35] Milazzo and Rizzo Nervo, 'Lucia', 95–135; *Sigeberts von Gembloux Passio Sanctae Luciae Virginis und Passio Sanctorum Thebeorum*, ed. E. Dümmler (Berlin, 1893); A. Kazhdan, 'Hagiographical notes', *Byzantion* 53 (1983), 538–58.

remain in Syracuse.[36] In the later twelfth century the bishop elect of Syracuse, the Englishman Richard Palmer, commissioned the creation of an arm reliquary to hold Marcianus' remaining limb. Significantly, in 1183 he seems to have taken the reliquary with him when he was transferred to Messina, where it is now found in the city's cathedral. It suggests that Marcianus' cult was not unequivocally bound to Syracuse and perhaps was used by Richard, also a powerful royal *familiaris*, to express Messina's pretensions to ecclesiastical supremacy, given Marcianus' historic role in the Sicilian Church.[37] Similar strategies may have coalesced with devotional trends to influence the promotion of cults at the great Greek-rite archimandrite monastery of San Salvatore di Messina. Built with the support of Roger II between 1122 and 1132, it was to be the region's leading Greek monastery, tasked with organizing the disordered (from the Latin perspective) state of Greek monasticism in Sicily and Calabria.[38] Liturgical works produced at the monastery commemorated in varying forms St Lucas di Isola di Capo Rizzuto, St Bartholomew of Simeri, St Filaretus, St Gregory bishop of Agrigento and St Leo of Catania.[39] Also, from its foundation charter (*typikon*) we know that the monastery went to great lengths to acquire an impressive library of sacred texts and to ensure it was 'adorned and beautified [. . .] with the most venerable relics of the great saints and with their sacred images', although their identities were not provided.[40] One by-product appears to have been the recovery or reproduction of information on Sicily's distant past, including its local Greek-rite saints. For example, the ninth-century encomium of St Pancratius of Taormina survived in the archives of a religious centre for it to be incorporated into a twelfth-century manuscript collection which appears to have subsequently found its way into the library at San Salvatore di Messina.[41] Furthermore, the monastery promoted the cult of St Philip of Agira, producing in the second half of the twelfth century a new *vita* and associated hymns. Undoubtedly a leading Greek monastic house would nurture genuine devotional interest for a pioneering figure of the island's early monastic history, but at the same time associating with the saint could express San Salvatore's hope to imitate the influence formerly

---

[36] Brodbeck, *Saints*, 72–3, 126.

[37] *I Normanni, popolo d'Europa*, ed. D'Onofrio, 520 no. 332 for an image of the arm reliquary; Loud, *Latin Church*, 234–6.

[38] Von Falkenhausen, 'I monasteri greci', 214–17.

[39] See the table in Pertusi, 'Rapporti', 492–3.

[40] 'Typikon of Luke for the monastery of Christ Saviour (San Salvatore) in Messina', trans. T. Miller, *Byzantine Monastic Foundation Documents*, ii. 645 no. 26.

[41] Stallman-Pacitti, 'Encomium', 340–5.

exerted by the monastery of S. Filippo di Agira in the Early Middle Ages.[42]

The transfer of St Marcianus' relic to Messina and the devotional strategies of San Salvatore di Messina show how both Latin-rite churchmen and Greek-rite monks utilized, and perhaps discarded, old Sicilian cults according to current need. Conversely, compelling local factors could explain why revival in the Norman period of the cult of Pancratius of Taormina was restricted to liturgical sources. During the ninth and tenth centuries the settlement of Taormina had repeatedly stood as the main Byzantine stronghold against Muslim advances. Even after its capitulation in 902, Taormina served as a bridgehead for potential Byzantine counter-campaigns. Consequently, Taormina remained in a frontier war zone and suffered great disruption: repeated attacks, a lengthy siege in 962 which led to resettlement by Muslim colonists, complete destruction and evacuation in the mid-960s, and repopulation by 976.[43] These conflicts appear to have been militarily and strategically motivated, but the Christian community was inevitably reduced as a consequence, and the city suffered again after offering stout resistance to the Normans in 1079. St Pancratius' shrine had clearly been thriving in the mid-ninth century – a contemporary encomium of Pancratius was tailored for the people of Taormina and the shrine was visited by St Elias of Enna – but in the ensuing century it could easily have been destroyed or fallen into disrepair. A second factor will have compounded this situation. Taormina's bishopric was not revived under Norman rule, and therefore there was less need in the late eleventh century to recover its early history and prestige. On the other hand, Agrigento had similarly been repopulated by Muslims, but the re-establishment of its bishopric in 1092 created potential new patrons for the cult of St Gregory, the early bishop of Agrigento, as evidenced in the production of the martyrology discussed earlier, and the acquisition by the city's bishop in 1178 of the Greek monastery of S. Gregorio di Agrigento.[44] Nevertheless, here the socio-religious make-up of the population was not straightforward. A thirteenth-century source noted that Gerlandus, the first bishop of the revived see, built his cathedral 'next to the citadel out of fear of the innumerable

[42] C. Pasini, 'Osservazioni sul dossier agiografico ed innografico di San Filippo do Agira', *Storia della Sicilia*, ed. S. Pricoco (Catania, 1988), 173–201, at 192–3.

[43] Metcalfe, *Muslims of Medieval Italy*, 28–31, 47, 51, 55–6, 59; Metcalfe, *Muslims and Christians*, 18–28.

[44] *Le più antiche carte dell'archivio capitolare di Agrigento (1092–1282)*, ed. P. Collura (Palermo, 1960), no. 32 pp. 78–80; Von Falkenhausen, 'I monasteri greci', 217.

Saracens living in Agrigento; indeed there were few Christians there before the death of King William II [in 1189]'.[45]

In some territories in Sicily the revival of Christian worship, and how it was articulated on a broader plane, clearly had to be negotiated in the context of multi-faith communities and religious pluralism. Some evidence exists for parallel and shared devotion operating between Christians and Muslims, while other evidence, supplied most notably on the city of Palermo by Hugo Falcandus, shows simmering interfaith tensions and periods of open hostilities; all in all a complex and shifting picture.[46] In the 1190s, the English chronicler Roger of Howden recorded news of an eruption at Etna, following which a 'multitude of pagans' (Muslims) fled to St Agatha's tomb at Catania and held up the saint's veil to divert the lava. This certainly mimicked the earliest hagiographical traditions of St Agatha's cult in which a year after the saint's death (AD 252) the people of Catania ran to her tomb and used her veil as protection from Etna's eruption. Among this crowd were pagans who were subsequently converted by Agatha's miraculous intervention.[47] As well as possible knowledge of these early traditions, Howden may also be providing a snapshot of the current socio-religious landscape in Catania in the later twelfth century. None of the traditions surrounding the cult's revival explicitly portray it as missionary in objective despite the presence of large Muslim communities, particularly to the south in the Val di Noto. This mirrors broader policy in Norman Sicily, where no consistent and widespread conversion programmes were aimed against the island's Muslims. Instead, evidence for conversion suggests it was a gradual process arising from long-term socio-cultural assimilation. The charter of privileges granted by the bishop of Catania in 1168 to the Catanesi allowed 'Latini, Graeci, Iudaei et Saraceni' to live according to their own law, demonstrating the religious eclecticism of the city, and the absence of discernible Latin Christian efforts to convert the infidel.[48]

Indeed, the socio-cultural history of Sicily made religious pluralism likely. The *vita* of St John Terista shows that, as the saint grew up in Muslim Palermo in the first half of the eleventh century, his Christian mother educated him in the Christian faith, and his Muslim stepfather

---

[45] *Più antiche carte dell'archivio capitolare di Agrigento*, 307.

[46] Liber de Regno, 56–7 (English trans: Tyrants, 109–10).

[47] For Roger's account, *Chronica Magistri Rogeri de Houedene*, iii. 53; *Bibliotheca Sanctorum*, 14 vols (Rome, 1961–87), i. 323.

[48] G. Fasoli, 'Tre secoli di vita cittadina catanese', in her *Scritti di storia medievale* (Bologna, 1974), Appendix, document II, pp. 400–1. In the 1150s the Muslim geographer Muhammad al-Idrisi recorded notable mosques in Catania: Idrisi, *La Première Géographie de l'Occident*, revised translation by H. Bresc et al. (Paris, 1999), 314.

taught him Arab–Islamic customs.[49] John's mother acted, it seems, partly against long-established norms for, as Ibn Hawqal's comments (in 973) on the frequency of interfaith marriage in Sicily show, the general practice was for boys to be raised as Muslims following their fathers, and girls as Christians like their mothers.[50] The existence of different faiths within kin groups and communities could only create multiple interconnections between Muslim and Christian forms of worship. Comparative evidence from the crusader states shows that there existed a number of sites of shared veneration not only between different Christian denominations but also between Muslims and Christians, including at the Holy Sepulchre, locations in Bethlehem, Mount Sinai and John the Baptist's birthplace at 'Ain Karim.[51] In the Holy Land there is evidence of Muslims participating in local Christian festivals, and recent anthropological fieldwork in Palestine has demonstrated a continuing stream of parallel devotion up to the present day, along with its significant social dimensions.[52] Some sites were clearly imbued with an aura of holiness and folkloric magnetism that appealed to people of all faiths, who each individually drew their own meanings from a spiritual space. The efficacy and protective powers of holy shrines could easily transcend religious affiliations, especially in a region dominated by the numinous dangers of Etna. Indeed, al-Harawi, a Muslim traveller who visited Sicily in the 1170s, noted an Islamic pilgrimage site, dedicated to thirty Muslim martyrs, in a cemetery in Catania.[53] While not spreading the faith directly, St Agatha may well have counted Muslims among her devotees, who were comfortable at utilizing different elements of both religions. Indeed, Roger of Howden's aforementioned account suggests such a scenario, and a large number of Muslim families fell under the lordship of the cathedral–monastery of St Agatha, providing the context in which cross-religious affinities could develop towards a saint whose feast days might mark important fiscal landmarks.[54] All of these factors shaped the visibility of

---

[49] Borsari, 'Vita', 137.
[50] *Book of Curiosities* [accessed on 10 May, 2012], Bk 2.12.
[51] For a stimulating analysis of such cross-cultural interaction see C. MacEvitt, *The Crusades and the Christian World of the East. Rough Tolerance* (Philadelphia, 2008), and particularly 126–30, 132–5. See also A. Jotischky, 'Pilgrimage, procession and ritual encounters between Christians and Muslims in the crusader states', *Cultural Encounters during the Crusades*, ed. K. Villads Jensen, K. Salonen and H. Vogt (Copenhagen, 2013), 245–62; I am grateful to Professor Jotischky for kindly allowing me to view the article in advance of publication.
[52] G. Bowman, 'Nationalizing the sacred: shrines and shifting identities in the Israeli-occupied territories', *Man: Journal of the Royal Anthropological Institute* 28 (1993), 431–60.
[53] Al-Harawi, *A Lonely Wayfarer's Guide to Pilgrimage*, trans. J. W. Meri (Princeton, 2004), 142.
[54] Metcalfe, *Muslims of Medieval Italy*, 116–19.

cults, feast-day processions and the practice of pilgrimage to shrines. In short, twelfth-century Sicily was full of disjointed cultic histories, some of which only carried limited relevance to the contemporary era, while others were located in a fluid socio-religious setting which necessitated 'pragmatic adaptations' and circumspection among the cult's promoters.[55]

Patron of Sicily: the cult of St Agatha of Catania

An analysis of the cult of St Agatha of Catania shows how restricted efforts were elsewhere in Sicily to revive other cults, or how limited the surviving evidence for them is. In the twelfth century, the cult of St Agatha of Catania represents the only documented case of a Sicilian shrine centre for which we are able to track the development over a number of decades; no other cult offers comparable insight into some of the processes behind the reassertion of Christianity in Sicily. The translation account and miracle collection, recorded by Bishop Maurice (c.1130), was later supplemented by the monk Blandinus (in the 1140s–1150s) with further accounts of miracles. Thereafter, a range of additional evidence attests both the saint's presence in the city and the geographic spread of her cult from its centre at Catania. Having already discussed the circumstances behind St Agatha's possible removal to Constantinople, we now turn to the process of the saint's revival in Sicily. The continued universal popularity of St Agatha and her earliest hagiographic traditions maintained the memory of her association with Catania, and would have been appealing to the city's emergent bishopric. Indeed, Bishop Maurice of Catania (c.1122–c.1141) was the central figure in the re-establishment of the cult, putting considerable energy into its promotion. He was a powerful and ambitious prelate, lord of the entire city of Catania; one of the earlier references to him in 1125 saw Roger II of Sicily bestow land between Catania and Lentini on the bishopric, and exempted the cathedral–monastery's ships from certain tolls, clear confirmation that Catania and its bishop were favoured at the highest levels.[56] Maurice, of course, was promoted to the bishopric shortly before the translation, and was the author of the translation text. Both the translation account and the miracle collection suggest his active involvement in the venture. Indeed, Maurice wrote himself into the translation script by sending monks to Messina to verify the

[55] See the valuable article by R. M. Hayden, 'Antagonistic tolerance: competitive sharing of religious sites in South Asia and the Balkans', *Current Anthropology* 43 (2002), 205–31; quotation at 219.

[56] *I diplomi greci ed arabi di Sicilia*, ed. S. Cusa (Palermo, 1868–82), 554–6; Loud, *Latin Church*, 320–1.

authenticity of the relics as they arrived in Sicily, and he then extended his account to record a collection of miracles worked by St Agatha, which was probably written by c.1130. It seems that his successor, Evenus, was in place by 1141, which means that Maurice supervised the crucial first decade and a half of the cult's re-establishment.[57]

Maurice's account of the translation detailed the return of St Agatha's relics to Catania in 1126. The translation was accomplished by two Latin Christians: Giselbertus, from France (*genere Gallus*), who occupied a military post within the Byzantine imperial household, and Goscelinus, a Calabrian (*Calabricus*).[58] St Agatha visited Giselbertus in a dream and appealed to him to return her body to Catania. The subsequent theft of the relics from a Constantinopolitan church and their transfer to Catania was a masterclass in improvisation. The two Latins placed St Agatha's head in two bowls and divided her limbs into two quivers. Having eluded a search party, they took to the sea, stopping at Smyrna (where they endured an earthquake), Corinth (where St Agatha helped both men find another boat) and the Methone littoral, before crossing the Adriatic with a group of merchants. The translation narrative is then interrupted with the description (perhaps a later interpolation) of a miracle worked by St Agatha at Taranto, where the men had arrived, which culminated with the depositing of a relic fragment in the city. From there, Giselbertus and Goscelinus traversed the dangerous Strait of Messina, navigating their way past the ancient 'sea monsters' Scylla and Charybdis. Having halted at Messina, Giselbertus proceeded ahead to Catania to notify the bishop of the imminent arrival. He found Bishop Maurice in the nearby *castrum* of Aci, who in response dispatched two of his monks to Messina to authenticate the relics. The authentication was duly accomplished, and the relics escorted into Catania on 17 August 1126 by a huge candlelit procession. The saint's arrival was accompanied by miraculous healings and exorcisms.

The arrival of a saint with Agatha's pedigree, her location at the heart of a large diocese and the timing of her return, represented a potent combination in the consolidation of Christian control over the island. By the 1120s the first phase of Sicily as a Christian island once more had passed; it had witnessed the first waves of Christian colonization, the revival of monastic centres, the establishment of diocesan structures, and Urban II's donation of the Apostolic Legateship to Count Roger I of Sicily. The development of this cult centre may be seen as a significant secondary phase of Christian consolidation, and this may explain why Agatha's cult was not overtly revived until as late as 1126. It would appear that the

---

[57] *Italia Pontificia*: x. 290–1 nos. 20, 22.
[58] For the translation narrative, *Epistola Mauritii*, 643–8.

leaders of the Church of Catania in the first decades of its re-establishment were in no position to create more ambitious agendas. St Agatha's return to Catania proved a great success and eventually she would become the island's leading saint: 'the sacred relic and benevolent patron of Sicily', in Bishop Maurice's words.[59] Let us first return to the two accounts, those of Bishop Maurice and of Orderic Vitalis, which recorded the alleged translation of St Agatha to Constantinople in c.1040. It is possible to apply their interpretations for her removal from Sicily in reverse and connect these to the situation in the island when both versions were written around 1130. Bishop Maurice, in claiming that St Agatha was moved to Byzantium to strengthen a failing empire, might be indirectly implying that her return in 1126 was a sign of Constantinople's final decay and the transfer of the saint's patronage to a youthful and expansive Christian Sicily. Orderic Vitalis suggested that St Agatha was removed by Maniakes to protect her remains from Muslim desecration. He too may implicitly invite the conclusion that the saint's return was a sign (at least from the perspective of external observers) that Sicily's Christianity was now secure from the infidel.

It was crucial for any cult to conform to a catalogue of universal models which signalled its authentic Christian credentials. Furthermore, it was vital that zones on the periphery of Christendom, such as Sicily, established exchange networks and reciprocal relationships with inner, core regions such as Rome or France. In both cases, St Agatha fulfilled the necessary criteria. The acquisition of relics from the city of Constantinople was a mark of their quality and, as Geary has shown, the *furta sacra* model was a widely accepted method for articulating to a wider audience that the saint had bestowed divine favour on her new home.[60] For St Agatha such messages were intensified by her established popularity across Europe, with widespread church dedications, and the fact that this 'relic theft' also represented a homecoming. In this instance, Catania benefited from its Christian past. It did not have to import an external cult, which was often necessary in other border regions of Christendom where, in the absence of 'native' cults, 'foreign' saints were crucial in the initial phase of institutionalizing Christian structures.[61] The path taken during the translation itself was also significant. Once into the orbit of southern Italy, associations were created between St Agatha's relics and the cities of Taranto,

---

[59] *Epistola Mauritii*, 643.
[60] Geary, *Furta Sacra*.
[61] See the example of Poland: N. Kersken, 'God and the saints in medieval Polish historiography', *The Making of Christian Myths in the Periphery of Latin Christendom (c.1000–1300)*, ed. L.-B. Mortensen (Copenhagen, 2006), 153–9, at 173.

Messina and the small settlement of Aci, near Catania. At Taranto, news of the translation was first made public. Here, according to the translation account, St Agatha's presence created a spiritually charged atmosphere culminating in the bestowal of a relic. At Messina the relics were finally back on Sicilian soil and were also authenticated in the city, while it was at Aci that the first glorious news of St Agatha's imminent arrival reached the bishop. As Turner and Turner noted in their classic study, circles of influence radiate out from a central shrine. In this outer orbit were found lesser shrines and chapels, encountered by the pilgrim on his route to the main shrine. These represented 'sacred valves and resistances [. . .] designed to build up a considerable load of reverent feeling', making the final experience on arrival at the saint's resting place fittingly transcendental.[62] In this case, Catania was the central shrine with potential staging-posts at Aci (a local settlement drawing in the rural population from Catania's hinterland), at Messina (the chief port of Sicily, attracting merchants and pilgrims) and at Taranto (a key mainland port). Certainly, other staging-posts would have arisen along different routes, but those associated with the translation carried greater resonance and connected the cult to an immediate wider zone. In this way, the cult of Catania, on the frontier of Latin Christendom, underwent a transformative process, which according to Geary was replicated across Europe. It became a new 'centre' on the edge of a world of which it was now an integral component.[63]

From these promising and solid foundations, the cult rapidly spread on both a local and international stage. The power of the bishopric of Catania, one of the largest ecclesiastical lordships on the island, assisted the spreading influence of St Agatha.[64] The collection of miracles worked by St Agatha, which was recorded by Bishop Maurice and Blandinus, reveals cultic connections spreading beyond the city.[65] The pilgrims visiting the shrine at Catania are explored in Chapter 6, but here it will still be useful to highlight some important themes. It is significant that the Church of Catania could claim the patronage of one of Sicily's few major

[62] Turner and Turner, *Image and Pilgrimage*, 23.
[63] P. Geary, 'Reflections on historiography and the holy: center and periphery', *The Making of Christian Myths in the Periphery of Latin Christendom (c.1000–1300)*, ed. L.-B. Mortensen (Copenhagen, 2006), 323–30, at 328.
[64] Malaterra, Bk IV.7, pp. 88–9, for the early privileges enjoyed by the bishops of Catania. See the studies by H. Bresc, 'Dominio feudale, consistenza patrimoniale e insediamento umano', 91–107 and E. Pispisa, 'Il vescovo, la città e il regno', 137–54 in *Chiesa e società in Sicilia: l'età normanna*, Atti del I convegno internazionale organizzato dall'arcidiocesi di Catania, 25–27 novembre 1992, ed. G. Zito (Turin, 1995).
[65] These miracles can be found in *Epistola Mauritii*, 645–8 and *S. Agathae Miracula, Descripta a Blandino Monacho*, AS February, i (Paris, 1863), 648–51.

landholders: Henry of Paternò, brother-in-law to Count Roger I of Sicily and later uncle of King Roger II.[66] Following a nocturnal apparition of St Agatha, Henry visited her shrine, an act which led to reconciliation with the cathedral monks at Catania, for whom, we are told, he had previously conceived a virulent hatred.[67] The saint's presence at Catania operated then as a neutral channel for peacemaking, forging a union between the city's Church and this powerful aristocrat. Indeed, this was a significant alliance, as Henry was responsible for the security of the territories around Catania, and it seems that he was able to influence the city's bishops to make donations to two of his favoured Holy Land churches.[68]

In the first few decades of the cult's development after 1126, the miracle records reveal repeated connections with the city of Messina, and with a number of pilgrims arriving from the city.[69] The concentration on Messina in the miracle records undoubtedly fulfilled some important requirements for St Agatha's cult and for the city of Catania. It strengthened the translation tradition in which Messina was established as a key staging-post of the cult. It also assisted in the quest for regional supremacy by trying to manifest Messina's spiritual subordination to Catania. Indeed, contemporaneous with these accounts, in the 1130s and the 1140s, the diocesan map of Sicily was being controversially restructured. If accomplished, Catania would become a suffragan see of the newly created archbishopric of Messina.[70] Messina's presence in the miracle collection also represented an attempt to generate support for the cult in the leading port of the island, a flourishing embarkation point for the growing pilgrim and crusader traffic to the Holy Land.[71] Indeed, the combined crusading forces of Richard I and Philip Augustus wintered on the island in 1190–1 and were based at Messina. As we shall see, the garrisoning of these Third Crusade forces in Sicily led to deeper awareness of Sicilian folklore and particularly of the cult of St Agatha in western Europe. Perhaps the desire to tap into these streams of commerce and pilgrimage, and to attach to a rival city's expanding communication

---

[66] Scalia, 'La traslazione', 95–6; Loud, *Age of Robert Guiscard*, 177, 180, 182.
[67] *Epistola Mauritii*, 646.
[68] Bresc, 'Dominio feudale', 93; G. A. Loud, 'Norman Italy and the Holy Land', *The Horns of Hattin*, ed. B. Z. Kedar (Jerusalem, 1992), 49–62, at 58–61.
[69] *Epistola Mauritii*, 646–8.
[70] The bishopric of Catania avoided subordination to Messina, and in 1168 was made directly subject to the papacy; however, in 1183 Catania was subordinated to the new archbishopric at Monreale: *Italia Pontificia*: x. 292 no. 25, 293 no. 27.
[71] Loud, 'Norman Italy', 52, 54, 56; see also the chapters by Houben, Luttrell and Franchetti Pardo in *Il mezzogiorno normanno-svevo e le crociate*, Atti delle XIV giornate normanno-sveve, Bari, 17–20 Ottobre 2000, ed. G. Musca (Bari, 2002), 251–88, 289–300, 301–23.

network, underlay the translation of 1126, in much the same way that Bari made the move for St Nicholas in 1087, ahead of their Venetian rivals.

References to the city of Syracuse might also be considered in a similar context. Although not as central to crusading and commercial traffic as Messina, Syracuse was another key port on the east coast of Sicily. By creating an association between that city and the cult of St Agatha, the Church of Catania could further advertise its ambitions for regional ascendancy. It should also be remembered that the hagiographical tradition of St Lucy of Syracuse stresses a dependence on St Agatha, and this may be reflected in the selection of particular miracles. Agatha's performance of an exorcism on the wife of the steward of the bishop of Syracuse implies that the ecclesiastical hierarchy in the latter city were informed on the power of the Catanese cult. Another woman from Syracuse was liberated from demonic possession at St Agatha's shrine on the feast day celebrating her return to Catania; the city was said to be filled with a huge crowd of Christians, precisely the sort of news which the establishment at Catania would hope to be communicated back to Syracuse and beyond.[72] Indeed, as one historian noted, religious processions reflected 'the increasing needs for a suitable arena to exchange information across wider distances'.[73] A much more overt message was offered by Blandinus in his miracle collection when he recorded a piratical raid by Iberian Muslims on Sicily in 1127. Catania was saved by St Agatha who alerted its inhabitants to the raiding party, allowing them to defend the city. However, on the same day, the Muslim force attacked Syracuse and massacred its population, leaving only the city walls standing.[74] At their core, the associations made with both Messina and Syracuse in St Agatha's hagiographical dossier might be seen to reveal Catania's fear that it was being overshadowed by the two cities, and indeed such fear was justifiable given that from the mid-twelfth century the Churches of Messina and Syracuse could both exert more economic and political influence in the island.

Blandinus' work attempts to evidence the broadening horizons of the cult. His records refer more frequently to innumerable crowds flocking to Catania and focus on episodes which are greater in magnitude. Blandinus placed St Agatha within the context of the aforementioned Muslim raid of 1127 and later did the same regarding a famine that spread across Sicily.[75] He also stated, under the year 1132, that the fame of Agatha's miracles

[72] *S. Agathae Miracula*, 645, 649.
[73] S. Menache, *The Vox Dei. Communication in the Middle Ages* (Oxford, 1990), 2.
[74] *S. Agathae Miracula*, 648–9.
[75] *S. Agathae Miracula*, 648–9.

brought devotees 'not only from the Sicilians, but also from inhabitants of foreign territories'.[76] A charter of Catanese privileges issued by Catania's bishop in 1168 granted free passage across the city's river to pilgrims, suggesting their numbers were sufficiently high to be included in such an important document.[77] However, a comparative analysis of the distances travelled by pilgrims recorded by both Maurice and Blandinus shows little difference, and if anything they are shorter in the latter's collection. A mixed message is presented of a cult broadening its fame and popularity in its early decades, yet its pilgrims appear to originate from a fairly consistent territorial sphere orbiting primarily around eastern and north-eastern Sicily. The actual origins of pilgrims may not, however, have been of particular significance to our Catanese hagiographers, for a recurrent feature of Agatha's miracle workings is their location at the shrine itself. The vast majority of miracles occurred before the saint's relics, and a number followed a period of incubation near the shrine.[78] A few pilgrims were healed or aided by St Agatha away from Catania, but importantly these events always occurred en route to the shrine: a paralytic carpenter had his donkey stolen, was miraculously lifted across a river and was able to walk the final two miles to St Agatha's shrine; a monk from Troina was healed and 'flown' to Catania; a woman sailing from Messina to the shrine at Catania was visited by Agatha who aroused her from a comatose state; and an old man had vision in one eye restored while journeying to St Agatha's shrine and the other cured on arrival.[79] The centrality of Agatha's shrine was made explicit: the most effective way to obtain the saint's aid was physical proximity to her relics. At the same time, this would expose visitors to other miracle stories and traditions relating to St Agatha, transmitted visually (through decorations and pilgrim offerings), orally (through liturgical services and encounters with shrine officials) and via written records (through the display of hagiographical texts). The woman at Messina, struck deaf because she refused to visit Agatha's shrine, is emblematic of the dominant message. The need to locate the intensity of the cult at its centre is indicative of the first stage of the development of a fledgling shrine.

Communication networks were of the utmost importance in the estab-lishment and development of cults. At Catania, evidence suggests that those supervising the cult attempted to attach it to existing communication

---

[76] S. Agathae Miracula, 649.

[77] Fasoli, 'Tre secoli', Appendix, document II pp. 400–1.

[78] For more on the practice of incubation see D. Mallardo, 'L'incubazione nella cristianita medievale napoletana', AB 67 (1949), 465–98.

[79] Epistola Mauritii, 646–8.

networks, while also creating new ones. The nobility, commerce, pilgrimage and the oral testimony of individuals enabled information exchange. The Church, staffed by a literate elite connected by channels of communication which transcended geographical frontiers, represented one of the medieval world's most effective conduits for information transmission. As we have seen in Chapter 1, the cult of St Agatha had from the Early Middle Ages attracted devotion from across the Christian world. At a more localized level, after 1126, the Sicilian ecclesiastical establishment was harnessed to the cult. As one of the island's leading ecclesiastical lords, the bishop of Catania enjoyed a prominent platform from which to disseminate knowledge of the city's saint. Also, as a cathedral–monastery, connections were evidently forged with both the secular and regular Church. Orderic Vitalis' knowledge of Sicilian affairs and St Agatha no doubt owed much to the connections that were established between his monastery in Normandy and South Italian Benedictine monastic houses. Significantly, the Church could also utilize visual media throughout its religious spaces. Although there is insufficient space here to trace the full range of her visual representations, St Agatha was depicted in two of the most famous Sicilian mosaic cycles. Her image adorned the interior of both the royal chapel in Palermo, the Cappella Palatina (decorated between c.1140 and c.1170), and the extravagant cathedral at Monreale (constructed c.1174–83), which was intended to serve also as a royal mausoleum.[80] On another level, recipients of St Agatha's miracles were drawn from ecclesiastical circles or interacted with them. Among those cured were the wife of the steward of the bishop of Syracuse, and Greek monks from Troina and Gerace in Calabria (or possibly Geraci in Sicily, seventy kilometres south-east of Palermo).[81] The latter are particularly interesting, suggesting that St Agatha's cult, centred in a city under the control of Latin Benedictine churchmen, was popular among the Greek Christian communities of southern Italy. Agatha's stay in Constantinople and her earlier connections to Byzantine Sicily may well account for this. Indeed, Messina, where some of St Agatha's miracles were directed, retained a large Greek Christian community throughout the twelfth century. Moreover, the aforementioned monk from Troina was healed of a swelling in his knee and miraculously transported the forty miles to Catania in the space of one hour. Maurice says that he accompanied seven fellow-monks and their Greek abbot, who had been inspired to visit the shrine after 'having discovered the news of the return of the most blessed virgin, and

---

[80] Demus, *Mosaics*, 327; Brodbeck, *Saints*, 314; for Monreale's historical context see Loud, *Latin Church*, 329–39.
[81] *Epistola Mauritii*, 647.

having heard of her wonders'.[82] The episode is of additional interest because a similar incident forms the first miracle in the *vita* of St Silvester, a monk of the Greek monastery of S. Michele at Troina who died at some point in the second half of the twelfth century. Silvester had been 'gripped with great desire to see the tomb of the divine Agatha, he received permission to go from his superior, [and] completed the journey, beyond the laws of nature, in the space of one hour'.[83] The two monks from Troina would thus appear to be one and the same, independently corroborated from two hagiographical texts. Echoing the relationship with St Lucy of Syracuse, St Agatha here is seen nurturing new forms of sanctity on the island of Sicily, contributing to the consolidation of a network of holy figures and shrines.

After the early phase of the revival of St Agatha's cult, increasing evidence suggests that in the second half of the twelfth century the shrine began to operate on a wider stage, in addition to the saint's long-established presence in church dedications, universal martyrologies, calendars and in place-names. Three developments primarily explain the saint's re-emergence onto the international stage. First, the growth of pilgrimage to the Holy Land and the evolution of the crusading movement provided sustained exposure for the cult. As already noted, cultic connections were immediately established with the city of Messina, which was increasingly a key node on a major Christian pilgrimage route. But it was an event of the magnitude of the Third Crusade that significantly boosted the international reputation of Agatha's cult. The Anglo-French crusading forces wintered near Messina in 1190–1 on their way to face Saladin in the East. As a result, a large number of western Europeans were exposed to a range of Sicilian traditions, customs and folklore, which then filtered westwards. The Englishman Roger of Howden, who accompanied Richard I on the Third Crusade, took a keen interest in St Agatha. He noted Agatha's ability to prevent eruptions from the nearby volcanic Etna, and how the saint's veil acted like a shield against the fiery lava. Roger recorded a specific occasion in which Agatha's veil was used to divert the volcanic fire into the sea, leaving some fish half-burned which could still be seen in the 1190s, fondly termed *pisces Sanctae Agathae*. From this incident, a local custom emerged in which any fisherman who caught one of the fishes immediately released it 'on account of reverence for Blessed Agatha'. The

[82] *Epistola Mauritii*, 647.
[83] *Vita Sancti Silvestri*, 177; for more on Silvester see *Bibliotheca Sanctorum*, xi. 1074–5; Scalia, 'La traslazione', 96–7.

chronicler here records some of the more quotidian and curious ways in which the cult infiltrated lay consciousness.[84]

The second significant development to boost St Agatha's international reputation can be identified from the mid-twelfth century, as the existence of the new Kingdom of Sicily was gradually accepted by medieval Europe's leading powers. As a result cordial diplomatic relationships were established above all with the Angevins in England, the Capetians in France and the popes in Rome.[85] Peter of Blois and Gervase of Tilbury were just two of the prominent authors who came into contact with the region through diplomatic ties, and recorded aspects of Sicilian life.[86] As we have seen, the Church of Catania had influence in the highest Sicilian circles, and two of its archdeacons during the 1140s and 1160s – Asclettin and the celebrated scholar Henry Aristippus – were royal chancellors and leading advisors to the king.[87] A chain of prominent communication channels thus connected St Agatha at Catania to a much wider audience. Indeed, Roger of Howden made a significant reference to the cult's growing repute: in 1190–1, with the crusader forces at Messina, King Tancred of Sicily and Richard I of England finally settled their differences and made a symbolic visit to Agatha's tomb.[88]

The third and final key factor connects to the first two: the crusading/pilgrimage movement and the creation of diplomatic links increased western European knowledge of Sicily. Above all, the message that returned westwards, from authors such as Peter of Blois, Roger of Howden, Walter Map, Conrad of Querfurt and Gervase of Tilbury, was of a strange and exotic land.[89] As will be explored further in Chapter 5, the region's landscape had a mystical quality – marked by fiery volcanoes, and the scars of terrible earthquakes. The dangerous seas around it hosted classical monsters such as Scylla and Charybdis. Here was found the new home of King Arthur in the caverns of Etna, and the battlefields of *chansons de geste*, waged against Muslim foes, most famously in the *Chanson d'Aspremont*. Some authors located the gateway to the Underworld in Mount Etna or

---

[84] *Chronica*, iii. 53; in the 1190s, Conrad of Querfurt, bishop of Hildesheim, visited Sicily and recorded a similar account of 'Saracens' turning to St Agatha for protection against Etna: *Arnoldi Chronica Slavorum*, ed. G. H. Pertz, MGH SS xxxiv (Hanover, 1868), Bk. 5, 195. In the mid-thirteenth century, Matthew Paris' strip-map also referenced St Agatha's veil protecting against Etna: S. Lewis, *The Art of Matthew Paris in the Chronica Majora* (Aldershot, 1987), 346 n. 54.

[85] See especially, G. A. Loud, 'The kingdom of Sicily and the kingdom of England, 1066–1266', *History* 88 (2003), 540–67, at 550–63.

[86] See Chapter 5.

[87] *Liber de Regno*, 11–13, 44–5 (Tyrants, 63–5, 98–9).

[88] *Chronica*, iii. 97.

[89] For full references in the following section see Chapter 5.

near Naples, and others placed the entrance to Purgatory in Sicily. Gervase of Tilbury, Alexander of Neckham and Conrad of Querfurt were fascinated by Virgilian legends associated with Naples. In addition, the continued presence of Muslim communities added to the region's pagan and supernatural undertones. These perceptions of a volatile southern Italy would cast into the limelight the role of any protector, and St Agatha was aptly placed to assume the task. The proximity of her shrine to the supernatural Etna, whose fame was known across the Christian and Muslim worlds, immediately placed Agatha in a perpetual struggle with this fiery entity. Roger of Howden commented on it, and Gervase of Tilbury noted that Saint Agatha 'preserves the city from fire by its protection'.[90] News of the catastrophic Sicilian earthquake of 1169, which almost destroyed Catania, further disseminated the image of Agatha operating in a world of powerful forces. The disaster occurred on 4 February, the vigil of St Agatha, collapsing the saint's church.[91] Commentators did not see such events as proof of saints' failure to protect, but of their powerful displeasure. The event was, according to Peter of Blois, St Agatha's punishment for a sinful episcopal election in Catania.[92]

St Agatha thus represented goodness and purity in a landscape of Hell, Purgatory, sinister natural forces and pagan communities. This combination undoubtedly attracted external interest and fascination. By 1200 the cult of St Agatha was firmly rooted both in its immediate locale and in the wider European consciousness. The revival of Agatha's cult uncovers the initial, prosaic renewal of the island's Christian identity. Standard techniques for propagating the shrine's popularity were utilized by a powerful episcopal centre, connected to the highest socio-political circles, building on a reputation already enhanced both in the Early Middle Ages and by the saint's residence at Constantinople. In addition, the patrons of the cult were able to channel wider Mediterranean movement and exchange into St Agatha's orbit, ensuring her fame spread beyond the island. The proximity to uniquely sinister, mythical forces, news of which was increasingly circulated across Europe, enabled Agatha to stand as a protector of the faith, and to allay external suspicions of an otherwise strange and semi-pagan island. In the process, medieval Sicily obtained a cult to rival the mainland shrines of St Nicholas at Bari and St Michael the Archangel at Monte Gargano, and firmly rooted itself within the broader topography of Christian pilgrimage.

[90] Gervase of Tilbury, *Otia Imperialia. Recreation of an Emperor*, ed. and trans. S. E. Banks and J. W. Binns (Oxford, 2002), Bk. II.12, pp. 334–5.
[91] Liber de Regno, 164–5 (Tyrants, 216–17, 243).
[92] *Petri Blesensis Opera Omnia*, Patrologia Latina 207 (Paris, 1855), no. 46 cols. 133–4.

New saints in Sicily   The old cult of St Agatha was thus revived during the Norman era under the direction of Latin Christian churchmen and with some appeal to both Muslim and Greek Christian communities. On the other hand, a striking feature of Sicilian sanctity during this period was its limited production of new saints. At first glance this represents a stark contrast to the preceding era, especially the ninth and tenth centuries when Sicily seemed full of saints. This is something of a smokescreen; as we have seen, the surviving information available to us shows that they all moved away from Sicily. In the eleventh century, in the twilight of Muslim control of the island, St John Terista and St Filaretus of Seminara similarly migrated to the mainland at an early age. We have to retreat to the pre-827 era to find saints who were firmly based in Sicily. In a reversal of the patterns evident in the ninth and tenth centuries, three twelfth-century hagiographies show new saints from the mainland visiting Sicily after the Norman conquest. When the hagiographical motifs are stripped away, these accounts reveal interesting glimpses of the island's religious make-up in the first decades of the twelfth century. In around the 1110s the Calabrian Greek St Lucas di Isola di Capo Rizzuto took his tireless missionary activities to Sicily, which was portrayed as 'unfaithful through the atheistic enemies who lived there'. This ambiguous phrase might suggest that the 'enemies' were Latin Christians, or lapsed Greek Orthodox, and Lucas's actions – ordaining priests in the cities he visited – suggest that the blurring of Christian rites rather than converting Muslims was his main concern.[93] Around a similar time, perhaps c.1120, St John of Matera's desire to live an extreme ascetic existence prompted him to spend over two years in Sicily as a hermit. The island, which had nurtured so many wandering eremitical saints, appears once again to attract this type of figure.[94] Neither Lucas nor John worked any miracles on the island, but they may have still presented useful exemplars to the reviving Christian communities there. On the other hand, St Bartholomew of Simeri experienced a short and eventful stay in Messina, where his biographer states he was acclaimed as a saint. Bartholomew, heir to the rich tradition of Italo-Greek eremitic saints, had been falsely accused of heresy, brought before Roger II's court at Messina and condemned. Fortunately, a column of fire rising from the saint's feet proved his innocence, at which point the whole city of Messina, Roger II and his magnates begged Bartholomew's pardon.[95] Indeed, Roger II entrusted to Bartholomew the development of the great monastery of San Salvatore di Messina, although

---

[93] *Vita di S. Luca,* 47, 90–1.
[94] *Vita S. Iohannis,* 37.
[95] Zaccagni, '*bios*', 267–71.

the saint's exact role in its foundation remains unclear. Bartholomew returned to Calabria where he died in 1130. Shortly afterwards, his cult developed and was nurtured at San Salvatore, but evidence for a popular cult in Sicily is lacking. Collectively, the brief experiences of the three mainland saints show a Sicily where variant forms of Christianity converged, a landscape that might once again attract ascetic holy men, and a policy of secular rulers hand-picking suitable candidates to revitalize Christian worship on the island.

While some new saints did appear on the island of Sicily in the twelfth century, they were only temporary visitors. The evidence for home-grown Sicilian saints is notably restricted, and not aided by the dearth of chronicle and other narrative sources on socio-religious change in twelfth-century Sicily. One would have expected that the period of Christian–Muslim military conflict arising out of the Norman invasion, followed by the pioneering endeavours of churchmen in territories in which the majority Muslim population might have left the Christian inhabitants vulnerable, would have offered fertile ground for the promotion of new saints.[96] Ottavio Gaetani's seventeenth-century collection of Sicilian *vitae* preserves record of a life of a St Chremes (d. c.1100), an abbot who apparently lived in Sicily during Muslim rule, spent time as a hermit, and obtained aid from Roger I to rebuild the monastery of S. Salvatore di Placa (near Messina), which was formally founded in 1092. Although a liturgical feast day for the saint exists, there is no further historical information on this figure.[97] Similar uncertainties arise from the *bios* of the virgin St Marina of Scanio (location unidentified) which states she was born in 1062 when Roger I had arrived to help the Christians in Sicily.[98] She entered a monastery at a young age, earned fame through miraculous healing, and then 'fleeing fame as one flees a serpent' elected to travel to Jerusalem, where she stayed for over three years, visiting the Holy Sepulchre and the River Jordan, developing close ties with a bishop of Tripoli and entering a monastery. Marina finally chose to return to Sicily where she died, and subsequently her relics worked various, unspecified, miracles. However, the work, which was probably produced in the twelfth century, offers no further firm historical information (such as the date of her death, although the reference to the bishop of Tripoli implies a date following the creation of the County of Tripoli in 1104 by

---

[96] Intriguingly, a Sicilian martyrology dating between 1101 and 1154 includes the death of Roger I of Sicily under 23 June, inviting the reader to consider him within the framework of sanctity: Aricò, 'Il martirologio', 2–3, 26.

[97] *Vitae Sanctorum Siculorum*, ii. 131–2; *Bibliotheca Sanctorum*, iv. 282–3.

[98] *Martirio di Santa Lucia: Vita di Santa Marina*, 83.

the Crusaders), and says almost nothing specific on Sicily in that period; indeed, a large part of the content is devoted to Marina's travels in the Holy Land.[99] Moreover, there is no other historical evidence for this saint or her cult prior to the production of the *bios*.

The best attested case of a saint definitely associated with this early period of Christian reconquest and consolidation is that of St Gerlandus. Originally from Besançon, he was recruited by Roger I who appointed him as first bishop (from 1092 until his death in 1104) of the revived see of Agrigento. Gerlandus found himself in the south-west of the island amidst large Muslim communities which would retain their numerical strength for most of the twelfth century.[100] Why he more than any other of his contemporary churchmen should have been later considered a saint is unclear. Unfortunately, evidence for the establishment of a cult as early as 1159 when Gerlandus' relics were allegedly translated by the ambitious bishop Gentilis of Agrigento (1154–71) remains unsubstantiated. However, Gerlandus appears as a saint in the mosaic cycles produced in the 1180s at Monreale where his location alongside St Marcianus of Syracuse, the founding father of the Sicilian Church, suggests, according to Sulamith Brodbeck's interpretation, that Gerlandus in turn was being portrayed as 'a new evangelizer'.[101] Greater evidence for the cult emerges mostly in the thirteenth century. A translation of Gerlandus' relics had occurred by 1219 and another in 1264, both corroborated by charter documentation.[102] In the same century a short biography of Gerlandus was included in the *Libellus de successione pontificum Agrigenti* in which the bishop was described as a saint.[103] Various charters from Agrigento in the thirteenth century also mention the feast day of St Gerlandus and commemorate his translation. The lack of other Sicilian saints from this early period of conquest and consolidation might offer another indication that religious tensions were relegated to the background, and that the strategies employed by the first generation of incoming churchmen were pragmatic and con- ciliatory – perhaps not the best ingredients for hagiographies and cults.

It is no exaggeration to say that the evidence relating to all of the other figures identified as new saints in twelfth-century Sicily is rather

---

[99] The first Latin bishop of Tripoli was Albert of St Erard (1104–10): B. Hamilton, *The Latin Church in the Crusader States* (London, 1980), 25.

[100] Malaterra, Bk IV.7, p. 89.

[101] Brodbeck, *Saints*, 126.

[102] *Più antiche carte dell'archivio capitolare di Agrigento*, no. 48 pp. 100–2, no. 74 pp. 148–50, no. 79 p. 173, no. 82 p. 178, no. 98 p. 222.

[103] The *libellus* is edited in *Più antiche carte dell'archivio capitolare di Agrigento*, 307; a short and problematic *vita*, *Translatio et Miracula B. Gerlandi Episcopi Agrigento*, was included in Gaetani's *Vitae Sanctorum Siculorum*, ii. 128.

unsatisfactory. In many cases specific dates are vague, biographical data minimal, evidence of miracle working limited and clear promotion of a cult appears to date from the Early Modern period. We are forced to rely on hagiographical texts, some of which are of late and uncertain provenance. Most were preserved only in Gaetani's *Vitae Sanctorum Siculorum*, from where some were copied into the *Acta sanctorum* series by the Bollandists. We encounter ephemeral figures such as Cosma of Palermo, who according to one tradition was sent as a missionary bishop to Africa by Roger I, although his date of death is given as 1160 by which point he had returned to Palermo. Another tradition claims he died in Africa and his relics were transferred to Sicily.[104] Most others were apparently a mix of monks and hermits, many based in north-east Sicily, the zone of heaviest Greek Christian settlement. Lawrence of Frazzano (near Messina) was a Greek monk who had spells in monasteries at Troina, at S. Filippo di Agira and at S. Filippo di Fragalà. He also spent time as a hermit on the slopes of Etna and restored a church in Calabria, all in the best tradition of the Italo-Greek saints. However, the church dedicated to this saint, and home to his relics, was built in Frazzano only in 1600.[105] Indicative of the problematic biographical data surrounding this group of Sicilian saints is the *vita* of a St Nicholas the Hermit which contains the standard hagiographic motifs found in many texts relating to earlier Italo-Greek saints: separation from kin and *patria*, solitary living on Etna, encounter with a demon and generic miracle working. The only chronological signpost provided, namely that Nicholas was born during the later part of Roger I's reign, seems to have led Gaetani to posit a date of death in 1167.[106] Even more challenging is the *vita* of a St Lucas Casali of Nicosia (north-eastern Sicily), a monk at S. Filippo di Agira who eventually became its abbot, who was a popular preacher who once miraculously made stones sing 'Amen', and who was buried in the monastery at Agira. Gaetani believed he died in 1164, other scholars claim he lived in the eighth century, and no certain evidence of his cult can be discerned before the late sixteenth century.[107] Of these twelfth-century eremitical monks, one of the more interesting appears to be St Silvester of Troina whom we have already met.[108] He apparently lived some time between c.1100 and c1180, and became a monk and then abbot of the Greek monastery of S. Michele di Troina. According to his *bios*, Silvester's charitable works and acts of

---

[104] *Vitae Sanctorum Siculorum*, ii. 144; *Bibliotheca Sanctorum*, iv.222.
[105] *Vitae Sanctorum Siculorum*, ii. 172–6; *Bibliotheca Sanctorum*, viii. 135.
[106] *Vitae Sanctorum Siculorum*, ii. 180.
[107] *Vitae Sanctorum Siculorum*, ii. 183–4; *Bibliotheca Sanctorum*, viii. 227–8.
[108] *Vita Sancti Silvestri*, 176–7.

healing established his reputation, and he visited the pope in Rome and healed the future King William II in his youth. We have already noted how Silvester appears to have been mentioned independently in the miracle collections (dating c.1130–c.1155) associated with St Agatha, where he made a miraculous journey to the saint's tomb.[109] Silvester's historicity is strengthened by this connection with Agatha and suggests that he was associated with saintliness while alive. Nevertheless, Silvester's cult only seems to have established itself firmly in the fifteenth century, when his body was rediscovered.[110]

The new Sicilian saints of the twelfth century are thus a shadowy group, defined by uncertain historical authenticity and minimal supporting evidence. The one positive distinguishing characteristic is the persistent association with Greek monastic/eremitical and saintly traditions which can be traced back to the pre-Muslim era on the island. At the very least this suggests the ongoing influence of Greek Christian monastic communities on Sicilian sanctity and hagiographical production in the twelfth century. Consequently, most of these saints originate from the north-eastern zone of the island; hence there is revealed in the renewed Sicilian sanctity of the Norman era an element of conservatism tied to centuries of tradition, which conversely through these same features chimed with the new reforming currents in the Western Church. The new demographic, religious and social transitions which were transforming Sicily do not appear to have produced new types of saint. The influx of Latin Christians and the emergence of a Latin Church did not lead to the emergence of new Latin saints of any prominence: the cults of Gerlandus, Rosalia of Palermo (see more later in this chapter) and possibly the Carmelite St Angelus (d. c.1220), who spent most of his life in Palestine but whose cult seems to have originated in Sicily, all seem to have been restricted or virtually non-existent in twelfth-century Sicily.[111] Furthermore, the hagiographies of these new saints offer little evidence that their subjects encountered Sicilian Muslims, in stark contrast to those of their ninth- and tenth-century saintly forerunners. Only brief references occur in the problematic *vitae* of St Chremes and of St Nicholas the Hermit to Roger I's victory over the Saracens, while St Gerlandus was said to have preached to Muslims.[112] This might be partially explained by the remote,

---

[109] *Epistola Mauritii*, 647.

[110] *Bibliotheca Sanctorum*, xi. 1074–5.

[111] L. Saggi, *S. Angelo di Sicilia* (Rome, 1962); again Angelo's *vita* is late, dating to the fourteenth or fifteenth century.

[112] *Vitae Sanctorum Siculorum*, ii. 128, 131, 180–2. Indeed, Gerlandus equally preached to Jews, and the Carmelite St Angelus allegedly converted 207 Jews at Palermo: *Vitae Sanctorum Siculorum*, ii. 196.

monastic settings, often in the Christian zones of the north-east, where most of these new saints operated. Indeed, barring St Gerlandus, and the revived cult of St Agatha, none of the new saints were explicitly associated with the island's urban communities in the twelfth century, probably because of the previous discontinuities in Christian urban life, and for the reason that communities were too ethnically and religiously mixed for any saints to be intrinsically identified with a city in its entirety. Thus, there was little opportunity for cults to establish popular, urban bases. Neither did any new Sicilian cult attain any real reputation beyond Sicily; it seems that the revival of St Agatha's at Catania cast all other cults into the shadows. It is certainly interesting to note that in the crusader states in the twelfth century, where a similar revival of the Church occurred in a landscape populated by varying Christian and non-Christian faiths, there was also a marked absence of new saints. Here, of course, any new cult faced the added challenge of competing with the Holy Sepulchre and any number of sacred biblical locations.

Aside from the works linked to St Agatha's return to Catania, new cults of 'old' Sicilian saints who were associated with the pre-Muslim era were not established during Norman rule. On mainland southern Italy cults of early medieval saints, such as Secundinus at Troia and St Cataldus of Taranto, who boasted no earlier firm evidence for their veneration, were effectively created in the eleventh century. Likewise, in the Duchy of Normandy the first evidence for a series of cults – for St Taurinus of Evreux, St Vigor of Bayeux, St Nicasius of Rouen and St Romanus of Rouen – appears in the eleventh century for saints who were claimed to have lived during Normandy's pre-911 past.[113] In Sicily, the eleventh- and twelfth-century use of the island's sacred past was more conservative, tending to build on devotion for pre-established cults of the Early Christian era such as St Agatha, St Lucy and St Marcianus, or on non-Sicilian universal saints. Indeed, the most popular church dedication in Norman Sicily was to the Virgin Mary, whose cult flourished in the twelfth century. Houses were established across the island in zones of Greek Christian (as in the Val Demone in the east), mixed-faith (as at the cathedral in Palermo) and Muslim settlement (as at Mazara in the west), while a mosaic at S. Maria di Monreale depicted Mary receiving the magnificent new cathedral from King William II.[114]

Palermo, the monarchy and national saints As the Kingdom of Sicily established itself as an efficient administrative state, the city of

---

[113] Herrick, *Imagining*, 4, 112–31.
[114] For Marian dedications see White, *Latin Monasticism*, 318–9.

Palermo gradually evolved into a royal capital of sorts. By the 1190s it was described by one contemporary as 'a city which deserves the unique privilege of rising above the entire kingdom'.[115] Palermo was the centre of royal power, the location of the main royal residence and of a cluster of royal pleasure complexes.[116] It was the centre of royal fiscal administration (the *diwan*) and the royal inner council (*familiares regis*).[117] The city was also home to some exquisitely decorated religious spaces, most notably the church of S. Maria dell'Ammariglio and the royal chapel (the Cappella Palatina), which served to articulate the Hauteville kings' ideals of sacral kingship. Thus Palermo itself expressed many facets of royal identity, mixing secular power and piety, and yet the kings did not elect to promote a Palermitan saint with royal associations who might have developed into a national saint, nor did any one saint emerge in the twelfth century as patron of the 'capital' city. The lack of initiative in this respect is at first glance unusual, for the kings were pioneers in so many other arenas of statecraft and cultural agenda, and the twelfth century saw monarchies begin to nurture, with local variations, the triangular relationship between kingship, royal city and national saint. The Capetian dynasty gradually established an increasingly fixed alliance with Paris and the cult of St Denis.[118] From the reign of Frederick Barbarossa (1155–90) the German monarchs promoted devotion to the Magi at the important city of Cologne as an expression of the cult of kingship, and supported the canonization of Charlemagne at Aachen to underline their imperial pretensions.[119]

Comparable developments failed to materialize in Palermo because of a range of factors. The city did not hold a prominent place in the history of sanctity, and even the most notable saints associated with Palermo carried problematic traditions or had their cult centres relocated elsewhere. The main patron saints of Palermo were Nympha, Olivia, Rosalia and Agatha, but the cults of the first three barely developed in the city before the thirteenth century and were truly established only in the Early Modern period. The virgin St Nympha was born at Palermo (possibly in the sixth

---

[115] By the anonymous author of 'A letter concerning the Sicilian tragedy to Peter, Treasurer of the Church of Palermo', in Liber de Regno, 172, and 177–86 for a description of the city (Tyrants, 254, and 258–62).
[116] Metcalfe, *Muslims of Medieval Italy*, 235–45.
[117] Takayama, *Administration*; Johns, *Arabic Administration*.
[118] G. M. Spiegel, *The Past as Text. The Theory and Practice of Medieval Historiography* (Baltimore, 1999), 138–62.
[119] On the Magi see especially H. Hofmann, *Die Heiligen Drei Könige. Zur Heiligenverehrung im kirchlichen, gesellschaftlichen und politischen Leben des Mittelalters* (Bonn, 1975); for comparative developments in Iberia see S. Barton, 'Patrons, pilgrims and the cult of saints in the medieval kingdom of León', *Pilgrimage Explored*, ed. J. Stopford (Woodbridge, 1999), 57–77.

century?) but, fleeing persecution in Sicily, she visited Rome and died nearby. Consequently her relics were venerated primarily at Rome, while fragments were later translated to the English abbeys of Glastonbury and Reading. Traces of her cult at Palermo are minimal before the relics were transferred there in the 1590s.[120] We have already seen in Chapter 1 the uncertainties surrounding the chronology of St Olivia's life, and again evidence for her cult at Palermo in the Central Middle Ages is restricted. An icon from the Palermitan church of S. Maria dell'Ammariglio, dating to the thirteenth century (possibly earlier), shows Olivia alongside St Rosalia and other saints, but further evidence for popular veneration is lacking, and the main texts associated with the cult date to the Late Middle Ages.[121]

St Rosalia would in fact eventually become the main patron saint of Palermo, but only in the Early Modern period, the era from which the main written sources appear to date.[122] These claim that Rosalia lived between c.1130 and c.1170, and had been the daughter of a leading noble Sicilian family, the Sinibaldi, who were related to the royal dynasty. Consequently, Rosalia spent time at the royal court and possibly served as maid to Queen Margaret (d.1183), before she decided to dedicate herself to God and a life of solitude. After some years practising eremitism she died in a cave in Monte Pellegrino overlooking Palermo. There are a number of problems surrounding these traditions, most notably the lack of evidence of a Sinibaldi family, and uncertainty over the exact nature of her religious practice. A thirteenth-century icon depicts her in the outfit of a Greek monk, although she seems to have been descended from a Norman family and was a rare case of an independent female hermit. There is a possibility that Rosalia might have been locally canonized by Archbishop Walter of Palermo (1169–91), while there is reference in 1196 to a tenement called 'Sancte Rosalee', but it was located in Calabria.[123] As we have already seen, an icon dating to the thirteenth century might suggest that her cult was established within approximately the century following her death, and churches dedicated to her are also attested in that century. However, Rosalia's great moment of fame suggests that the cult

[120] D. Bethell, 'The making of a twelfth-century relic collection', *Studies in Church History* 8 (1972), 61–72, at 69–70.

[121] G. Agnello, 'La S. Oliva di Palermo nella storia e nelle vicende del culto', *Archivio storico siciliano* 8 (1956), 151–93; *Bibliotheca Sanctorum*, ix. 1165–9; V. Noto, *Santa Rosalia* (Milan, 2008), 35.

[122] *De S. Rosalia virgine Panormitana* in *Vitae Sanctorum Siculorum*, ed. O. Gaetani (Palermo, 1657), ii. 147–65. For an overview see Noto, *Santa Rosalia*.

[123] *Constantiae Imperatricis et Reginae Siciliae Diplomata (1195–1198)*, ed. T. Kölzer, Codex Diplomaticus Regni Siciliae, Ser. II.i (2) (Cologne, 1983), no. 30 pp. 111–12; Noto, *Santa Rosalia*, 26, 36.

was far from popular prior to 1624 when her relics were rediscovered following a series of apparitions, and then used in a procession to save Palermo from a terrible plague. Indeed, St Rosalia should be added to the catalogue of new, but shadowy, Sicilian saints of the twelfth century. Like them her sanctity was defined by an attraction to the eremitic or monastic life, and her cult was not firmly established until some centuries later. Only St Agatha's cult offers discernible traces in twelfth-century Palermo, despite the uncertain tradition of her birth there. The quarter surrounding the gate of St Agatha, with the nearby church of Sant'Agatha la Pedata, offered a localized zone for the cult, but from 1126 onwards the saint was firmly aligned with Catania and there appears to have been no overt Palermitan counter-initiative. In short, the Norman monarchy did not have great material to work with if it had wanted to promote devotion for a Palermitan saint; traditions were patchy, relics transferred elsewhere, or the cult (in the case of Rosalia) was far too recent.

However, this in itself was not an insurmountable problem. The monarchy could have imported a saint's cult into the city through a relic translation. The famous *furta sacra* of St Nicholas by the Baresi provided a local example, and the arrival of the Magi at Cologne a more recent one. Relics do appear to have been collected within the royal complex at Palermo. Two side altars within the Cappella Palatina appear to have contained relics of Saints Barnabas, Philip, Sebastian and Stephen.[124] William II's mother, Margaret of Navarre, owned a hanging reliquary containing shards of the blood-soaked vestments of Thomas Becket, sent to her by Reginald, archbishop of Bath (1174–91).[125] It was also claimed that Emperor Henry VI, after conquering the kingdom, found a fragment of the True Cross among other relics in the Palermitan royal palace.[126] But overall, only small glimpses of relic movement into the capital are evident, and some were not necessarily driven by the monarchy. At some point in the mid-twelfth century part of St Cataldus' pastoral crook was transferred to Palermo, and a church built in his honour by Maio of Bari, a chief royal minister who was assassinated in 1160. Later, the saint would appear in the mosaic cycles of the Cappella Palatina and the cathedral at Monreale, both expressions

---

[124] Tronzo, *Cultures*, 91–92.
[125] *I Normanni, popolo d'Europa*, ed. D'Onofrio, 518 no. 329.
[126] A. Frolow, *La Relique de la vraie croix* (Paris, 1961), 352 no. 388. Perhaps among these were fragments of the relics of St Clement which Roger II requested from the monks of Casauria in 1140: *Chronicon Casauriense*, 889. According to another source an arm of St Agnes had been housed in the Cappella Palatina before it turned up at Mont St Michel, Normandy, in 1184: Bethell, 'Making of a twelfth-century relic collection', 70 n. 5; and in 1160 relics of St Christine were also brought to Palermo: Brodbeck, *Saints*, 42.

of royal piety and power.[127] It is unclear why Cataldus, more than any other cult situated in the kingdom, should have attracted the attention of the elite in Palermo. Also, Archbishop Alfanus of Capua donated the relics of the Campanian St Castrensis to King William II, probably in 1177, and the saint also features prominently in the Monreale mosaics.[128] Nevertheless, neither cult became notably popular within Palermo, nor attracted greater patronage from the monarchy.

This is not to say that the monarchy did not promote or cultivate links with saints. In a Sicilian, and specifically Palermitan, setting we can see this reflected in the magnificent decorative schemes of the Cappella Palatina (dating to c.1140–c.1160), and particularly at Monreale (in the 1180s) some five kilometres outside Palermo. In the latter case, Sulamith Brodbeck has recently analysed some of the political, diplomatic and propagandistic dimensions behind the appearance of saints in the decorative cycles.[129] A number of early northern European saints appear with greater prominence, in part linked to new foreign political relationships. From the mid-1170s the Sicilian monarchy moved closer to the Plantagenets, consolidated by the marriage in 1177 of William II to Joanna, sister of the future King Richard I. Thus, St Hilary of Poitiers, whose cult was centred in the territory of Eleanor of Aquitaine, mother of Joanna, appears in the mosaic decorations of Monreale. Also depicted at Monreale, and found in other South Italian liturgical texts, are other ancient saints who were primarily popular in the Anglo-Norman and French sphere: Lambert of Maastricht, Ursin of Bourges, Foy of Conques and Leodegarius of Autun, to name but a few. The earliest extant image of St Thomas Becket (canonized in 1173) is also located in the decorative programme at Monreale. Becket's early appearance here testifies to the close contacts with both the papal and Plantagenet courts – for he was adopted as a symbol of the struggle for ecclesiastical independence, but also, surprisingly, became a favoured royal saint of Henry II after the king completed his penance.[130] Furthermore, in line with the Sicilian rapprochement and marriage alliance with the previously hostile German Empire in the 1180s, new saints appeared in the Monreale decorations whose cult centres were based within the territories of the German Empire, including St Boniface of Mayence and St Odile of Alsace.

The differences between the decorative schemes at the Cappella Palatina and at Monreale suggest some revealing transitions across the

[127] Brodbeck, *Saints*, 152, 386–9; Demus, *Mosaics*, 327.
[128] Galdi, *Santi*, 186; Brodbeck, *Saints*, 160–1, 376–7.
[129] Brodbeck, *Saints*, especially, 85–115.
[130] Brodbeck, *Saints*, 95–8; F. Barlow, *Thomas Becket* (London, 1986), 251–75.

decades separating their creation. At Monreale, although the doctors of the Greek Church, eastern stylites and Byzantine holy warriors retain their centrality as they do in the Cappella Palatina, most of the saints are Latin from the early Christian period, and a number are associated with Benedictine monasticism or originated from northern Europe. As importantly, a sizeable number of the new saints added at Monreale come from southern Italy, particularly via Campanian channels (Ianuarius and Restituta from Naples, Germanus from Capua, Sabinus from Canosa, Cataldus from Taranto, Eleutherius from Troia, Cassius, Castrensis and Castus from Campania), and from Sicily itself (Marcianus from Syracuse, Euplus and Agatha from Catania, Gerlandus from Agrigento, the hermit Calogerus). The selection of saints at Monreale suggests a monarchy gradually turning away from the eastern Mediterranean and looking instead towards western Christendom, to conform and to promote rapprochement. But at the same time, the inclusion of more saints from the constituent parts of the Kingdom of Sicily does indicate that the monarchy attempted to cultivate a shared identity across the diverse territories under its control.[131]

Nevertheless, the Monreale mosaics show that no one South Italian saint was given special status by the monarchy. It could have 'adopted' a saint in a more abstract way that did not require a relic transfer, but which still carried great resonance, much like the Lombards did with St Michael the Archangel at Monte Gargano; but it did not. Similarly, it could have built on Bishop Maurice's attempts to present St Agatha as patron of Sicily, but again it did not. On the mainland the Norman rulers had been adept at displaying their piety through the promotion of cults, and at utilizing them to communicate power and legitimacy. In the twelfth century, the Sicilian kings certainly appreciated the multifaceted value of nurturing ties with saints' cults. Roger II, for example, could employ local saints as diplomatic vessels for reconciliation. Following Pope Innocent II's recognition of the Kingdom of Sicily in 1139, Roger was able to conduct a ceremonial entry into the city of Benevento, a papal enclave within the new realm, where he performed highly resonant symbolic acts at some of the city's main religious spaces associated with local cults: he prayed for his salvation in the church of St Bartholomew the Apostle, visited the monastery of Santa Sophia (with its celebrated relic collections) and prostrated himself before St Mercurius' altar.[132] A year later, when consolidating control in the Abruzzi, Roger cemented an alliance with the monastery of S. Clemente a Casauria with a charter of

[131] Brodbeck, *Saints*, 42–5, 70–84, 114, 145–57.
[132] Falco, 224.

protection, but also at the same time initiated a symbolic union by praising a painting of St Clement found above the altar, and requesting a fragment of the patron saint's relics. That these acts were important is confirmed by their entry in the monastery's chronicle.[133] The stability and protection provided by the new monarchy earned it the support of Casauria and its patron saint: in the 1180s King William II was portrayed on the abbey's bronze doors directly below St Clement.[134] The international promi- nence of St Nicholas, whose relics were brought to Bari during the Norman period, offered a particularly obvious candidate for royal prefer- ence. Dating from the 1130s, a rare image from Bari of Roger II depicts the king alongside St Nicholas, and the city's royal charter of privileges of 1132 protected the honour of the shrine. In a late-life wave of pious activity Roger II also invested heavily in the foundation of the church of St Nicholas at Messina.[135] Later, in the 1180s, William II undertook a pilgrimage to the Barese shrine.[136] The Sicilian monarchy displayed deep respect for the cult, but the interrelationship was rarely made explicit. Similarly, the distinctive ties between Robert Guiscard and St Matthew of Salerno were barely advanced by his royal descendants. Roger II donated a silver panel to the shrine but the Sicilian kings tended merely to articu- late their devotion to the saint in a formulaic manner when conferring privileges on the archbishopric of Salerno.[137] Indeed, in 1162 when William I threatened to punish Salerno for its involvement in a rebellion, one narrative source showed St Matthew in open opposition to the mon- archy, brewing up a storm that compelled the royal forces to withdraw from the city.[138]

The interrelationship between monarchs and saints was fraught with complexities: cults could bolster royal authority and power, but they could also be employed to attack and critique it. The nature of this double-edged sword was especially apparent in a handful of hagiograph- ical texts produced by promoters of shrine centres associated with con- temporary South Italian saints. We have already seen in the decade before the monarchy was created how Roger II's attitude to St Bartholomew of Simeri, as displayed in the saint's *bios*, was an equivocal one. Roger reluctantly agreed to condemn Bartholomew as a heretic, before a miracle

---

[133] *Chronicon Casauriense*, 889; Loud, *Latin Church*, 280.
[134] Bloch, *Monte Cassino*, i. 589–91.
[135] Romuald, 236.
[136] CDBV, no. 147.
[137] Romuald, 236; see King Tancred's donation in 1190: *Tancredi et Willelmi III Regum Diplomata*, ed. H. Zielinski, Codex Diplomaticus Regni *Siciliae*, Ser. I.v (Cologne, 1982), no. 1 pp. 4–5.
[138] Romuald, 251.

changed his mind and prompted Roger to enlist Bartholomew's counsel in the foundation of a major new Sicilian monastery at Messina.[139] In the *vita* of St John of Matera, officials of Roger II were depicted arresting and torturing a debtor, and the hagiographer's sympathies lay with Pope Innocent II, the rival to Pope Anacletus II who had Roger's backing. St John, after his death, intervened in the disagreement between the king and the monks of Pulsano over the nature of royal intervention in the election of John's successor, Abbot Jordan. In this episode, St John acted as a mediator facilitating compromise, and although the hagiography refers to Roger redeeming certain of his own 'excesses', it also portrays him as a guardian of the monastery.[140] Roger II also appears as a positive force in the *vita* of St William of Montevergine; at one point his rule on the mainland was portrayed as the antidote to endemic brigandage.[141] However, two episodes in the *vita* detail more ambiguous encounters between Roger II and William on the mainland. Both see Roger examine William's spiritual credentials.[142] On one occasion, the king apparently enlisted a prostitute, a standard hagiographical ruse, to tempt the saint. The trick was, of course, unsuccessful, and Roger thereafter held William in such high esteem that 'he did not cherish any other religious man in the kingdom more and he listened to him humbly and devotedly as if Peter the Apostle was speaking to him'. Indeed, the *vita* claimed Roger later founded a monastery at Palermo in St William's honour.[143] These encounters reveal underlying tensions which are eventually resolved positively. Importantly, both episodes appear to be the work of a later author, added to the text in c.1170. Thus their historicity is highly dubious, and they should be read as appeals from Montevergine for patronage and good conduct from the current king, William II.[144] Finally, the *vita* of St John of Tufara claimed that the monks of S. Matteo di Sculgola had to beseech King William three times, followed by the saint's intervention, before he confirmed the monastery's earlier privileges.[145] Collectively, these hagiographies are full of didactic messages and derivative hagiographical conventions, but they reveal the perceived importance of contact with the monarchy and how the ideal of royal protection needed to be balanced against the potential danger of too much secular intervention. In other words, the interrelationship between monarchy and saint had to be crafted

---

[139] Zaccagni, '*bios*', 267–70.
[140] *Vita S. Iohannis*, 44, 46, 49–50; Vuolo, 'Monachesimo', 107–11.
[141] *Vita et Obitus Sancti Guilielmi*, 10.
[142] *Vita et Obitus Sancti Guilielmi*, 26–29, 38–43.
[143] *Vita et Obitus Sancti Guilielmi*, 42–3.
[144] *Vita et Obitus Sancti Guilielmi*, xlix.
[145] Galdi, *Santi*, 65–6.

sensitively; any misunderstanding could be damaging to both. Indeed, while the widespread South Italian veneration for St Thomas Becket (see Chapter 2) might reflect attraction to the model of the 'reforming bishop', it could equally be interpreted as approval for resistance to royal authority.

Such sensitivities might explain why the kings appeared reluctant to identify any one saint too closely with the monarchy or with the kingdom, let alone the fact that in Palermo there were few suitable saints available. To show preference for one saint would have required settling on a defined identity for the king and his realm which might have alienated any number of the diverse groups found in southern Italy. It must be remembered that the kingdom was a new creation without precedent in southern Italy. Its legitimacy was disputed, its rulers potential usurpers, and its lands an amalgam of disparate political, socio-cultural and religious communities. The varied territories and communities within the kingdom claimed their own histories and traditions, and the monarchy notoriously absorbed traditions and cultural influences from a host of western and eastern sources. Creating one shared history, which electing a national saint would have threatened to do, was impracticable and potentially incendiary. South Italian historiography of the twelfth century markedly avoided confronting its awkward past and its complex present.[146] It operated a code of silence which circumvented the region's pre-Norman past, and focused instead on contemporary royal affairs rather than on contemporary socio-religious interactions. By contrast, the alliance of St Denis and the Capetians developed in the context of a shared past stretching back to Charlemagne, which was increasingly used to inform a present common French identity. Alternatively, it might be argued that the English monarchy failed to establish a prominent London-based or national cult before the thirteenth century, because the kingdom's legal and political identity was so cohesive, in stark contrast to Capetian France. The famous cult of Thomas Becket was always associated more with the ideal of freedom from lay oppression than with national identity, although Londoners did clearly adopt the cult by c.1200, and Henry III's personal promotion of the cult of Edward the Confessor in the thirteenth century moved it towards the status of a national cult.[147] Nevertheless, a truly national saint, deemed to protect the nation and reflect its identity, emerged in the form of St George only in the Later Middle Ages.[148] The Kingdom of

---

[146] T. S. Brown, 'The political use of the past in Norman Sicily', *Perceptions of the Past in Twelfth-Century Europe*, ed. P. Magdalino (London, 1992), 191–210.

[147] D. A. Carpenter, *The Reign of Henry III* (London, 1996), 427–59; D. Keene, 'London from the post-Roman period to 1300', *The Cambridge Urban History of Britain, Vol. I 600–1540*, ed. D. M. Palliser (Cambridge, 2000), 187–216, at 211–12.

[148] Good, *Cult of St George*.

Sicily could not easily look back nor could it expect to form a common 'national' identity in such a short time span, two factors which would have made promoting a national saint based at Palermo very problematic. The monarchy could not even do this for the island of Sicily alone, as Catania had stolen a march and presented St Agatha to the outside world as the protector of the island. Indeed, according to Roger of Howden, it would appear that Richard I presented Excalibur to King Tancred at Catania; an emotive symbol which could draw parallels with the French royal flag (the oriflamme) which was kept in the monastery of St Denis.[149]

In the Kingdom of Sicily 'royal sanctity, national loyalty, religious personality, and historical identity' could not be drawn together in the way Spiegel identified for Capetian France.[150] Perhaps the Norman kings did not want this in any case. Evidence for other royal strategies, in relation to the kingdom's religious minorities and mainland urban communities, suggests that they were willing to take a minimalist approach that allowed for de facto freedoms in return for the recognition of subservience to the crown.[151] The administrative superstructure of the kingdom was effective not because it was repressively controlling, but because it delegated and supervised power flexibly. This system provided the only real chance for cohesion across the kingdom, and a 'national' saint could have done little to enhance this further. The Norman kings had a theocratic understanding of their kingship, which may also have made them unwilling to present themselves symbolically as vassal to any saint (and, by extension, to the religious house in which the shrine was based). The famous mosaic image of King Roger II being crowned by Christ in the church of S. Maria dell'Ammariglio demonstrated the monarchy's ideology, influenced by Byzantine imperial practice, that its direct relationship with God allowed no room for intermediaries.[152] Consequently, we do not see a Palermitan equivalent of the Lombard relic-removal programme which created a sacred capital at Benevento, buttressed by the omnipotent protection of St Michael the Archangel. The challenges associated with the development of royally sponsored saints' cults at Palermo emerged out of past discontinuities, fluid identities in the present and the need for ongoing compromise, patterns which broadly defined the revival of sanctity in Sicily under the Normans.

---

[149] *Chronica*, iii. 97
[150] Spiegel, *Past as Text*, 162.
[151] See Metcalfe, *Muslims of Medieval Italy*, 102–8 and Oldfield, *City and Community*, chs. 3 and 4.
[152] Houben, *Roger II*, 113–15.

Part II

Pilgrimage

5   Bridge to salvation and entrance to the underworld: Southern Italy and international pilgrimage

The interplay between pilgrimage and southern Italy must be placed within the wider psychological and physical climate of the medieval world. How the region fitted into broader patterns of movement and was understood and experienced by external visitors carried important implications for local shrines, for the extent to which southern Italy was integrated into the universal community of Christendom and for stimulating cross-cultural interaction.

Southern Italy: a bridge to salvation

(i)   *Connecting Rome and Jerusalem*

Medieval pilgrimage was shaped by its start and end points, the two spots on the map which separated the pilgrim's home from his spiritual goal. However, it was the challenges and the symbolic acts that occurred in the spaces between, during the journey itself, which generated the core experience of pilgrimage. It was here that the individual truly became a pilgrim, metamorphosing into what Turner and Turner famously termed a 'liminoid' state, both psychologically and physically, as new landscapes were traversed.[1] The pilgrim both looked backwards to the 'roots' of Christian heritage and forwards to an eschatological destination; both were linked by the 'dynamic of journey', which framed pilgrimage in metaphorical 'death and rebirth'.[2] Philosophical and Christological traditions merged here alongside worldly realities. In the late twelfth century Alan of Lille's hexameter poem, the *Anticlaudianus*, offered a vivid account of the link between a spiritual journey and the creation of the 'perfected' man.[3]

---

[1] Turner and Turner, *Image and Pilgrimage*, 6–11.
[2] J. Inge, *A Christian Theology of Place* (Aldershot, 2003), 92–6. For further revisions of these themes see J. Eade and M. J. Sallnow (eds.), 'Introduction', *Contesting the Sacred. The Anthropology of Christian Pilgrimage* (London, 1991), 4–5, 23.
[3] Alan of Lille, *Anticlaudianus*, trans. J. J. Sheridan (Toronto, 1973), especially Bk. VII, pp. 173–88.

Furthermore, already from the late eleventh century many pilgrims/ Crusaders bound for Jerusalem undertook their journey in the spirit of 'Christomimesis' – the imitation of Christ – which could only have intensified the individual's transitory self-identity.[4] So too did the very real experience of detachment from homeland, kin group and an established status, as the pilgrim encountered unfamiliar territories, cultures and languages. All of these are important considerations for understanding the pilgrim's experience in alien lands.

The strategic setting of southern Italy was of central importance in drawing pilgrims to and through the region. It was located at the crossroads of the major commercial routes of the Mediterranean. Of equal significance, southern Italy also occupied an integral position in the 'Christianized topography' of medieval Christendom. Cult centres often emerged at key nodes of passage and communication – islands and peninsulas were thus endowed with particular sacred qualities. Many early eastern Christians who were subsequently considered saints allegedly sought refuge in southern Italy. Thus, from the early medieval period, southern Italy functioned as a fulcrum for movement around the Mediterranean Sea, which itself was seen as a 'medium of grace' for those on pilgrimage.[5] Without doubt, the cult centres of southern Italy represented the end points of many a foreign pilgrim's travels. From the Early Middle Ages distant visitors were specifically attracted to a number of shrines within the region, which carried appeal throughout Christendom. However, for even more pilgrims, southern Italy was experienced as part of that crucial transitional phase which created the penitential dimensions of a journey which had its destination elsewhere. In this context the passing pilgrim might have encountered South Italian shrines which thus served to build the spiritual anticipation en route to his transcendental final destination.

From at least a century before the commencement of the crusading movement, the practice of pilgrimage, particularly to Jerusalem, experienced a striking revival, and southern Italy and its maritime links were of central importance in the Christian pilgrimage network. Indeed, when the Norman rulers of southern Italy began to dominate the central Mediterranean shipping routes, freeing East–West transit from Muslim piracy, sea routes were safeguarded and then expanded upon by the North

---

[4] W. J. Purkis, *Crusading Spirituality in the Holy Land and Iberia c. 1095–c. 1187* (Woodbridge, 2008), 59–85.

[5] P. Horden and N. Purcell, *The Corrupting Sea. A Study of Mediterranean History* (Oxford, 2000), 438–52. Famed early medieval pilgrims such as the Anglo-Saxon Willibald ('The Hodoeporicon of St Willibald', in *The Anglo-Saxon Missionaries in Germany*, trans. and ed. C. H. Talbot (London, 1981), 160, 172) visited shrines in southern Italy.

Italian cities.[6] Furthermore, the rising popularity of the shrines at Rome, and the city's development as the headquarters of an increasingly assertive papacy, brought more visitors to the Italian peninsula who were often tempted to include South Italian shrines on their itineraries, as Abbot Suger of St Denis did in 1123; this was even more likely if they were continuing their journey on to the eastern Mediterranean.[7] Southern Italy thus functioned as an integral transit point for traffic en route to Rome and the Holy Land. This was intensified in the eleventh century by the increased instability of pilgrimage routes through Asia Minor, the growing naval power of Norman Italy and, from 1095, by the evolution of the crusading movement. Following the success of the First Crusade and the establishment of Christian territories in the Levant, southern Italy was the closest western European territory to the crusader states. Scores of pilgrims and Crusaders (technically armed pilgrims) passed through southern Italy, most notably during major expeditions such as the First and Third Crusades. While long-distance pilgrimage always remained in some senses a minority pursuit, certainly in comparison with short- and medium-distance pilgrimage, some regions experienced the former phenomenon with intensity, often because of their geographical location and earlier Christian traditions. Marcus Bull is certainly right to identify the greatest concentrations of pilgrim traffic in the later eleventh century as being in Gascony and Galicia, both routes running to Santiago de Compostela, and also in the northern approach roads to Rome.[8] Southern Italy should also be included here. By the twelfth century, long-distance pilgrim movement through the region became increasingly prevalent. The continuator of the Chronicle of William of Tyre, a key source on the crusader states, was in no doubt about the number of pilgrims involved when he recorded the impact of King William II of Sicily's preparations for a great naval assault on the Byzantine Empire in 1185. It was said that in recruiting his naval force the king 'retained the pilgrims from other lands who were passing through his territories. And so for two years he prevented the passage so that no one could cross to Outremer'. It was even suggested that this was responsible for the catastrophic Christian defeat by Saladin at Hattin in 1187.[9]

---

[6] See Stanton, *Norman Naval Operations*, especially chapter 4.

[7] Suger, *The Deeds of Louis the Fat*, trans. R. C. Cusimano and J. Moorhead (Washington, DC, 1992), ch. 27 p. 126; D. J. Birch, *Pilgrimage to Rome in the Middle Ages. Continuity and Change* (Woodbridge, 1998).

[8] M. Bull, *Knightly Piety and the Lay Response to the First Crusade. The Limousin and Gascony, c.970–c.1130* (Oxford, 1998), 234, 248.

[9] *La Continuation de Guillaume de Tyr (1184–1197)*, ed. M. Morgan (Paris, 1982), ch. 72 p. 82.

(ii)   South Italian routeways and itineraries

Many arrived in southern Italy from north of the Alps via Rome, usually travelling along the increasingly busy Via Francigena which linked the city to northern Europe. The Via Francigena then connected into the South Italian road system [see Map 2]. The eleventh-century French chronicler Adhemar of Chabannes noted the integral role of these South Italian routeways in the international pilgrimage network, naming one of them the Via Hierosolimae when reporting its disruption in c.1016 due to warfare between Normans and Byzantines in Apulia.[10] The pilgrim to Jerusalem could leave Rome and take either the Via Appia or Via Latina as far as Capua and (passing Montecassino) branch across the Apennines on the Appia or Via Traiana through Benevento, which functioned as a prominent crossroads. From there two main routes continued onwards, the Appia carried on via Venosa to Taranto and finally the port of Brindisi; the other ran along the Via Traiana (also known as the 'southern' Via Francigena) into northern Apulia, where at Troia an important intersection was located with the Via Peregrinorum leading to the shrine of St Michael the Archangel at Monte Gargano. The Traiana then continued down the coast passing a number of embarkation ports, including Trani, Bari, Brindisi and Otranto.[11] The Icelandic abbot Nikulas of Munkathvera seems to have taken a variation of the latter route when he travelled to Jerusalem in the 1150s, but also to have known about the former. He appears to have passed Capua, Montecassino and Benevento, before moving down the Apulian coast via Siponto, Barletta, Trani, Molfetta and Bari, whereas he also mentioned a second route passing Gaeta on the Tyrrhenian coast, Capua, Benevento, Monopoli and Brindisi.[12]

There was still another route through southern Italy, used mostly by those who had arrived from a western Mediterranean port. This usually entailed halts at Salerno and other settlements running down the Tyrrhenian and Calabrian coastlines, incorporating stretches of the Via Popillia which ran to Reggio in Calabria, and heading for Messina in Sicily and hence onwards into the eastern Mediterranean.[13] Indeed, one of the

---

[10] *Ademari Historiarum Libri III*, ed. G. Pertz, MGH SS iv (Hanover, 1841), Bk III, p. 140.

[11] R. Stopani, *La Via Francigena. Una strada europea nell'Italia del medioevo* (Florence, 1988), 29 n. 1; see also P. Dalena, *Dagli itinera ai percorsi: viaggiare nel mezzogiorno medievale* (Bari, 2003) and the same author's article, 'Percorsi e ricoveri di pellegrini nel mezzogiorno medievale', *Tra Roma e Gerusalemme*, ed. M. Oldoni, 3 vols (Salerno, 2005), i. 227–53.

[12] Extracts from Nikulas's travel diary are found in *Jerusalem Pilgrimage 1099–1185*, trans. J. Hill et al. (London, 1988), 215–16.

[13] The famous pilgrimage of the Anglo-Saxon St Willibald in the eighth century had already traversed a broadly equivalent southward itinerary from Rome: 'Hodoeporicon of St Willibald', 159–60.

origin narratives of the Norman arrival in southern Italy presented Norman pilgrims stopping at Salerno on their return from the Holy Sepulchre.[14] In other instances travellers sailed directly to Messina. Both routes usually involved a voyage through the dangerous Strait of Messina, which was, according to Charles Stanton, the principal 'choke-point' of the Mediterranean and one of the busiest waterways of the Middle Ages.[15] Messina with its excellent port facilities boomed. The medieval commentators Hugo Falcandus, Ibn Jubayr and Muhammad al-Idrisi all supply portraits of the city in the second half of the twelfth century which show it to be the meeting point of travellers and traders of all faiths, origins and backgrounds.[16] The crusading forces of Richard I and Philip Augustus both sailed from Marseilles to Messina in 1190, where they halted until spring 1191, but on Philip's return journey in October 1191 he opted for the land route across the South Italian peninsula, almost following in reverse the path taken by Nikulas of Munkathvera in the 1150s.[17] According to the account formerly attributed to Benedict of Peterborough and now believed instead to have been the work of Roger of Howden, the Capetian king landed at Otranto and his South Italian itinerary included, among others, Brindisi, Bari, Trani, Barletta, Troia, Benevento, Capua and Montecassino.[18] There existed therefore two primary routes to pass through southern Italy, with inevitable variations according to individual circumstances. In the mid-thirteenth century Matthew Paris's strip-map itinerary from London to the Holy Land via southern Italy provided vivid illustration of these two main routes. It created a visual image of southern Italy, and the port of Otranto in particular (to which the reader was guided by a special symbol and a picture of a boat), as a crucial stage in the passage to the Holy Land. It also confirmed the prominence of the other key route via the Strait of Messina, on which two boats were pointedly depicted.[19]

The majority of pilgrims/Crusaders who passed through southern Italy en route to the Holy Land did not leave precise itineraries, but many

---

[14] Amatus, Bk I.17–19, pp. 249–51.

[15] J. Pryor, *Geography, Technology, and War. Studies in the Maritime History of the Mediterranean 649–1571* (Cambridge, 1988), 7, 90–3; Stanton, *Norman Naval Operations*, 117, 180.

[16] Liber de Regno, 108 (Tyrants, 156); *The Travels of Ibn Jubayr*, trans. R. J. C. Broadhurst (London, 1952), 338–9; Idrisi, *La Première*, 312.

[17] For a detailed itinerary of Richard I's journey see *The Crusade of Richard Lion-Heart by Ambroise*, trans. M. J. Hubert (New York, 1941), Appendix B.

[18] *Gesta Regis Henrici Secundi Benedicti Abbatis*, ii. 227–8.

[19] D. K. Connolly, *The Maps of Matthew Paris. Medieval Journeys through Space, Time and Liturgy* (Woodbridge, 2009), 77–8, 84–6; Lewis, *Art of Matthew Paris*, 323–32, 346–7.

passed through one of the main Apulian ports.[20] The examples are too many to note more than the most high-profile cases: during the First Crusade the contingents led by Count Robert of Flanders sailed from Bari, while Duke Robert of Normandy and the chronicler Fulcher of Chartres eventually departed from Brindisi.[21] Commenting on the same expedition, Guibert of Nogent said that 'many journeyed to Brindisi, pathless Otranto accepted others, and the fishy waters of Bari welcomed still more'.[22] The English pilgrim Saewulf initially sailed to the Holy Land in 1102 from Monopoli before a storm forced a second embarkation at Brindisi, and he also noted ships leaving from Bari, Barletta, Siponto, Trani and Otranto.[23] On the Second Crusade, a large body of Louis VII's forces passed through Apulia and Brindisi, while during the Third Crusade Duke Leopold of Austria, and contingents from Cologne and the Lower Rhineland, also sailed from Brindisi.[24] Indeed, the volume of traffic had become so significant that in 1192 King Tancred of Sicily dispatched orders to the archbishop of Brindisi to look after overseas pilgrims ('de ultra marinis partibus') arriving at the port.[25] Already, in the 1170s, the Jewish traveller Benjamin of Tudela had reported crowds of pilgrims, bound for the Holy Land, congregating at the port of Trani.[26] In the other direction, Peter the Hermit's putative journey to Jerusalem prior to the First Crusade included a stop at Bari on the return leg, Earl Rögnvaldr of Orkney's return trip from Jerusalem in the mid-twelfth century saw him land in Apulia, and the port of Otranto received Philip Augustus on his return journey from the Holy Land in the 1190s.[27]

During the late eleventh and twelfth centuries the increasing significance of long-distance pilgrimage saw the development of more sophisticated

---

[20] For examples of the movement of individuals and groups through the region see F. Vanni, 'Itinerari, motivazioni e status dei pellegrini pregiubilari. Riflessioni e ipotesi alla luce di fonti e testimonianze del e sul meridione d'Italia', *Tra Roma e Gerusalemme*, ed. M. Oldoni, 3 vols (Salerno, 2005), i. 71–156.

[21] *The First Crusade. The Chronicle of Fulcher of Chartres and Other Source Materials*, trans. E. Peters (Philadephia, 1971), Bk I.7–8, pp. 60–1.

[22] Guibert de Nogent, *Dei Gesta per Francos*, ed. R. B. C. Huygens, Corpus Christianorum. Continuatio Mediaevalis 127 A (Turnhout, 1996), Bk II, p. 135.

[23] *Peregrinationes Tres: Saewulf, John of Würzburg, Theodericus*, ed. R. B. C. Huygens with study by J. H. Pryor, Corpus Christianorum. Continuatio Mediaevalis 139 (Sydney, 1994), 35–7, 59 lines 6–12.

[24] Odo of Deuil, *De Profectione Ludovici VII in Orientem*, ed. and trans. V. G. Berry (New York, 1948), Bk IV, pp. 68–9; *Die Chronik Ottos von St. Blasien und die Marbacher Annalen*, ed. and trans. F.-J. Schmale (Darmstadt, 1998), ch. 33 p. 94, and ch. 40 p. 121 for German pilgrims sailing from Brindisi and Siponto in the mid-1190s.

[25] *Codice diplomatico brindisino, vol. 1 (492–1299)*, ed. G-M. Monti (Trani, 1940), no. 29.

[26] *The Itinerary of Benjamin of Tudela*, trans. M. N. Adler (London, 1907), 66.

[27] Albert of Aachen, *Historia Ierosolimitana*, ed. and trans S. B. Edgington (Oxford, 2007), 6; *Icelandic Sagas, Vol. 3, The Orkneyingers' Saga*, trans. G. W. Dasent (London, 1894), 182.

overland travel and communication networks in southern Italy. The research of Dalena has revealed much on their structure and operation. From the late eleventh century hospitals, inns, bridges and religious houses appeared with increasing frequency along the region's key roads and on the approach routes to leading shrines, although it is often difficult to distinguish the precise functions of the various *xenodochia* and *hospitia* mentioned in the documentation.[28] The main hot spots for these services were the Capua and Benevento junctions, the northern Apulian inter-section between the Via Traiana and the Via Peregrinorum heading to Monte Gargano, and the major Apulian and Sicilian ports. The South Italian monastic revival played its part; the expansion of major monastic orders – Montecassino, Cava and Montevergine – from the mid-eleventh century to the early thirteenth saw the emergence of more monastic hospitals which provided shelter for pilgrims. The phenomenon was particularly profound in the region of Monte Gargano. Between 1098 and 1100, and therefore as the First Crusade climaxed, Count Henry of Monte Sant'Angelo built a hospital to receive pilgrims at Monte Sant'Angelo, on the slopes of Monte Gargano near to the sanctuary of St Michael the Archangel. It was later donated to Montecassino and bequests poured in for this pilgrim hospital.[29] A number of hospitals and monasteries appeared in the twelfth century along the Via Peregrinorum leading to Monte Gargano. At the emerging settlement of Foggia, between Troia and Monte Gargano, a hospice was recorded in 1125, while Spanish pilgrims almost certainly founded the monastery of S. Michele Arcangelo di Orsara in the first quarter of the twelfth century near to Troia; in 1159 its abbot received confirmation of the right to receive bequests from those (presumably including pilgrims) who had died in the monastery's hospital.[30] Still on the same route to Monte Gargano the monastery of S. Leonardo was founded near Siponto, or, more accurately, 'iuxta stratam peregrinorum inter Sipontum et Cabdelarium', probably in the first decade of the twelfth century.[31] S. Leonardo soon had an attached hospital and became a major land-owner in the Monte Gargano region.[32] St John of Matera founded in 1129

[28] Dalena, 'Percorsi e ricoveri', 227–53; and also generally Dalena, *Dagli itinera*.

[29] *Le colonie cassinesi in Capitanata*, ed. T. Leccisotti, 4 vols (Montecassino, 1937–57), ii. 2–32, nos. 5, 8, 13.

[30] R. Hiestand, 'S. Michele in Orsara. Un capitolo dei rapporti pugliesi – iberici nei secoli xii–xiii', *Archivio storico pugliese* 44 (1991), 67–79; *Chartes de Troia*, no. 76.

[31] *Regesto di S. Leonardo di Siponto*, ed. F. Camobreco (Rome, 1913), no. 6, see also no. 124 for a similar reference.

[32] H. Houben, '"Iuxta Stratam Peregrinorum": la canonica di S. Leonardo di Siponto (1127–1260)', *Rivista di storia della chiesa in Italia* 56 (2002), 323–48.

the monastery of S. Maria di Pulsano about nine kilometres south-west of Monte Sant'Angelo. It appears that part of the monastery's function was to receive pilgrims bound for the shrine on Monte Gargano.[33] By the twelfth century an additional route named the Via Sacra was established to the north of the Via Peregrinorum which passed a number of local churches and monasteries.

Already in the eleventh century at Montecassino itself Abbot Desiderius had built a vast hospital and guesthouse to accommodate the rising number of pilgrims visiting St Benedict's tomb, which for many was undoubtedly one stage on a longer itinerary.[34] The city of Capua, an important station on the pilgrimage routes south from Rome, boasted at least five hospitals by around 1200.[35] Capua's bridges spanning the Volturno also formed an integral component of those routes, and their value to pilgrimage was implicitly acknowledged by the bequest of a Capuan doctor in 1183 which provided funds 'for the poor and the maintenance of bridges'.[36] Indeed, Desiderius' *Dialogues* records a bishop 'ex Galliae partibus' who stayed in Capua on his journey to St Michael's shrine at Monte Gargano.[37] Given their more direct role at the vanguard of the travel, communication and supply routes to the crusader states, the major Apulian and Sicilian ports hosted a network of hospitals and inns. An 'ospitalium Sancti Nicolai' was recorded at Bari in a document of 1101 and by the 1130s it was referenced in a charter as the 'hospital of pilgrims ["hospitalis peregrinorum"] which is located in the city of Bari in the courtyard of the church of blessed Nicholas where his holy relics lay'.[38] Molfetta seems to have specialized in providing hospital care; a hospital attached to Santa Maria de Martiribus and the hospital of St James were found within its vicinity in the second half of the twelfth century, and possibly three more had been founded by 1200.[39] Also within these port cities, the military monastic orders – the Hospitallers, Templars and Teutonic Knights – and a number of Holy Land religious establishments

---

[33] *Vita S. Iohannis*, 40; Vuolo, 'Monachesimo', 74–5.
[34] 'xenodochium maximum ad susceptionem peregrinorum', Chron. Cas., Bk III.33, pp. 407–8. Another 'pilgrim hospital' was found at nearby San Germano.
[35] *Le pergamene normanne della Mater Ecclesia capuana (1091–1197)*, ed. G. Bova (Naples, 1996), nos. 12, 30, 33; *Le pergamene sveve della Mater Ecclesia capuana*, ed. G. Bova, 2 vols (Naples, 1998–9), ii. no. 8; *Le pergamene di Capua*, ed. J. Mazzoleni, 3 vols (Naples, 1957–8), i. 110–2 no. 52, ii. 22–4 no. 102; Oldfield, *City and Community*, 221 n. 258; Loud, *Latin Church*, 409.
[36] *Pergamene normanne*, no. 23.
[37] Desiderius, Bk II.10, pp. 1131–2.
[38] CDBV, nos. 34, 82; other charter references include nos. 83, 85, 88, 91.
[39] *Le carte di Molfetta (1076–1309)*, ed. F. Carabellese, Codice diplomatico barese VII (Bari, 1912), no. 102; Dalena, *Dagli itinera*, 157.

had by the late twelfth century built up a patrimony of dependencies, which included churches, land and pilgrim hospitals.[40]

It should be emphasized that southern Italy's connective role also extended to the maritime travel network. The traveller/pilgrim/Crusader arriving at a South Italian port could readily find local ships which were bound for the eastern Mediterranean. The region had established its own direct links with the Levant well before 1000; ships from the port cities of Amalfi, Gaeta and Bari were active there, and southern Italy's relative proximity to the eastern Mediterranean and the crusader states resulted in a range of interrelationships and cultural crossovers. Amalfitan kin groups were known to facilitate pilgrimage travel to the East and to offer shelter in hospitals which they had founded there.[41] As already noted, the rise of Norman naval power assisted the emergent commercial power of the North Italian maritime cities – Genoa, Pisa and Venice. All three steadily increased their presence in the ports of southern Italy in the Central Middle Ages, with the region becoming the nexus of their wider maritime activities in the Mediterranean. Venetian ships, for example, regularly included Apulia on a trading circuit which might also incorporate Acre and Alexandria.[42] The pilgrim travelling through southern Italy would have been able to utilize integrated, secure and well-informed local and North Italian shipping services.

(iii)   Protecting the pilgrim

As a result of such high levels of pilgrim, Crusader and commercial traffic, the port cities of Apulia flourished along with Messina in Sicily. The urban development of Barletta, for instance, was closely linked to the city's relationships with the Holy Land and its role as a European headquarters for a number of religious institutions based in the crusader states.[43] These cities increasingly hosted diverse and transient populations, and legislative activity emphasizes the growing need to address some of the consequences of rising pilgrimage traffic. In the twelfth

---

[40] See the articles by H. Houben and A. Luttrell in *Il mezzogiorno normanno-svevo e le crociate*, Atti delle XIV giornate normanno-sveve, Bari, 17–20 Ottobre 2000, ed. G. Musca (Bari, 2002), 251–88, 289–300; Loud, 'Norman Italy', 55–61. Dalena, 'Percorsi e ricoveri', 243–5, lists further hospitals along the Adriatic coast.

[41] Amatus, Bk VIII.3, pp. 480–3.

[42] *Documenti del commercio Veneziano nei secoli XI–XIII*, ed. R. Morozzo della Rocco and A. Lombardo, 2 vols (Rome, 1940), i. nos. 41, 63, 136, 306, 325, 397, 409–10, 437, ii. nos. 544, 569, 626.

[43] V. Pace, 'Echi della Terrasanta: Barletta e l'Oriente crociato', *Tra Roma e Gerusalemme*, ed. M. Oldoni, 3 vols (Salerno, 2005), ii. 393–408.

century agreements and customs recorded at Salerno, Troia, Benevento, Barletta and Brindisi, all sitting at important junctions, dealt variously with the protection of pilgrims, their burial and the execution of their wills if they died within these cities.[44] When in 1130 the South Italian mainland and the island of Sicily were incorporated into a new kingdom, a superstructure was created which theoretically offered greater security to foreign travellers. Roger II's chief apologist, the chronicler Alexander of Telese, depicted him protecting pilgrims on mainland southern Italy, who, he claimed, before his control of that area were subjected to robbery and assassination.[45] The hagiographer of St William of Montevergine also believed that the robbery of the saint while travelling through Apulia as a pilgrim occurred because Roger II – 'the exterminator of all evils and the best patron of peace and tranquillity' – had yet to establish his rule there.[46] Roger's legislative activities suggest that these literary portrayals were not entirely erroneous: in the 1130s he took all of the houses of the order of St John of Jerusalem, including its hospitals, important refuges for pilgrims, under special royal protection.[47] Similar to Alexander of Telese, the great Cluniac abbot Peter the Venerable's praise for Roger II's efforts to create security within his realm appears to be more than mere encomium.[48] Later, in 1178, William II went to great lengths to maintain the appearance of safe transit through his kingdom by the very public punishment of those found guilty of attacking Frederick Barbarossa's envoys as they passed through southern Italy.[49] Indeed, one chronicler claimed that during William II's reign, 'the traveller did not fear the robber's ambush, nor the sailor injury from pirates by sea'.[50] It is clear that the Sicilian monarchs understood that their status could be measured by their ability to provide security for foreign visitors.

---

[44] F. Giunta, 'Documenti su Salerno normanna', *Byzantino-Sicula II. Miscellanea di scritti in memoria di Giuseppe Rossi Taibbi* (Palermo, 1975), 277–83; *Chartes de Troia*, no. 50; *Le più antiche carte del capitolo della cattedrale di Benevento (668–1200)*, ed. A. Ciarelli, et al. (Rome, 2002), no. 89; *Tancredi*, no. 1 pp. 4–5; *Codice diplomatico brindisino*, nos. 26, 28.

[45] Al. Tel., Prologue, p. 3 and Bk I.21, pp. 18–9.

[46] *Vita et Obitus Sancti Guilielmi*, 10.

[47] *Rogerii II*, no. 43 pp. 119–23; that these 'houses' were visited by foreigners is clear from the clause in the document (at p. 122) relinquishing alms to the order which had been donated by 'indigenis aut alienigenis de universis provinciis venientibus'.

[48] *The Letters of Peter the Venerable*, ed. G. Constable, 2 vols (Cambridge, Mass., 1967), i. 330–3 no. 131.

[49] Romuald, p. 296.

[50] *Rycardi de Sancto Germano Notarii Chronica*, ed. C. A. Garufi, RIS 8 (i) (Bologna, 1937), 4.

(iv)   Salvation and pilgrim saints

Despite the monarchy's best efforts and the creation of suitable infra-structures, it is clear that internal security within the Kingdom of Sicily was not always guaranteed, and that pilgrims were taken advantage of.[51] Periods of civil war in the mid-twelfth century caused inevitable travel disruption; William of Tyre commented on the problematic effects of disorder in southern Italy in 1155–6 for travellers attempting to pass through the region.[52] The recurrent record of the vulnerability and death of pilgrims in the legislation demonstrates the ongoing hazardous nature of pilgrimage. Robbery, shipwreck and illness were ever present dangers, and no wonder pilgrims often travelled in groups.[53] St William of Vercelli cancelled his pilgrimage to Jerusalem after being attacked at Oria.[54] Moreover, many pilgrims sought cures for debilitating conditions, and therefore were least able to endure the rigours of medieval travel. One of the justifications presented by the *Adventus Sancti Nycolai* for the trans-fer of St Nicholas's patronage to Benevento was the depiction of pilgrims enduring a dangerous journey to a squalid Bari; a polemical tool no doubt, but one that carried impact because it was formed from a common experience of perilous travels and threatening, unfamiliar cities.[55] As will be seen, a number of recipients of healing acts in South Italian miracle collections were stricken pilgrims passing through the region, and the dissemination of this type of positive news served to promote the benefits of the South Italian route. Many others, however, did not survive their pilgrimage. The most high-profile of travellers were not spared; for instance Bishop Odo of Bayeux, half-brother of William the Conqueror, died in Palermo in 1097 while travelling to the East on the First Crusade. Unfortunately, only glimpses of the fate of the masses of low-ranking pilgrims were recorded. Fulcher of Chartres, for instance, witnessed the drowning of 400 pilgrims when a boat sank leaving the harbour at Brindisi on the First Crusade.[56]

---

[51] We have already noted that rulers conscripted pilgrims into their armies, something replicated in the crusader states. William II appears to have recruited many for his naval expedition against Byzantium in the 1180s, while Henry VI's invasion force was bolstered in the 1190s by German pilgrims moving through southern Italy.

[52] Guillaume de Tyr, *Chronique*, ed. R. B. C. Huygens, Corpus Christianorum. Continuatio Mediaevalis 63 A (Turnhout, 1986), 18.7, p. 819.

[53] Dalena, *Dagli itinera*, 119–39.

[54] *Vita et Obitus Sancti Guilielmi*, 10.

[55] Cangiano, 'Adventus', 149.

[56] *Ecclesiastical History*, v. Bk X, 208–10; iii Bk V, 166 records the death in Apulia of a young Norman knight heading for Jerusalem; *The First Crusade. The Chronicle of Fulcher of Chartres*, Bk I.8, pp. 60–1.

Some who faced death could at least have hoped that their endeavours had earned them salvation and a lasting reputation for piety. Fulcher reported that many of the dead bodies rescued at Brindisi were discovered with crosses imprinted on the skin of their shoulders, proof according to the chronicler that they 'had already by God's mercy obtained the peace of everlasting life'. Indeed, in 1162 the church of Santa Maria de Martiribus was founded near Molfetta 'where the bodies of the pilgrim martyrs of Christ lay', honouring those who had died while travelling through Apulia.[57] The perils of pilgrimage combined with southern Italy's centrality within the matrix of sacred journeying meant that the region became the point of a presumed eternal salvation for many pilgrims. The iconography within churches and manuscript illuminations contributed to a transcendental atmosphere. Indeed, the foundation and rebuilding of a number of cathedrals, along with the translation of relics within them, a phenomenon particularly marked in Apulia in the late eleventh and early twelfth centuries, might also be viewed in terms of its relationship to pilgrimage traffic. Many of these buildings, such as the cathedrals at Troia and Trani, were very close to major travel routes. It was undoubtedly desirable to attract greater numbers of visitors to enhance the prestige of a particular see or city, while these sanctuaries embedded within the pilgrim a deeper self-identity. Images of Christ often depicted him as a pilgrim on the path to eternal life.[58] Mola's work has revealed the presence of themes of salvation in the iconographic decoration of churches close to pilgrim routes, such as at Santa Maria delle Cerrate at Squinzano between Brindisi and Lecce, at S. Leonardo di Siponto on the Via Peregrinorum to Monte Gargano, and at S.Giovanni in Tumba at Monte Sant'Angelo itself. The choice of imagery appears to have deliberately targeted the pilgrim, just as church architecture in western Tuscany, which was located close to pilgrim routes heading for Jerusalem, was often adorned with sculpted lintels depicting the Mission of the Apostles and the Entry into Jerusalem.[59]

Furthermore, according to their hagiographical traditions some South Italian saints were originally foreign pilgrims who died unexpectedly in

---

[57] A hospital was later attached to this church, see L. M. De Palma, 'Santi martiri crociati? Storia e leggenda di un culto medievale', *Verso Gerusalemme: pellegrini, santuari, crociati tra X e XV secolo*, ed. F. Cardini et al. (Bergamo, 2000) available at www.enec.it/Verso Gerusalemme/08LUIGIMICHELEDEPALMA.pdf (accessed on 18 October 2011).

[58] M. Gargiulo, 'L'iconografia del pellegrino', *Tra Roma e Gerusalemme*, ed. M. Oldoni, 3 vols (Salerno, 2005), ii. 435–87.

[59] S. Mola, 'L'iconografia della salvezza sulle strade dei pellegrini', *Tra Roma e Gerusalemme*, ed. M. Oldoni, 3 vols (Salerno, 2005), ii. 489–527; D. F. Glass, *Portals, Pilgrimage and Crusade in Western Tuscany* (Princeton, 1997), 22–4, 57, 67.

the region. A consequence of southern Italy's connective role in international pilgrimage was its provision of a space to transform pilgrims into saints, who in turn augmented the map of South Italian shrines. This formed part of the increasingly standard 'hagiographic profile' which frequently incorporated travel to holy shrines within it.[60] In addition to its location on the Rome–Jerusalem axis, southern Italy also presented a dangerous landscape of fiery volcanoes, imposing mountains and treacherous seas, along with supernatural and non-Christian perils, an ideal cocktail of the sacred and the penitential for any aspiring saint. The Greek Nicholas the Pilgrim died at Trani in 1094 while undertaking a pilgrimage to Rome. His sanctity was acknowledged before the end of the century, and his shrine in Trani developed close associations with Holy Land pilgrimage traffic. St William of Vercelli had already visited the shrine of St James at Compostela by the time he passed through southern Italy in the early twelfth century heading for Jerusalem. While in the region, a fellow saint-in-the-making, John of Matera, encouraged him to remain where he was and adopt an eremitical existence. This William did, ultimately founding the great monastery of Montevergine near Avellino, and he was considered a saint almost immediately after his death in 1142.[61] Another example is offered by the monk Conrad of Bavaria, the son of the duke of Bavaria, who left the Cistercian house of Chiaravalle in controversial circumstances to visit the Holy Land. When he eventually returned to Europe he landed at Bari and visited St Nicholas's shrine. Conrad decided to assume the eremitical life and withdrew to a cave at Modugno (about ten kilometres inland from Bari) where he died soon after in 1154/5. Subsequently, at an unknown date, his saintly virtues were acknowledged and his body was transferred to the cathedral of Molfetta, perhaps because this port city enjoyed greater exposure to pilgrim and commercial traffic than Modugno.[62]

Some of the traditions of these pilgrim saints are late, confused or ambiguous. Such problems surround the figure of Bernerio, an Iberian wandering hermit, who wanted to see the major shrines, visited Rome and then stopped at Eboli just south of Salerno where he undertook a life of penitence and prayer in a cave. After his death, possibly in the late twelfth century, his body was buried in a church annexed to the monastery of S. Pietro in Eboli, where he was soon allegedly considered a saint.[63] The

---

[60] See A. Galdi, 'Pellegrinaggi e santità nelle tradizioni agiografiche', *Tra Roma e Gerusalemme*, ed. M. Oldoni, 3 vols (Salerno, 2005), i. 305–8.
[61] See Chapter 2.
[62] *Historia Welforum*, ed. E. König (Sigmaringen, 1978), 26, 28; L. M. De Palma, *San Corrado il Guelfo: indagine storico-agiografico* (Molfetta, 1996).
[63] *Vita S. Bernerii*, AS October, vii (Brussels, 1845), 1187–8; *Bibliotheca Sanctorum*, iii. 77.

contamination and blurring of hagiographical traditions is most conspicuous in the accounts of a group of putative English pilgrim saints who
were believed to have died in southern Italy, all within the northern zone
of Campania. Bernard of Arpino was claimed to have died in the region on
his return from Jerusalem in the twelfth century, and Folco of Aquino
similarly died there after visiting the Holy Land. Their legends seem to
have been mixed with those of Arduin of Ceprano, most likely a seventh-
century Anglo-Saxon pilgrim returning from Palestine, and of Gerard of
Gallinaro, a youth from Auvergne who died on his way to Jerusalem in the
early twelfth century, and who was rediscovered twenty-five years later by
a passing pilgrim who had received a vision while unwittingly sleeping on
his grave.[64] There are many other cases of alleged pilgrim saints in southern Italy, and while extracting fragments of reliable historical information
from this problematic material is difficult, the recurrent paradigm of the
holy pilgrim passing through southern Italy is a conspicuous one.

(v)   Pilgrim traffic

As a communication and service network evolved in southern Italy which
enabled and further stimulated pilgrimage traffic, it provided the tangible
counterpart to the metaphorical image of southern Italy as a bridge to
Christian salvation, a fundamental channel between the two great
Christian centres of Rome and Jerusalem. Nevertheless, some of the
South Italian shrines were already well known across Europe even before
the great resurgence of long-distance pilgrimage in the twelfth century.
This provided additional impetus for pilgrims to use the South Italian
'bridge', visiting and further enhancing the reputations of its main sacred
centres, while also as a by-product nurturing its smaller local cults. The
process of visiting shrines, and indeed resting at monastic houses, during a
pilgrimage played a crucial role. These breaks represented spiritual release
points which built towards the transcendental release at the final destination. South Italian shrines were thus boosted and given precious exposure
to a wider audience, while the region itself acted like a transformative
nucleus for international pilgrimage. In this context, a number of southern Italy's cult centres developed into classic roadside shrines, especially
those on or near to the two main routeways through the region. Evidence
from hagiographical works and from individual itineraries suggests that

---

[64] For these saints see: *Bibliotheca Sanctorum*, ii. 385–6, iii. 61–3, v. 955–6, vi.186–7; Galdi,
Santi, 66–92; St Cataldus of Taranto was also considered, in one dubious early modern
tradition, to have been an Irish pilgrim returning from Palestine in the Early Middle Ages
who settled at Taranto.

foreign travellers were conscious of the cult centres they were passing in southern Italy, and visited them, although often only the major shrines seemed worthy of record. Nikulas of Munkathvera, strangely, mentioned Montecassino and the presence of relics belonging to St Matthew without noting the presence of St Benedict. He also referred to the famous medical traditions of Salerno but not to the relics of St Matthew housed in the city cathedral. Nikulas did, however, record the shrine of St Michael at Monte Gargano and the presence of St Nicholas at Bari.[65] The itinerary followed by Philip Augustus and recorded by the Englishman Roger of Howden referenced the presence of three holy bodies: St Nicholas at Bari, St Bartholomew at Benevento and St Benedict at Montecassino.[66] It is hard to conceive that either party passed through the other settlements on their itinerary – including Trani, Troia, Capua and Messina – without encountering at least some of the local shrines. The same could be said of the pilgrims referred to by the Jewish traveller Benjamin of Tudela at Trani, 'where all the pilgrims gather to go to Jerusalem', and at Messina, at which 'most of the pilgrims assemble to cross over to Jerusalem, as this is the best crossing'.[67]

More explicit allusions to the magnetism of lesser South Italian shrines are provided in a range of hagiographical accounts. So recurrent is this theme, with its underlying tone of competition with other pilgrimage centres, that it must be considered a standard hagiographical motif; however, the material supplied suggests that the authors had no difficulty in finding relevant examples to construct this common theme.[68] The *miracula* in St Nicholas the Pilgrim's hagiographical dossier indicate that his shrine in the magnificent cathedral on the city's harbourside acted as a beacon to attract passing pilgrims, and was adorned by some of them with wax votives. Many of the saint's posthumous miracles saved pilgrim ships returning from the Holy Land. Other miracles recorded the healing of a man from Flanders who then continued his journey to Jerusalem, and told of a wealthy man from Gaul who went blind on his return journey from Jerusalem, was cured at Trani and vowed to build a church dedicated to St Nicholas the Pilgrim in his homeland.[69] The *Adventus Sancti Nycolai in Beneventum* represents an unapologetic attempt by Benevento to siphon off for its own civic shrines the pilgrimage traffic which was

---

[65] *Jerusalem Pilgrimage*, 215–16.

[66] *Gesta Regis Henrici Secundi Benedicti Abbatis*, ii. 227–8.

[67] *Itinerary of Benjamin of Tudela*, 66, 137. Arnold of Lübeck recorded many German Crusaders arriving at Messina in 1197 from where they would sail to Acre, *Arnoldi Chronica Slavorum*, Bk. V, p. 204.

[68] For more on using hagiographical texts to understand pilgrimage see Chapter 6.

[69] *Vita S. Nicolai Peregrini*, 241, 244–5; Oldfield, 'St Nicholas the Pilgrim', 175–6.

passing through the city heading for the shrine of St Nicholas at Bari.[70] The construction of the *miracula* in the translation account of St Agatha of Catania also indicates that the authors understood the significance for their shrine of tapping into the heavy concentration of pilgrimage movement at nearby Messina, and they provide sufficient evidence, alongside some chronicle accounts, to suggest that pilgrims did detour to Catania from Messina.[71] Isolated examples also occur for other lesser shrine centres. The *inventio* of St Secundinus of Troia, composed in the 1020s or 1030s, recorded a man from Aquitaine travelling to St Michael the Archangel's shrine at Monte Gargano, but, having heard of the 'fama sanctitatis venerabilis Christi famuli Secundini episcopi', he visited the saint's shrine at Troia where he was cured of his semi-paralytic condition.[72] Similar episodes were recorded at the shrine of St Cataldus at Taranto in a miracle collection of the mid-twelfth century: a Lombard returning from the Holy Sepulchre developed epilepsy while in the Apulian port of Monopoli, heard of the miracles of St Cataldus and was healed in Taranto; a master of the liberal arts from Gaul was returning from the Holy Land 'and other places' when he was saved in a shipwreck by invoking St Cataldus; and a German, who 'had sought the blessing of a cure throughout the earth without success', was cured of his physical deformity at St Cataldus' shrine.[73] The mid-twelfth-century image of St Cataldus found at the Church of the Nativity, Bethlehem, is quite probably connected to the movement of pilgrims to the Holy Land via Taranto.[74]

Comparisons can be made with other pilgrimage networks elsewhere in Europe. The continued popularity of the great cult centre at Santiago de Compostela was responsible for the success of some southern French shrine centres which were situated on the main routeways to Galicia. The development in the twelfth century of the renowned Marian cult at Rocamadour in south-west France owed much to its relationship with the pilgrim roads heading to Santiago, and superseded Rocamadour's own in-house saint, Amator, who was a rather less conspicuous figure on the Christian map of sanctity.[75] However, Cohen has demonstrated that the most enduringly successful within this group of southern French shrines were those located on the sections of routeways which also functioned as key trade routes and which continued to expose the shrines to visitors and

---

[70] For more see Chapter 2.
[71] For more see Chapter 4.
[72] D'Angelo, 'Inventio', 850.
[73] *Historia S. Cataldi*, 571, 573–4.
[74] Jotischky, *Perfection of Solitude*, 88.
[75] *The Miracles of Our Lady of Rocamadour*, trans. M. Bull (Woodbridge, 1999), 73–4.

their wealth after the decline of Santiago de Compostela.[76] The two main South Italian routes which formed part of the wider pilgrimage itinerary to the Holy Land were, at the same time, the key commercial and military arteries of the region. Conclusive evidence of this convergence can be found in 1194 as Henry VI's invasion force moved into southern Italy, and was reinforced by German pilgrims heading along the same routes towards the Holy Land.[77] The shrines that lay along them simultaneously tapped into fluctuating spiritual and economic flows, either of which could compensate for the loss of the other should it occur.

(vi)   *South Italian shrines within the topography of international pilgrimage*

In the framework of international pilgrimage movements, the prosperity of a number of southern Italy's shrines was associated with their passive role as roadside or subsidiary cults and, in the cases of the holy pilgrims cited earlier in this chapter, some actually originated in this context. However, southern Italy did also boast shrines of true international significance which attracted distant pilgrims, and which notably enriched the texture of southern Italy's sacred landscape. Certainly, in this context southern Italy could not call upon a body of travel and pilgrim literature to match the scope and ambition of the varied medieval guides to Rome, or of the *Liber Sancti Jacobi* which comprised a pilgrim guide and hagiographical and liturgical texts for visitors to the shrine of St James at Compostela.[78] But the quantity of pilgrim and commercial traffic passing through southern Italy would have disseminated oral accounts across Christendom, and a range of useful if often brief travel accounts and excerpts from other sources, such as those of Nikulas of Munkathvera and various crusading narratives, were also in circulation.[79] Some of those foreign pilgrims may have still been heading elsewhere, but in many cases it is reasonable to assume that an informed decision had been taken to include these more renowned South Italian shrines on their itineraries in advance, which may well have shaped the broader contours of their journey. The major shrine centres in southern Italy were St Matthew at

[76] E. Cohen, 'Roads and pilgrimage: a study in economic interaction', *SM* 21 (1980), 321–41.
[77] *Chronik Ottos von St. Blasien*, ch. 40 p. 121.
[78] See for example: Master Gregorius, *The Marvels of Rome*, ed. and trans. J. Osborne (Toronto, 1987); *Liber Sancti Jacobi. Codex Calixtinus*, vol. 1, ed. W. Muir Whitehill (Santiago de Compostela, 1944).
[79] J. Richard, *Les Récits de voyages et de pèlerinages*, Typologie des Sources du Moyen Âge Occidental 38 (Turnhout, 1981), shows that across western medieval Europe pilgrim and travel accounts were relatively rare and that most lacked detail.

Salerno (which revived notably after 1080), St Benedict at Montecassino, St Agatha at Catania (from 1126), St Nicholas at Bari (from 1087) and St Michael at Monte Gargano. Of course church dedications and listings in martyrologies and calendars existed across Europe for all these saints, proof of their international profile, but evidence indicates that foreign visitors also frequented their main cult centres in southern Italy on a regular basis and that awareness of these shrines' geographic coordinates was acutely present in the medieval European consciousness.

Admittedly, it is difficult to extricate the success of these South Italian shrines in their own right from the benefits which accrued to them from their proximity to the Rome, Constantinople and Holy Land pilgrimage itineraries. Montecassino and Bari sat directly on one main artery. The former was visited for example by Count Robert of Flanders, Duke Robert of Normandy and Count Hugh of Vermandois during the First Crusade expedition in 1096 when they commended themselves to St Benedict, whereas Gonario II of Torres, a ruler of one of Sardinia's five *guidicati* (kingdoms), visited Montecassino on his return from the Second Crusade and paid reverence to St Benedict.[80] We examine the nature of pilgrim influx into Bari in detail in the next section, but other shrines also benefited from their proximity to international pilgrimage channels. St Agatha's shrine at Catania clearly tapped into nearby Messina's pivotal position in the Mediterranean (for more see Chapter 4). Even St Michael the Archangel at Gargano only required a minor detour from the central routes along the branch road named the Via Peregrinorum. These shrines attained prominence on the Christian pilgrimage map, and indeed Bari was known across Europe simply as *portus Sancti Nicholai*.[81] We have already seen how many of these main South Italian sites were referenced in itineraries through the region. Their popularity was encapsulated by Abbot Suger of St Denis, who, having attended the First Lateran Council at Rome in 1123, subsequently visited all of these major shrines, except for St Agatha's whose relics were not yet *in situ*.[82] The fantastical itinerary of a twelfth-century pilgrim, recorded in the *miracula S. Enimiae*, included a visit to St Matthew's shrine at Salerno, which significantly took its place on this tour alongside some of the shrines which were most highly esteemed in western Europe, from Jerusalem, Bethlehem and Constantinople in the East to Rome, Venice, Paris, Tours and Santiago in the West.[83] In addition to such itineraries, legislative

---

[80] Chron. Cas., Bk IV.11, p. 476; Dormeier, *Montecassino*, 182.
[81] See, for example, *Gesta Regis Henrici Secundi Benedicti Abbatis*, ii. 206.
[82] Suger, *Deeds*, ch. 27 p. 126.
[83] C. Brünel, 'Vita, Inventio et Miracula Sanctae Enimiae', *AB* 57 (1939), 236–98.

decrees, miracle collections, and the presence of buildings and infrastructure connected to pilgrimage, a plethora of inferential evidence confirms the importance of several South Italian shrines beyond their localized orbits. As it had done in the Early Middle Ages, Montecassino continued to receive a multitude of foreign, often high-ranking visitors, as a result of both its eminent status in western monasticism and its political influence. In the eleventh century figures such as the emperors Henry II and Conrad II, the Church reformer Peter Damian and the Cluniac abbot Hugh all visited the monastery. In most of these cases, political, ecclesiastical and diplomatic business appears to have brought the individuals to the monastery, and although a visit to St Benedict's shrine is rarely mentioned explicitly it would be hard to conceive that these individuals failed to make such a visit.[84] In the case of Henry II a distinct connection was made with venerating the relics of St Benedict, when he was healed by the saint, and this was undoubtedly recorded by the monks of Montecassino as a weapon to ward off the rival claims of the French abbey of Fleury over Benedict's remains.[85]

Pilgrimage could be incorporated and subsumed within other activities, and often lost from record. At Montecassino this would seem to have been a particularly marked phenomenon. There is a surprisingly limited number of overt records of pilgrims such as the monk from Jerusalem who in the early eleventh century travelled to Montecassino on account of his reverence for St Benedict and donated a fragment of the cloth used by the Apostles to wash Christ's feet, or the Spanish brothers who, yearning for heaven, visited the home of St Benedict during the abbacy of Oderisius I (1087–1105) and donated a church which they had built in their homeland.[86] St Agatha's at Catania and St Matthew's at Salerno are perfect examples of shrines which clearly attracted foreign visitors, the evidence for which is, however, only indirect. Chapter 4 mapped the dissemination of St Agatha's cult onto an international platform through the combination of a series of exchanges between the shrine and Sicilian folklore, on the one hand, and Crusaders, foreigners resident on the island and merchants, on the other. Moreover, St Matthew's undoubtedly benefited

[84] Chron. Cas., Bk III.20, p. 386 for one of Peter Damian's visits; Desiderius, Bk I.9, pp. 1123–4 for a visit by Conrad II; the Montecassino Chronicle said of Hugh of Cluny's visit in 1083 that 'ad patris Benedicti limina valde devotus advenit', suggesting attendance at the shrine: Chron. Cas., Bk III.51, p. 433. Cowdrey, *Age of Abbot Desiderius*, 33.

[85] Chron. Cas., Bk II.43–4, pp. 247–52; Amatus, Bk I.28, pp. 257–8; Loud, 'Monastic miracles', 121–2.

[86] Chron. Cas., Bk II.33, pp. 229–30; Bk IV.92, p. 553. Peter the Deacon also included in his compilation of holy monks of Montecassino a certain Fortunatus from Spain who 'came to the body of St Benedict in order to undergo a pious conversion': *Petri Diaconi Ortus et Vita*, 75.

from Salerno's growing importance to Mediterranean trade and in particular from the commercial activities of Genoa and Pisa. Amatus of
Montecassino offered an anecdotal report of Prince Gisulf II of
Salerno's abuse of some Pisan merchants, revealing that the latter
believed that St Matthew had saved them from a storm in the waters
outside Salerno and in gratitude 'they went barefoot to the church of
St. Matthew [and] at the altar where lay his most holy body they placed
a cloth and a beautiful lamp, and they decorated the entire church'.[87]
Implicit within this account were the evident gains to be made from the
devotion and patronage of wealthy merchants who visited Salerno on their
trading circuit, and the likelihood that this type of encounter was far
from uncommon. It should be no surprise that church dedications to
St Matthew are attested in the port cities of Pisa and Genoa in the eleventh
and twelfth centuries.[88]

(vii)   Monte Gargano and Bari

Within the elite group of South Italian pilgrimage centres, two stand out
as the most popular on the international stage: St Michael the Archangel
on Monte Gargano and St Nicholas at Bari. Both fitted neatly into the
Rome–Jerusalem pilgrimage matrix. The early traditions of the shrine at
Monte Gargano were woven around ancient healing legends, apparitions
of St Michael and the saint's military prowess.[89] As Arnold suggests, the
emptiness of the Archangel's cave-shrine on Monte Gargano imitated
the 'truth of the Resurrection' and the Holy Sepulchre; thus at Gargano
'an eschatological Jerusalem' and a most powerful call for veneration
could be found.[90] The shrine was receiving Anglo-Saxon pilgrims as
early as the eighth century, its popularity subsequently spread throughout the Carolingian Empire, and by the tenth century it formed part of a
network of shrines dedicated to the saint, with key nodes in Normandy
(Mont-Saint-Michel), the western Pyrenees (Saint-Michel-de-Cuxa)
and Piemonte (S. Michele della Chiusa). It was accessible by the Via
Peregrinorum which branched eastwards off the Via Traiana at the
northern Apulian city of Troia. From the eleventh century evidence for
the popularity in western Christendom of long-distance pilgrimage is
more common, and Monte Gargano, already a renowned cult centre,

---

[87] Amatus, Bk VIII.4, pp. 483–4.
[88] Galdi, 'La diffusione del culto del santo patrono', 188–90.
[89] For more see Chapter 1 and also the articles collected in *Culte et pèlerinages*.
[90] J. C. Arnold, 'Arcadia becomes Jerusalem: angelic caverns and shrine conversions at
Monte Gargano', *Speculum* 75 (2000), 582–7.

certainly benefited from this revival. Furthermore, the shrine's popularity in the twelfth century was undoubtedly boosted by the crusading movement, although not as directly as the shrine of St Nicholas at Bari. Proof of the international dimensions of Monte Gargano's attraction is provided from a range of channels: inscriptions by distant travellers found within the grotto at Monte Gargano, iconographic decorations and church dedications spread across Europe and the increased use of St Michael in preaching material are but a few. William of Apulia's account of the Norman arrival in early eleventh-century southern Italy claimed that some Norman pilgrims 'had climbed to the summit of Monte Gargano, to you, Michael the Archangel, to fulfil a vow which they had made'; if it was a fictitious episode it was certainly symbolic of the shrine's international status.[91]

The influence of Mont-Saint-Michel in Normandy may explain, to a large extent, the presence of pilgrims arriving from the region of modern-day France. In the 1020s the abbot of St Michel of Verdun visited Monte Gargano, and the *Montecassino Chronicle* recorded the penitential journey of a virtuous bishop 'de Galliarum partibus', who might have been the same French pilgrim bishop referenced later by Abbot Desiderius in his *Dialogues*.[92] The *inventio* of St Secundinus of Troia, dating to the 1020s or 1030s, recorded a man from Aquitaine travelling to the Archangel's shrine 'as was the custom of that people', as did Godfrey Martel, count of Anjou, with his wife in 1046–7.[93] Leading figures of the medieval world visited Monte Gargano: German emperors such as Otto III in 999 and Lothar III in 1137, and popes such as Leo IX who journeyed 'ad oratorium Sancti Angeli' three times between 1049 and 1051.[94] We have already seen that twelfth-century travellers – Nikulas of Munkathvera, Philip Augustus and Abbot Suger of St Denis – included the shrine in their own itineraries. Even the compiler of the *Liber de Existencia Riveriarum et Forma Maris Nostri Mediterranei*, a Pisan maritime map dating to the late twelfth century, broke off from his navigational recording of commercial routes and coastal ports to note the location of the shrine of Monte Gargano.[95]

---

[91] Wil. Apulia, Bk. I, p. 98 lines 11–13.

[92] *Chronicon S. Michaelis Monasterii in pago Virdunensi*, ed. G. Waitz, MGH SS iv (Hanover, 1841), 82; *Chron. Cas.*, Bk II.55, p. 270; Desiderius, Bk II.10, pp. 1131–2. St Dominic of Sora also cured a Fulco the Frank en route to Monte Gargano: Howe, *Church Reform*, 120.

[93] D'Angelo, 'Inventio', 850; M. D'Arienzo, 'Il pellegrinaggio al Gargano tra XI e XVI secolo', in *Culte et pèlerinages*, ed. P. Bouet et al. (Rome, 2003), 219–44, at 223.

[94] *Vita S. Nili*, 314; *Die Reichschronik des Annalista Saxo*, ed. K. Nass, MGH SS xxxvii (Hanover, 2000), 606; O. Bertolini, 'Gli *Annales Beneventani*', BISIME 42 (1923), 136. Urban II (in 1093) and Alexander III (in 1177) also visited Monte Gargano.

[95] P. Gautier Dalchè, *Carte marine et portulan au XIIe siècle (Pise, circa 1200)*, (Rome, 1995), lines 1525–6 p. 155. Visitors from central and northern Italy were also notable: in the

Indeed, it was during the eleventh and twelfth centuries that a pilgrimage infrastructure of satellite hospitals and monasteries was established on the approach routes to the shrine, and a second major roadway called the Via Sacra was established to the north of the Via Peregrinorum. The establishment of this pilgrimage network was partly achieved through the South Italian monastic revival, but also by the control exerted over this zone of southern Italy by the dukes of Apulia in the early twelfth century and the concomitant cultivation of the vast Tavoliere plain to the west of the Gargano peninsula.[96]

A compelling sign of the esteemed status of St Michael's shrine at Monte Gargano is its appearance in several *vitae* (from outside southern Italy), in which it is visited by a saint. In c.1050, St Gerard of Corbie visited Rome, Montecassino and Monte Gargano (and later appears to have travelled to Jerusalem), while around a century later the hermit saint Albert of Sens

went to the churches of the holy apostles at Rome, then took himself to Apulia to visit the temple of St Michael located on Monte Gargano; finally he saw the relics of St Mark at Venice. Then he sailed to Palestine.

Albert's hagiographer recorded a subsequent visit to St James at Compostela and therefore placed the Gargano shrine within an itinerary of Christendom's top-ranking pilgrim sites.[97] Similarly, towards the end of our period, Saint Bona of Pisa (1115–1207) undertook a life of perpetual pilgrimage, the main staging posts of which were Monte Gargano, Rome, the Holy Land and Compostela, whereas the theologian St Martin of Léon (d. 1203) travelled from Compostela to Rome, Monte Gargano, St Nicholas at Bari and then onwards to the Holy Land.[98]

Further south in Apulia, the cult centre of St Nicholas at Bari, a city located on the Via Traiana, flourished from the moment of the translation of 1087. Bari thereafter rapidly rivalled Monte Gargano in attracting international pilgrims to southern Italy. Soon the translation was being recorded in historical accounts all across medieval Christendom and the

---

twelfth century a Popino of Poppi in Tuscany visited Monte Gargano twice, as well as the shrines at Rome twice and Santiago once. Also from Tuscany, all the *burgenses* of San Qurico d'Orcia undertook a collective pilgrimage to Monte Gargano in c.1124: G. Cherubini, 'Una nota sui tempi di viaggio dei pellegrini', *Studi in onore di Giosuè Musca*, ed. C. D. Fonseca and V. Sivo (Bari, 2000), 105–15.

[96] Martin, 'Les Normands', 356–8; J.-M. Martin, *Foggia nel medioevo* (Rome, 1998), 29–53.
[97] *Vita S. Geraldi Abbatis*, AS April, i (Paris, 1866), 414–15; see also Bull, *Knightly Piety*, 128–34; *De B. Alberto Eremita in Territorio Senensi*, AS January, i (Paris, 1863), 402.
[98] A. Vauchez, 'Du Gargano à Compostelle: la sainte pelerine Bona de Pise (v. 1115–1207)', *Puer Apuliae*, ed. E. Cuozzo et al., 2 vols (Paris, 2008), ii. 737–43; *Vita Beati Martini Legionensis*, Patrologia Latina 208 (Paris, 1855), 213.

label *portus Sancti Nicholai* was adopted as a synonym for Bari.[99] A separate study would be required to track the spread of St Nicholas's cult across medieval Europe in its entirety but, in summary, the saint's wider popularity beyond the bounds of southern Italy owed a great deal to monastic networks and to his relocation to one of the major ports on the Adriatic which sat on an expanding commercial and pilgrimage route.[100] In the decades following the translation of 1087 the mercantile cities of Genoa and Venice coveted and claimed (in the latter's case) ownership of the remains of St Nicholas. A range of attempted relic thefts, some allegedly successful, also saw minor cult centres emerge across Europe, particularly in northern France. There was also a marked increase in church dedications to St Nicholas. We know, for example, that the viscount of Turenne, in the Limousin, ordered a church to be dedicated to St Nicholas in 1091, by which point he himself (or a close associate) had apparently undertaken a pilgrimage to Bari.[101] Alison Binns's study on dedications of monastic houses in medieval England and Wales illuminates not only the spread of Nicholas's cult to the further reaches of Europe, but also the mechanics of this dissemination.[102] Nicholas's cult was established in England before 1087, as evidenced for instance by the presence of a relic at Exeter, and monastic dedications in England and Wales between 1066 and 1216 indicate that Nicholas's popularity continued to grow. Among the identifiable monastic dedications, Nicholas was the sixth most popular saint, numbering sixteen dedications in total, which made him the 'most popular non-biblical patron-saint of monastic houses' in the region during that period. In some cases a monastic dedication to Nicholas, as at Pembroke and Spalding, can be seen to be influenced by the particular house's subordination to a continental monastery with more direct ties to the cult of Nicholas. Pembroke was given to the abbot of Sées who had been present in 1092 at the donation of an alleged relic of Nicholas to the monastery at Noron, while Spalding was a dependant of the monastery of St Nicholas at Angers, which had been founded by Fulk Nerra and was destined to become an important centre for the saint's cult. Exchange networks transmitted devotional trends

---

[99] As early as the first quarter of the twelfth century the chronicler *Albert of Aachen* (p. 824) was calling Bari 'civitatem beati Nicolai'.

[100] C. W. Jones, *Saint Nicholas of Myra, Bari and Manhattan. Biography of a Legend* (Chicago, 1978), offers a broad examination; G. Cioffari, *Storia della basilica di S. Nicola di Bari. I. L'epoca normanno- sveva* (Bari, 1984) provides useful material on the medieval cult.

[101] Bull, *Knightly Piety*, 214–5.

[102] A. Binns, *Dedications of Monastic Houses in England and Wales, 1066–1216* (Woodbridge, 1989), especially 18–39.

across Europe, and the monastic one was perhaps the most effective channel of all, especially when it involved the movement of liturgical texts between houses.

To understand fully its prominence on the map of international pilgrimage, a few further examples of the geographic range of St Nicholas's cult will suffice. Orderic Vitalis' record of attempted thefts of Nicholas's relics suggests that the cult's renown was firmly rooted in northern France, and this is confirmed by the twelfth-century collection of *miracula* attributed to the saint, which was compiled by a monk of Bec and situated the miracle working mostly in and around the vicinity of the abbey.[103] The twelfth-century *Vita Wulfstani* by the English chronicler William of Malmesbury equated Bishop Wulfstan of Worcester's miraculous saving of a ship bound for Ireland with the works of St Nicholas, and interestingly attempted to promote St Wulfstan's renown by implying its dissemination to the major centres of the Christian world, which were listed as Rome, Bari and Jerusalem. In addition, the *Portiforium* of Wulfstan, dated between 1062 and 1092, added the foreign saints Jerome, Martin and Nicholas into the English catalogue of saints.[104] In the early thirteenth century, the Cistercian monk Caesarius of Heisterbach compiled his *Dialogue on Miracles*, a collection of homiletic *exempla* for novices in his monastic house based near Bonn in the Rhineland, in which the cult of St Nicholas features frequently. Some of the exemplars record the celebration of St Nicholas's feast day, and churches dedicated to him at Cologne and Lübeck; others show the saint performing a range of miracles, often for individuals who harboured a special devotion for Nicholas.[105] He is associated with the saving of a ship from a piratical raid on the Rhine, an image of the saint in a monastery near Aix-la-Chapelle was believed to have curative powers, and he was also credited with the healing of a sick boy in Saxony and the saving of a thief from the gallows near Cologne.[106] This is not to deny that other saints feature in the works by William of Malmesbury and Caesarius of Heisterbach, but St Nicholas is certainly positioned among the main cast of Christian saints. In the *Dialogue on Miracles* one story concluded with a priest of the region of Gröningen stating 'I hold

[103] *Ecclesiastical History*, iv. 4 Bk VII 70–2; A. Poncelet, 'Miracula Sancti Nicolai a Monacho Beccensi', *Catalogus Codicum Hagiographicorum Latinorum Bibliotheca Nationali Parisiensi*, vol. 2 (1890), 405–32.

[104] *The Vita Wulfstani of William of Malmesbury*, ed. R. R. Darlington, Camden third series 40 (London, 1928), 60, 90; Binns, *Dedications of Monastic Houses*, 24.

[105] Caesarius of Heisterbach, *The Dialogue on Miracles*, trans. H. von E. Scott and C. C. Swinton Bland (London, 1929), vol. 1 Bk V.27, p. 355, Bk VI.8, p. 414, Bk VII.46, p. 530.

[106] Caesarius, vol. 1 Bk VII.38, pp. 515–6; vol. 2 Bk VIII.72–6, pp. 73–7, Bk XI.45, p. 275.

St Nicholas the equal of many of the apostles', and another claimed that 'St. Nicholas is represented in churches both in sculpture and in pictures more frequently than any other pontiff'.[107] We certainly should not dismiss Caesarius' material because it is framed within *miracula* and moralizing *exempla*; historical relevance was a vital ingredient within both these literary genres, employed to elucidate the meaning of the fantastic and didactic elements of their content for the audience. Indeed, evidence in the Later Middle Ages from the Low Countries, a region covered in Caesarius' *exempla*, shows that St Nicholas's shrine at Bari was one of the main destinations for pilgrimages imposed as judicial punishments.[108] Although Nicholas's cult already had a popular base across Europe before 1087, subsequent developments in commercial and monastic networks, alongside the emergence of crusading, aided the deeper diffusion of Nicholas's cult far beyond southern Italy.

Such wide renown brought an influx of visitors and pilgrims to Bari. As at Monte Gargano, the records show a heavy preponderance from the area of modern-day France. Perhaps this could be attributed to links with the Normans in southern Italy, and could also confirm a marked proclivity among people of France to go on crusade. The Anglo-Norman monk Orderic Vitalis, who included in his *Ecclesiastical History* an abbreviated version of John the Archdeacon of Bari's account of the translation of 1087, recorded the theft of an arm of St Nicholas by a monk from the monastery dedicated to the saint at Angers and that of a tooth by a knight from Normandy, which allegedly found its way to a church at Noron in northern France.[109] The *Adventus Sancti Nycolai in Beneventum*, dating probably from the late eleventh century, recorded groups of pilgrims, including *transalpini*, passing through Benevento for Bari.[110] Of greater significance is the collection of miracles attributed to St Nicholas which was compiled by a monk of the abbey of Bec in Normandy and which not only reveals St Nicholas's popularity in northern France, where many of the miracles were worked, but also a network of movement and information linking the abbey and its world to Bari and the Mediterranean.[111] Some of the miracles were recounted by eye-witnesses who were present in Bari, who were all pilgrims and presumably visited St Nicholas's shrine in the process. The account of three ships heading for Jerusalem in 1136

[107] Caesarius, vol. 1 Bk VII. 46, p. 530; vol. 2 Bk VIII.75, p. 76.
[108] Van Herwaarden, 'Pilgrimages and social prestige. Some reflections on a theme', *Wallfahrt und Alltag in Mittelalter und früher Neuzeit*, ed. G. Jaritz and B. Schuh (Vienna, 1992), 27–79, at 34–5.
[109] *Ecclesiastical History*, iv. Bk VII, 54–70, 70–2.
[110] Cangiano, 'Adventus', 149–50.
[111] Poncelet, 'Miracula', 405–32.

which were saved from a storm by the saint and guided safely to Bari was told by one of the passengers who later became a monk.[112] The author from Bec learned of the healing of a blind pilgrim at Bari from an Anglo-Norman monk named Alboldo who was in the city at the time when 'the Christian nations began the journey to Jerusalem', that is during the First Crusade.[113] A failed attempt to steal some of St Nicholas's relics in the 1120s was reported by a certain Rainerius who was in Bari returning 'from the path to Jerusalem', while another miracle, dated to 1129, was related by Abraham, a cleric of the diocese of Rouen.[114]

In many cases it is not possible to know if the pilgrim's end destination was Bari, or whether the shrine fitted into a wider pilgrimage; but certainly a large proportion of the pilgrimage movement to Bari was linked to Jerusalem or a Crusade, as the preceding miracles recorded at Bec suggest. Because the translation of St Nicholas to Bari took place so close to the beginning of the crusading movement, and the two events are so complementary on a number of levels, it is difficult to measure the international popularity of the shrine in isolation from the Crusades. Furthermore, while some foreign pilgrims might have visited the shrine in the period 1087 to 1095, pilgrimage to Jerusalem was already popular by this stage; this only complicates any attempts to differentiate pilgrim types at Bari. Certainly the contemporary accounts of St Nicholas's translation, written before 1090 by John the Archdeacon and Nicephorus, record, with but a few exceptions, a host of South Italians as the main initial group to visit the relics. The early promotion of the cult at Bari clearly required focus to be placed on Nicholas's relationship with his new South Italian home which seems to have overruled the need at this stage to advertise the saint's broader, pre-established popularity across Europe.[115]

It is only with the commencing of the Crusades that we are on firmer ground in identifying foreign visitors to Bari, but still a number of cases do not make explicit reference to a visit to St Nicholas's shrine. It would appear, however, that the shrine's popularity was already on an upward trajectory which was then boosted by the international character of crusading. These two combined developments probably explain the absence in the twelfth century of new hagiographical sources and *miracula* composed by the guardians of the cult in Bari. The cult had evidently attained universal appeal and did not need further reinforcing, which does unfortunately mean that we must rely only on scattered references

---

[112] Poncelet, 'Miracula', 405.
[113] Poncelet, 'Miracula', no. 26 p. 422.
[114] Poncelet, 'Miracula', nos. 27, pp. 422–3 and 31 pp. 425–7.
[115] For more on this see Chapter 6.

throughout a range of sources across Europe to track pilgrim movement to the shrine. Peter the Hermit's possibly apocryphal journey to Jerusalem prior to the First Crusade included a stop at Bari on the return leg, and it is from among the ranks of the First Crusaders that we can locate with authority some of the earliest known foreign pilgrims to the shrine.[116] The contingent including Duke Robert of Normandy, Count Robert of Flanders and the chronicler Fulcher of Chartres reached Bari, where they visited the church of St Nicholas and 'prayed to God effusively'.[117] Other First Crusade commentators, such as Guibert of Nogent, noted Bari among the Apulian embarkation ports chosen by the First Crusaders.[118] Thereafter, contingents from all the major Crusade expeditions of the twelfth century, and a constant stream of pilgrims bound for Jerusalem, such as the Englishman Saewulf in 1102, the Spaniard St Teotonio of Coimbra in 1130 and the Icelander Nikulas of Munkathvera in the 1150s, passed through, or recorded, Bari on their itineraries.[119] Services and accommodation were adapted in the city to cater for a new transient population. The basilica housing St Nicholas's relics was reconstructed to provide passageways and spaces suitable for large crowds of visitors, and it is from the 1130s that the first documented evidence appears of a 'hospitalis peregrinorum' at Bari.[120] Both Monte Gargano and Bari clearly operated in an international setting; much of the evidence for this however is surprisingly inferential and sporadic. For example, Anselm of Canterbury participated in the papal council held by Urban II in 1098 at Bari and advertised as being 'before the body of St Nicholas'; the implication must be that the participants also worshipped at St Nicholas's shrine.[121] There is also a marked paucity of charter evidence in the form of bequests to either shrine, which would provide unambiguous testimony to the presence and motivations of foreign pilgrims. A rare exception is a revealing charter of 1189 in which a group of German pilgrims heading for the Holy Land to assist in the recovery of the Holy Sepulchre made a bequest to the church of S. Nicola. Count Bertold, his son Henry and four other companions, described as 'teotonici et peregrini', declared themselves ready to sail on a ship belonging to the church of S. Nicola, which was destined for 'the Holy Sepulchre in Jerusalem which because of our sins is now controlled

[116] Albert of Aachen, p. 6.
[117] *The First Crusade. The Chronicle of Fulcher of Chartres*, Bk I.7, p. 60.
[118] Guibert de Nogent, Bk II, p. 135.
[119] *Peregrinationes Tres*, 35–7, 59 lines 6–12; *Vita S. Teotonio*, AS February, iii (Paris, 1865), 108–22.
[120] CDBV, no. 82.
[121] *Eadmer's Historia*, 108–14.

by a pagan race'. They donated to the church of S. Nicola forty-four olive trees which they had purchased in the territory of Bari, made confession at St Nicholas's altar, and asked in return for a candle to be lit permanently before the altar on their behalf.[122]

Southern Italy: entrance to the Underworld

Logistically and spiritually, southern Italy and its shrines occupied a prominent place within the Christian topography of pilgrimage. Its dual importance lay in connecting major international pilgrimage centres while also offering its own array of shrines for the foreign pilgrim to attend. These local shrines, and especially those with established international reputations, were integral to the pilgrim's spiritual experience while travelling. But pilgrimage itself proposed the dichotomy of the joy in redeeming sins and the need to suffer to obtain that redemption. Southern Italy's geographic setting and its own shrines assisted in the path towards salvation, and as penitential pilgrimage functioned most effectively at sites which were liminal and hazardous, they offered an environment in which the crucial penitential element of the pilgrimage could be performed.[123] The dangers inherent in medieval travel provided the tangible framework for the sacrifice necessary for redemption. Jacques de Vitry, one of the greatest preachers of the thirteenth century, emphasized the spiritual rewards gained through the ordeals of pilgrimage.[124] We have already encountered some of these hazards: roadside attacks and the need to legislate for the protection of pilgrims, shipwreck, and the omnipresent prospect of illness and death. Charter records demonstrate that many pilgrims preparing for their journeys were well aware of the likelihood that they might perish on their travels. Southern Italy also presented its own unique features which helped construct the penitential dimension of pilgrimage and at the same time induced marvel and horror in the foreign visitor. The region formed a dangerous landscape and was surrounded by unforgiving seas, both of which were overlaid with a set of supernatural, classical and folkloric traditions. As these traditions were transmitted across western Europe by the increased movement of travellers and texts, they might well have shaped the sense of anticipation generated in many visitors to the region, and even

---

[122] CDBV, no. 154.
[123] R. Bartlett, *The Making of Europe. Conquest, Colonization and Cultural Change 950–1350* (London, 1993), 294–5.
[124] D. J. Birch, 'Jacques de Vitry and the ideology of pilgrimage', *Pilgrimage Explored*, ed. J. Stopford (Woodbridge, 1999), 79–93.

attracted some pilgrims eager to face fear and suffering. Indeed, the imagined – supernatural forces, portentous signs, shadows in dark forests, evil spirits and demons waiting in ambush – could be deemed as one of the greatest threats to the medieval traveller.[125] Therefore, to understand fully southern Italy's role in international pilgrimage, we must look beyond shrines and religious centres, and consider these topographical characteristics, cultural perceptions and imagined landscapes which provided the substantive psychological backdrop to many a pilgrim's experience of the region. For some it must have created a land of contradictions, a staging post to salvation set alongside a gateway to damnation.

(i)   Dangerous landscapes

The South Italian landscape was marked by natural features which were endowed with numinous properties that could elicit fear, wonder and curiosity in the minds of some foreign visitors. Above all, southern Italy was a land shaped by its relationship to the surrounding seas, bodies of water which could be dangerous to navigate. As we have seen, many pilgrims at some stage of their journeys experienced the seas around southern Italy and Sicily. Thousands traversed the waters of southern Italy peacefully leaving no record of their trouble-free travels. But many instances also indicate that the experience of sea travel around the South Italian peninsula could be a harrowing affair. Fulcher of Chartres witnessed the drowning of some 400 pilgrims as their vessel sank in Brindisi harbour in 1096.[126] It was from the latter port that the English pilgrim Saewulf set sail for the Holy Land in 1102, after his first attempt from Monopoli ended in shipwreck in the Adriatic.[127] The body of miracles performed by saints such as Nicholas the Pilgrim and Cataldus which rescued seafarers suggest that shipwreck was sufficiently commonplace for it to provide a resonant message in hagiographical texts.

The seas around Sicily posed particular problems. The Strait of Messina was notoriously treacherous but, as it offered a direct route across the Mediterranean, it was used by many seafarers. The well-informed author of a late twelfth century Pisan maritime map warned of the torrid

---

[125] Indeed, the chronicler William of Newburgh recorded an episode in the 1190s in which a pilgrim heading from Le Mans to Jerusalem was attacked and burned with a fiery cloak by a demon, but was saved through the timely intervention of St James: *The History of William of Newburgh*, trans. J. Stevenson (London, 1856), 632–3.

[126] *The First Crusade. The Chronicle of Fulcher of Chartres*, Bk I.8, pp. 60–1.

[127] *Peregrinationes Tres*, 35–7, 59 lines 6–12.

nature of the strait.[128] The Muslim traveller Ibn Jubayr offered a vivid description of the dangers of sea-travel in the region. Travelling through the Strait of Messina which 'boils like a cauldron', his ship was driven onto the shoreline and all aboard prepared 'to meet death'. Fortunately, the passengers were saved by a Sicilian rescue party.[129] The whirlpools and tidal rips in the strait contributed to the creation of the ancient legend of Scylla and Charybdis, two sea monsters which were said to inhabit those waters. Virgil, following Homer's *Odyssey*, described Charybdis as a whirlpool devouring ships, and Scylla as a sea creature with wolves in its womb pulling vessels onto the rocks.[130] As we shall see later in this chapter, curiosity for classical traditions was partly responsible for the medieval interest in Scylla and Charybdis, legends which were known across the Christian world and associated with Sicily. However, oral accounts and first-hand experience of the strait confirmed its dangers, regardless of any belief in the genuine presence of monsters. Ibn Jubayr and Gervase of Tilbury both understood the menace of the strait in nautical and geological terms, but the latter still recorded the legends of Scylla and Charybdis and intimated that many seafarers believed in them.[131] Bishop John of Norwich endured a treacherous crossing of the strait in 1176, and chose to frame it around the presence of the 'rocks of Scylla and the watery chasms of Charybdis', while Jacques de Vitry also referenced them as he passed the island in the early thirteenth century.[132] These traditions were also perpetuated from within southern Italy by individuals and communities who were more accustomed to the strait's whirlpools and tidal rips, seemingly as a way of emphasizing the extreme dangers to be encountered there. The late eleventh-century chroniclers William of Apulia and Geoffrey Malaterra both commented on the dangers of Scylla and Charybdis in ambiguous ways which avoided explicit rejection of the actual existence of sea monsters. One purpose of their works, it must be remembered, was to entertain courtly circles.

---

[128] Gautier Dalchè, *Carte*, 26 lines 158–2 p. 157. Pryor, *Geography, Technology, and War*, 7, 13–14, 90–3.

[129] *Travels of Ibn Jubayr*, 335–7.

[130] Virgil, *Aeneid*, trans. D. West (London, 2003), Bk III, 410–30; he also alludes to the presence of the Sirens on an unidentified stretch of the South Italian coastline: Bk V. 865–6.

[131] Gervase, BkII.12, pp. 340–3. Walter Map, a courtier at Henry II of England's court, also recorded similar traditions on the sea monsters and the nautical curiosities of the straits in his *De Nugis Curialium. Courtiers' Trifles*, ed. and trans. M. R. James et al. (Oxford, 1983), 367–9, 504–5.

[132] *Radulfi de Diceto Decani Lundoniensis Opera Historica*, ed. W. Stubbs, 2 vols, RS 68 (London, 1876) i. 416–7; *Lettres de Jacques de Vitry*, ed. R. B. C. Huygens (Leiden, 1960), 79–97 no. 2.

The twelfth-century author of the translation of St Agatha to Catania described the saint's return to Sicily via the Strait of Messina 'which contains Charybdis and Scylla, who it is said are girded with raging dogs and cause shipwrecks'.[133] Furthermore, the volcanic islands of Lipari were situated only approximately thirty kilometres north of Sicily on the approach routes to the strait, their smouldering peaks signifying a gateway to the approaching perils and augmenting their psychological dangers. Many observers commented on them. The anonymous author of the *Itinerarium peregrinorum et Gesta Regis Ricardi* wrote of the sighting of the ever burning volcanoes on the islands by Richard I's fleet as it approached Messina, whereas Caesarius of Heisterbach included among his *exempla* the eerie experiences of northern European pilgrims returning from Jerusalem as they sailed around these infernal volcanic islands.[134]

Away from the seas, southern Italy was also characterized by its mountainous terrain – especially the Apennines and hinterlands of Calabria and Sicily – which appeared to offer ascent to the heavens but also the prospect of plummeting into the deep bowels of the earth: a challenging dichotomy. The great pilgrim centres at Compostela and Rome required most pilgrims to cross daunting mountain ranges – the Pyrenees and the Alps – which contributed to the penitential dimension of the pilgrimage. Indeed, while we have little in the way of specific comment on the torments of the South Italian Apennines, we do know that Conrad of Querfurt, the chancellor of Henry VI of Germany, spoke of the difficulty of crossing the mountain range during his journey down the peninsula in 1194, and a hospital was built at San Germano to host pilgrims who were unable to climb up to the heights of the shrines at Montecassino, itself located in the Apennine foothills.[135] Medieval travellers passing through the Alps recorded their experiences with emotive and significant language which could well represent a common understanding of mountain travel further south in the Italian peninsula. In 1128 the abbot of St Trond and the bishop of Liege crossed the Great St Bernard Pass where they experienced 'the jaws of death' and feared avalanches which would 'bury them in the depths of hell', while later in 1188 a monk from Canterbury described his reaction to traversing the same pass as 'on the one hand looking up to the heavens of the mountains, on the other shuddering at the hell of

[133] Wil. Apulia, Bk III, p. 174 lines 190–4; Malaterra, Bk II.I, p. 29; *Epistola Mauritii*, 644.
[134] *Chronicle of the Third Crusade. Itinerarium Peregrinorum et Gesta Regis Ricardi*, trans. H. J. Nicholson (Aldershot, 1997), Bk II.10, p. 154; Caesarius, vol. 2 Bk XII.7–9, pp. 298–9, Bk XII.12–13, pp. 300–2.
[135] 'Epistola Conradi cancellarii', in *Arnoldi Chronica Slavorum*, 192.

the valleys'.[136] If at the least such vocabulary was employed merely as a literary device, it nonetheless created a mental climate which encouraged associations with salvation and damnation.

Earthquakes and volcanic eruptions also made particularly volatile contributions to the South Italian landscape, which has historically experienced high levels of seismic activity.[137] South Italian historical works contain sporadic records of these events. Benevento was struck by an earthquake in 1094, and the chronicler Falco recorded the devastation wrought by another in his city in 1125, along with a terrifying series of aftershocks.[138] The *Chronicle* attributed to Archbishop Romuald of Salerno noted a great earthquake throughout Apulia in 1087, and another hit eastern Sicily in 1169, severely damaging Syracuse and Messina, and almost completely razing Catania, killing 15,000 inhabitants, an event which reverberated across Europe. The *Pisan Annals* commented dramatically that 'since the time of Sodom and Gomorrah, there had never occurred such amazing and incredible wonders as took place on the island of Sicily'.[139] Entries in South Italian annals confirm the dates of these earthquakes and offer further record of seismic activity: the *Annales Casinenses*, for instance, record a plethora of seismic episodes in 1117 (described as 'huge', they collapsed buildings, killed men and disturbed the seas), 1141, 1152, 1172 and in 1184/5 (a 'terrible and violent earthquake spread throughout Calabria', destroying churches and killing people within, including the archbishop of Cosenza).[140] The English chronicler Ralph of Diceto also noted the latter earthquake and recorded the impact spreading to the Adriatic coast where cities, with their populaces asleep at night, collapsed into subterranean chasms.[141] In addition, the region was host to a number of active volcanoes – Lipari, Vulcano and Stromboli on the islands of Lipari, Ischia in the gulf of Naples, and more famously Vesuvius and Etna – which, as we shall see later in this chapter, were often commented on by foreign observers. Episodic eruptions occurred in the medieval period. The *Annales Casinenses* noted an eruption of Vesuvius in 1037, and Amatus of Montecassino recorded another from the same volcano in c.1060, when volcanic ash covered Campania,

---

[136] G. B. Parks, *The English Traveller to Italy. First Volume: The Middle Ages (to 1525)* (Rome, 1954), 194–7; Birch, *Pilgrimage to Rome*, 56–7.

[137] E. Guidoboni and J. E. Ebel, *Earthquakes and Tsunamis in the Past. A Guide to Techniques in Historical Seismology* (Cambridge, 2009), 261.

[138] Bertolini, 'Gli *Annales Beneventani*', 149; Falco, 82.

[139] Romuald, 198; Liber de Regno, 164 (Tyrants, 216–18); see also *Roberti de Monte Cronica*, 518; *Gli Annales Pisani di Bernardo Maragone*, ed. M. Lupo Gentile, RIS 6 (ii) (Bologna, 1936), 47.

[140] *Annales Casinenses*, ed. G. H. Pertz, MGH SS xix (Hanover, 1866), 305, 308–13.

[141] *Radulfi de Diceto*, ii. 37.

and parts of Calabria and Apulia.[142] Falco of Benevento noted a huge eruption of Vesuvius in 1139 which spewed out fire and flame for eight days and cast black ash into the sky as far as Salerno, Capua and Benevento.[143] Over a dozen eruptions have been catalogued for Mount Etna prior to 1284, although the limitations of medieval source material suggest that more undoubtedly occurred. For instance, both Ibn Jubayr's commentary on Mount Etna in the 1180s, and Roger of Howden's discussion of the protective powers of St Agatha of Catania, set in the 1190s, imply that the volcano had erupted within living memory.[144]

(ii)   *The natural and the supernatural within southern Italy*

The medieval mind interpreted such natural phenomena in a dichotomous framework awash with ambiguity; they were understood in their natural scientific context and partially desacralized but at the same time traditional views persisted which interpreted them as portentous divine signs. The physical experience of challenging landscapes or natural disasters combined with the psychological trials inherent in understanding these features or events as imbued with divine resonances left a profound impression. The record of an earthquake in 1117 in the *Annales Casinenses* pointedly referred to the shaking of the lamps in the churches, implying that the equilibrium within Christian sanctuaries was being disturbed.[145] Falco of Benevento called the 1125 earthquake at Benevento an 'unknown prodigy', and described the fear of his fellow-citizens as they sought out the apotropaic qualities of the city's holy shrines.[146] Two commentators on the earthquake at Catania in 1169 testify to beliefs that the event carried deeper meaning. Hugo Falcandus noted that one court faction at Palermo was 'frightened by these and other portents, and they thought that these unprecedented happenings foretold great calamities for Sicily', while Peter of Blois, with his own axe to grind, interpreted the catastrophe as St Agatha's judgement on a sinful episcopal election in the city.[147]

It remains uncertain just how far South Italians truly considered these natural disasters as supernatural events, and to what extent the region's

---

[142] *Annales Casinenses*, 306; Amatus, Bk V. 5, pp. 391–2.
[143] Falco, 218 (also recorded in the *Annales Casinenses*, 309).
[144] E. Guidoboni and C. Ciuccarelli, 'First historical evidence of a significant Mt. Etna eruption in 1224', *Journal of Volcanology and Geothermal Research* 178 (2008), 693–700; *Travels of Ibn Jubayr*, 343–4; for Roger of Howden see more later in this chapter.
[145] *Annales Casinenses*, 308.
[146] Falco, 82–4.
[147] *Liber de Regno*, 164–5 (Tyrants, 218); *Petri Blesensis*, no. 46 cols 133–4.

inhabitants engaged with the new naturalizing scholarly enquiries of the twelfth century. To unravel the nuances of such a question would require a study to match Carl Watkins's magisterial work on medieval England.[148] For now, it will suffice (at the admitted risk of generalization) to note that our South Italian commentators were surprisingly laconic when discussing natural disasters. When they did record them, the phenomena were interpreted either as generic prophetic symbols or simply in a neutral framework; they recorded the event and its geological characteristics but offered no further clarification of any theological meaning underpinning it. The prevailing mindset remained equivocal in its understandings of these events. Parallel developments were occurring in other parts of western Europe, where conflicting and unresolved discourses were evolving around the natural and the wondrous as explanatory tools for a range of events. Twelfth-century Europe, as Watkins explains, was still very much caught between these two traditions.[149] The real significance for our present study lies in the integration of information on the apparent supernatural elements of the South Italian landscape into the broader European discourse on the natural and the wondrous. Foreign commentators displayed a close interest in the unique features of southern Italy's topography and folkloric traditions, drawing much of their material from local sources and introducing it to a wider audience, a part of which was likely to encounter the region directly at some point.

(iii)   The Classical world of the south

The South Italian material included within these external accounts shows that individuals did not necessarily see the natural and the wondrous as mutually exclusive spheres. They also reveal other important trends in European thought, namely the revived, but contentious, interest in Classical learning and the emerging centrality of Purgatory, as Europe grappled with its understanding of how and where sins were redeemed.[150] In both cases, southern Italy was called on to illuminate these debated spaces, and in doing so was depicted as a magical and sinister arena, with the audience often left to decide how far this might be real or imagined. Interest in the Classical past focused understandably on the ancient treasures of the city of Rome, the production of 'tourist guides'

---

[148] C. S. Watkins, *History and the Supernatural in Medieval England* (Cambridge, 2007).

[149] Watkins, *History and the Supernatural*, 171.

[150] J. Le Goff, *The Birth of Purgatory*, trans. A. Goldhammer (Aldershot, 1991); Watkins, *History and the Supernatural*, 171–82; B. P. McGuire, 'Purgatory and the communion of saints: a medieval change', *Viator* 20 (1989), 61–84; G. R. Edwards, 'Purgatory: "birth" or "evolution"', *Journal of Ecclesiastical History* 34 (1985), 634–46.

such as Master Gregory's *Narracio de mirabilibus urbis Romae* extolling the wonders within the city, much as Robert of Clari did for the city of Constantinople in 1204.[151] But southern Italy was also steeped in Classical traditions which were deemed both alluringly enchanting and dangerously pagan. Gervase of Tilbury took a keen interest in the more mainstream Classical traditions of southern Italy, referencing Scylla and Charybdis as the ancient sea monsters patrolling the Strait of Messina and the devastation they wrought. However, the Englishman's desire to disenchant certain aspects of the wondrous led him to classify the sea monsters as whirlpools created by trapped winds in the bowels of the earth and he explained that this 'is the origin of the notion that it is the dogs of Scylla barking, when people sailing past at a distance are terrified by the roar of the waves which the seething water hurls together as the whirlpool gulps them down'. Within his explanation, Gervase reveals that some seafarers might have believed in the existence of Scylla and Charybdis. He also briefly noted that Sicily was once the home of the Cyclopes, and made a subtle link to widespread twelfth-century perceptions of the island and its rulers by stating that it 'has ever afterwards been the nurse of tyrants'.[152]

However, Gervase devoted most space to the legends surrounding Virgil at Naples, which appear to have been current among the local community. The legendary magician, poet and author of the *Aeneid* was believed to have been buried near Naples from where his protective powers were deemed to extend over the city. Gervase recorded a host of local traditions on this subject: Virgil's miraculous preservation of meat in the city market, his protection of the city from snakes, his garden with magical plants, the story of an English master seeking Virgil's bones during the reign of Richard I and finding them with a book of magic which Gervase claimed to have seen, and the city gate where Virgil bestowed good fortune on those entering through it on the correct side (which Gervase was glad to report that he had unwittingly passed through himself). Gervase's personal experience of elements of these legends challenged his attempts to fit them into a neatly delineated taxonomy of the natural and supernatural.[153] He and Conrad of Querfurt, bishop of

---

[151] Master Gregorius, *The Marvels of Rome*; Robert de Clari, *La Conquête*, chapters 80–92 pp. 169–85.

[152] Gervase, Bk II.12, pp. 332–5, 340–3; the so-called 'Hugo Falcandus' also highlighted the Sicilian link with tyranny in his work: Liber de Regno, 6 and also 176 (Tyrants, 58, 257); see also H. Wieruszowski, 'Roger of Sicily, *Rex Tyrannus*, in twelfth-century political thought', *Speculum* 38 (1963), 46–78. Parallels were clearly being drawn with the 'tyrants' Dionysius I and II who ruled Syracuse from 405 to 357 BC.

[153] Gervase, Bk III.12–13, pp. 576–85; 112, pp. 802–3.

Hildesheim and vice-regent of the Kingdom of Sicily under Emperor Henry VI, were among the first medieval commentators to write down these Virgilian legends, in c.1210 and 1195 respectively; but also from the mid-twelfth to the early thirteenth century writers such as the English philosopher John of Salisbury and Alexander Neckham, an English master at the University of Paris, also recorded an interest in Virgilian traditions which revealed their independent circulation throughout Europe.[154] That the legends were already flourishing within southern Italy is apparent in the work of the South Italian abbot Alexander of Telese (composed by c.1136) which included two references to Virgil's rule over Naples.[155] Conrad of Querfurt recorded legends similar to those found in Gervase's work, but added a few extra ones, particularly on Virgil's gift of a model city within a small glass bottle which would safeguard Naples. Interestingly, the highly educated Conrad had followed Henry VI's orders in dismantling the city's walls; however, by asserting that the glass bottle containing Virgil's model had a crack which therefore rendered it impotent, he refused to dismiss the authenticity of this legend. He also recorded that the imperial soldiers charged with destroying the city's walls feared that in doing so they would break Virgil's charm which was believed to have enclosed all the snakes within the region under the Porta Ferrea city gate. Conrad also added that he had seen the skies darken and a storm arise, which indicated that Virgil's bones, believed to be encased in a castle out at sea, had been exposed to air.[156]

Conrad is of great interest because he recorded the Virgilian traditions of southern Italy in a letter written as he travelled through the region in 1194 leading the victorious invasion forces of Henry VI, which also contained an account, framed by his fascination with the region's Classical legacies, of the landscape he encountered. Conrad drew from a mixture of authentic Greek mythologies, authentic home-grown Italic and Roman traditions, and uncritically from efforts in Late Antiquity or afterwards to locate in southern Italy traditions which were previously associated with the Eastern Greek world.[157] Among the many Classical reference points, he noted Ovid's home at Sulmona in the Abruzzi, Chieti where Achilles' mother kept him in hiding, and Canne where Hannibal was famously victorious. Conrad also located Mount Olympus in southern Italy, and

---

[154] See also the erudite work of D. Comparetti, *Vergil in the Middle Ages*, trans. E. F. M. Benecke (London, 1895, reprinted 1966), especially Part II chapters 2 and 3, pp. 257–89.

[155] Al. Tel., Bk III.19, pp. 69–70 and 'Alloquium', p. 89.

[156] 'Epistola Conradi cancellarii', in *Arnoldi Chronica Slavorum*, pp. 194, 196.

[157] I would like to express my extreme gratitude to Mr Ian Moxon for providing his extensive expertise on the Classical world.

the place where Paris abducted Helen was identified (entirely errone-ously) near Naples. Having passed through the fearsome torments of Scylla and Charybdis to arrive at Sicily, Conrad saw the Minotaur's Labyrinth at Taormina, and nearby the spot where Icarus plummeted to his death, the last two traditions relocated to Sicily again on dubious grounds.[158] Conrad here indulges in the aura and power of Classical traditions which are given their potency, like holy relics, through being observed and accessed in a physical landscape.

(iv)   *Locating the Christian Afterlife: interchanges between Hell, Purgatory and King Arthur*

The developing awareness of southern Italy's Classical past was not restricted to recounting ancient curiosities for the purpose of entertain-ment or indeed to elucidate the broader boundaries between the natural and supernatural. The core underpinning a number of southern Italy's Classical traditions was fused with and applied to developing Christian concepts of Purgatory and the Afterlife. Increased interest in the Neapolitan traditions of Virgil also meant increased knowledge of his works, particularly the *Aeneid*, in which the hero Aeneas journeyed through the Underworld. Aeneas appears to have accessed the gateway to Hell close to Lake Avernus, near Pozzuoli, and subsequent tradition tended to record the entrance to the Underworld within the vicinity of the Bay of Naples.[159] The presence of various ancient underground passages in this part of southern Italy, particularly Roman military tunnels, no doubt consolidated these accounts.[160] Southern Italy's complement of volcanoes and Classical traditions intensified connections between the region and the Underworld, and this was absorbed into medieval thinking. In his *Dialogues*, Gregory the Great emphasized this perception, writing of 'fire-spitting cauldrons' and 'infernal torments' in Sicily, while the author of the eighth-century text the *Hodoeporicon of St Willibald* recorded the journey of the English pilgrim St Willibald through southern Italy and described the volcanoes of the Lipari islands in hellish terms.[161] Gregory the Great in fact went further; by noting that the Arian king Theodoric (d. 526) was thrust into the burning Mount Vulcano because of his sins, he linked the

---

[158] 'Epistola Conradi cancellarii', in *Arnoldi Chronica Slavorum*, 192–6. Comparetti, *Vergil*, 257–9.

[159] Virgil, *The Aeneid*, Bk VI, lines 199–243.

[160] R. J. Clark, 'Conrad of Querfurt and Petrarch on the location of the Vergilian under-world', *Papers of the British School at Rome* 64 (1996), 261–4.

[161] Gregory the Great, *Dialogues*, iii. Bk IV.4, pp. 33–7; 'The Hodoeporicon of St Willibald', 171–2.

region's geophysical attributes to religious and eschatological dimensions.[162] Other commentators did the same: according to the ninth-century *Gesta Dagoberti* the Merovingian king Dagobert I (603–39) was more fortunate for his soul was recovered from Vulcano by his protectors, Saints Denis, Maurice and Martin.[163]

The reviving interest in Classical learning in the Central Middle Ages ensured that such associations continued to be made. In the eleventh century, the *vita* of St Odilo, abbot of Cluny (994–1049), recounted a hermit's vision of one of the islands of Lipari where 'the lamentations of the dead can be heard emerging from the crater of a mountain inside which the dead are purged'.[164] The diplomat and poet, Peter of Blois, having left Sicily in acrimonious circumstances in the 1160s, lambasted the island as an 'infernal place, which devours its inhabitants', the mountains of which 'are the gates of death and hell, where men are swallowed by the earth and the living sink into hell'.[165] Gervase of Tilbury noted the assertion that from Vesuvius 'a vent of the terrestrial hell blasts out', and recorded another tale about the bishop of Pozzuoli in the 1130s who heard the 'spine-chilling cries of lamenting souls' near Lake Avernus and saw within its waters 'broken-down bronze gates and iron bars' which were 'the gates of Hell'.[166] Moreover, Gervase had previously recounted another story about the same bishop who heard the wailing of souls from a nearby mountain, and who encountered one soul who had been sentenced 'to the severe penal fires of Avernus': this experience made it clear to the prelate that the cries came from souls found in the 'places of punishment' ('in locis penalibus') which bordered on the margins of this world. In the same passage Gervase used the term *purgatorium* (Purgatory).[167] The transmission of these traditions varied in detail but retained their core themes. Conrad of Querfurt, for example, identified the island of Ischia, in the Bay of Naples, as the place where 'it is claimed that the mouth of hell is and where the painful places ["loca penalia"] are recorded to be'.[168] Another German, Caesarius of Heisterbach, included in his *Dialogue of Miracles* a series of tales of Swedish, Flemish and German pilgrims sailing along the peninsula's

162 Gregory the Great, *Dialogues*, iii. Bk IV.31, pp. 104–6; S. Boesch Gajano, 'Agiografia e geografia nei Dialoghi di Gregorio Magno', *Storia della Sicilia*, ed. S. Pricoco (Catania, 1988), 209–20, at 215.
163 *Gesta Dagoberti I, Regis Francorum*, ed. B. Krusch, MGH Scriptores Rerum Merovingicarum ii (Hanover, 1888), 421.
164 Le Goff, *Birth of Purgatory*, 201.
165 *Petri Blesensis*, no. 46 cols 133–4; no. 93 cols 291–3.
166 Gervase, Bk III.14, pp. 584–5; 19, pp. 590–1.
167 Gervase, Bk III.17, pp. 588–90.
168 'Epistola Conradi cancellarii', in *Arnoldi Chronica Slavorum*, 196.

coastline, and passing the volcano of Stromboli where voices were heard welcoming the damned into the infernal world within. Caesarius also recorded a story of voices arising from Etna which were heard preparing a great fire for the tyrannical duke of Zähringen. In answering whether these volcanoes represented Purgatory or Hell, Caesarius responded through his fictional monk who interpreted each episode: 'they are said to be the jaws of hell, because none of the elect, but the wicked only are sent into them'.[169] As we shall see, the great Sicilian volcano of Etna boasted a rich corpus of supernatural traditions.

The works of Conrad, Gervase and Caesarius clearly allude to the location in southern Italy of the entrance to Purgatory, which itself was becoming ever more central to twelfth-century theological thinking, and also increasingly understood beyond the ecclesiastical world.[170] In addition to the entrance to Purgatory being located both on the islands of Lipari and near Naples, the volcanic Mount Etna was also identified as the specific point at which the present and the Afterlife converged. Classical traditions had always affirmed the existence of sinister fiery forges within Etna, and its numinous qualities continued to awe both Christian and Muslim commentators. When the Muslim traveller Ibn Jubayr passed through Sicily in 1184–5 he marvelled at Allah's creation of 'the Mountain of Fire, the famous volcano of Sicily'.[171] In the Middle Ages new Christian and other folkloric traditions were embedded within the legends to provide more depth to the charged environment in and around Etna.[172] One of the sermons of the Benedictine monk, Julien de Vézelay (d. 1160), made an overt etymological link between Etna and Gehenna, and Matthew Paris's strip-map of the thirteenth century referenced beliefs that Etna was 'a mouth of Hell'.[173] Gervase of Tilbury included a report of a marvellous episode associated with Etna, which revealed a strange and intermediate Otherworld in Sicily which in turn alluded to Purgatory. The report, drawn from local and contemporary sources, recorded the discovery of King Arthur recovering in the caverns of the volcano, and added that some locals had actually seen gifts sent by Arthur to the bishop of Catania.[174] Typically, Gervase appears equivocal in his interpretation of this news on Arthur. He included additional

---

[169] Caesarius, vol. 2 Bk XII.7–9, pp. 298–9, Bk XII.12–13, pp. 300–2.
[170] See the important discussion in Le Goff, *Birth of Purgatory*, 177–208.
[171] *Travels of Ibn Jubayr*, 335, 343–4. In the preceding decade, another Muslim visitor to Sicily, Al-Harawi, noted the fires of Etna, Al-Harawi, *Wayfarer's Guide*, 144.
[172] A. Pioletti, 'Artù, Avallon, l'Etna', *Quaderni medievali* 28 (1989), 6–35.
[173] Julian de Vézelay, *Sermons*, ed. D. Vorreux, 2 vols (Sources chrétiennes 192) (Paris, 1972), ii. Sermo XXI pp. 456–9; Connolly, *Maps of Matthew Paris*, 80.
[174] Gervase, Bk II.12, pp. 334–5.

evidence to verify it, but later said it had a 'legendary ring' and subsequently offered a naturalistic explanation of Etna's volcanic activity. For Gervase the fires of Etna provided 'an image of Gehenna' because the cavernous and sulphurous nature of the island of Sicily created a volatile cocktail of wind pressure, steam and flames. Gervase's account is the earliest surviving reference to the transmigration of Arthurian myths to Sicily. The arrival of the Normans in Sicily was almost certainly responsible for introducing this new shift in Arthurian myth. Roger of Howden augmented the legend by claiming that Richard I gave Excalibur to King Tancred of Sicily when the English monarch was passing through the island on the Third Crusade.[175] Interest in Arthur's Sicilian domicile appears to have remained mostly within the domain of western Europe's literary elite, but the creation of the remarkable Tree of Life mosaic floor in Otranto cathedral in the 1160s suggests a more popular dissemination. The cathedral offered a sanctuary for pilgrim traffic heading for the city's port, and its prominent mosaic floor was adorned with Arthurian imagery alongside Classical, biblical, Scandinavian and Islamic motifs.[176] The Sicilian dimension of the Arthurian legend served to provide an additional and beguiling layer to Sicily's Otherworldly associations.[177]

By the thirteenth century esteemed writers such as Caesarius of Heisterbach and Stephen of Bourbon recorded revised accounts of Arthur's Sicilian residence which linked it more firmly to the place of Purgatory. Stephen's account, for instance, explicitly identified the Sicilian volcano as 'locus purgatorii'.[178] However, ultimately the trend to place Purgatory in Sicily was only a transitional phase in the evolution of medieval Christian theology; in the Later Middle Ages, St Patrick's in Ireland was more widely acknowledged as the entrance site for Purgatory. Sicily's intimate and long-standing infernal associations proved problematic in a world which required greater delineation between Hell and Purgatory. As Le Goff has summed up: 'the ancient Hell stood in the way of the youthful Purgatory'.[179] The researches of scholars such as Pioletti and Schmitt offer further support. They demonstrate how versions of the Arthurian legends at Etna gradually diabolized the British king and

---

[175] *Chronica Magistri Rogeri de Houedene*, iii. 97.
[176] G. Gianfreda, *Il mosaico pavimentale della basilica cattedrale di Otranto*, 2nd edn (Frosinone, 1970); C. Settis Frugoni, 'Per una lettura del mosaico pavimentale della cattedrale di Otranto', *BISIME* 80 (1968), 213–56.
[177] In the thirteenth century, the French romance *Floriant et Florete* built on these interconnections to recount a journey made by Arthur to Sicily where the fairy Morgan resided within Etna: *Floriant et Florete*, ed. H. F. Williams (Ann Arbor, 1947).
[178] Pioletti, 'Artù, Avallon, l'Etna', 34.
[179] Le Goff, *Birth of Purgatory*, 208.

ultimately substituted him for Satan and his infernal world, as if Sicily consumed Arthur's virtuous attributes.[180] Caesarius in particular depicted Arthur as an 'ambivalent king of the dead' who was associated with the devil, and the Otranto mosaic depicts Arthur ambiguously riding on a goat but places him next to biblical scenes redolent with Christian symbolism.[181] It seems Sicily simply could not shake off its relationship with the more sinister realms of the Otherworld.

(v)   *Islam, exoticism and the otherness of southern Italy*

Southern Italy's ongoing association with Islam deepened its exotic and dangerous presentation to the outside world. Latin Christendom's interest in and understanding of Islam underwent significant and conflicting transitions in the late eleventh and twelfth centuries, in correlation with the emergence of the crusading movement and of the danger of heresy within Europe. The Muslim truly emerged onto the mental landscape of Christian Europe. *Chansons de geste* viewed Muslims as 'exotic reflections of the Christian knight', whereas other western sources, such as the travesties of Muhammad's life, presented Islam in terms which imitated Christian heretical groups.[182] The continued presence of a sizeable Muslim community in Sicily, which appeared to be tolerated (if only superficially) by the Norman rulers, and the Arab–Islamic imagery utilized by the Norman kings of Sicily induced some uncertainty. Unfortunately we know little about how far this information was available across Europe, and many writers simply chose to overlook what was undoubtedly a difficult subject. Occasionally scraps of evidence do suggest some awareness. The *Saxon annals* denounced King Roger II as 'a semi-pagan tyrant', and an indifferent attitude to crusading while ruling over a pariah state in western Europe would not have helped. During the Third Crusade, the English and French forces developed a perception of the inhabitants of Messina as 'a wicked bunch', many of whom were the 'offspring of Saracen fathers and [...] were absolutely opposed and hostile towards our people'.[183] The evident sense of difference and otherness

---

[180] Pioletti, 'Artù, Avallon, l'Etna', 9–16.

[181] J.-C. Schmitt, *Ghosts in the Middle Ages. The Living and the Dead in the Middle Ages*, trans. T. Lavender Fagan (Chicago, 1998), 116–18.

[182] S. Kangas, '*Inimicus Dei et Sanctae Christianitatis?*: Saracens and their prophet in twelfth-century crusade propaganda and western travesties of Muhammad's life', *The Crusades and the Near East*, ed. C. Kostick (London, 2011), 131–60, quotation at 152. For the broader context see also J. V. Tolan, *Saracens. Islam in the Medieval Imagination* (New York, 2002), chs 5 and 6.

[183] *Die Reichschronik des Annalista Saxo*, p. 608; *Itinerarium Peregrinorum et Gesta Regis Ricardi*, Bk II.12, pp. 155–6.

recorded on this occasion converged with Europewide paranoia on internal enemies; the hybridized Greek–Islamic population of Sicily might thus represent another problematic phalanx among the ranks of Latin Christendom's deviant foes. The region's Islamic past was also anchored in the present through its use as a setting for some popular *Chansons de geste*. Most famously the late twelfth-century *Chanson d'Aspremont* saw Charlemagne's liege Roland seek revenge in Calabria against the Saracen king Agolant, who ruled from Reggio.[184] The passage of the Third Crusade aroused greater European interest in Sicily, and the chroniclers of the expedition recorded a number of local traditions, while demonstrating their awareness of the *Chanson* by noting Reggio as Agolant's residence.[185] It is also significant that Conrad of Querfurt included in his tour of the region's Classical curiosities a reference to the ability of the island's Saracens to kill animals with their spit, a phenomenon which he then connected to their veneration of Paul the Apostle who, it was claimed, enjoyed supernatural powers over serpents.[186] An uncertain world emerges where boundaries between Christian and non-Christian appear to be dangerously fused. Under Christian rule, Sicily even retained a place within the Islamic topography of pilgrimage. The late twelfth-century Muslim travellers Al-Harawi and Ibn Jubayr discovered functioning Islamic pilgrimage sites in settlements such as Marsala and Catania, and one near Palermo. At the last, Ibn Jubayr tells us, were 'numerous tombs of ascetic and pious Muslims, and it is known for its grace and blessedness, being visited by men from all countries'.[187] Many Crusaders passing through this island must have struggled with a series of paradoxes on the nature of faith, encountering an eclecticism that they would only meet again when in the Holy Land.

To add further conflicting messages, underground grottos were a prominent feature throughout southern Italy, mostly in Apulia and Sicily; only parts of Iberia and Cappadocia in Asia Minor could offer parallels. These were for the most part ancient natural cavities extended by human initiative, which offered refuge to holy men and variously housed shrines (most famously that of St Michael the Archangel at Monte Gargano), churches and chapels which continued to flourish in

---

[184] *The Song of Aspremont.*
[185] *Itinerarium Peregrinorum et Gesta Regis Ricardi*, Bk II.11, p. 154, Bk V.21, p. 300; *The Crusade of Richard Lion-Heart by Ambroise*, p. 48 line 516.
[186] 'Epistola Conradi cancellarii', in *Arnoldi Chronica Slavorum*, 196; G.-C. Di Scipio, 'Saint Paul and popular traditions', *Telling Tales. Medieval Narratives and the Folk Tradition*, ed. F. Canadé Sautman et al. (London, 1998), 189–208 reveals a strong current of Pauline popular traditions in Sicily and Apulia.
[187] Al-Harawi, 142, 144; *Travels of Ibn Jubayr*, 345.

the Central Middle Ages. Most were replete with representations of saints, often, and unsurprisingly, including St Michael the Archangel. Some, the rock city of Matera and the famous catacombs at Naples and Syracuse, were surely known to foreign travellers. In other words, a distinctive component of the matrix of Christian worship in southern Italy also took place in subterranean spaces.[188] However, the landscape was interpreted, it was unique and had undeniably challenging characteristics, and to many external observers it encapsulated an overriding perception of southern Italy. Medieval mapmakers provide the most vivid proof. In their works they enshrined what Licini calls 'a whole network of implicit, unexpressed, cultural and historical connotations, a kind of ultra-textual code'.[189] While the narrow South Italian peninsula usually left little room to insert imagery, and often lost space to depictions of nearby Rome, the triangular body of Sicily lying conspicuously at the heart of the Mediterranean exerted a natural magnetic pull for both the mapmaker and viewer. The famous Hereford Mappa Mundi, created in the late thirteenth century, offers a striking symbolic depiction of Sicily with a fiery Mount Etna at its heart, and flanked on either side by the two Classical sea monsters, Charybdis and Scylla. Earlier maps from the twelfth century, such as the Imago Mundi of Honorius Augustodunensis and the Sawley Abbey map, include similar imagery for Sicily.[190] It seems that landscape, an exotic, but dangerous pagan past and contemporary Otherworld associations largely shaped how southern Italy and Sicily were perceived throughout Latin Christendom.

In many areas of the medieval world, as Graham Loud has shown even for England and Normandy, alternative and accurate knowledge simply did not exist in sufficient quantity or quality to revise such stereotypes.[191] The emerging genre of *Chansons de geste*, for example, deepened the region's romantic and sinister associations at the expense of veracity, and influenced a host of medieval French commentators from Guy of Bazoches (d.1203) to Robert of Auxerre (d.1212).[192] Of course, despite all these uncertainties, many individuals, usually from the elite levels

[188] Messina, *Sicilia Rupestre*.

[189] P. Licini, 'A multi-layered journey. From manuscript initial letters to encyclopaedic *mappaemundi* through the Benedictine semiotic traditions', *The Hereford World Map. Medieval World Maps and their Context*, ed. P. A. Harvey (London, 2006), 269–92, at 277.

[190] E. Edson, *Mapping Time and Space. How Medieval Mapmakers Viewed Their World* (London, 1997), 114–5.

[191] Loud, 'The Kingdom of Sicily and the Kingdom of England', 540–67.

[192] On this general theme, see the collection of articles in *Il mezzogiorno normanno-svevo visto dall'Europa e dal mondo mediterraneo*, Atti delle XIII giornate normanno-sveve Bari, 21–24 ottobre 1997, ed. G. Musca (Bari, 1999).

of medieval society, visited the region and experienced it in a less threatening, and more positive and conventional, way. Following Norman intervention, southern Italy and Sicily represented a market for commercial opportunity for enterprising North Italian merchants, a land for the advancement of political and ecclesiastical careers for ambitious foreign administrators and churchmen, and an environment for intellectual enrichment for leading scholars. Indeed, as the twelfth century progressed, southern Italy and Sicily were becoming more Latinized and homogenized, more conformist to western European patterns. But this was a slow, incremental process, and those foreigners who experienced all of the above developments and opportunities were still too few to send a sufficient body of accurate information on the region back to their homelands. Indeed, as we have already seen, many of these high-level foreigners were actually responsible for the perpetuation of deep-rooted perceptions and stereotypes: Peter of Blois, Roger of Howden, Gervase of Tilbury, Conrad of Querfurt, and even within southern Italy itself the caustic commentary of Hugo Falcandus. It would seem that Jacques de Vitry's complaint that people desired to travel out of curiosity, in order to experience the absurd, was well founded.[193] Roger of Howden, for example, copied into his *Chronicle* what appears to be a version of a literary tourist guide to southern Italy, and suggested that King Richard I visited sites associated with Pontius Pilate, the sons of Aymon (legendary French heroes from the Carolingian era who were said to be buried in the Neapolitan catacombs) and Virgil.[194]

The movement of foreign pilgrims to South Italian shrines, and the dissemination of all the aforementioned and varied Christian, Classical and folkloric traditions, indicates an extraordinary diversity of cross-cultural exchanges arising out of the mechanics of international pilgrimage and travel. In its totality, these interactions presented southern Italy as neither completely Christian nor completely of this world; like the many pilgrims who travelled through it, the region occupied a permanent liminal state. As Kathy Lavezzo has demonstrated for medieval England, 'wondrous aspects of alterity' combined with 'geographic otherness' to produce conflicting notions of a barbarous yet blessed region, and comparable confluences occurred in southern Italy.[195] If indeed many pilgrims by the nature of their endeavours suspended

---

[193] *La Traduction de l'Historia Orientalis de Jacques de Vitry*, ed. C. Buridant (Paris, 1986), ch. 82 pp. 131–2; Van Herwaarden, 'Pilgrimages and social prestige', 47.

[194] *Chronica*, iii. 41. Matthew, *Norman Kingdom of Sicily*, 114.

[195] K. Lavezzo, *Angels on the Edge of the World. Geography, Literature, and English Community, 1000–1534* (Ithaca, 2006), 18–20.

their normative behaviour and beliefs, so as to be able to override their rationalized personal experience of the region, passing through southern Italy could well have been a cognitively dissonant and eschatologically charged undertaking. Here, in this land, could be found worldly routes to life and death, and eternal pathways to salvation and damnation, all assembled in an uneasy juxtaposition.

6   Pilgrims at South Italian and foreign
shrines: origins, identities, destinations

Recording pilgrimage: problems and patterns

Some of the shrines of southern Italy occupied a prominent place in the wider Christian topography of pilgrimage, and others benefited immensely from increasing international pilgrimage traffic through the region. The growing popularity of long-distance pilgrimage in the Middle Ages generated much comment and attention, but arguably this was disproportionate to the overall numbers participating. Most shrines drew the majority of pilgrims from their immediate geographic orbit; unfortunately these short- and medium-range pilgrimages, more inconspicuous and quotidian, often escaped record. The evidence available on the origins and identities of pilgrims to South Italian shrines suggests that, while highly visible foreign pilgrims were a consistent and advantageous presence, it was the more local pilgrims who were responsible for most movement. It would seem true of all areas of medieval Europe that most pilgrimages were performed across a short space in a short time span. Equally, the available evidence suggests that South Italian shrines followed the normative pattern across western Christendom in attracting (or in being seen to attract) an eclectic body of pilgrims from all social backgrounds. Pilgrimage also remained a polyvalent act, confirmed by the lack of consistent terminology associated with it. Pilgrimage could be carried out alongside other activities, and could be undertaken in vastly differing spiritual and devotional spaces and contexts, from penitential journeys across an entire continent to visiting a shrine located within one's own settlement. The one constant, presence at a shrine, will thus be the base point for categorizing pilgrim status in what follows.

(i)   South Italian hagiographies

The body of material on pilgrims visiting South Italian shrines poses challenges, and perhaps explains why few scholars have attempted to explore the subject in depth. In many respects, the corpus of South

Italian hagiographical texts, *vitae* and *miracula*, represents the best opportunity to understand pilgrimage movement in southern Italy. Their information is invariably more explicit and, unlike much of the material utilized in the preceding chapter, focuses on both foreign and local patterns of pilgrimage. However, the consistency of coverage even for the region's main shrines can be irregular, and our understandings, particularly in the case of lesser shrines, hampered by exiguous records, minimal anecdotal material and at best one hagiographical text, which preserves a single developmental phase in the shrine's life cycle. There are certainly no miracle collections comparable to the detailed accounts recorded in the *Liber Sancti Jacobi* for St James's shrine at Compostela or to those on which Ronald Finucane was able to base his statistical analyses of pilgrimage activity at a selection of English medieval shrines.[1] In each English case, a minimum of 100 posthumous miracles were preserved in record (115 for St William of Norwich, 703 for Thomas Becket in the first decade after his murder, 244 for Godric of Finchale, 108 for St Frideswide of Oxford).[2] If the inconsistency of the material and in some cases its fragmentary nature are taken into account, for no South Italian shrine of this period can we count on more than 40 specific posthumous miracles, and in many cases the figure is around a mere 10 or less. Some of the major shrines are especially disappointing in this respect, although, as we shall see, other opportunities to identify pilgrims are available. But such limitations mean that pilgrimage can be explored only at a select group of South Italian shrines. Consequently, the geographic spread of this selection is dictated by the available source material and requires that the greatest focus is on shrines in Apulia, and less so in Campania, with only minimal evidence drawn from a few sites in Calabria and a solitary shrine in Sicily.

At two of southern Italy's major shrines, St Michael's on Monte Gargano and St Benedict's at Montecassino, there is surprisingly little in the way of concentrated hagiographical accounts which might illustrate pilgrimage patterns. There are no surviving miracle collections composed within southern Italy for the shrine at St Michael's, and the records of foreign pilgrim visits to both Monte Gargano and Montecassino must be found in a range of other sources. Certainly there is plenty of evidence for foreign pilgrims at Monte Gargano, directly through accounts of individual journeys and inscriptions at the shrine, and indirectly through the emergence of a network of pilgrimage services in the surrounding region.

---

[1] *Liber Sancti Jacobi*, Bk II, pp. 259–87.
[2] R. Finucane, *Miracles and Pilgrims. Popular Beliefs in Medieval England* (London, 1977), 113–29.

But, rather surprisingly, in very few cases can we unequivocally identify South Italian pilgrims visiting Monte Gargano. It is not possible, therefore, to establish any localized geographic patterns of pilgrimage to the shrine, which could complement the more certain evidence for Europeanwide interest. It might be suspected that Monte Gargano was too well established in this period to require the creation of a dedicated body of literature to record the experiences of its visitors, and that, in addition, shorter-distance pilgrimage by South Italians to the shrine was considered too routine to justify comment alongside the array of high-profile visitors. Furthermore, St Michael appeared at Monte Gargano in the form of an apparition, leaving no bodily remains. The cult of St Michael was thus irrevocably centred at the shrine in southern Italy; the only relics that could be dispersed (fragments of the red altar cloth and the stone imprints of the Archangel's footprints) were secondary ones firmly associated with the grotto on Monte Gargano, meaning that other centres which acquired them implicitly enhanced its prominence rather than competing with it, further negating the need of the shrine's guardians to record systemati-cally the presence of pilgrims.[3] The impressive spread of churches and subterranean cave chapels dedicated to Saint Michael across southern Italy also served as local poles of devotion dissuading South Italians from visiting the main centre at Monte Gargano, while more distant travellers would have been attracted by the sacrifice inherent in a longer journey. In addition, St Michael's shrine was not located within the heart of an urban community, and the nearest settlement, Monte Sant'Angelo, did not have urban traditions and a population size comparable to other major cult centres in Salerno and Bari. There was not a ready-made body of *cives* supplying core visitors and supporters for the shrine. A final factor should not be discounted: while St Michael's shrine continued to flourish during the Norman period, there is little evidence that the Normans themselves were particularly motivated to promote the cult over others. This is surprising given St Michael's popularity in Normandy and his warrior image. Whatever the reason, intentional or not, the saint's role in the political and military sphere as protector of southern Italy receded during the Norman era. The opportunity was not taken to consolidate a national shrine with an intimate relationship with its people, which might well have encouraged the maintenance of more records on pilgrimage to the shrine.[4] In this sense, the shrine became more homogeneous and universal, and

---

[3] For the tradition of the transfer of these contact relics see *Revelatio Ecclesiae Sancti Michaelis (in Tumba)*, ed. and trans. P. Bouet and O. Desbordes, in 'Les Sources' in *Culte et pèlerinages*, ed. P. Bouet et al. (Rome, 2003), 14 VI.

[4] Martin, 'Les Normands', 341–3.

rather detached from the South Italian people because it was claimed by the wider European community instead.

The evidence for pilgrims attending the shrine of St Benedict at Montecassino is also problematic, but does offer wider scope for investigation. Montecassino was responsible for a great deal of hagiographical output particularly in the second half of the eleventh century, most of which was produced for other communities and cult centres across southern Italy. However, the composite text known as the *Montecassino Chronicle* and Abbot Desiderius' own *Dialogues* (completed c.1076–9) do provide some focus on pilgrimage to the monastery. Although the primary aim of the *Montecassino Chronicle* was not to record pilgrimage movement to the monastery, it does still incorporate some important evidence on the subject.[5] The *Dialogues*, on the other hand, was an overtly hagiographical text, which recorded miracles performed by St Benedict, and visitors to his shrine, in the early and mid-eleventh century.

It is apparent that the status of Montecassino and its own agendas did not necessitate the systematic recording of pilgrim attendance at St Benedict's tomb. High-profile, mostly foreign, visitors were noted at Montecassino, but the pilgrimage dimension of their presence was usually subordinated to other concerns. Positioning Montecassino favourably within both the ecclesiastical and political hierarchies and defending its rights and patrimony were key strategies which influenced what sort of information was retained by the monastery's historians, and this spilled over into the way St Benedict's relationship with his devotees was depicted. This is true of the *Montecassino Chronicle*, Desiderius' *Dialogues* and Amatus of Montecassino's *History*. The miraculous cure of Henry II at Benedict's shrine, for example, was recounted by both Amatus and the author of the *Montecassino Chronicle*, not only because of his imperial status but also because it gave the former author the chance to stress that Montecassino was the rightful home of St Benedict and the latter a platform to denounce the rival claims of Fleury over the saint's relics.[6] The underpinning messages within the miracles and stories recounted in Desiderius' *Dialogues*, as Graham Loud has conclusively shown, focus on St Benedict's protection of Montecassino, alongside the spiritual qualities of the monastic community and the enforcing of discipline within it. It was a pattern replicated at other South Italian monasteries, such as San Clemente a Casauria, Cava and

---

[5] Some in fact was drawn from Desiderius' *Dialogues* itself, at least in the original section of the *Chronicle* composed in c.1100, but thereafter the continuation of the chronicle provides further, original material: A. M. Fagnoni, 'I "Dialogi" di Desiderio nella "Chronica Monasterii Casinensis"', *SM* 34 (271), 65–94.

[6] Amatus, Bk I.28, pp. 257–8; Chron. Cas., Bk II.43–4, pp. 247–52.

especially Pulsano where monks were the subject of nineteen of St John of Matera's twenty-six recorded miracles[7] Consequently, stress on the curative powers of St Benedict (a recurrent attraction for pilgrims visiting any site) is restricted, despite the *Dialogues*' composition in the immediate aftermath of the rediscovery of St Benedict's tomb in 1068 when the monastery was being rebuilt.

It appears that by the eleventh and twelfth centuries the shrines of St Michael and St Benedict boasted distinctive identities and an established status of the highest order, and that this explains the paucity of evidence on pilgrimage to these sites. Montecassino's rivalry with Fleury was a threat, and must be linked to some of the hagiographical output and building works at Montecassino in the mid- to late eleventh century. But it could never damage the primacy of Montecassino's relationship with Benedict, which continued to buttress the South Italian monastery's claims to hold the saint's relics. Perhaps in their formative eras both of these cult centres would have benefited from recording pilgrims and miracles at their shrines, and perhaps they did but the records are no longer extant. In any case this would be an anachronistic line of enquiry: the genre of *miracula* collections, and their full significance, only really came into genuine fruition from the eleventh century onwards. Certainly by the Central Middle Ages the aspirations of each of these cult centres extended far beyond the need to compile authenticating pilgrim lists, which instead was the domain of emergent cults which were more vulnerable and unsure of their self-identities.

Southern Italy was home to at least three further cult centres – St Nicholas at Bari, St Matthew at Salerno and St Agatha at Catania – which, being founded on a universal appeal across Christendom, could expect to receive a notable influx of pilgrim numbers, and which, significantly, were all based within large and expanding urban settlements. The patterns and record of pilgrim activity at these shrines are best understood in the way each was established and subsequently developed. St Nicholas might best be termed a new arrival in the South Italian pilgrimage network, following the translation of his relics to Bari in 1087. Conversely, the key characteristics of the cults of St Matthew and St Agatha in the Central Middle Ages were shaped by the revival of old shrine centres which had previously experienced dormant periods and disjunctures with the past. St Matthew's relics were translated to Salerno in 954 and the cult steadily developed thereafter. But the

---

[7] Loud, 'Monastic miracles', 109–22; at Cava, for example, only a few cases of curative miracles were recorded at the shrines of the monastery's saint-abbots, and most involved monks of Cava, although one episode recorded a 'worker' (*faber*) who healed an eye complaint by rubbing powder from the tomb of St Constable in the eye: VQPAC, especially, 33–4.

reinvention of Matthew's relics in 1080 was tacit acknowledgement of the previous limits of the cult's role in Salerno and beyond. As for St Agatha, according to one tradition, her relics may have been still *in situ* in Catania as late as c.1040, but if this were the case, the cult seems to have been increasingly neglected in Sicily by that point with the relics forgotten or displaced. Technically, the return translation of St Agatha to her native city in 1126 should be classed as a revival of the cult, following an absence which appears to have cemented discontinuities in the cult's traditions which were already apparent in Catania by the mid-eleventh century.

Certainly, the respective dates of 1080 (at Salerno), 1087 (at Bari) and 1126 (at Catania) should not be taken as the de facto points of inauguration for these shrine centres. Each, including St Nicholas at Bari, could call on earlier traditions of devotion for the particular saint within their cities, which helped consolidate their subsequent development. Nevertheless, the dates do provide undeniable poles around which the cults were reinforced and expanded to new dimensions in an era which facilitated this far more than previously. All have in common a burst of promotional activity in the decades immediately after their arrivals and revivals, a phenomenon replicated at new cult centres across Europe, and most prominently for the cult of St Thomas Becket at Canterbury. The process of reviving an old cult or authenticating the arrival of a new one was predicated on past and future uncertainty. Hence, the guardians of these cult centres resorted to the use of a combination of strategies which were especially significant given the international stature of the saints in question and the undeniable importance of creating and identifying to wider circles the existence of pilgrimage activity in order to validate their emergent shrines. The strategies encompassed the creation of hagiographical dossiers, especially *translationes* and *miracula* at Bari and Catania, although not significantly at Salerno, but also saw the production of poetical and liturgical works, the construction of grandiose new buildings to house the relics, and the insertion of these cults at the centre of evolving regional religious and political landscapes.

The arrival of St Nicholas's relics at Bari in 1087 was followed shortly after by the composition in the city of two competing accounts of the translation by the cleric Nicephorus and by John the Archdeacon which offer rich detail on movement to the shrine, although only for the first week after the translation. Nicephorus recorded over 100 healings during that time, but only discussed a small selection of these in detail.[8] The aims

---

[8] Nitti di Vito, 'La traslazione', 350–3; the *Jerusalem Legend* of the translation calculated 125 healings (Corsi, *La traslazione*, 81) within the first week, and *The Russian Legend* put the figure at 110 (Corsi, *La traslazione*, 121).

of both authors were not only to assert which faction within the city deserved guardianship of the relics but also to authenticate the cult's location in its new-found home in Bari, and by extension raise the status of the city and prevent future rival claims to St Nicholas. Besides these agendas, the material recorded by both authors is clearly shaped by the logistics of dissemination of information across time and space. Both John the Archdeacon and Nicephorus ended their accounts almost immediately after the translation, and even when the additional time to compose the works is added, it is unlikely to have been sufficient to allow for information to be received in more distant regions, legitimated and then acted on in the form of pilgrimages to the shrine, or, on the other hand, for news to return to Bari of distant miracles taking place. Revised twelfth-century versions of John's and Nicephorus' works, the Beneventan Continuation and the Jerusalem Legend, offer only minor additions.[9] The case of the cult of St Agatha at Catania provides a body of hagiographical material with evident similarities to the situation at Bari. The promoters of St Agatha, led initially by Catania's bishop Maurice, recorded a collection of miracles intended to authenticate the saint's presence in the city, to solidify her relationship with the faithful among the urban populace, and to assert regional religious and political ascendancies. Whereas at Bari, John the Archdeacon and Nicephorus recorded pilgrim activity only up to a week after St Nicholas's arrival, Bishop Maurice's account of St Agatha's translation (composed c.1130) and the continued documentation of miracles by the monk Blandinus (concluded at the latest in the early 1150s) stretch over the first decades of the cult's development.[10] Together they uncover deeper patterns of pilgrimage activity during a period of foundation and consolidation.

The material on pilgrimage to the shrine of St Matthew at Salerno is quite different from that at Bari and Catania in both type and context. There are no surviving miracle collections composed within southern Italy for the shrine, and Salerno was not a renowned centre for hagiographic production. In fact, only a few miracles were recorded in the wake of the initial translation of 954 and this pattern continued even after the cult's revival in the second half of the eleventh century.[11] It is even possible that curative miracles (one of the most common contexts for pilgrimages) may have been an infrequent occurrence at St Matthew's shrine because visitors could seek instead the medical knowledge of the physicians in the city's famous medical school. Indeed, that there was an

---

[9] Nitti di Vito, 'La traslazione', 353–6; Corsi, *La traslazione*, 80–4.
[10] See the *Epistola Mauritii* and *S. Agathae Miracula*.
[11] For the cult in the tenth century see Galdi, 'Il santo', 50–7.

interrelationship between medical expertise and miraculous cures is evident in the *vita* of St Alferius, abbot of the great monastery of Cava, near Salerno: a monk who had been afflicted by painful teeth initially turned for a remedy to the *ars medicorum*, clearly from the Salernitan school, but having met with no success he was cured at St Alferius' tomb.[12] This then implies that the regular type of pilgrim visit to St Matthew's was devotional, and less likely to attract comment. Other sources from within the city portrayed St Matthew as a devoted civic patron saint while also simultaneously being a leading Apostle for all Christendom.[13] Moreover, Salerno had no other genuine competitors for the possession of the main core of St Matthew's relics. The conviction brought by this set of attributes might partly explain the limited attestation of specific pilgrimages to his shrine: Matthew's place on the landscape of pilgrimage appears to have been so implicitly entrenched that it did not need volumes of corroborating textual evidence to be advertised to both a local and distant audience.

The challenges posed by our sources are accentuated for those shrines in southern Italy which were not as renowned and more often than not drew their pilgrims predominantly from a localized geographic radius. Without much influence on an international level, and lacking real financial muscle, these shrines often left limited records, minimal anecdotal material, and often merely one hagiographical text replete with complications, such as the work on St Gerard of Potenza.[14] The hagiographical texts of many of the region's Greek saints contain only sparse evidence on the post-mortem development of saintly cults, including pilgrimage patterns. As they have survived to us, the *bioi* of St Bartholomew of Simeri and of St Cyprian of Reggio both end with the deaths and the ceremonial burials of their respective subjects, with no posthumous miracles or evidence for pilgrimage thereafter; this silence is perhaps connected to the more remote locations of their shrines.[15] Saint Agatha's cult at Catania is effectively the only centre in Sicily where the evidence permits us to establish a satisfactory understanding of pilgrim activity on the island; all lesser shrine centres are silent on the subject. Nevertheless, less high-profile shrines should not be discounted entirely; there are certainly some exceptions on mainland southern Italy where material is relatively extensive, can reveal

---

[12] VQPAC, 11.

[13] For more on this see Chapters 2 and 5.

[14] St Gerard's hagiographer only speaks of a monk being healed at the shrine, and thereafter generically of unspecified miracles and visits to the saint's sepulchre: *De S. Gerardo*, 468–9.

[15] Zaccagni, 'bios', 273–4; Schirò, 'Vita', 97. Similarly, the hagiographical text on St John Terista ends with the saint's death, and records only one posthumous miracle: Borsari, 'Vita', 150–1.

international connections, and does assist in moving towards a more satisfactory understanding of pilgrimage activity in southern Italy. Prominent examples can be found for the cults of St Nicholas the Pilgrim at Trani, Saints Maurus, Pantaleon and Sergius at Bisceglie and St Cataldus at Taranto.

St Nicholas the Pilgrim, like his more famous namesake at Bari, was a new arrival to the region; he died at Trani in 1094. Unlike St Nicholas at Bari, he was a contemporary saint and therefore there was no pre-established devotion for St Nicholas the Pilgrim. Perfectly timed to coincide with the rise of the crusading movement, and perfectly positioned to benefit from its movement, St Nicholas the Pilgrim's cult was also a manifestation of civic pride and the emulation and competition which undoubtedly developed between Trani and Bari. In this climate, the production of hagiographical texts and the authentication bestowed by the written word were essential. The saint's hagiographical dossier provides plentiful evidence on pilgrimage, and in itself is more extensive than the comparable material emanating from Salerno and Bari. These last two, however, boast reams of corroborative external and anecdotal evidence to set pilgrimage activity firmly into its broader context. The hagiographical works for St Nicholas the Pilgrim offer two snapshots of the cult's development. First in c.1098 a *vita* and collection of miracles were composed by Adelferius, a *famulus* (servant) of the archbishop of Trani, and this text was probably the one handed to Urban II to promote the saint's canonization; secondly in 1142 Amandus, a deacon of the Church of Trani, composed an account of the saint's translation within the city's refurbished cathedral along with a set of attendant miracles.[16] Collectively, both authors offer twenty-three individual post-mortem miracles worked by St Nicholas the Pilgrim, many rich in detail and affecting large groups of people, along with a wealth of further complementary information on pilgrimage patterns. Amandus further enhanced his hagiographic portfolio in the late 1160s when, as bishop of Bisceglie, he authored an account of the discovery, translation and posthumous miracles of Saints Maurus, Pantaleon and Sergius which took place in 1167. It is a lengthy and laborious work replete with detail and evidence on pilgrim activity in the region of Bisceglie, but still framed, and in places restricted by, the usual hagiographic conventions.[17] A final hagiographic text of note within this category is the *Invention and Translation of St Cataldus*, written by a learned layman called Berengarius some time after 1151 when St Cataldus had been translated

---

[16] *Vita S. Nicolai Peregrini*, 241, 243–6.
[17] *Inventio, Translationes, et Miracula*; Head, 'Discontinuity', 203–07.

to a new shrine in Taranto.[18] It records over thirty miracles, with some revealing incidental information on pilgrimage included. A few of the miracles occurred after the rediscovery in the second half of the eleventh century, with most on the eve of, during or subsequent to the translation in 1151. In addition, a conflicting tradition of a translation of St Cataldus in 1094, recorded in the *Sermo de inventione sancti Kataldi* (composed between 1094 and 1174), offers six further miracle cases.[19] Together, they present a diverse body of evidence to evaluate pilgrimage movement in a variety of dimensions. Ordinarily, however, in the more standard type of hagiographic source, coverage tended to offer fewer examples of, and less content on, individual pilgrimages to shrines. The *Translation of SS Eleuterius, Pontianus and Anastasius* to Troia in 1104, composed some time in the twelfth century by a Roffredus, *precentor* of the city's bishopric, concentrated almost entirely on the transfer of the relics from Rome to Troia and recorded only eleven miracles which followed the event.[20] Likewise, Leo of Ostia's version of the translation of St Mennas to Caiazzo (in 1094) and then to S. Agata dei Goti (in 1110) highlighted a mere eight miracles which clearly were deemed sufficient authentication.[21] The *bios* of St Lucas, bishop of Isola di Capo di Rizzuto, written by an anonymous author probably between 1116 and 1120, is one of the richest sources for pilgrimage to a shrine of an Italian–Greek saint in the period 1000 to 1200 and yet records only eight miracles associated with the cult.[22]

In addition to the specific challenges presented by South Italian hagiographical material, these sources must also be used with caution and an understanding of both the genre and the contemporary context in which they were produced. As Marcus Bull put it, the hagiographer 'would be locating himself in a tradition of earlier writings as much as he would be engaged in contemporary "reportage" of events known to him'.[23] In identifying a diverse body of devotees, both geographically and socially, the author conformed to the needs of the hagiographical genre, and material on visitors to shrines was constructed for particular strategies. Information was carefully selected, concealed and also manipulated to present a particular message, both didactic and promotional. Often, it seems that such selections concealed the more mundane pilgrimage activity that took place within the local community itself. It is also important to recognize that dissonant religious discourses could exist between

[18] Historia S. Cataldi, 569–74.
[19] Hofmeister, 'Sermo', 110–14.
[20] Poncelet, 'Translation', 424–6.
[21] Hoffman, 'Translationes', 476–81.
[22] *Vita di S. Luca*, 115–25.
[23] *Miracles of Our Lady of Rocamadour*, 14–15.

pilgrims visiting the shrine and the guardians of it; hagiographers were usually drawn from the latter. For example, the pilgrims might prefer a 'pragmatic miracle discourse', searching for divine intervention in the present, while the guardians (and hagiographers) were as likely to promote the 'transcendent, sacrificial discourse' emphasizing the redemptive and grace-giving powers of a shrine.[24] In his account of the translation and miracles of St Nicholas the Pilgrim of Trani, the deacon Amandus drew his material from sources which were likely to emphasize different perspectives and meanings. On the one hand, he recorded incidents that he deemed believable 'from the fact that many people tell the story', or which he heard direct 'from the mouth' of those involved, in other words from sources external to the cult's guardians.[25] On the other hand, Amandus was a deacon of Trani cathedral, a man from the 'inside' as it were, who recorded his own eyewitness accounts, and who also tellingly assured the reader that in some cases he 'ascertained [news of the miracles] by the true method. For these miracles which the present narrative preserves, I drew with greedy heart from the mouth of the lord Russo, venerable priest, who is the guardian of that holy body [of St Nicholas] and is *primicerius* of our church'.[26]

Whatever the case may be, the individual pilgrims recorded were unlikely to have been purely fabricated; rather they represented assiduous authorial selections from a wider pool of pilgrims. Indeed, at one point in the *Chronicle* of S. Clemente a Casauria in the Abruzzi the author limited himself to recording merely three episodes of miraculous cures for fear that the reader would tire of further examples, and John the Archdeacon was apologetic and candid about his choice to record a mere fragment of the vast numbers of pilgrims arriving at St Nicholas's shrine at Bari.[27] Moreover, the core information on pilgrims within these accounts could be deemed real to the extent that it was often believed to be so by those who supplied the information and those who recorded it. The potency of this reality is strengthened by its need to have some rigour in the face of the widespread evidence within hagiographical works for scepticism and alternative opinions. Indeed, while much of our information on pilgrim visits to shrines is located within artificially constructed literary frameworks often associated with curative and biblical miracles, we must neither overlook the significance of the author's need to adhere to routine historical realities in order to authenticate the more fantastical elements of their

---

[24] Eade and Sallnow (eds), *Contesting the Sacred*, 10–16.
[25] *Vita S. Nicolai Peregrini*, 244 (at chapters 57 and 58), 245 (chapter 66).
[26] *Vita S. Nicolai Peregrini*, 245 (chapter 62).
[27] *Chronicon Casauriense*, 854–5; Corsi, *La traslazione*, 66.

works, nor fail to appreciate that these realities were often the products of exchanges with lay people.[28] Thus the surrounding secular world helped shape the attributes of a particular shrine, and provided additional parameters within which the hagiographer had to work. The autonomy of the hagiographer was therefore restricted in a number of ways.

(ii)   Supplementary sources on pilgrimage activity

In many cases, the deficiencies within South Italian hagiographical sources are mitigated by the existence of other material, including charters, chronicles, pilgrim itineraries, liturgical and poetical works, buildings and services associated with the shrine and pilgrimage, and also by texts from other regions. Much of this material was produced externally to the place where the shrine was located or outside the immediate circle of those who promoted it. These additional sources are not without their own problems, and they are often not available for the region's lesser shrines. Charter documentation and bequests are particularly sporadic. However, on the whole what does survive can provide new perspectives and fill some significant gaps. An understanding of pilgrimage patterns at Bari, Montecassino and particularly at Salerno and Monte Gargano is certainly dependent on such material. At Bari, for instance, we can utilize the collection of miracles composed by a monk of Bec from Normandy in the twelfth century which recorded a multitude of men of diverse ages converging on St Nicholas's shrine.[29] At Monte Gargano pilgrim itineraries, chronicle accounts, inscriptions, incidental references in foreign hagiographies and the development of a pilgrimage-service network represent almost the entirety of evidence on pilgrimage.

It is crucial to recognize that a great deal of pilgrimage activity was also masked by other actions and exchanges which were conducted in and around the vicinity of a cult centre; this was certainly the case at Montecassino where symbolic acts of power, patronage, reconciliation and collaboration were recorded to have taken place within the monastery without direct reference to a concomitant pilgrimage to St Benedict's shrine, which in most cases would have been a crucial component within such episodes. Heinrich Dormeier's methodical study reveals a range of interrelationships between Montecassino and the laity. Between 1039 and 1125, 193 religious houses were donated to the monastery by laypeople, and many more of the latter featured in Montecassino's necrology, joined the monastery's brotherhood, took on the monastic habit or were buried

---

[28] *Miracles of Our Lady of Rocamadour*, 32–7, 92.
[29] Poncelet, 'Miracula', 405–32.

in the monastic grounds.[30] In all of these cases, the relationship or event was extrinsically founded on devotion to St Benedict, and in at least a proportion of these a visit to the saint's tomb must have been integral. Indeed, Stephen D. White has shown how the medieval practice of donating to religious institutions, and by extension to saints, was a highly ritualized ceremony, with the final stage often taking place at the high altar, where saintly relics were usually housed, and was therefore intertwined with the act of pilgrimage.[31] Individuals entered in necrologies and confraternities (like the *Liber Confratrum* of St Matthew's at Salerno containing over 13,000 names), taking part in religious processions and festivities or conferring payments on feast days, might all have undertaken in these circumstances acts which could represent pilgrimage. Similarly, when King Tancred was reconciled with Richard I in 1191 and allegedly received Excalibur as confirmation, the reconciliation almost concealed the Angevin king's contemporaneous visit to St Agatha's tomb at Catania.[32] Indeed, devotional practices undertaken as part of royal and aristocratic itineraries might often be better understood in the context of a continual cycle of pilgrimages.[33]

It is unfortunate that many medieval authors were reluctant to apply explicit and consistent nomenclature to the pilgrim. *Peregrinus* is used relatively infrequently in the South Italian material, and other more neutral terms are often preferred. Individuals are often simply said to be 'going' to a shrine, 'approaching' or 'moving towards' it without any more distinct connections to the language of pilgrimage. In two separate and rare cases, both from Taranto, hagiographers recorded a woman from Cosenza and a French painter visiting St Cataldus' shrine 'in pilgrim dress', but the actions and experience of these pilgrims appeared to be no different from others without the *peregrinus* label who were recorded at the shrine.[34] Amandus was understandably keen to stress that St Nicholas the Pilgrim (*Peregrinus*) protected *peregrini*. Yet most of the individuals visiting his shrine were not labelled as pilgrims, and Amandus seems to have preferred to give the specific term only to travellers on ships; here he

---

[30] Dormeier, *Montecassino und die Laien*, 28–52, 108–21, 154–95.

[31] S. D. White, *Custom, Kinship, and Gifts to Saints. The Laudatio Parentum in Western France, 1050–1150* (Chapel Hill, 1988), 31–2. M. McLaughlin, *Consorting with Saints. Prayer for the Dead in Early Medieval France* (Ithaca, 1994), 170, 251, similarly shows how a variety of relationships between the laity and religious houses were intrinsically founded on shared associations with the 'community of the saints'.

[32] *Chronica*, iii. 97.

[33] See N. Vincent, 'The pilgrimages of the Angevin kings of England', *Pilgrimage. The English Experience from Becket to Bunyan*, ed. C. Morris and P. Roberts (Cambridge, 2010), 20–8.

[34] *Historia S. Cataldi*, 572; Hofmeister, 'Sermo', 118.

interchanged between *peregrini* and *palmiferi*, the latter applied to Holy Land pilgrims.[35] In short, the body of evidence for pilgrimage in southern Italy throws up several challenges, most of which can be overcome through recourse to a wider, less orthodox range of sources.

Pilgrim origins and identities

(i)   Insiders: citizens and natives

Closer proximity to a shrine was the most effective way to cultivate a stronger connection between the individual and the saint. From the most sacred space in and around the saintly tomb, pulses of spiritual energy radiated outwards into the wider world, gradually losing their charge as the distance from the shrine increased. At the same time, and as outlined in Chapter 2, the local community, both religious and secular, stood to gain an array of benefits if the shrine within their midst proved to be popular. These two forces together, along with the simple logistics of contact and communication, ensured that the largest number of pilgrims to most sites originated from the settlement in which the shrine was located, or were from its immediate hinterland. Unfortunately, the sources often choose not to dwell on this aspect of pilgrimage for long, or even at all. Some accounts appear to take for granted the presence of pilgrims from the local community. Others flag up native pilgrims at the outset, clearly reflecting the obvious realities behind the development of a cult and also wishing to demonstrate popular support for it; but they tend to overlook the role of these native devotees thereafter and focus instead on the arrival of pilgrims from outside the local community. The latter were a sign of prestige, and represented pilgrimage in its more identifiable guise; however, certainly the more long-distance pilgrims were only a small minority of pilgrimage movement overall. As will be seen in what follows, at some South Italian shrines hagiographers attempted to identify a pattern which is standard across medieval Christendom. Local inhabitants were understandably the first visitors recorded at the shrine, but in progressive stages over time pilgrims arrived from the shrine's immediate hinterland, then from the wider zone, followed sometimes by visitors from beyond southern Italy. Pierre-André Sigal's study on the miracles of Saint Gibrien, whose relics were translated to Reims in 1145, shows the cult's orbit initially operating in a radius of around thirty kilometres from the city before gradually expanding to distances of up to sixty kilometres

---

[35] *Vita S. Nicolai Peregrini*, 244–6.

away.[36] Over half of the recorded pilgrims to the shrine of St William of Norwich in England were from Norwich or from within ten miles of the city, while a quarter of British pilgrims recorded in the first decade after the death of Thomas Becket came from Kent or Canterbury. However, in both cases, as time passed, the proportion of pilgrims from further afield increased, spectacularly so in the case of Becket's shrine.[37] Clearly, the need to develop the intensity of the cult at its centre is indicative of the first stage of the growth of fledgling shrines which gradually reach maturity as pilgrims are attracted from further distances. But the intensity apparent at the centre of a new cult was hard to sustain. The accessibility of the saint to the local population may have generated a casual air of entitlement among native pilgrims which did not end devotional activity but made it less likely to create new miracles worthy of record. In short, local devotion and pilgrimage remained a constant feature of most cults, but its repetitive nature over time, and the natural development of a shrine, placed it at the margins of the material included in many of our sources.

At the leading shrines a diverse body of pilgrims from a range of territories could be expected. But in many cases, especially in major urban centres like Bari, Catania and Salerno, the arrival of these overlaid the core support from the native community. At Bari, Nicephorus offers a detailed breakdown of the miraculous healings occurring in the city within the week subsequent to St Nicholas's arrival.[38] Within roughly twenty-four hours of the translation Nicephorus claimed forty-seven people of both sexes and of diverse ages were cured: all were inhabitants from various parts of Bari, including a Pisan and a man considered to be among the most noble of the city. Thereafter, Nicephorus' analysis of the week tracked the cult's extension beyond the confines of Bari to attract pilgrims from increasingly greater distances. There was only a solitary further reference to the healing of a young Barese girl (on the Wednesday after the translation) which served to remind the reader of the cult's core following within the city. The week ended with the healing of eleven more individuals, but the fact that no more detail is provided here may suggest that they were Baresi, that native pilgrims continued to visit the shrine in numbers, and that this consistent presence was already relegated to the background. Nicephorus' calculations and descriptions are not entirely lucid, but at their base he picked out 101 miraculous healings within the first week of the translation, of which he discussed directly only a small

---

[36] P.-A. Sigal, 'Maladie, pèlerinage et guérison au XIIe siècle: les miracles de Saint Gibrien à Reims', *Annales: Economies, Sociétés, Civilisations* 24 (1969), 1533–9.

[37] Finucane, *Miracles and Pilgrims*, 161–66.

[38] Nitti di Vito, 'La traslazione', 350–3.

selection, while hinting at reams of additional miracles and pilgrims. It seems reasonable to suggest that the majority of these partly and wholly unrecorded pilgrims were native to the city and its immediate environs.

John the Archdeacon offers less detail than Nicephorus and more apologies for his ability to record only a segment of the pilgrimage activity.[39] His information follows a similar pattern to that of Nicephorus, but it differs in some instances, and suggests that the cult's renown spread faster and further. Aside from recording thirty healings on the first day, John does not attempt any further quantification and instead resorts to expressions of wonder at the infinite number of miracles that occurred. He discusses just four healings in depth, only one of which concerned a resident of Bari, who, however, originally came from Ancona. Despite their ambiguous language and concealed motivations, the accounts by Nicephorus and John together demonstrate that the main worshippers at the shrine were the people of Bari; their passion and commitment were vividly portrayed during the initial drama of the translation and the arrival of the relics in the city. The Baresi are understandably the first visitors recorded at the shrine and, although as time progressed pilgrims arrived from further away, there is enough supplementary evidence of the Baresi's devotion (such as bequests and the creation of the so-called society of S. Nicola) to be confident that they remained at the core of pilgrimage activity at the shrine throughout our period.

As at Bari, the promoters of St Agatha's recorded a collection of miracles which attempted to glorify the cult and, by extension, Catania. However, both Maurice and Blandinus fail to label specifically any pilgrim or recipient of a miracle as being from Catania, a surprising omission and highly unusual for an urban South Italian shrine. It would be absurd to suggest the cult did not draw pilgrims from the city, and Maurice and Blandinus certainly imply that citizens were a consistent component of pilgrimage traffic to St Agatha's shrine. Some half a dozen miracles involved individuals with no designated origin, who might therefore have been understood as being from Catania, while both authors must have included local citizens in their thoughts when offering their general statements on crowds of pilgrims flocking to the shrine. Geographically, the pilgrims recorded by Maurice and Blandinus originate almost exclusively from Sicily, and in particular the eastern zone of the island with prominent hot spots found in the port cities of Messina and Syracuse. As we shall see, the focus on Messina and Syracuse fits with broader strategies developed at Catania and represents one example of the way hagiographers selected

---

[39] Corsi, *La traslazione*, 66–8.

their material, in this case perhaps to the detriment of the recording of the presence of Catanesi at the shrine.

In certain respects the evidence for the role of native pilgrims at St Matthew's shrine at Salerno is much clearer than at Catania, even though the source material initially appears to be deficient. While hagiographical sources are largely absent, in this particular case their absence may represent an advantage by removing layers of camouflage and allowing other forms of evidence into the foreground. We have already noted that the presence of the famed Salernitan medical school would have discouraged some from within the city from turning to holy relics for cures, and this may explain the lack of curative miracles occurring among the Salernitani. On the other hand, the surviving record of the organization of St Matthew's feast-day procession in Salerno involved churchmen and communities from both the city and the entire archdiocese of Salerno, and indicates that the act of pilgrimage was built into the festivities.[40] Over 13,000 names of laymen and clerics are also contained within the *Liber Confratrum*, the cathedral confraternity dating from c.1000 and dedicated to St Matthew. As Vitolo concluded, the *Liber* is testament to the vast capacity which St Matthew's cult had to draw in the faithful, not only from the city but also from Salerno's archdiocese.[41] The individuals listed had made donations to the cathedral and could thereafter enjoy the spiritual rewards associated with the shrine centre. It must be assumed that many visited St Matthew's shrine either before, during or after their donations were made. St Matthew's Salernitan civic identity was not a new phenomenon in itself, but it was certainly revitalized with greater intensity in the second half of the eleventh century. The evidence, discussed in Chapter 2, demonstrates that the urban populace of Salerno developed a profound affinity with their saint, and was therefore the primary body of worshippers to visit the shrine.

The hagiographical sources at some of the lesser South Italian shrines, for St Nicholas the Pilgrim at Trani, St Cataldus at Taranto and Saints Maurus, Pantaleon and Sergius at Bisceglie, reveal the presence of pilgrims from the wider region and from beyond the limits of southern Italy. Nevertheless, alongside this non-local devotion, the presence of native pilgrims is visible and significant. In all three cases, their fortunate geographic location on the Apulian coastline at a time of urbanization and of increasing pilgrimage and commercial traffic suggests that the hagiographical texts may be offering a reasonably representative cross-section of pilgrimage activity at these ostensibly less well-known shrines.

---

[40] Vitolo, 'Città e chiesa', 134–45.
[41] *Necrologio del Liber Confratrum*; Vitolo, 'Città e chiesa', 141.

Adelferius, St Nicholas the Pilgrim's earliest hagiographer, utilized the stock techniques of his profession by aiming to establish the popular base of devotion for a newly established cult: the citizens gathered as one at the saint's tomb immediately after his death, earlier scepticism towards St Nicholas from among the city's inhabitants duly evaporated, and people from the surrounding territories flocked into the city. The earliest attendees whom Adelferius recorded at St Nicholas the Pilgrim's shrine are from Trani: a girl, a boy, two women and a youth from a noble family within the city. Only subsequently did Adelferius note the spreading fame of the saint, proved by the arrival of visitors from other territories.[42] The miracles added by Amandus some forty years later move the cult, and its pilgrim types, in new directions.[43] There is only one explicit reference to a devotee from Trani at St Nicholas the Pilgrim's shrine; otherwise the presence of the local inhabitants is merely implied. The implication from Amandus' information is quite clear. Now, in the mid-twelfth century, the proportion of pilgrims arriving from beyond Trani has increased, while St Nicholas the Pilgrim moves beyond the boundaries of his shrine to work miracles in the wider world. However, Amandus does not conversely suggest that the real numbers of native pilgrims decreased, and evidence from the year 1180 on the saint's feast-day festivities, where special masses and confession for 'those going to St Nicholas the Pilgrim' were offered, shows that local veneration and pilgrimage remained a potent force.[44]

At Taranto, Berengarius' record of over thirty miracles worked by St Cataldus notes only five explicit cases in which the recipients were from the city.[45] Nevertheless, their inclusion is spread evenly across the entire record of miracles, rather than, for example, being grouped at the start. In some sense, the presence of these inhabitants of Taranto binds the text together, and the events connected to the miraculous interventions associated with them confer further prominence. A tanner from Taranto was healed by St Cataldus and tried to sneak out of the shrine without alerting anybody to the event. Consequently, the church doors refused to open and allow his exit, compelling the man to inform everyone present about the miracle. This episode seems to have been recorded to encourage the locals to communicate their experiences at the shrine along with their gratitude, suggesting that some locals neglected to publicize or appreciate their visits.[46] One of the more dramatic

---

[42] *Vita S. Nicolai Peregrini*, 241.
[43] *Vita S. Nicolai Peregrini*, 243–6.
[44] Trani, no. 70.
[45] The *Sermo de Inventione Sancti Kataldi* does not record any directly from Taranto, see Hofmeister 'Sermo'.
[46] Historia S. Cataldi, 570.

incidents in Berengarius' account saw St Cataldus safely steering a ship of sailors from Taranto through a storm and the crew subsequently visited his shrine in gratefulness, while another high-profile miracle involved a *miles* from the city who had translated a work from Greek into Latin for the king, was healed while journeying to Palermo and who was almost certainly Berengarius himself.[47] Thus, although recorded in only limited numbers, the Tarantini were presented as an integral component in the miracle-working and pilgrimage activities connected to St Cataldus' shrine.

Finally, Bishop Amandus of Bisceglie's detailed record of miracles and visits to the shrines of Saints Maurus, Pantaleon and Sergius presents similarities with St Cataldus and Taranto. Among over forty separate records of miracles and visits to the shrine of the three saints, only five unequivocally related to people from Bisceglie.[48] In contrast to the accounts of Tarantini interacting with their local shrine, those from Bisceglie broadly represent standard, low-key episodes which do not stand out from the rest of the account. On the other hand, Amandus makes it clear that the people of Bisceglie were especially devoted to their new saints, and this was often expressed in collective action. As the bodies were discovered and translated to different locations, the people of Bisceglie flocked to the shrine. When the relics were translated from the rural church of S. Fortunato to S. Bartolomeo, 'a great multitude of people from Bisceglie and neighbouring lands' visited the new shrine, and when Amandus decided to build a new oratory for the saints near the city cathedral, all the inhabitants of Bisceglie, from the 'least to the greatest', worked day and night on the construction.[49] Similarities are clear with the record of Roffredus on the miracles and devotional activities at Troia following the translation of the relics of Saints Eleutherius, Pontianus and Anastasius in 1104. Only two of the eleven recorded miracles involved inhabitants of Troia, but they were nonetheless depicted in the work as the main body of devotees.[50] In the case of each of the shrines at Trani, Taranto, Bisceglie and Troia, ecclesiastical officials were clearly motivated to harness to their churches the emergent sense of civic and communal identity via these cults. How far we should trust the details of these particular records is perhaps not as significant as the fact that their strategies were aimed in this direction, which suggests that creating and cultivating streams of pilgrimage from within the local community was deemed to be both integral and achievable.

---

[47] Historia S. Cataldi, 572.
[48] *Inventio, Translationes, et Miracula*, 362.
[49] *Inventio, Translationes, et Miracula*, 363, 367.
[50] Poncelet, 'Translation', 422–6.

(ii)   *Outsiders: regional and foreign pilgrims*

If the more quotidian features of pilgrimage activity were founded, in most cases, on devotees drawn from the immediate community, visitors from further away were often more likely to be noted. Their presence signified many things, above all the growing renown of a cult but also ongoing interactions and encounters between different communities on a wider plane. Evidence from the major shrines at Bari, Catania, Montecassino, Monte Gargano and Salerno attests the presence of a large body of medium-distance pilgrims from other regions of southern Italy as well as a significant number of foreign pilgrims, as discussed in Chapter 5, who originated from territories beyond southern Italy. In each of these cases, the cult boasted a universally popular saint, and was located near to key travel routes. An international dimension to these cults was therefore largely assured.

While lacking a defined localized body of lay devotees, pilgrimage to the shrines at both Monte Gargano and Montecassino prominently featured visitors arriving from medium and long distances. Indeed, St Michael's at Monte Gargano should be ranked alongside St Nicholas's at Bari as the leading South Italian shrine for foreign, long-distance pilgrims. Foreign visitors to Monte Gargano were recorded in a geographically diverse body of material, within which a large number, including Normans, came from modern-day France, while others included German emperors, popes, Crusaders and a range of wandering saints from across Europe. On the other hand, and taking into account the limited evidence on the shrine which emanates from southern Italy itself, it still remains surprising that in very few cases can we unequivocally identify South Italian pilgrims visiting Monte Gargano. In the early eleventh century, at Monte Gargano, a group of Norman pilgrims met the Lombard rebel Melus, a member of the urban patriciate of Bari. William of Apulia's (possibly invented) set piece for the Norman arrival in southern Italy suggests the meeting was a chance one and, by extension, that Melus was visiting the shrine.[51] That St Michael was seen as the Lombard national saint may both strengthen the case for Melus' presence and weaken it at the same time, because the episode proffers the conveniently resonant message that the new power in the south rose at the spiritual centre of a people who were soon to become subjects. However, evidence for South Italian Lombards visiting the shrine post-1000 is virtually non-existent, and information on any South Italian pilgrims relates almost exclusively to high-profile visitors. For

---

[51] Wil. Apulia, Bk I, pp. 98–100 lines 11–16.

example, late in the eleventh century, the wealthy merchant Pantaleon of Amalfi donated the beautiful bronze doors which adorn the sanctuary, and which had been built at Constantinople. Pantaleon had clearly visited the shrine as a pilgrim, and engraved on the doors were both his name and the exhortation: 'I ask all who come here to pray that first you should inspect such a beautiful work.'[52] In the twelfth century, St John of Matera stayed at the shrine for a whole year in the 1120s, and Henry, prince of Capua, the younger brother of King William II, visited Monte Gargano in 1172.[53] Beyond this meagre haul little more is known of the pilgrim activity of South Italians at the shrine.

The evidence at Montecassino is largely more promising. In Chapter 5 we noted the visits of French nobles, German emperors, leading churchmen, and of individuals from as far away as Iberia and Jerusalem. Some arrived in the guise of Crusaders, diplomats or benefactors of the monastery, most seem also to have simultaneously undertaken pilgrimage to St Benedict's shrine, and this was the case also for visitors from within southern Italy. During the abbacy of Richer (1038–55) the brothers of the counts of Aquino were reconciled with the monastery following the abduction of Montecassino's abbot by one of their brothers, who had since died. The record of their visit to Montecassino carries all the hallmarks of a penitential pilgrimage: 'They soon hastened to the monastery with ropes tied round their necks, confessing with loud voices how they had gravely sinned against such a great man and had wickedly harmed so venerable a place.'[54] It is hard to conceive that this staged resolution of conflict did not involve the performance of any symbolic acts at St Benedict's tomb. The same could be inferred from several other episodes, such as when in the 1120s Rao son of Rahel, a local nobleman, 'came to the monastery and renounced to the Blessed Benedict by charter' the contested ownership of some men from Teano.[55]

Other passages in Desiderius' *Dialogues* confirm that St Benedict's tomb was frequently visited by pilgrims from within southern Italy. According to the *Dialogues* several miracles occurred *ad sepulcrum beati Benedicti*, suggesting movement and, in this context, pilgrimage: a secular priest was cured, a boy was released from the control of a lionlike demon, and another similarly from a demon in the form of an Ethiopian.[56] Another demon was exorcised from an old man from the region of

---

[52] D'Arienzo, 'Il pellegrinaggio', 224.
[53] *Vita S. Iohannis*, 39–40; Romuald, 261.
[54] Chron. Cas., Bk II.69, pp. 306–7.
[55] Chron. Cas., Bk IV.92, p. 553.
[56] Desiderius, Bk.II.9, p. 1131, 14–5 pp. 1134–5.

Marsia (central-eastern Italy), who had heard that many ailments were healed at St Benedict's threshold.[57] Other cures involved a highly esteemed nephew of a monk at Montecassino, and the son of a peasant (*rusticus*) from one of the monastery's local *castella* who was freed from the grip of a demon after sleeping at St Benedict's tomb.[58] The *Montecassino Chronicle* and its Continuation, dated mostly to the 1120s, recorded further healings before St Benedict's body: a monk from Bari (256 kilometres away) was brought by his kinsmen before St Benedict's altar where he was cured; around 1070 a *rusticus* also from Apulia was freed from demonic possession when 'he was laid before the body of Father Benedict'; in 1112 a *transalpinus miles* in the service of the count of Teano was healed after falling from his horse; in c.1120 another knight was freed from captivity by the saint, and travelled from Apulia to St Benedict's tomb.[59] In total, the number of pilgrims recorded at St Benedict's shrine is rather low and details are minimal; certainly individual pilgrimages were not the main concern of the various authors in question. What can be gleaned from the surviving material? As with St Michael's at Monte Gargano, there was no large and proximate urban community to supply a constant stream of visitors; however, St Benedict's shrine certainly attracted a localized core of devotees primarily from the sizeable territories of Montecassino itself, but also from neighbouring lands, which like those of the counts of Aquino might be only about 15 kilometres away. These were supplemented by a notable stream of foreign pilgrims, who were more likely to be recorded. The old man from Marsia, and the monk, peasant and knight based in Apulia, present cases of mid-range pilgrimage, those from Apulia possibly linked to the spread of Montecassino's dependencies there; pilgrims from other regions in southern Italy are absent from our records.

Of the major city-based shrines, Salerno is undoubtedly the most disappointing for direct evidence of pilgrimage activity of all ranges. While there is enough material to be certain that the Salernitan community regularly visited St Matthew's shrine, the evidence is incredibly meagre on pilgrimage from other areas of southern Italy or from further afield. The surviving formula of St Matthew's feast-day celebrations within the city suggests pilgrims arrived from throughout the archdiocese, and the necrology and *Liber Confratrum* of S. Matteo include individuals

---

[57] Desiderius, Bk II.16, p. 1135. It should be noted that there was a strong influence from the Marsia region at Montecassino, including the chronicler Leo Marsicanus, and members of the comital family of Marsica, to which Abbot Oderisius I (1087–1105) was related: Howe, *Church Reform*, 132–9.

[58] Desiderius, Bk II.17–18, pp. 1135–7.

[59] Chron. Cas., Bk II.48, pp. 258–9, III.38, p. 414, IV.44, pp. 512–3, IV.58, pp. 521–2.

from beyond Salerno, many of whom must have visited the shrine.[60] In 1120 Count Roger of San Severino, a powerful nobleman in the principality of Salerno, agreed not to disturb the 'pilgrims, clerics, monks, merchants, and women' of the church of St Matthew of Salerno.[61] Amatus of Montecassino recorded Pisan merchants at the shrine in the eleventh century, and a miracle attributed to Troia's saints Eleutherius, Pontianus and Anastasius was worked on a monk from Narni in Umbria (281 kilometres north of Salerno) while he was returning from a visit to St Matthew's shrine; however, overall this is very limited information, both in quantity and quality, for such an established shrine.[62]

Fortunately, evidence from the shrines at Bari and less so at Catania demonstrates the presence of regional and foreign visitors far more clearly than is the case at Salerno. We have already noted how the works of both Nicephorus and John the Archdeacon reveal that the immediate devotional activity at the shrine at Bari arose from the local citizenry. However, within a matter of days of the translation, both authors recorded the geographic expansion of the cult and the arrival of pilgrims from outside Bari. By the following Tuesday Nicephorus commented that the cult had already begun to extend beyond the confines of Bari to attract villagers and inhabitants from surrounding settlements. He recorded twenty-three miracles from among the crowds, most replications of biblical healings, but only one was identified more closely as affecting a woman from Giovinazzo (17 km away). On the Wednesday a further twenty-nine individuals were healed, and their origins indicate that the shrine's orbit of influence had moved further from Bari: Bitonto (14 km), Terlizzi (26 km), San Vito near Montescaglioso (65 km), Taranto (78 km) and Ascoli Satriano (108 km). Thursday saw a monk receive a cryptic vision from St Nicholas and the recording of only one healing of a youth who was blind, mute and possessed. On Friday, Nicephorus recorded the recognition of the cult by some of the key ecclesiastical officials of the diocese of Bari: the bishop of Bitonto led a great procession to the shrine, while the bishop of Bari, accompanied by the archbishop of Brindisi (106 km), the bishop of Conversano (28 km) and three more unidentified bishops, led an immense crowd to adore the holy relics. The week ended with the healing of eleven more, anonymous, individuals. The number of miracles recorded by Nicephorus diminished as the days passed, perhaps because,

---

[60] Vitolo, 'Città e chiesa', 134–45; see examples from the index in *Necrologio del Liber Confratrum*.
[61] Giunta, 'Documenti', 277–83.
[62] Amatus, Bk VIII.4, pp. 483–4; Poncelet, 'Translation', 426.

once the occurrence of miracles had been established, their quantity was less important than their quality and widening geographic pull.[63]

John the Archdeacon's account is more brief, but certainly suggests that the cult's renown spread faster and further, reaching all parts of Italy within a mere few days.[64] He covered only four healings in depth, relating to a man from Ancona (who seems to have been a resident of Bari), a priest from the territory of Camerino in the Marches (384 km away), a young boy conveyed from Amalfi (197 km) and a baby brought from an unidentified settlement. Later versions of the accounts of Nicephorus and John, the Beneventan Continuation and the Jerusalem Legend, provide only a few additional miracles. The Beneventan Continuation extolled the rapid dissemination of the shrine's fame across the world, and included additional cases of pilgrim activity such as the poor servant of a citizen of Siponto (96 km) in northern Apulia who went on pilgrimage to Bari by ship with other pilgrims from the same city; however, from further afield it could offer only the single example of a poor man and wife who sailed across the Adriatic from Durazzo.[65] The Jerusalem version added some colourful accounts and recorded pilgrims from Benevento (173 km) and its zone, but no specific cases were recorded of more distant pilgrims.[66]

Associations with maritime commerce, with the crusading movement, with wide-ranging monastic networks and with France in particular, ensured the shrine's growing success and an influx of foreign visitors, as has been outlined in Chapter 5. Such a broad stamp of approval also probably explains why no further hagiographical accounts were produced at Bari in the twelfth century. Although this lacuna can be circumnavigated to some extent in the case of foreign visitors, it means that little consistent information survives on patterns of South Italian pilgrimage to the shrine in the later eleventh and twelfth centuries. Thus, while we know that the influx of foreigners to the shrine rapidly increased after 1095, and French, Anglo-Norman, North Italian and German pilgrims are all attested at the shrine in the eleventh and twelfth centuries, many journeying to the Holy Land, mere scraps of information alone remain for South Italian pilgrims visiting St Nicholas's shrine.

Aside from references to hospitals and other possible pilgrimage services, the charter documentation from Bari offers little assistance in mapping pilgrimage activity of any sort in the city. A bequest made to the shrine of St Nicholas by aristocratic German pilgrims heading to the Holy

---

[63] Nitti di Vito, 'La traslazione', 350–3.
[64] Corsi, La Traslazione, 66–8.
[65] Nitti di Vito, 'La traslazione', 353–6.
[66] Corsi, La traslazione, 80–4.

Land in 1189 was noted in Chapter 5, and it is only this form of high-status presence that remains in the Barese cartularies. A document from the early twelfth century reveals that a grandson of one of Robert Guiscard's elder brothers was buried in the cemetery of the church of St Nicholas, and implies an ongoing relationship with, and, by extension, pilgrimages to, the shrine by members of the Hauteville dynasty.[67] King William II issued a charter in 1182 recording his pilgrimage 'ad limina beati Nicolai' and Henry VI, newly crowned as king of Sicily, surely attended the shrine in April 1195 when he confirmed, on account of his devotion to St Nicholas, the church of S. Nicola's rights in the city of Matera, held the Diet of Bari and almost certainly took his oath to go on Crusade.[68] Identifying the act of pilgrimage within some of this material must remain conjecture. The same can be said of other evidence. When Roger II attempted to incorporate the mainland into his new kingdom in the 1130s he visited Bari on at least three occasions, and issued a charter of privileges to the city which expressed the protection of the cult of St Nicholas as a royal priority. An enamel plaque at the high altar in the basilica of S. Nicola, dating probably to the 1130s, depicts the saint holding the king's crown on his head; it would be almost unthinkable that Roger had not therefore visited the shrine, especially when we know, according to Falco of Benevento, that he toured the holy places of Benevento in 1139 when a diplomatic settlement enabled him to enter that city.[69] Similarly, when William I razed the city of Bari in 1156, the basilica of S. Nicola was spared, possibly revealing a personal devotion to the shrine. This Sicilian royal activity may well fit with Nicholas Vincent's findings on the pilgrimages of the Angevin kings of England. For the Angevins, visits to relics and shrines were a standardized feature of royal itineraries; they sanctified their passage through their territories and many of their normal devotional acts could in fact be considered as pilgrimages.[70]

Sources external to the city of Bari offer some useful information on pilgrimage to St Nicholas's shrine. We have already noted references to the visits of foreigners to Bari which are found in a wide range of sources, although, as they often record crusading expeditions, information on pilgrimage to St Nicholas's shrine is usually incidental. Likewise, accounts of miracles at other South Italian shrine centres noted that recipients had initially visited St Nicholas's shrine at Bari – this was the

[67] CDBV, no. 50.
[68] CDBV, no. 147; CDBVI, no. 1.
[69] *Rogerii II*, 54–6 no. 20; Houben, *Roger II*, 115–17; Falco, 224.
[70] Vincent, 'Pilgrimages', 20–8.

case for a woman healed by St Mennas at S. Agata dei Goti and another from Manopello healed at Troia by the city's saints; these accounts thus inadvertently acknowledged the popularity and esteem of St Nicholas's shrine at Bari.[71] The collection of miracles composed by the monk of Bec, however, represents a work devoted to the cult of St Nicholas. It presents vast numbers of visitors of diverse ages converging at the shrine at Bari, a standard hagiographical claim for sure. However, it also added individual examples, some of which shed more light on South Italian pilgrims at Bari. One case confirmed that many pilgrims travelled in groups and were inspired by the actions of those around them: it concerned a blind man from Calabria who heard of some of his neighbours' plans to visit St Nicholas's shrine, joined their company (*comitatus*) and was healed at Bari.[72] Another told of a young man (*juvenis*) in 1129 who on account of his crimes was ordered by his bishop to do penance and to visit various holy places; he did so wearing an iron ring around his stomach. After he had offered prayers at St Nicholas's shrine the ring miraculously broke. The young man's origins are not stated and, while the information was related by an eyewitness, a cleric of the diocese of Rouen, it does not necessarily follow that the *juvenis* was foreign.[73] The iron ring, an overt symbol of the penitential pilgrimage, may suggest however that the man travelled from some distance, and Bari was indeed a common destination for penitential pilgrimages imposed as judicial punishment. At Bari the combined evidence suggests a broad spectrum of people visited St Nicholas's shrine, and that wider European developments drove much of this activity. In truth, a paradox sits at the core of this activity as it is poorly documented and often appears to be clouded by varying shades of uncertainty. Any conclusions must be tempered by the flawed nature of the extant material. It is clear that a framework existed which enabled Bari to develop as a thriving pilgrimage centre: externally because of the city's geographic location, St Nicholas's broad appeal in western Christendom and transitions in Christian religious devotion; internally because of the evolution of pilgrimage services within the city, the enlarging of the basilica, and evidence for royal and aristocratic veneration alongside that of the local Barese community with its society of S. Nicola. However, the detail within this framework is limited; intimate records of pilgrim experiences at the shrine are in increasingly short supply after the initial translation, thus denying the opportunity to construct deeper insight into

---

[71] Hoffmann, 'Translationes', 476–7; Poncelet, 'Translation', 426.

[72] Poncelet, 'Miracula', no. 26 p. 422.

[73] Poncelet, 'Miracula', no. 27 pp. 422–3; indeed the previous miracle concerning the Calabrian was related by an Anglo-Norman monk.

the nature of pilgrimage movement at one of western Christendom's greatest shrines.

It will be useful to incorporate here comparative evidence of pilgrimage to another South Italian shrine of St Nicholas: the sanctuary at the Beneventan church of S. Nicola della Torre Pagana. The movement of pilgrims to the sanctuary was recorded in the polemical work known as the *Adventus Sancti Nycolai in Beneventum* which purported to recount the transfer of the saint's patronage from Bari to Benevento at some point shortly before the text was composed around 1100. Underlying the obvious political overtones of the work is an interesting account of miracles worked from the new shrine centre and of pilgrimages to it. The *Adventus* employs the usual hagiographic strategies to denote authenticity and popularity: the miracles selected for recording often had biblical resonances, and the pilgrims arrived from all parts, beyond the seas, from north of the Alps and from most regions of southern Italy. The information on the *transmarini* and *transalpini* who were said to have flocked to the sanctuary in Benevento is very laconic, lacking almost any additional detail. The same is true for the South Italian groups listed: the *apuli* (Apulians), *tetini* (from modern Chieti in the Abruzzi), *salernitani* (Salernitans), *amalfitani* (Amalfitans), *capuani* (Capuans) and *napoletani* (Neapolitans). None of the miracle/pilgrim stories relates to an individual from any of these regions, although it seems that it was primarily in Campania and regions north of Benevento that the author of the text envisaged the influence of the cult as having the most force.[74] The potential for pilgrims from Calabria, who were recorded at St Nicholas's shrine at Bari, and from Sicily appears to be disregarded. The miracles which were recounted in detail involved movement to the sanctuary from zones neighbouring Benevento, or implied a localized origin for the recipient. One miracle recounted the healing of a deaf man from an unknown, presumably local, *castellum*, while others involved a mother and baby from the Valle Caudina region (c.20 km west of Benevento) and a father and son from S. Agata dei Goti (25 km west). Towards the end of the work, a Count Eribert of Ariano (c.40 km east of Benevento) was recorded visiting the sanctuary twice, the first time to hear from the guardians of the church about the miraculous healings, the second time returning barefoot and singing psalms, and accompanied by Bishop Sarulus of Ariano and the clergy and people of the county.[75] It would appear then that, despite grander pretensions, the collector of the miracle stories relied on only relatively localized examples, probably because such information was

---

[74] Cangiano, 'Adventus', 149–51.
[75] Cangiano, 'Adventus', 153–5.

more readily available and because the majority of pilgrims to this parvenu shrine centre were undoubtedly local. It is equally significant that further detail on foreign pilgrims, which would have been an attractive promotional tool, was not simply fabricated.

The case of the cult of St Agatha at Catania suggests that, as at Bari, medium-distance pilgrims from beyond the city's immediate hinterland were a significant feature of pilgrimage traffic. The pilgrims included in the hagiographical works authored by Maurice and Blandinus originate predominantly from eastern Sicily, especially from the key coastal cities of Messina and Syracuse. This is in stark contrast to St Nicholas at Bari where evidence of efforts to make firm connections between the shrine and its major neighbouring, and competitor, urban settlements – places such as Trani and Brindisi – are minimal. Through miracle workings at St Agatha's and the focus on medium-distance pilgrimage we are able to glimpse the interactions, relationships and rivalries operating between emergent cities.[76] The recording of pilgrims from Messina and Syracuse served to assert the prominence of Catania's political and ecclesiastical rank within Sicily. Cultivating devotion to St Agatha in Messina, the foremost port city in Sicily, and one of the main transit ports in the Central Mediterranean, represented the chance to tap into a large urban community, with an increasingly international, heterogeneous and transient population with thriving communication networks. Contemporary depictions provide vivid illustration of a frenetic entrepôt, and Benjamin of Tudela was clear that it was where most of the pilgrims convened on their journey to Jerusalem.[77] Unfortunately, there is only limited record of those travellers and pilgrims actually visiting St Agatha's shrine. As is often the case, visits are implied, and only the higher-profile cases made it into some form of record. In around 1170, for instance, Prior Theobald of Vermandois of the Cluniac house of Saint-Arnoult at Crepy-en-Valois appears to have undertaken a diplomatic mission to the Holy Land which might have entailed a visit to Sicily, and if so this must have been via Messina. White put forward the plausible case that, as the church of Saint-Arnoult at Crepy-en-Valois claimed to have acquired relics of St Agatha, Theobald may have visited the shrine at Catania where he was able to procure the sacred objects from his fellow Benedictine monks at the cathedral.[78] Certainly, the crusading forces of Richard I and Philip

---

[76] For more see Chapter 4.

[77] Liber de Regno, 108 (Tyrants, 156); *Travels of Ibn Jubayr*, 338–9; *Itinerary of Benjamin of Tudela*, 137.

[78] White, *Latin Monasticism*, 50 n. 8. Robert of Cricklade, the scholarly Augustinian prior of St Frideswide of Oxford, visited Catania in 1156, p. 50.

Augustus stayed in Sicily in the winter of 1190–1 and were based at Messina. Evidence suggests that some of these Crusaders visited Catania, and the encounters with the local inhabitants which occurred during this expedition undoubtedly further stimulated the transmission of knowledge of Sicilian folklore and of St Agatha's cult throughout western Europe. The English historian Roger of Howden, who accompanied Richard I on the Third Crusade, took a keen interest in the folklore surrounding St Agatha, which he clearly obtained from local sources and might suggest he attended the saint's shrine. It is also Roger who recorded the visit of King Richard I to St Agatha's shrine as part of the diplomatic rapprochement with King Tancred of Sicily.[79]

Messina then was clearly viewed from Catania as a fundamentally important channel through which pilgrims could be directed to St Agatha's shrine. Indeed, Messina was woven into St Agatha's translation account of 1126 as an important staging post in the journey. It was the point where St Agatha's relics first returned to Sicily, and the location of their authentication by church officials from Catania.[80] The message reinforced Messina's subsidiary role as a conduit for devotion to St Agatha, and acted as a signpost diverting travellers south to Catania. Indeed, by the twelfth century there was a church of S. Agata in Messina and one miracle actually involved the woman who had initially provided shelter in Messina for the two men who were transporting the relics to Catania.[81]

The continuation of the miracle records by the monk Blandinus does indicate a shift in emphasis. The horizons of the cult were perceptibly broadened according to this hagiographer. He made several references to vast crowds heading to Catania and said that in 1132 visitors to the shrine came 'not only from the Sicilians, but also from inhabitants of foreign territories'.[82] However, the specific pilgrims recorded by Blandinus conflict with his portrayal of the cult's expanding geographic pull. The earlier material provided by Maurice included individuals from Consentina (Cosenza? in Calabria, 225 km) and Gerace (in Calabria, 131 km; or possibly Geraci in Sicily, 91 km), as well as from Messina (87 km), Syracuse (49 km) and Troina (53 km) in Sicily. Those pilgrims for whom Blandinus supplied details also included people from Messina, Syracuse and Palatolium (possibly Palazzolo Acreide, 52 km). It appears from both Maurice's and Blandinus' accounts that pilgrims primarily originated from a consistent territorial zone based on eastern and north-

[79] *Chronica*, iii. 97.
[80] *Epistola Mauritii*, 644–5.
[81] White, *Latin Monasticism*, 148, 240; *Epistola Mauritii*, 646.
[82] *S. Agathae Miracula*, 649.

eastern Sicily. An important charter of 1168 freed pilgrims from paying river tolls at Catania, and implied their high numbers, but unfortunately it offers no indication as to their origins.[83]

Pilgrims from other areas of southern Italy were a prominent presence at some of the region's lesser shrines. Primarily they originated from a core zone orbiting around the shrine, which usually stretched up to c.40 km, followed by more sporadic numbers at distances between 40 km and 100 km, with only very limited numbers from distances further afield which were still within the territories of southern Italy and Sicily. Pilgrims from foreign territories also visited some of these lower-ranking shrines. As the majority of the lesser shrines for which we have sufficient evidence are located on or near to major commercial and pilgrim route-ways, the presence of foreign pilgrims should not be dismissed as purely hagiographical topoi. This also suggests that many of the longer-distance pilgrims might not initially have been heading for the shrines at which they subsequently appeared, and the examples in the hagiographies often con-firm this. The hagiographers of St Nicholas the Pilgrim at Trani set out a progressive expansion of the cult's influence, in a pattern similar to that for St Nicholas at Bari. The earliest attendees whom Adelferius recorded at St Nicholas the Pilgrim's shrine are all from Trani, but subsequently he noted the spreading fame of the saint, proved by the arrival of visitors from other territories. These included pilgrims from the relatively close settlements of Bisceglie (8 km) and Terlizzi (19 km), and others from Mottola (88 km), whose journey would have required passing St Nicholas' shrine at Bari, from Calabria and even from Flanders.[84] Adelferius explic-itly framed the pilgrimage of Andrew from Flanders around the increasing dissemination of St Nicholas's renown throughout the whole of Italy. Having been exorcised of a demon at the saint's shrine, Andrew was ordered by the city's archbishop to proceed to Jerusalem to give further thanks to God, an event which might otherwise conceal the likelihood that Andrew was heading there already and only heard of St Nicholas the Pilgrim's shrine as he moved along the Apulian coast.

The miracles added by Amandus some forty years later map the cult's continued, gradual expansion. With only one explicit reference to a devotee from Trani at St Nicholas the Pilgrim's shrine, Amandus presents a picture of increased interaction between the cult and the wider world. Pilgrims arrive from distances similar to those recorded by Adelferius – from Bisceglie (8 km), Corato [?] (14 km), Ruvo (19 km), Salpi (29 km approximately), Ascoli Satriano (72 km), Potenza (86 km) and from

[83] Fasoli, 'Tre secoli', Appendix, document II, pp. 400–1.
[84] *Vita S. Nicolai Peregrini*, 241.

France – but now they form a more conspicuous element of visitors to the shrine.[85] At the translation in 1142, Amandus recorded the ceremonial visit of church dignitaries, including the archbishop of Brindisi (147 km) and the bishops of Ostuni (115 km), Ariano (112 km), Rapolla (71 km) and Andria (11 km). Also at this celebration 'almost the entirety of Apulia was roused up'; 'each *urbs*, *vicus*, and *municipium* sent their people to honour the holy man, for there was such an assembly of people that the space of the city could hardly contain them'.[86] There are some notable omissions in the accounts of Adelferius and Amandus. No pilgrims are recorded from Barletta (11 km) or Molfetta (17 km), two neighbouring competitor port cities. Perhaps the parvenu saint at Trani simply did not exert sufficient pull for the inhabitants of either settlement to overcome local rivalries, and one would have expected Adelferius and Amandus to jump at the chance to assert St Nicholas the Pilgrim's influence in either location. Also missing are any references to Bari (40 km) or to pilgrims from the city. It would have been highly unlikely for a Barese to spurn the protection of St Nicholas of Myra for a 'lesser' St Nicholas at one of his main rival cities in Apulia.[87] In remaining silent on Bari, both Adelferius and Amandus appear to have also declined an obvious head-to-head clash in which they were unlikely to offer any convincing proof of ascendancy. The main target audience for the guardians of St Nicholas the Pilgrim was within the medium to small settlements of central Apulia. However, references to Brindisi and Mottola in southern Apulia, to Ascoli Satriano in northern Apulia, to pilgrims in Lucania (from Potenza) and Calabria, as well as from beyond the Alps, suggest plausible currents of wider dissemination.

Indeed, this is confirmed by the appearance of miracles performed by St Nicholas the Pilgrim away from Trani, which also show the impact of the rising pilgrimage and crusading movement on this port city. First, in Amandus' account, St Nicholas the Pilgrim frees prisoners and saves ships carrying pilgrims.[88] The latter is an appropriate calling for this saint and may reveal a not so subtle attempt to tap into pilgrimage traffic, and to compete with St Nicholas of Bari, also known for his protection of sailors. Benjamin of Tudela had noted in c.1170 the crowds of pilgrims assembling at Trani for the voyage to the Holy Land, and the reconstruction of the city's cathedral on the harbourside must have served as a beacon advertising the shrine to travellers. Twice St Nicholas the Pilgrim

---

[85] *Vita S. Nicolai Peregrini*, 243–6.
[86] *Vita S. Nicolai Peregrini*, 244 (at chs 69 and 60).
[87] For more on this rivalry see Chapter 2.
[88] *Vita S. Nicolai Peregrini*, 243–6.

appeared on board ship to save vessels returning from Syria full of *palmiferi* (pilgrims to Jerusalem), one of whom had been Amandus himself. These actions, however, appear to have created an obligation to visit the saint's shrine, at least by the captains of the ships. One of the aforesaid vessels had been guided to safety at Syracuse in Sicily and yet Amandus claimed to have heard the story from the ship's captain, suggesting he had fulfilled a vow to visit St Nicholas the Pilgrim's shrine. A third account of a ship saved by the saint ended with the captain leaving at the shrine a wax model ship with St Nicholas the Pilgrim at the helm.[89]

This last case is of further interest as Amandus said that the ship, which a storm had forced onto the Dalmatian coastline, was full of 'people making for the holy shrine of the man [St Nicholas the Pilgrim]'.[90] It implies that demand was sufficient to create maritime pilgrim traffic to the shrine from destinations where coastal travel was more expedient than travel overland. At the very least, this was the impression Amandus hoped to convey. Although in total Adelferius and Amandus specifically record only two visitors to St Nicholas's shrine from beyond Italy – the man from Flanders, and a man from France who was returning from Syria and vowed to build a church in the saint's honour in his homeland – it is enough to suggest that some of the ships of *palmiferi* did visit St Nicholas the Pilgrim's shrine. Amandus noted other hallmarks of a flourishing shrine drawing a steady stream of pilgrims. By the 1140s a huge quantity of wax and silver figurines hung from the ceiling of the crypt housing St Nicholas's relics in the cathedral church, placed there in gratitude for miracles worked. Also, Amandus referred to the presence of pilgrims wearing iron bands as a sign of penance, who by their very nature were likely to have travelled longer distances.[91]

At the shrine of St Cataldus at Taranto there is even greater evidence for regional and foreign pilgrims. Berengarius recorded pilgrims from relatively short distances – from Massafra (16 km), Lizzano [?] (21 km), Mottola (24 km), Oria (35 km), Baresentio (35 km) and Ostuni (40 km) – and a number of visitors from unidentified settlements may also have travelled from comparable distances.[92] Four of the miracles recorded by the author of the *Sermo* also suggest that the visitors arrived from small, local

[89] *Vita S. Nicolai Peregrini*, 244 (ch. 57).
[90] *Vita S. Nicolai Peregrini*, 244 (ch. 57). The term *sanctum sepulchrum* used here is not to be confused with the Holy Sepulchre, Jerusalem; as further confirmation, Amandus did not call the pilgrims *palmiferi*, as he had done for those on ships which were returning from Syria.
[91] *Vita S. Nicolai Peregrini*, 243 (ch. 56).
[92] Historia S. Cataldi, 570, 572–3.

settlements.[93] A sizeable number of visitors to St Cataldus' shrine arrived from greater distances across southern Italy, from between around 50 and 150 km away, indicating that it exerted influence beyond the territories Taranto dominated as the main urban centre. Indeed, Berengarius clearly asserted that the shrine's fame pushed beyond the confines of Apulia into Calabria, and he attested other visitors from Lucania and Campania.[94] Thus, pilgrims arrived from Conversano (55 km), Pomarico in Lucania [?] (58 km), Brindisi (62 km), San Nicandro di Bari (69 km), Roseto Capo Spulico in Calabria [?] (76 km), Salandra in Lucania (77 km), Gallipoli (79 km), Trani (112 km), Alessano near Otranto [?] (114 km), Cosenza in Calabria (154 km), Crotone in Calabria (155km) and Benevento in Campania (218 km).[95] With apparent exceptions, St Cataldus' shrine attracted pilgrims primarily from central and southern Apulia, southern Lucania and the northern half of Calabria. Unsurprisingly for a major Apulian port, foreign pilgrims were also present. A man from Lombardy returning from the Holy Sepulchre suffered an epileptic seizure at the port of Monopoli (54 km away) before being healed at St Cataldus' shrine.[96] A young man from France, a master of the liberal arts, returning from the Holy Sepulchre, was the only survivor of a shipwreck off the Calabrian coast thanks to his prayers to St Cataldus, whose shrine he subsequently visited.[97] The *Sermo* also recorded the pilgrimage of a French painter to St Cataldus' shrine.[98] Finally, a German who had unsuccessfully sought a cure from many shrines was at length healed at Taranto.[99] Within the miracle stories relating to these pilgrims, we also see the miraculous powers of St Cataldus, in similar manner to St Nicholas the Pilgrim and others, moving beyond the confines of his shrine: the route between Mottola and Massafra, the settlement of Oria, the Ionian Sea and Sicily were all stages for St Cataldus' intervention, which in every case was followed by the recipient's pilgrimage to Taranto.[100]

Evidence on medium- and long-distance pilgrims at Bisceglie points to some similarities with pilgrimage to the shrines at Trani and Taranto, but also to a notable difference primarily associated with the smaller stature of the former settlement. Like other less renowned shrines, Bisceglie still

---

[93] Hofmeister, 'Sermo', including a woman 'de castello sancti Paris', and a man 'de castello quod Clavis dicitur', 111–12.
[94] Historia S. Cataldi, 571 ch. 17.
[95] Historia S. Cataldi, 569–73.
[96] Historia S. Cataldi, 571.
[97] Historia S. Cataldi, 573.
[98] Hofmeister, 'Sermo', 113–14.
[99] Historia S. Cataldi, 573.
[100] Historia S. Cataldi, 570, 572–3.

attracted foreign pilgrims to the shrine of its saints, no doubt assisted by its coastal location. Amandus identified no less than six individuals broadly originating from modern-day France (*Gallico genere, Normandus genere, ex genere Gallico, de Gallorum genere, Francigenus, ex Gallicorum*) who received cures at Bisceglie. Furthermore, a German (*Teutonicus*) was also healed at the shrine.[101] In only two cases, however, were these individuals specified as arriving from outside southern Italy. The *Francigenus* had his eyesight restored at the shrine at Bisceglie after being visited by Saints Pantaleon and Sergius in a dream while staying in a Greek port on return from the Holy Sepulchre.[102] In the other instance, a 'Gaul', who had visited the Holy Sepulchre, and later suffered an injury when fighting the 'Saracens', returned west, landed at Brindisi, heard of the discovery and translation of the saints of Bisceglie (some 138 km north-west) and was healed at their shrine.[103] In the remaining cases, however, the earlier movements of these foreign-born pilgrims were not traced, and in some instances they might have settled in the region already. Indeed, one man (*ex genere Gallico*) was said to have dwelled for a long time at nearby Trani.[104]

There was an international flavour to Bisceglie's pilgrims, as recorded by Amandus, which certainly built on a core of localized devotees both from Bisceglie and from lands up to c.40 km away. There were repeated accounts of pilgrims from Trani, as well as references to other connections with this city which was only 8 km up the coast. Amandus' respect for Trani through his earlier affiliations and the city's proximity explain this, but it is also possible to detect assertions of independence from, and not deference to, the spiritual authority of Trani. Amandus chose to stage the final celebration ceremony of the saints' translation when the archbishop of Trani was in Constantinople on royal business (and the archbishop of Bari was also absent in Palermo).[105] Furthermore, the account of the healing of the 'Gaul' who had been resident at Trani, and who 'rejoiced in sharing the same name as St Nicholas', suggests Trani's patron saint was at the least complicit with the workings of the saints at Bisceglie.[106] Another episode recounted the experience of a woman from Trani who mocked the saints at Bisceglie; consequently her young son was struck half-dead, only to be healed after the mother repented of her faithlessness.[107]

[101] *Inventio, Translationes, et Miracula*, 363–5, 369–70.
[102] *Inventio, Translationes, et Miracula*, 369.
[103] *Inventio, Translationes, et Miracula*, 370.
[104] *Inventio, Translationes, et Miracula*, 364.
[105] *Inventio, Translationes, et Miracula*, 368.
[106] *Inventio, Translationes, et Miracula*, 364.
[107] *Inventio, Translationes, et Miracula*, 366.

The majority of the other South Italian pilgrims to Bisceglie hailed from a similarly localized radius based on central Apulia: from Corato (13 km), Terlizzi (13 km), Ruvo (14 km), Giovinazzo (15 km), Andria (18 km), Barletta (19 km), Bitonto (21 km), the parish of Bari ['Barensis parochiae'] (32 km), Canosa (37 km) and Spinazzola (46 km). Aside from an isolated pilgrim from Monopoli (73 km), and some of the ecclesiastical officials who attended the translation ceremony – from Polignano (66 km), Vieste [?] (76 km) and Melfi (76 km) – South Italian visitors from such distances and beyond are absent, unlike at Trani and Taranto. It would seem then that a heavily localized pattern of pilgrimage dominated the shrine at Bisceglie, perhaps characteristic of many well-established shrines based in smaller settlements, but that the city's fortuitous position on the Apulian coast attracted some foreign pilgrims to endow the shrine with more eclectic features. The pilgrims attracted to the shrine of St Lucas di Isola di Capo Rizzuto may represent the more standard case of a smaller shrine which functioned almost exclusively within a restricted space. While the exact location of St Lucas's shrine is debated (sites near Isola di Capo Rizzuto, Rossano and Amaroni have all been suggested), it was certainly somewhere in central Calabria. As far as it is possible to identify the origins of the handful of pilgrims who were recorded at the shrine in St Lucas's *bios*, some came from central Calabria (Cassano Ionio near Cosenza, Placa near Isola di Capo Rizzuto, Gagliano near Catanzaro), others from southern Calabria (Seminara and Briatico), and one travelled from Sicily (Taormina).[108] Apart from the last, the shrine did not attract pilgrims from longer distances, and its isolated location along with the cult's limited appeal to wider communities may explain this.

(iii)   Social identities

The leading shrines, at Bari, Montecassino, Monte Gargano, Catania and Salerno, attracted the very apex of the elite, but aside from these exceptional instances the social composition at most South Italian shrines was broadly comparable. Most shrines in southern Italy appear to have drawn their pilgrims from the entire social spectrum, or at least aimed to present this as being the case. On the one hand, the devotion and patronage of the nobility conferred connections and power on a shrine, while on the other, evolving theological doctrines of the later eleventh and twelfth centuries promoted a cult of poverty which began to shape attitudes on the 'poor' in a more positive framework, earning

---

[108] *Vita di S. Luca*, 11, 16–41, 114–125.

greater empathy and acknowledgement at shrine centres.[109] Moreover, the less-privileged elements of communities, in greater need of support and protection, were always going to be a major presence at any shrine. Unfortunately, beyond the occasional urge to advertise the devotion of a noble patron and to demonstrate a saint's protection of the weak, those who recorded pilgrimage to South Italian shrines appear to have been disinclined to label consistently a pilgrim's social status. Rarely do our hagiographers demonstrate interest in the variety of socio-political groupings among the laity, particularly in its urban context.[110] Therefore, it is inevitable that most often the powerful and influential can be identified visiting shrines, and those who are less so fade into the background. Thus, the social status of those recorded pilgrims at Monte Gargano is very high. This might well be expected, particularly of foreign pilgrims – most notably the emperors, popes and leading churchmen such as Abbot Suger of St Denis who made pilgrimages there – but it was also the case for those few pilgrims from southern Italy whom we might identify with some level of confidence. The Lombard rebel Melus, who apparently met the Normans while visiting Monte Gargano, was a leading member of the urban patriciate of Bari. Of a similar standing at Amalfi was the wealthy merchant Pantaleon who donated to the sanctuary its magnificent bronze doors.[111] Of even higher status was Henry, prince of Capua, the younger brother of King William II, who visited the shrine in 1172.[112] By virtue of the records on Monte Gargano and its renown on the international stage, pilgrims below the level of the urban and ecclesiastical elites barely make any appearance.

The source material from Montecassino offers a more rounded picture, but one which is still dominated by elite pilgrimage. That Montecassino was also a powerful political force induced the arrival for varying reasons of high-level figures who were also likely to incorporate into their visit the act of pilgrimage to St Benedict's shrine. A range of high-profile foreign and South Italian pilgrims were noted visiting the shrine of St Benedict, from Emperor Henry II to Abbot Suger of St Denis. We have already discussed various figures from the South Italian nobility who visited and interacted with Montecassino, such as the counts of Aquino, while Dormeier's work potentially illuminates numerous other examples. But the *Montecassino Chronicle* and the *Dialogues* do provide snapshots of other

[109] M. Mollat, *The Poor in the Middle Ages. An Essay in Social History*, trans. A. Goldhammer (Yale, 1986), 106.
[110] For a North Italian comparison see Webb, *Patrons and Defenders*, 45–50.
[111] D'Arienzo, 'Il pellegrinaggio', 224.
[112] Romuald, 261.

types of pilgrim. These include secular and regular churchmen, a respected nephew of a monk at Montecassino, knights and peasants.[113]

A similar broad social spectrum emerges at Bari and Catania, where pilgrims of the highest levels were recorded alongside those in the lowest ranks of society. At Bari, members of the Hauteville dynasty, Sicilian kings, leading Crusaders and foreign noblemen, and high-ranking churchmen all appear to have visited St Nicholas's shrine. The hagiographical sources add little on the social status of pilgrims, but enough to confirm a standard picture. Nicephorus mentions the healing of one of the most noble men of Bari, as well as that of a poor beggar.[114] The Beneventan Continuation noted a poor man and wife from Durazzo, and a poor servant from Siponto, and the Jerusalem *Legend* added news of a noble Beneventan family who visited St Nicholas's shrine.[115] Likewise at Catania, King Richard I visited St Agatha's shrine according to Roger of Howden, while Bishop Maurice apparently recorded the presence of one of Sicily's leading noblemen: the North Italian Henry of Paternò, brother-in-law to Count Roger I of Sicily and ruler of one of the few major lordships on the island.[116] Henry's visit to St Agatha's shrine followed a nocturnal vision of the saint. This pilgrimage interestingly appears to have cemented a reconciliation with the cathedral monks at Catania, which in the future would develop into a close relationship with the city's church.[117] Both Maurice's and Blandinus' accounts of St Agatha's miracles reveal a diverse social mix among the pilgrims: the poor, the rich, craftsmen and urban inhabitants, churchmen, the young and old, men and women.

At southern Italy's less well-reputed shrines the overall evidence is again meagre, but the fragmentary picture that does emerge is a familiar one of social diversity, except that there is no representation from the apex of the social hierarchy. Kings, queens, popes and leading members of the nobility and the crusading movements were not as inclined to visit such sites for obvious reasons. At Trani, our hagiographers offered little information on the social background of visitors to the shrine, aside from references to a demoniacal slave and to the noble traits of a youth from Trani and a pilgrim from France.[118] Recording the two extremes of the social spectrum seemed to justify silence on all those in between. At Bisceglie, not even a single attendant at the shrine of Saints Maurus, Pantaleon and

[113] Desiderius, Bk II.9, p. 1131; II.14–15, pp. 1134–5; II.16, p. 1135; II.17–18, pp. 1135–7. Chron. Cas., Bk II.48, pp. 258–9; III.38, p. 414; IV.44, pp. 512–13; IV.58, pp. 521–2.
[114] Nitti di Vito, 'La traslazione', 350–1.
[115] Nitti di Vito, 'La traslazione', 355–6; Corsi, *La traslazione*, 81.
[116] Scalia, 'La traslazione', 95–6; Loud, *Age of Robert Guiscard*, 177, 180, 182.
[117] *Epistola Mauritii*, 646; Loud, 'Norman Italy', 58–61.
[118] *Vita S. Nicolai Peregrini*, 241, 243, 245.

Sergius was directly described as being poor, and Amandus in fact provides little on social backgrounds. Priests visited the shrine, sailors were saved, and many of the recipients of miracles had already consulted doctors, a not inexpensive option.[119] A very old woman from Corato was deemed to have led a commendable and virtuous life, and a skilled gold-smith was healed by the saints of Bisceglie.[120] Overall, a small return from an otherwise detailed collection of miracles. The account of the miracles worked by St Mennas after his translation to S. Agata dei Goti is slightly more informative, but still exceedingly limited. Recipients of miracles who visited the shrine all appear to have been of reasonably high social standing: they included the daughter of a knight, a noble woman, two canons of the church where St Mennas' relics lay and Count Robert of Alife himself.[121]

Fortunately, the hagiographers of St Cataldus offer rather more infor-mation on the social status of some of the pilgrims who visited Taranto. Surprisingly, there are only two direct references to poor people (a *paupercula* from Lizzano and a blind beggar from Salandra who nonetheless had managed to visit the Holy Sepulchre); otherwise many of the pilgrims appear to be from relatively stable or wealthy socio-economic backgrounds.[122] Craftsmen, such as a tanner and a carpenter, and sailors were attested, as were nuns and priests.[123] Also, a number of pilgrims appear to have been affluent enough to first seek the help of doctors.[124] Indeed, the parents of a blind girl from Brindisi, who had tried doctors without success before finding a cure at St Cataldus' shrine, were able to offer to the saint a votive in the shape of eyes cast out of silver rather than the more common and cheaper wax.[125] Berengarius also recorded individuals with more overt wealth and social standing. A man from Pellicorio was described as 'moral and wealthy'; an 'excellent knight' (Berengarius himself!) worked in royal service and translated books from Greek to Latin.[126] A young 'Gaul' was a master of the liberal arts, a paralysed girl from Trani was 'from parentage of unique nobility' who had spent a great amount on doctors' fees, whereas St Cataldus healed the son of the 'distinguished' lord of San Nicandro (near Bari).[127] The *Sermo* adds to these 'a most skilful artist' from France who was

[119] *Inventio, Translationes, et Miracula*, 363–7.
[120] *Inventio, Translationes, et Miracula*, 363, 65.
[121] Hoffmann, 'Translationes', 476–81.
[122] Historia S. Cataldi, 570, 572.
[123] Historia S. Cataldi, 570–3.
[124] Historia S. Cataldi, 571.
[125] Historia S. Cataldi, 571.
[126] Historia S. Cataldi, 570–2.
[127] Historia S. Cataldi, 572–3.

asked to decorate the new church dedicated to St Cataldus at Taranto with an image of one of his miracles, and also the pilgrimage of a very noble knight (apparently from the Taranto region).[128] The latter derided the citizens of Taranto for venerating St Cataldus, subsequently received a nocturnal visit from the saint and consequently visited his shrine and donated money; a practice which the knight performed regularly thereafter for as long as he lived. The message is clear, as is the call for patronage from the elites.

From the restricted evidence, a picture emerges of a broad spectrum of people visiting most shrines, with the leading cult centres able to also attract the genuine elites. Certainly female pilgrims were a conspicuous feature of the miracle records for St Agatha of Catania and undoubtedly illuminate gender-based affinities. However, whereas it is possible to say, for instance, that the shrine of St William of Norwich in England drew a preponderant number of merchants and artisans, and that two-thirds of pilgrims to Godric of Finchale's shrine were female and the overall majority were lower class, the material from the South Italian shrines, though certainly illuminating, is not sufficiently consistent to yield comparable conclusions.[129]

Boundaries and connections in southern Italy

With some notable exceptions, most South Italian shrines attracted the core of pilgrims from within the immediate surrounding lay community. In addition, most also drew a sizeable segment of their pilgrims from a radius of up to forty kilometres. Clearly the majority of pilgrimage activity in southern Italy was relatively localized, functioning over short spaces, and this conformed with most shrine centres across Europe. In the peculiar geopolitical context of southern Italy, South Italian pilgrimage activity may have consolidated the fragmentary and dissonant features which many historians have long identified within southern Italy, bolstering certain visible and invisible internal boundaries, and obstructing the formation of a common identity among the region's inhabitants. Certainly, we find virtually no South Italian pilgrims moving from one end of the region to the other, from Sicily to northern Campania for example. The great distances involved would largely explain this; in the entire survey, only one Sicilian pilgrim was attested on the mainland, and this was an individual travelling from the Greek zone of Taormina to a Greek zone in Calabria.[130] Calabrian pilgrims were attested at Catania, Taranto, Bari

---

[128] Hofmeister, 'Sermo', 113.
[129] Finucane, *Miracles and Pilgrims*, 121, 127.
[130] *Vita di S. Luca*, 125.

and Trani, but do not appear to have headed further north. The author of
the miracle works of St Nicholas at Benevento does not seem to have even
considered Calabrians as potential pilgrims to the city. The miracles
reported at Troia after the translation of 1104 show a target zone north
and west of the city, and no connection to central and southern Apulia,
Lucania, Calabria or Sicily.[131] St Agatha's shrine at Catania drew mostly
eastern Sicilians. If individuals from Calabria also visited Catania, they
were moving between zones with some history of shared Greek Christian
cultural traditions, and the same could be said to a lesser extent of the
Calabrians who visited Taranto, Bari and Trani. It might be added that the
famously diverse body of pilgrims attending Thomas Becket's shrine at
Canterbury initially included few visitors from more distant zones of
England such as Devon and Northumbria. Pilgrims instead originated
primarily from a shared cultural zone pivoting around south-east England
and northern France, and did little to dissolve the so-called English
North–South divide.[132]

On the other hand, we should not underestimate the impact of pilgrimage
movement that is apparent in the South Italian sources. Even if some of
this movement occurred within broad cultural zones which were familiar
to the pilgrim, some of the distances travelled were still considerable, and
in some cases pushed the traveller to the periphery of that zone or beyond.
This may be observed at the shrines of St Cataldus at Taranto, St Nicholas
at Bari and St Benedict at Montecassino, where South Italian pilgrims
travelled in excess of 100 kilometres and some over 200 kilometres. The
major shrines at Salerno and especially Monte Gargano almost certainly
attracted South Italians from greater distances too, but the evidence is too
lacunose to track more than a few isolated examples. While there is also
compelling general evidence (see Chapter 3) to show that sanctity was a
force for syncretism between Latins and Greeks in southern Italy, there is
very little direct information to explore how often South Italian Greek and
Latin pilgrims visited the same shrines.[133] The Calabrian pilgrims at Bari,
Taranto and Trani were not explicitly identified as Greek or Latin, but all
three shrines could have had resonance for Greeks: St Nicholas of Myra,
St Nicholas the Pilgrim, and the cities of Bari, Taranto and Trani all
had distinctive Greek Christian heritages, and Greek was still spoken in

[131] Poncelet, 'Translation', 424–6.

[132] Finucane, *Miracles and Pilgrims*, 164. However, early pilgrims from York were noted, perhaps to emphasize Canterbury's primatial ascendancy over the archbishopric of York.

[133] In the late tenth century, the Calabrian St Fantino the Younger and companions went on pilgrimage to Monte Gargano: *Vita di S. Fantino*, ch. 26 p. 431; other potential parallel devotions include a Latin from Briatico at St Lucas of Isola di Capo di Rizzuto's shrine (*Vita di S. Luca*, 122–3) and Muslims at St Agatha's at Catania (see Chapter 4).

Taranto during the later twelfth century. On the other hand, the guardians of each of the shrines at Bari, Taranto and Trani were Latin churchmen based within large Latin communities, and likewise, although the South Italian Greek visitors to St Agatha's shrine at Catania were moving in a territory with strong Greek traditions, and worshipping a saint with Byzantine connections, we should not forget that Latin Benedictine churchmen controlled that shrine too.

Moreover, in a region divided by imposing topographical features, such as the Apennines, the Strait of Messina and mountainous hinterlands in Calabria and Sicily, the main routeways, traversed so heavily by pilgrims and merchants, were a force for connectivity. As both pilgrimage and a range of South Italian cults were founded, revived or expanded from the eleventh century onwards, another channel of movement was opened up for South Italians of all social ranks. Furthermore, many South Italian pilgrims could avoid long and arduous land journeys by taking the quicker option by ship along the coast: we have seen that pilgrims were attested sailing along the Adriatic for the shrine at Trani, others from Salpi to St Nicholas's at Bari, from Gallipoli to St Cataldus' at Taranto and from Messina to St Agatha's at Catania. It is also clear that knowledge of other South Italian shrines passed along these land and sea routes; many a pilgrim was diverted to another shrine having heard of its fame whilst staying in a different settlement. Contact with the stream of pilgrims, both foreign and indigenous, moving through the region and disseminating traditions encountered at different shrine centres, did not produce shared identities spanning the entirety of southern Italy and Sicily, but it would have cultivated a broader awareness among South Italians of the interrelationships between the diverse constituent parts of the region, of their own position in a wider landscape, and of increased familiarity with difference. Thus, certain features of South Italian pilgrimage suggest that important aspects of interaction and connection were fostered across zones – however blurred, arbitrary and artificial these were – and between communities which were otherwise separated by significant distances and cultural divergences.

South Italians and pilgrimage abroad

South Italians did not just seek shrine centres within southern Italy; some travelled much further, and a complete picture of their pilgrimage patterns must consider this aspect. It is true that, compared with other regions, South Italians were not the most active travellers to foreign shrines. This is all the more apparent when contrasted with the number of foreign pilgrims to South Italian shrines. Furthermore, it has long been noted that South Italians individually played little part in the crusading move-ment and, by implication, in pilgrimage to the Holy Sepulchre. It seems surprising given the geographic setting of southern Italy, and there may be a number of extenuating circumstances: the proximity of internationally significant shrines in southern Italy itself, the impact of acculturation with local Greek Orthodox and Muslim communities, and the belief among South Italians that they were contributing to the effort on a supply and transit level. However, an extensive search through a fragmented and diverse body of sources shows that in real terms South Italians did engage in long-distance pilgrimage, and in relatively large numbers.

The most striking feature of South Italian pilgrimage abroad is the apparently restricted destinations chosen. While it has been impossible to search exhaustively through the archives of every European shrine, the picture that nonetheless emerges suggests that South Italians mostly vis-ited one or other of two of the greatest medieval Christian shrines: St James's at Compostela and the Holy Sepulchre, Jerusalem. Surprisingly little evidence exists for South Italian pilgrimage to the other great shrine centre at Rome, although visits were made, most notably by Siculo-Calabrian saints like Nilus of Rossano and Silvester of Troina.[134] It may well be that Rome was not considered sufficiently long-distance, which meant that it did not confer the additional sacrifices and rewards, and was thus seen as broadly comparable to some of the leading South Italian shrines which were more attractive through their familiarity. References to other shrines are also rare. In the late twelfth-century *Miracula beati Prosperi episcopi et confessoris* a paralysed man from Benevento intended to visit the shrine of St Martin of Tours, before the fame of the shrine of St Prosperus persuaded him to detour to Reggio Emilia where he was subsequently healed.[135] Liturgical sources and decorative works from elsewhere in southern Italy confirm that the cult of St Martin attracted devotion, particularly in the Terra d'Otranto in southern Apulia.[136] Elsewhere, the Anglo-Norman chronicler William of Malmesbury reported Bohemond's tour of France in 1106 during which he attended at Noblac the shrine of St Leonard, patron saint of prisoners. There Bohemond deposited some chains in gratitude for his release from captivity in a Turkish prison in the Near East.[137] A range of liturgical documents and church dedications suggests St Leonard's popularity in southern Italy but

[134] *Vita S. Nili*, 313; *Vita Sancti Silvestri*, 176–7.
[135] M. Mercati, 'Miracula B. Prosperi Episcopi et Confessoris', *AB* 15 (1896), 161–256, 212.
[136] A. Jacob, 'Le Culte de Saint Martin de Tours dans la terre d'Otrante hellénophone', *Puer Apuliae*, ed. E. Cuozzo et al., 2 vols (Rome, 2008), i. 345–56.
[137] William of Malmesbury, *Gesta Regum Anglorum*, vol. 1 Bk IV.387, pp. 690–3.

Bohemond's pilgrimage to Noblac was clearly an exceptional episode. Later on in the twelfth century, a father and son from near Termoli in Molise were cured of their illnesses by drinking water from Thomas Becket's tomb at Canterbury.[138]

Overall, there is limited evidence of South Italian pilgrimage north of the Alps, although the miracle collection of Saint Ouen of Rouen in Normandy might suggest otherwise. One miracle, recorded in the section of the collection written before 1092, recounts how an Italian pilgrim from Monte Gargano, who was suffering from paralysis, met some Normans in Rome 'ad limina apostolorum' (before the shrines of St Peter and St Paul). On the recommendation of these Normans, the pilgrim visited the shrine of St Ouen where he was healed.[139] Another episode in the collection, from a set of additional miracles recorded in the late eleventh century, depicts another South Italian from Andria who had been encouraged by South Italian Normans to visit St Ouen, where he too was healed.[140] As Elisabeth Van Houts has shown, these episodes need to be treated with caution and might reflect 'Rouen counterpropaganda against the Normans in Italy'.[141] It is perhaps significant that the first pilgrim came from the great shrine centre of Monte Gargano, implying he could not be healed there, while when both pilgrims returned to southern Italy they advertised the virtues of St Ouen and questioned the sanity of those Normans who had abandoned their patron saint in Rouen ('cur scilicet proprium ac specialem patronum beatum Andoenum deserentes').

Lingering links between Normandy and migrant South Italian Normans may have stimulated some pilgrimage activity to northern Europe for a brief period, but on the whole South Italian pilgrimage was largely framed by the Mediterranean. Indeed, there is more evidence of South Italian activity at the shrine of St James at Compostela, which experienced a remarkable growth in popularity during the twelfth century. In the *Liber Sancti Jacobi*, the main contemporary source for activity at the shrine of St James, a miracle dated to 1106 involved an ailing Apulian knight who received a vision from St James and was promptly restored to health on visiting his shrine.[142] From the same composite source, the

---

[138] *Materials for the History of Thomas Becket*, ed. J. Craigie Robertson, 7 vols, RS 67 (London, 1875–85), i. 165–6.

[139] *Miracula Sancti Audoeni*, AS August, iv (Paris, 1867), 829–30.

[140] *Miracula Sancti Audoeni*, 838.

[141] E. Van Houts, 'Rouen as another Rome in the twelfth century', *Society and Culture in Medieval Rouen, 911–1300*, ed. L. Hicks and E. Brenner (Turnhout, 2013). I would like to thank Professor Van Houts for alerting me to these pilgrims at Rouen and for allowing me to see her article in advance of publication, 101–24.

[142] *Liber Sancti Jacobi*, Bk II. XII, pp. 273–4.

author of the *veneranda dies* sermon emphasized the international stature of the shrine by listing *apuli*, *kalabriani* and *siciliani* among those visiting, and implied the accustomed nature of their presence at Compostela.[143] A search through South Italian charters reveals further evidence: a man from Molfetta 'compelled by divine inspiration', went to the shrine in 1148, a merchant from Benevento was preparing to go in 1183, in 1202 a subdeacon from Aversa was making similar plans, and so too in 1208 a man from Mercogliano, near Avellino.[144] The *vita* of the Apulian St Lawrence the Hermit recounts his visit to the shrine at some point before 1209.[145] Thus, while only sporadic cases survive, these apparently reflect wider South Italian patterns of devotion.

The shrine most frequented by South Italian pilgrims was of course the Holy Sepulchre in Jerusalem. Owing to the numerous interconnections between southern Italy and the eastern Mediterranean, journeying there was far easier than to St James's shrine in Galicia. Some of this activity pre-dates the crusading movement. Famously, by the early to mid-eleventh century Amalfitan merchants had established trading colonies in the Holy Land, and thereafter founded hospitals and churches.[146] Their presence and commercial networks would have opened up greater possibilities for South Italian pilgrims. Amatus discussed the role of one Amalfitan kin group as facilitators of Holy Land pilgrimage and the renown this engendered. Pantaleon, son of Mauro, offered shelter, financial aid and transport to travellers to the Holy Sepulchre. His kin group had also constructed hospitals at Antioch and Jerusalem which received pilgrims.[147] We know a number of individual cases of Holy Land pilgrimages, many undertaken by South Italian churchmen, especially monks, whether directly connected to Amalfitan activities or not. In the last decades of the tenth century Montecassino monks were recorded on pilgrimages to the Holy Sepulchre, one returning with a fragment of the True Cross.[148] From the early decades of the eleventh century, Amatus of Montecassino recounted the journey to Jerusalem of a celebrated youth from Capua who later

---

[143] *Liber Sancti Jacobi*, Bk I. XVII, p. 148.

[144] *Le carte di Molfetta*, no. 17; *Le più antiche carte del capitolo della cattedrale di Benevento*, no. 112; *Codice diplomatico svevo di Aversa (parte prima)*, ed. C. Salvati (Naples, 1980), no. 26 *Codice diplomatico verginiano*, ed. P. M. Tropeano, 13 vols (Montevergine, 1977–2001), xiii. no. 1273.

[145] *Vita Beati Laurentii Eremitae Confessoris*, AS August, iii (Paris, 1867), 304.

[146] A. O. Citarella, 'Patterns in medieval trade: the commerce of Amalfi before the Crusades', *Journal of Economic History* 28 (1968), 531–55.

[147] Amatus, Bk VIII.3, pp. 480–3. The hospital at Jerusalem later became the main house of the Knights Hospitaller.

[148] Chron. Cas, Bk I.6; II.12, pp. 189–90; II.22, p. 206.

became a monk at Montecassino.[149] Greek Orthodox monks also visited Jerusalem: in 1058 Lucas, the hegumen of the Calabrian monastery Sant'Anastasio di Carbone, went there.[150] A number of South Italian bishops undertook the pilgrimage: Alfanus, archbishop of Salerno, in the 1060s and John, archbishop of Amalfi, between 1071 and 1080, while Archbishop Urso of Bari was preparing to visit Jerusalem when news broke of the arrival of St Nicholas's relics in 1087.[151]

Snapshots from events which attracted deeper comment also hint at the regularity of pilgrimage to the Holy Land. One tradition of the translation of St Nicholas from Myra to Bari indicated that two Barese priests, on returning from pilgrimage to the Holy Sepulchre, joined the Barese party of translators at Antioch.[152] Amatus of Montecassino, in discussing Gisulf II's alleged feigned pilgrimage to the Holy Sepulchre in 1062, presented devotional travel to the Holy Land as a highly laudable but regular affair.[153] Such trends among the laity were intensified after the commencement of the crusading movement, although from this point travel to the Holy Land could more than ever merge pilgrimage into any number of activities motivated by political, military and economic considerations. The presence of South Italians in the First Crusade and thereafter in the crusader states is well known.[154] During the First Crusade, Bohemond's contingent included several high-ranking South Italians, such as his Hauteville relatives Tancred and Roger of Salerno, as well as the counts of Buonalbergo, Canne, Caiazzo, Molise, Montescaglioso and the principate, and Roger de Barneville from Sicily.[155] The author of the *Gesta Francorum* was almost certainly also a South Italian. Bishops from southern Italy participated as well, including those of Ariano and Martirano in Calabria.[156] Some returned home, while others settled in the East, in the newly formed principality of Antioch, in the regions of Galilee and also in the Kingdom of Jerusalem. Alan Murray has recently demonstrated that more South Italians entered the royal administration in Jerusalem in the 1110s and 1120s, in the wake of the abortive marriage between Baldwin I and

---

[149] Amatus, Bk IV.28.
[150] Vanni, 'Itinerari', 109.
[151] Amatus, Bk IV.37, pp. 373–5; Vanni, 'Itinerari', 110; Nitti di Vito, 'La traslazione', 365. Urso completed the pilgrimage according to the *Inventio S. Sabini*, 280.
[152] Corsi, *La traslazione*, 72.
[153] Amatus, Bk IV.34–37, pp. 372–5.
[154] For a clear overview see Loud, 'Norman Italy', 49–62; A. V. Murray, *The Crusader Kingdom of Jerusalem. A Dynastic History 1099–1125* (Oxford, 2000), 103–4, 180–1, 225–6.
[155] *Gesta Francorum*, 7–8; for Tancred see *The Gesta Tancredi of Ralph of Caen*, trans. B. S. Bachrach and D. S. Bachrach (Ashgate, 2005).
[156] *Gesta Francorum*, 93–4; Loud, 'Norman Italy', 48–9.

Adelaide del Vasto (mother of Roger II of Sicily).[157] Later, in the second half of the twelfth century some South Italian political exiles sought refuge in the Kingdom of Jerusalem.[158] Although their numbers begin to dwindle as one moves through the twelfth century, and the intense connections evident during the First Crusade were not replicated later, the list of South Italian settlers and visitors in the Holy Land could be extended much further: from the continued presence of Amalfitans in several cities of the crusader states to colonists (in c.1155 a man from Barletta was attested at al-Bira, a village owned by the Church of the Holy Sepulchre) and witnesses in charters (such as a John of Brindisi in 1138, and a chaplain named Alexander *Apuliensis* in 1153).[159] It is important to emphasize the consistency and number of South Italians, because at least a proportion clearly included the act of pilgrimage within their wider pursuits in the Holy Land, while for others it would seem a near certainty. The author of the *Gesta Francorum* detached himself from Bohemond's retinue in order to fulfil his pilgrim vow at Jerusalem.[160] Tancred de Hauteville participated in the capture of Jerusalem and, according to the panegyric in the *Gesta Tancredi*, shortly before its fall he vowed 'to give up his life for the light if he might be permitted to kiss the base of Calvary [believed to be located in the Holy Sepulchre]'.[161] If nothing else such passages attest the ritual value of attending the shrine, and it is hard to imagine that he and other South Italian visitors to the city – his cousin Bohemond and the count of Buonalbergo also eventually made their way there – did not go to the Holy Sepulchre.

There is more firm evidence from charter material for South Italian pilgrimage to the Holy Sepulchre after the establishment of the crusader states. Shortly after the First Crusade a nobleman called Defensor of Vaccarizza in northern Apulia went on pilgrimage, and in the early twelfth century William Tassio, based in the Abruzzi and a member of a branch of the Hauteville family, also made the journey; both returned to southern

---

[157] On Antioch see T. Asbridge, *The Creation of the Principality of Antioch, 1098–1130* (Woodbridge, 2000), 163–8; A. V. Murray, 'Norman settlement in the Latin Kingdom of Jerusalem, 1099–1131', *Archivio normanno-svevo* 1 (2008), 71, 75–82. Bishop Aschetin of Bethlehem (1109–c.1128) was almost certainly a South Italian, p. 70.

[158] Such as a royal justiciar named Florius of Camerota (see Oldfield, *City and Community*, 93). In 1132 Count Tancred of Conversano, as the price for his role in a rebellion against Roger II, pledged to go into exile as a pilgrim to Jerusalem but later reneged: Al. Tel., Bk II.21, pp. 31–2.

[159] J. Prawer, *Crusader Institutions* (Oxford, 1980), 127; *Regesta Regni Hierosolymitani (1097–1291)*, ed. R. Röhricht, 2 vols (Innsbruck, 1893), i. no. 35 p. 5, no. 180 p. 45, no. 253 pp. 63–4, no. 284 p. 72, no. 372 p. 98, no. 380 p. 100, no. 388 p. 102, no. 690a p. 183.

[160] *Gesta Francorum*, 90–3, 98–101, suggests he accomplished this.

[161] *Gesta Tancredi*, 130.

Italy to discover that in their absence difficulties had arisen relating to their landed estates.[162] Also between 1105 and 1107 a Sicilian–Greek monk from the monastery of S. Filippo di Fragalà departed on pilgrimage to Jerusalem, as did the (Greek?) abbess of a nunnery at Taranto at some point prior to 1126.[163] Two pilgrims from near Avellino in Campania left in the 1130s, a deacon from Trani was about to depart for Jerusalem in 1168, and a knight from Caiazzo went on the pilgrimage in the late twelfth century.[164] Further information emerges in hagiographies where normative patterns and behaviours are often incorporated to anchor supernatural episodes in reality. One of the miracles worked in the twelfth century by St Cataldus of Taranto restored sight to a man from the Lucania region who had previously been forced to beg in order to visit a host of shrines including the Holy Sepulchre.[165] After 1137, St Albert of Montecorvino exorcised a female demoniac who subsequently visited the Holy Sepulchre on Albert's advice, while the late hagiographical tradition for St Richard, bishop of Andria, claimed he spent the first six years (1158–64) of his episcopate in the Holy Land.[166]

Finally, the twelfth-century *vita* of St Marina, a Sicilian saint believed to have been born in 1062, narrates her visit to the Holy Land. If we may doubt the historicity of the events described, the text at least hints at one particular ideal of pilgrimage in the Holy Land as understood in the twelfth century. For Marina, pilgrimage was an act of purification in which God moved closer to those who were metaphorically and literally searching for him.[167] In the Holy Land she located a spiritual master (a bishop of Tripoli) and worshipped at the Holy Sepulchre. Marina also visited the Jordan, 'the most holy of rivers', and then entered a nearby monastery where she served the monks for three years.[168] Following a brief visit to Sicily, Marina re-entered the monastic community for a further five years before returning to die in Sicily.[169] The account also uncovers some of the realities of long-distance pilgrimage: the exposure to pilgrimage traffic in South Italian ports, the sight of which stimulated Marina's desire to depart; potential dangers at sea (in this case covetous sailors); and the insecurities faced by female travellers (Marina was forced

[162] Loud, 'Norman Italy', 53–4: Loud, 'Monastic chronicles', 121, 23–4, 131.
[163] *Byzantine Monastic Foundation Documents*, ii. 623, 632 no. 26; Loud, *Latin Church*, 503.
[164] Loud, 'Norman Italy', 54; Trani, no. 59.
[165] Historia S. Cataldi, 572.
[166] *Vita S. Alberti*, 434; Martin, 'Modèles', 80.
[167] *Martirio di Santa Lucia: Vita di Santa Marina*, 95, 99.
[168] *Martirio di Santa Lucia: Vita di Santa Marina*, 101, 103.
[169] *Martirio di Santa Lucia: Vita di Santa Marina*, 103–7.

to disguise herself as a monk).[170] As Marina's itinerary shows, other destinations were attended in the Holy Land, and the appearance of St Cataldus of Taranto in the mid-twelfth-century frescoes of the Church of the Nativity may suggest that South Italians visited Bethlehem.[171] Collectively, the evidence for South Italian pilgrims to the Holy Land shows that they were drawn from all regions of southern Italy, and that most appear to be high-ranking members of their communities, a natural consequence perhaps of the nature of records on long-distance pilgrimage. The limited appearance of South Italians across a broad range of European shrines is a notable feature, but it must be balanced by evidence which suggests that many visited the great shrines at Compostela and Jerusalem. Long-distance pilgrimage for South Italians seems to have functioned largely in a Mediterranean context. The combination of the popularity of local pilgrimage punctuated by evidence for visits to the greatest shrine centres in Christendom in fact conforms to pilgrimage patterns found elsewhere in Europe, and in this respect southern Italy was neither marginal nor unorthodox.

---

[170] *Martirio di Santa Lucia: Vita di Santa Marina*, 95–101.
[171] Jotischky, *Perfection of Solitude*, 88.

Conclusion

Sanctity in medieval southern Italy during the eleventh and twelfth centuries was marked by its linkage to Christianity's distant sacred past. Many cults continued to promote saints who were rooted in Late Antiquity and the Early Middle Ages. Often these figures were the putative founding or early bishops of ancient sees (e.g. St Barbatus of Benevento or St Ianuarius of Naples/Benevento), were early Christian martyrs (such as St Agatha of Catania or St Lucy of Syracuse) or pioneering hermits (St Benedict of Montecassino or St Elias of Enna). Some, such as St Matthew at Salerno, St Bartholomew at Benevento and St Michael at Monte Gargano, were apostolic or biblical saints of the very highest rank. However, the outward presentation of continuity inherent in South Italian sanctity in the Central Middle Ages should not lead us to the conclusion that it was conservative and static. In a society experiencing rapid and profound transitions these old cults were renewed and reconfigured to reflect a new landscape. Here we see neither retreat nor defence but innovation and informed response to a new world. Indeed, many of southern Italy's revived cults of the eleventh and twelfth centuries pretended to an ancient heritage which in reality they could not claim. The cults of a number of early medieval saints – St Secundinus at Troia, St Cataldus at Taranto and St Lawrence at Siponto, among others – show no certain sign of existence before the eleventh century; if anything, they emerged out of the disjuncture between past and present, and should arguably be classed as new cults responding to the needs of a new environment. Even those well-established cults dating to the Early Middle Ages (St Agatha at Catania, St Sabinus at Canosa, St Matthew at Salerno) were redeveloped and renewed in order to harmonize more appropriately with the present, while the arrival of St Nicholas brought the relics of an early Christian bishop to Bari: the city subsequently formed into the centre of a new cult shaped fundamentally by the socio-religious landscape of the late eleventh and twelfth centuries.

In addition, southern Italy produced a range of new, contemporary saints. It is true that, with the possible exception of St Nicholas the

Pilgrim of Trani, none of these were comparable with the new breed of urban lay saints who were briefly so prominent in northern Italy around c.1200. Some instead were bishop-saints, products of the region's diocesan reorganization, who displayed reforming ideals to varying degrees. Others might be termed monastic/eremitical saints, many of whom (St John of Matera, St Bruno of Cologne, St William of Montevergine) were influenced by both preceding and current generations of Greek-Italian saints and hermits. At the same time they espoused innovatory forms of spirituality and worship which were at the forefront of the more radical changes in the Western Church. In this context there were evident parallels with contemporary figures in other regions of Europe, who would subsequently be deemed saints; people such as Godric of Finchale (d.1170) in England, and a series of Cistercian monastic saints based in France: St Alberic of Citeaux (d. 1108), St Robert of Molesme (d.1111), St Stephen Harding (d.1134) and most famously St Bernard of Clairvaux (d.1153).

Some of the new forces which dictated the transitions in the make-up of South Italian sanctity in the Central Middle Ages were the rise of new secular powers, Church reform and urbanization. All were common to the rest of western Europe and thus, sitting alongside the weight of centuries of cultic traditions, shaped the parameters of sanctity in southern Italy along comparable lines. These forces stimulated pulses of activity at various shrine centres. The Norman takeover awoke the cult of St Matthew at Salerno from decades of dormancy, it provided the framework for the re-emergence of monastic patron saints at Montecassino and San Clemente a Casauria, and it roused into action a programme of cultic revival on the island of Sicily as it fell once again under Christian rule. The broad impact of Church reform reorganized southern Italy's episcopal sees, fortifying them and enhancing their aspirations – many combined the material revival of their dioceses with a spiritual reawakening centred on new or revitalized cathedral shrine centres. As discussed, reforming ideals also featured in varying guises in the lives of a number of southern Italy's contemporary episcopal, monastic and eremitical saints. Church reform also mirrored an upsurge in lay piety which, when concentrated in ever expanding urban settlements, exhibited a potent energy. Apulia's and Sicily's main ports and the larger Campanian cities experienced significant demographic growth across the eleventh and twelfth centuries. When more assertive episcopal sees and other religious houses promoted cults in their midst, urban communities (notably at Bari, Trani and Benevento) connected with and vigorously supported and shaped them as a way of articulating their own identities, faith and status.

Although similar developments, with their localized variations, were evident in other regions of medieval Europe, where South Italian sanctity and pilgrimage differed markedly was in its simultaneous interface with the Greek Christian, Latin Christian and Islamic worlds. Here, it was at the vanguard of some of the great confrontations of the medieval world. The evolution of Greek Christian saints in southern Italy, the worship of ancient eastern saints, and the dissemination, through both, of Greek Christian spiritual ideals situated South Italian sanctity firmly at the heart of what was developing into the great East–West schism, and showed that on a local, personalized level Greek and Latin could cohabit the same spiritual and physical space. Similarly, proximity to Rome brought direct papal input and claims against Constantinople over the disputed jurisdictional zones of southern Italy; supporting a new diocesan map augmented with new shrine centres, many consecrated by the pope, was one channel for doing so. Another channel was reconciliation, and Urban II's role in the apparent canonization of St Nicholas the Pilgrim at Trani might represent one of its clearest examples. In the conquest of Islamic Sicily, South Italian saints and their cults were employed to re-Christianize a territory, which significantly aided the expansion of the Latin Christian frontier. However, the reserved nature of the cultic revival on Sicily suggests that acculturation and collaboration between Latin, Greek and Arab-Islamic communities imparted a telling influence on the devotional map of Christian Sicily.

Inherent in its location at these key socio-religious frontiers was the significance of southern Italy's strategic setting at the Mediterranean crossroads for commercial and pilgrimage traffic, and its geographic and liminal setting provided it with a unique dimension. The region and its forms of sanctity were thus open to the widest possible spectrum of influences and, at the same time, it was exceptionally well placed to disseminate knowledge of its own cults. This underlying theme of movement was accentuated by the consistent rise of pilgrim traffic to South Italian shrines, which reached its apogee in the twelfth century after the beginning of the crusading movement. Crowds of visitors equally contributed towards the revival and expansion of saints' cults in southern Italy, particularly at places like Salerno, Benevento, Troia, Trani, Bari and Catania which were on or near to key pilgrimage routes. Pilgrims brought funds and an audience for hagiographical output, and alongside the increased participation of the urban laity, they assisted in the creation of the visual and textual dimensions of cults. Many pilgrims were local inhabitants or came from a neighbouring region in southern Italy, but there is evidence that some South Italians travelled significant distances to visit shrines elsewhere in southern Italy (and abroad), and further contributed to cross-cultural interaction and the breaking down of some of the internal frontiers across southern Italy.

An increasingly large number of pilgrims, however, were foreign, travelling great distances. Southern Italy's routeways ranked among the most frequented pilgrim and crusading itineraries in medieval Europe. Some aimed for the leading shrine centres of southern Italy – St Nicholas's at Bari, St Matthew's at Salerno, St Benedict's at Montecassino, St Michael's at Monte Gargano – others visited these en route to Jerusalem, Constantinople and Rome. Southern Italy responded to this increased movement by developing pilgrimage infrastructures and services, and offering its own shrine centres to enrich the pilgrim's experience. In many respects, southern Italy thus acted as a bridge to salvation, and indeed was the space in which many pilgrims perished and hoped to obtain eternal life. But, as ever, southern Italy presented its own unique paradoxes and challenges. For the region's traditions were composed of layers of supernatural, folkloric, classical and pagan histories which were fused on to a numinous landscape of earthquakes, volcanoes, subterranean spaces and dangerous waters. According to some traditions, the entrance to the Underworld and to Purgatory could be located in southern Italy, and the growing number of travellers and pilgrims seemed to have eagerly disseminated this news back to the West. Southern Italy offered a veritable adventure theme park for the aspiring penitential pilgrim, its landscape charged with religious and eschatological power; it is no surprise that a number of its new saints in the eleventh and twelfth centuries had been pilgrims. Everywhere one turned in medieval southern Italy, sanctity and pilgrimage functioned in contested spaces which, on closer inspection, offered the chance to nurture positive interrelationships between past and present, between different faiths and communities, and between diverse territories. In this respect South Italian saints and shrines were a ubiquitous presence, playing an integral role in mediating the destiny of a region at the core of some of the most profound transitions experienced in the Central Middle Ages.

Bibliography

MANUSCRIPT SOURCES

London, British Library, Add MS 23776.
Cava dei Tirreni, Archivio della badia di S. Trinità, *Arca* xxiv. no. 30, xxxiii. no. 38.
Manchester, John Rylands Library, MS 1.

PRINTED PRIMARY SOURCES

Acconcia Longo, A., 'La vita di s. Leone vescovo di Catania e gli incantesimi del mago Eliodoro', *Rivista di studi bizantini e neoellenici* 26 (1989), 3–98.
Les Actes grecs de S. Maria di Messina, ed. A. Guillou (Palermo, 1963).
Ademari Historiarum Libri III, ed. G. H. Pertz, MGH SS iv (Hanover, 1841).
Aimé du Mont-Cassin, *Ystoire de li Normant*, ed. M. Guéret-Laferté (Paris, 2011).
Alan of Lille, *Anticlaudianus*, trans. J. J. Sheridan (Toronto, 1973).
Albert of Aachen, *Historia Ierosolimitana*, ed. and trans. S. B. Edgington (Oxford, 2007).
Alexandri Telesini Abbatis Ystoria Rogerii Regis Sicilie Calabrie atque Apulie, ed. L. De Nava, FSI 112 (Rome, 1991).
Anastasius Bibliothecarius, *Sermo Theodori Studitae de Sancto Bartolomeo Apostolo*, ed. U. Westerbergh (Stockholm, 1963).
Andreae Danduli Ducis Venetiarum: Chronica per Extensum descripta (AD 460–1280), ed. E. Pastorello, RIS 12 (i) (Bologna, 1938–58).
Annales Casinenses, ed. G. H. Pertz, MGH SS xix (Hanover, 1866).
Gli Annales Pisani di Bernardo Maragone, ed. M. Lupo Gentile, RIS 6 (ii) (Bologna, 1936).
Antiche cronache di terra di Bari, ed. G. Cioffari and R. Lupoli Tateo (Bari, 1991).
Arnoldi Chronica Slavorum, ed. G. H. Pertz, MGH SS xxxiv (Hanover, 1868).
Bede's Ecclesiastical History of the English People, ed. and trans. B. Colgrave and R. A. B. Mynors (Oxford, 1969).
Bertolini, O., 'Gli Annales Beneventani', *BISIME* 42 (1923), 9–163.
The Book of Curiosities: A Critical Edition, ed. E. Savage-Smith and Y. Rapoport, available at www.bodley.ox.ac.uk/bookofcuriosities (March 2007) (accessed 10 May 2012).
Borsari, S., 'Vita di S. Giovanni Terista. Testi greci inediti', *ASCL* 22 (1953), 136–51.
Brünel, C., 'Vita, Inventio et Miracula Sanctae Enimiae', *AB* 57 (1939), 236–98.
Byzantine Monastic Foundation Documents, ed. and trans. J. Thomas and A. C. Hero et al., 5 vols (Washington, DC, 2000).

Caesarius of Heisterbach, *The Dialogue on Miracles*, trans. H. von E. Scott and C. C. Swinton Bland (London, 1929).

Cangiano, G., 'L'Adventus Sancti Nycolai in Beneventum', *Atti della società storica del Sannio* 2 (1924), 131–62.

The Capture of Thessaloniki by Eustathios of Thessaloniki, trans. J. R. Melville Jones (Canberra, 1988).

I carmi di Alfano I, arcivescovo di Salerno, ed. A. Lentini and F. Avagliano, Miscellanea Cassinese 38 (Montecassino, 1974).

Le carte che si conservano nell'archivio dello capitolo metropolitano della città di Trani (dal IX secolo fino all'anno 1266), ed. A. Prologo (Barletta, 1877).

Le carte di Molfetta (1076–1309), ed. F. Carabellese, Codice diplomatico barese VII (Bari, 1912).

Les Chartes de Troia. Édition et étude critique des plus anciens documents conservés à l'archivio capitolare, 1 (1024–1266), ed. J-M. Martin, Codice diplomatico pugliese XXI (Bari, 1976).

Chronica Magistri Rogeri de Houedene, ed. W. Stubbs, 4 vols, RS 51 (London, 1868–71).

Chronica Monasterii Casinensis, ed. H. Hoffmann, MGH SS xxxiv (Hanover, 1980).

Chronicle of the Third Crusade: Itinerarium Peregrinorum et Gesta Regis Ricardi, trans. H. J. Nicholson (Aldershot, 1997).

Chronicon Casauriense, ed. L. A. Muratori, RIS 2 (ii) (Milan, 1726).

Chronicon S. Michaelis Monasterii in Pago Virdunensi, ed. G. Waitz, MGH SS iv (Hanover, 1841).

Chronicon Salernitanum, ed. U. Westerbergh (Stockholm, 1956).

Die Chronik Ottos von St. Blasien und die Marbacher Annalen, ed. and trans. F.-J. Schmale (Darmstadt, 1998).

The Codex Benedictus. An Eleventh-Century Lexionary from Monte Cassino, Vat Lat 1202, ed. P. Meyvaert, 2 vols (New York, 1982).

Codice diplomatico brindisino, vol. 1 (492–1299), ed. G-M. Monti (Trani, 1940).

Codice diplomatico salernitano del secolo XIII, vol. 1 (1201–1281), ed. C. Carucci (Subiaco, 1931).

Codice diplomatico svevo di Aversa (parte prima), ed. C. Salvati (Naples, 1980).

Codice diplomatico verginiano, ed. P. M. Tropeano, 13 vols (Montevergine, 1977–2001).

Le colonie cassinesi in Capitanata, ed. T. Leccisotti, 4 vols (Montecassino, 1937–57).

Constantiae Imperatricis et Reginae Siciliae Diplomata (1195–1198), ed. T. Kölzer, Codex Diplomaticus Regni Siciliae, Ser. II.i (2) (Cologne, 1983).

La Continuation de Guillaume de Tyr (1184–1197), ed. M. Morgan (Paris, 1982).

Corsi, P., *La traslazione di San Nicola: le fonti* (Bari, 1988).

The Crusade of Richard Lion-Heart by Ambroise, trans. M. J. Hubert (New York, 1941).

D'Angelo, E., 'Inventio Corporis et Miracula Sancti Secundini Troiani Episcopi', *Scripturus Vitam: lateinische Biographie von der Antike bis in die Gegenwart – Festgabe für Walter Berschin zum 65. Geburtstag*, ed. D. Walz (Heidelberg, 2002), 841–54.

De B. Alberto Eremita in Territorio Senensi, AS January, i (Paris, 1863), 402–4.

Deeds of John and Manuel Comnenus by John Cinnamus, trans. C. M. Brand (New York, 1976).

De Rebus Gestis Rogerii Calabriae et Siciliae Comitis, Auctore Gaufredo Malaterra, ed. E. Pontieri, RIS 5 (Bologna 1927–8).

De S. Eleutherio, AS April, ii (Paris, 1865), 525–39.

De S. Gerardo Episcopo et Confessore Potentiae in Italia, AS October, xiii (Paris, 1883), 464–72.

Desiderius, *Dialogi de Miraculis Sancti Benedicti*, ed. G. Schwarz and A. Hofmeister, MGH SS xxx (2) (Leipzig, 1934).

De S. Joanne Episcopo Confessore Civitatis Montis Marani, AS August, iii (Paris, 1867), 510–13.

De S. Rosalia Virgine Panormitana in Vitae Sanctorum Siculorum, vol. 2, ed. O. Gaetani (Palermo, 1657).

De Translationibus S. Leucii, AS January, i (Paris, 1863), 672–3.

I diplomi greci ed arabi di Sicilia, ed. S. Cusa (Palermo, 1868–82).

Documenti del commercio veneziano nei secoli XI-XIII, ed. R. Morozzo della Rocca and A. Lombardo, 2 vols (Rome, 1940).

Eadmer's Historia novorum in Anglia, trans. G. Bosanquet (London, 1964).

The Ecclesiastical History of Orderic Vitalis, ed. and trans. M. Chibnall, 6 vols (Oxford, 1968–80).

Epistola Mauritii Cataniensis Episcopi de Translatione S. Agathae Virginis, AS February, i (Paris, 1863), 643–8.

Ex Miraculis Sancti Agrippini, ed. G. Waitz, MGH SRLI (Hanover, 1878).

Falcone di Benevento, *Chronicon Beneventanum*, ed. E. D'Angelo (Florence, 1998).

The First Crusade: the Chronicle of Fulcher of Chartres and Other Source Materials, trans. E. Peters (Philadephia, 1971).

Floriant et Florete, ed. H. F. Williams (Ann Arbor, Mich., 1947).

Gautier Dalché, P., *Carte marine et portulan au XIIe siècle (Pise, circa 1200)* (Rome, 1995).

Gervase of Tilbury, *Otia Imperialia: Recreation of an Emperor*, ed. and trans. S. E. Banks and J. W. Binns (Oxford, 2002).

Gesta Dagoberti I, Regis Francorum, ed. B. Krusch, MGH Scriptores Rerum Merovingicarum ii (Hanover, 1888).

Gesta Episcoporum Neapolitanorum, ed. G. Waitz, MGH SRLI (Hanover, 1878).

Gesta Francorum, ed. and trans. R. Hill (Oxford, 1972).

Gesta Regis Henrici Secundi Benedicti Abbatis, ed. W. Stubbs, 2 vols, RS 49 (London, 1867).

The Gesta Tancredi of Ralph of Caen, trans. B. S. Bachrach and D. S. Bachrach (Ashgate, 2005).

Giunta F., 'Documenti su Salerno normanna', in *Byzantino-Sicula II. Miscellanea di scritti in memoria di Giuseppe Rossi Taibbi* (Palermo, 1975), 277–83.

Gregory the Great, *Dialogues*, ed. A. de Vogue, 3 vols (Sources Chretiennes 251) (Paris, 1978–80).

Grundmann, H., 'Zur Biographie Joachims von Fiore und Rainiers von Ponza', *Deutsches Archiv für Erforschung des Mittelalters* 19 (1960), 437–546.

Guibert de Nogent, *Dei Gesta per Francos*, ed. R. B. C. Huygens, Corpus Christianorum. Continuatio Mediaevalis 127 A (Turnhout, 1996).

Guillaume de Pouille, *La Geste de Robert Guiscard*, ed. and trans. M. Mathieu (Palermo, 1961).

Guillaume de Tyr, *Chronique*, ed. R. B. C. Huygens, Corpus Christianorum. Continuatio Mediaevalis 63 A (Turnhout, 1986).

Al-Harawi, *A Lonely Wayfarer's Guide to Pilgrimage*, trans. J. W. Meri (Princeton, 2004).

Historia et Inventionis et Translationis S. Trophimenae, AS July, ii (Paris, 1867), 233–40.

Historia Inventionis Corporis S. Secundini, AS February, ii (Paris, 1864), 530–5.

Historia Inventionis et Translationis S. Cataldi, AS May, ii (Paris, 1866), 569–74.

Historia Inventionis S. Prisci, *AS September*, i (Paris, 1868), 216–18.

La Historia o Liber de Regno Sicilie e la Epistola ad Petrum Panormitane Ecclesie Thesaurium di Ugo Falcando, ed. G. B. Siragusa, FSI 22 (Rome, 1897).

Historia Translationis S. Viti, ed. G. H. Pertz, MGH SS ii (Berlin, 1829).

Historia Welforum, ed. E König (Sigmaringen, 1978).

The History of the Tyrants of Sicily by 'Hugo Falcandus', 1154–1169, trans. G. A. Loud and T. Wiedemann (Manchester, 1998).

The History of William of Newburgh, trans. J. Stevenson (London, 1856).

The Hodoeporicon of St Willibald, in The Anglo-Saxon Missionaries in Germany, trans. and ed. C. H. Talbot (London, 1981), 153–77.

Hoffmann, H., 'Die Translationes et Miracula Sancti Mennatis des Leo Marsicanus', *Deutsches Archiv für Erforschung des Mittelalters* 60 (2004), 441–81.

Hofmeister, A., 'Sermo de Inventione Sancti Kataldi', *Münchener Museum für Philologie des Mittelalters und der Renaissance* 4 (1924), 101–14.

The Hystoria Constantinopolitana of Gunther of Pairis, ed. and trans. A. J. Andrea (Philadelphia, 1997).

Icelandic Sagas, vol. 3: The Orkneyingers' Saga, trans. G. W. Dasent (London, 1894).

Idrisi, *La Première Géographie de l'Occident*, revised translation by H. Bresc *et al.*, (Paris, 1999).

Inventio S. Sabini in *Antiche cronache di Terra di Bari*, ed. G. Cioffari and R. Lupoli Tateo (Bari, 1991).

Inventio, Translationes, et Miracula SS. Mauri, Pantaleonis, et Sergii, AS July, vi (Paris, 1868), 359–71.

Italia Pontificia, ed. P. F. Kehr, 10 vols (Berlin, 1905–75): viii. Regnum Normannorum – Campania, ed. P. F. Kehr (1961); ix. Apulia-Samnium ed. W. Holtzmann (1963); x. Calabria, Insulae, ed. D. Girgensohn (1975).

The Itinerary of Benjamin of Tudela, trans. M. N. Adler (London, 1907).

Jerusalem Pilgrimage 1099–1185, trans. J. Hill *et al.* (London, 1988).

John Skylitzes, *A Synopsis of Byzantine History, 811–1057*, trans. J. Wortley (Cambridge, 2010).

Julian de Vézelay, *Sermons*, ed. D. Vorreux, 2 vols (Sources chrétiennes 192) (Paris, 1972).

The Letters of Peter the Venerable, ed. G. Constable, 2 vols (Cambridge, Mass., 1967).

The Letters of Pope Gregory the Great, trans. J. R. C. Martyn, 3 vols (Toronto, 2004).

Lettres de Jacques de Vitry, ed. R. B. C. Huygens (Leiden, 1960).

Il lezionario e l'evangeliario di Messina, ed. F. Terrizzi (Messina, 1985).

Liber de Apparitione Sancti Michaelis in Monte Gargano, ed. G. Waitz, MGH SRLI (Hanover, 1878).

Liber Sancti Jacobi, Codex Calixtinus, vol. 1, ed. W. Muir Whitehill (Santiago de Compostela, 1944).

Lupus Protospatharius, *Annales*, ed. G. H. Pertz, MGH SS v (Hanover, 1844).

Master Gregorius, *The Marvels of Rome*, ed. and trans. J. Osborne (Toronto, 1987).

Martirio di Santa Lucia: Vita di Santa Marina, ed. and trans. G. Rossi Taibbi (Palermo, 1959).

Martyrologium Hieronymianum, AS November, ii (ii), ed. H. Quentin (Brussels, 1931).

Martyrologium Pulsanensis Cenobii Sancte Cecilie de Fogia (Sec. XII), ed. G. De Troia (Brindisi, 1988).

Materials for the History of Thomas Becket, ed. J. Craigie Robertson, 7 vols, RS 67 (London, 1875–85).

Mercati, M., 'Miracula B. Prosperi Episcopi et Confessoris', *AB* 15 (1896), 161–256.

The Miracles of Our Lady of Rocamadour, trans. M. Bull (Woodbridge, 1999).

Miracula Sancti Audoeni, AS August, iv (Paris, 1867), 824–40.

Missale Antiquum S. Panormitanae Ecclesiae, ed. F. Terrizzi (Rome, 1970).

Necrologio del Liber Confratrum di S. Matteo di Salerno, ed. C. A. Garufi, FSI 56 (Rome, 1922).

Nitti di Vito, F., 'La traslazione delle reliquie di San Nicola', *Iapigia* 8 (1937), 295–411.

O City of Byzantium. Annals of Niketas Choniates, trans. H. J. Magoulias (Detroit, Mich., 1984).

Odo of Deuil, *De Profectione Ludovici VII in Orientem*, ed. and trans. V. G. Berry (New York, 1948).

Orlandi, G., 'Vita Sancti Mennatis. Opera inedita di Leone Marsicano', *Istituto lombardo, Accademia di scienze e lettere, Rendiconti, Classe di lettere* 97 (1963), 467–90.

Peregrinationes Tres: Saewulf, John of Würzburg, Theodericus, ed. R. B. C Huygens with study by J. H. Pryor, Corpus Christianorum. Continuatio Mediaevalis 139 (Sydney, 1994).

Le pergamene del duomo di Bari (952–1264), ed. G. B. Nitto de Rossi and F. Nitti di Vito, Codice diplomatico barese I (Bari, 1867).

Le pergamene di Capua, ed. J. Mazzoleni 3 vols (Naples, 1957–8).

Le pergamene di S. Nicola di Bari. Periodo normanno (1075–1194), ed. F. Nitti di Vito, Codice diplomatico barese V (Bari, 1902).

Le pergamene di S. Nicola di Bari. Periodo svevo (1195–1266), ed. F. Nitti di Vito, Codice diplomatico barese VI (Bari, 1906).

Le pergamene normanne della Mater Ecclesia capuana (1091–1197), ed. G. Bova (Naples, 1996).

Pergamene salernitane (1008–1784), ed. L. E. Pennacchini (Naples, 1941).

Le pergamene sveve della Mater Ecclesia capuana, ed. G. Bova, 2 vols (Naples, 1998–99).

Petri Blesensis, Opera Omnia, Patrologia Latina 207 (Paris, 1855).

Petri Diaconi Ortus et Vita Iustorum Cenobii Casinensis, ed. R. H. Rodgers (Berkeley, Cal., 1972).

Pirri, P., 'Translatio Corporis S. Andree Apostoli de Constantinopoli in Amalfiam', in his *Il duomo di Amalfi ed il chiostro di paradiso* (Rome, 1941), 135–48.

Le più antiche carte dell'archivio capitolare di Agrigento (1092–1282), ed. P. Collura (Palermo, 1960).

Le più antiche carte del capitolo della cattedrale di Benevento (668–1200), ed. A. Ciarelli *et al.* (Rome, 2002).

Poncelet, A., 'Miracula Sancti Nicolai a Monacho Beccensi', *Catalogus Codicum Hagiographicorum Latinorum Bibliotheca Nationali Parisiensi*, vol. 2 (Paris, 1890), 405–32.

Poncelet, A., 'La Translation des SS. Éleuthère, Pontien et Anastase', *AB* 29 (1910), 409–26.

Radulfi de Diceto Decani Lundoniensis Opera Historica, ed. W. Stubbs, 2 vols, RS 68 (London, 1876).

Regesta Regni Hierosolymitani (1097–1291), ed. R. Röhricht, 2 vols (Innsbruck, 1893).

The Register of Pope Gregory VII – 1073–1085, trans. H. E. J. Cowdrey (Oxford, 2002).

Regesto di S. Leonardo di Siponto, ed. F. Camobreco (Rome, 1913).

Die Reichschronik des Annalista Saxo, ed. K. Nass, MGH SS xxxvii (Hanover, 2000).

Revelatio Ecclesiae Sancti Michaelis (in Tumba), ed. and trans. P. Bouet and O. Desbordes, in 'Les Sources' in *Culte et pélerinages*, ed. P. Bouet *et al.* (Rome, 2003).

Robert de Clari, *La Conquête de Constantinople*, ed. and trans. J. Dufournet (Paris, 2004).

Roberti de Monte Cronica, ed. L. C. Bethmann, MGH SS vi (Hanover, 1844).

Rogerii II Regis Diplomata Latina, ed. C.-R. Bruhl, Codex Diplomaticus Regni Siciliae, Ser. I.ii (1) (Cologne, 1987).

Romualdi Salernitani Chronicon, ed. C. A. Garufi, RIS 7 (i) (Città di Castello, 1935).

Rycardi de Sancto Germano Notarii Chronica, ed. C. A. Garufi, RIS 8 (i) (Bologna, 1937).

S. Agathae Miracula, Descripta a Blandino Monacho, AS February, i (Paris, 1863), 648–51.

Schirò, G., 'Vita inedita di S. Cipriano di Calamizzi dal cod. Sinaitico 522', *Bullettino della badia Greca di Grottaferrata* 4 (1950), 65–97.

Sigeberts von Gembloux Passio Sanctae Luciae Virginis und Passio Sanctorum Thebeorum, ed. E. Dümmler (Berlin, 1893).

The Song of Aspremont (La Chanson d'Aspremont), trans. M. A. Newth (New York, 1989).

Suger, *The Deeds of Louis the Fat*, trans. R. C. Cusimano and J. Moorhead (Washington, DC, 1992).

Tancredi et Willelmi III Regum Diplomata, ed. H. Zielinski, Codex Diplomaticus Regni Sicilae, Ser. I.v (Cologne, 1982).

La Traduction de l'Historia Orientalis de Jacques de Vitry, ed. C. Buridant (Paris, 1986).

Translatio Corporum SS duodecim Fratrum, AS September, i (Paris, 1868), 142–55.

A Translation of Abbot Leontios' Life of Saint Gregory, Bishop of Agrigento, trans. J. R. C. Martyn (Lampeter, 2004).

Translatio Sancti Severini, ed. G. Waitz, MGH SRLI (Hanover, 1878).

Translatio Sancti Sosii, ed. G. Waitz, MGH SRLI (Hanover, 1878).

Translatio S. Mercurii, ed. G. Waitz, MGH SRLI (Hanover, 1878).

Translatio SS Ianuarii, Festi, et Desideri, AS September, vi (Paris, 1867), 888–91.

The Travels of Ibn Jubayr, trans. R. J. C. Broadhurst (London, 1952).

Usuardi Martyrologium, Patrologia Latina 213–14 (Paris, 1852).

Virgil, *Aeneid*, trans. D. West (London, 2003).

Vita Barbati Episcopi Beneventani, ed. G. Waitz, MGH SRLI (Hanover, 1878).

Vita Beati Laurentii Eremitae Confessoris, AS August, iii (Paris, 1867), 304–9.

Vita Beati Martini Legionensis, Patrologia Latina 208 (Paris, 1855).

Vita Berardi, AS November, ii (i) (Brussels, 1894), 128–34.

La vita di San Fantino il Giovane, ed. E. Follieri (Brussels, 1993).

Vita di S. Luca, vescovo di Isola Capo Rizzuto, ed. and trans. G. Schirò (Palermo, 1954).

Vitae Quatuor Priorum Abbatum Cavensium, ed. L. Mattei-Cerasoli, RIS 6 (v) (Bologna, 1941).

Vitae Sanctorum Siculorum, ed. O. Gaetani, 2 vols (Palermo, 1657).

Vita et Obitus Sancti Guilielmi, in *Scrittura agiografica nel mezzogiorno normanno: la vita di San Guglielmo da Vercelli*, ed. F. Panarelli (Lecce, 2004).

Vita et Translatio S. Athanasii Neapolitani Episcopi (BHL 735 e 737), ed. A. Vuolo (Rome, 2001).

Vita Inventio et Translatio S. Sabini, AS February, ii (Paris, 1864), 324–9.

Vita S. Alberti Episcopi Montis Corvini, AS April, i (Paris, 1866), 433–6.

Vita S. Bernerii, AS October, vii (Brussels, 1845), 1187–8.

Vita S. Eliae Junioris, AS August, iii (Paris, 1867), 489–509.

Vita S. Eliae Spelacotae, AS September, iii (Paris, 1868), 848–87.

Vita S. Geraldi abbatis, AS April, i (Paris, 1866), 412–28.

Vita S. Iohannis a Mathera, AS June, v (Paris, 1867), 36–50.

Vita S. Leonis Lucae Corilionensis Abbatis, AS March, i (Paris, 1865), 98–102.

Vita S. Lucae Abbatis Armenti, AS October, vi (Paris, 1868), 337–41.

Vita S. Nicolai Peregrini, AS June, i (Paris, 1867), 231–46.

Vita S. Nili, AS September, vii (Paris, 1867), 262–320.

Vita S. Philareti Monachi, AS April, i (Paris, 1866), 602–15.

Vita Sancti Silvestri Trainensis, in *Vitae Sanctorum Siculorum*, vol. 2, ed. O. Gaetani (Palermo, 1657).

Vita S. Sturmi, ed. G. H. Pertz, MGH SS ii (Berlin, 1829).

Vita S. Teotonio, AS February, iii (Paris, 1865), 108–22.

Vita S. Vitalis Abbatis, AS March, ii (Paris, 1865), 26–35.

Vita, Translatio et Miracula B. Gerlandi Episcopi Agrigento, in *Vitae Sanctorum Siculorum*, vol. 2, ed. O. Gaetani (Palermo, 1657).

The Vita Wulfstani of William of Malmesbury, ed. R. R. Darlington, Camden third series 40 (London, 1928).

Walter Map, *De Nugis Curialium: courtier's trifles*, ed. and trans., M. R. James *et al.* (Oxford, 1983).

Webb, D., *Saints and Cities in Medieval Italy* (Manchester, 2007).

William of Malmesbury, *Gesta Regum Anglorum*, ed. and trans. R. A. B. Mynors, R. M. Thomson, M. Winterbottom, 2 vols (Oxford, 1998–99).

Zaccagni, G., 'Il bios di San Bartolomeo da Simeri (BHG 235)', *Rivista di studi bizantini e neoellenici* 33 (1996), 193–274.

SECONDARY SOURCES (*INDICATES THAT THE ITEM CONTAINS EDITED DOCUMENTS)

Agnello, G., 'La S. Oliva di Palermo nella storia e nelle vicende del culto', *Archivio storico siciliano* 8 (1956), 151–93.

Albu, E., *The Normans in their Histories: Propaganda, Myth and Subversion* (Woodbridge, 2001).

Angold, M., 'Knowledge of Byzantine history in the west: the Norman historians (eleventh and twelfth centuries)', *Anglo-Norman Studies* 25 (2002), 19–33.

Aricò, F., 'Il martirologio di Usuardo della biblioteca comunale di Palermo (sec. XII)', *Schede medievali* 43 (2005), 1–45.

Arnold, J. C., 'Arcadia becomes Jerusalem: angelic caverns and shrine conversions at Monte Gargano', *Speculum* 75 (2000), 567–88.

Asbridge, T., *The Creation of the Principality of Antioch, 1098–1130* (Woodbridge, 2000).

Babudri, F., 'Sinossi critica dei traslatori nicolaiani di Bari', *Archivio storico pugliese* 3 (1950), 3–94.

Barlow, F., *Thomas Becket* (London, 1986).

Bartlett, R., *The Making of Europe. Conquest, Colonization and Cultural Change 950–1350* (London, 1993).

——*England under the Norman and Angevin Kings, 1075–1225* (Oxford, 2000).

Barton, S., 'Patrons, pilgrims and the cult of saints in the medieval kingdom of León', *Pilgrimage Explored*, ed. J. Stopford (Woodbridge, 1999), 57–77.

Bethell, D., 'The making of a twelfth-century relic collection', *Studies in Church History* 8 (1972), 61–72.

Bibliotheca Sanctorum, 14 vols (Rome, 1961–87).

Binns, A., *Dedications of Monastic Houses in England and Wales, 1066–1216* (Woodbridge, 1989).

Birch, D. J., *Pilgrimage to Rome in the Middle Ages. Continuity and Change* (Woodbridge, 1998).

——'Jacques de Vitry and the ideology of pilgrimage' *Pilgrimage Explored* ed., J. Stopford (Woodbridge, 1999), 79–93.

Bloch, H., *Monte Cassino in the Middle Ages*, 3 vols (Cambridge, Mass., 1986).

——'Peter the Deacon's vision of Byzantium and a rediscovered treatise in his "Acta S. Placidi" ', *Bisanzio, Roma e l'Italia nell'alto medioevo*, vol. 2, Settimane di studio del centro italiano di studi sull'alto medioevo 34 (Spoleto, 1988), 797–847.

——*The Atina Dossier of Peter the Deacon of Montecassino. A Hagiographical Romance of the Twelfth Century* (Vatican City, 1998).

Boesch Gajano, S., 'Agiografia e geografia nei Dialoghi di Gregorio Magno', *Storia della Sicilia*, ed. S. Pricoco (Catania, 1988), 209–20.

Borgia, S., *Memorie istoriche della pontificia città di Benevento dal secolo VIII al secolo XVIII*, 3 vols (Rome, 1763–9).

Borsari, S., *Il monachesimo bizantino nella Sicilia e nell'Italia meridionale prenormanne* (Naples, 1963).

Borsook, E., *Messages in Mosaic. The Royal Programmes of Norman Sicily (1130–1187)* (Oxford, 1990).

Bottiglieri, C., 'Literary themes and genres in southern Italy during the Norman age: the return of the saints', *Norman Tradition and Transcultural Heritage*, ed. S. Burckhardt and T. Foerster (Farnham, 2013), 97–124.

Bowman, G., 'Nationalizing the sacred: shrines and shifting identities in the Israeli-occupied territories', *Man: Journal of the Royal Anthropological Institute* 28 (1993), 431–60.

Boynton, S., *Shaping of a Monastic Identity. Liturgy and History at the Imperial Abbey of Farfa, 1000–1125* (Ithaca, NY, 2006).

Bresc, H., 'Dominio feudale, consistenza patrimoniale e insediamento umano', *Chiesa e società in Sicilia*, ed. G. Zito (Turin, 1995), 91–107.

Brodbeck, S, *Les Saints de la cathédrale de Monreale en Sicile* (Rome, 2010).

Brown, P., *The Cult of the Saints. Its Rise and Function in Latin Christianity* (Chicago, 1981).

Brown, T. S., 'The political use of the past in Norman Sicily', *Perceptions of the Past in Twelfth-Century Europe*, ed. P. Magdalino (London, 1992), 191–210.

Bull, M., *Knightly Piety and the Lay Response to the First Crusade. The Limousin and Gascony, c.970–c.1130* (Oxford, 1998).

Campione, A., 'Note sulla vita di Sabino di Canosa: inventio et translatio', *Vetera Christianorum* 25 (1988), 617–39.

Caravale, M., *Il regno normanno di Sicilia* (Rome, 1966).

Carpenter, D. A., *The Reign of Henry III* (London, 1996).

Caruso, S., 'Crucisque signo munitus. Luca da Dèmena e l'epopea anti-saracena italo-greca', *Byzantion* 73 (2003), 319–38.

Castelfranchi Falla, M., 'Continuità dall'antico: la basilica di San Leucio a Canosa. Nuove acquisizioni', *Vetera Christianorum* 22 (1985), 387–94.

Catallo, T., 'Sulla datazione delle "vitae" di Lorenzo vescovo di Siponto', *SM* 32 (1991), 129–57.

Chadwick, H., *East and West. The Making of a Rift in the Church. From Apostolic Times until the Council of Florence* (Oxford, 2003).

Cherubini, G., 'Una nota sui tempi di viaggio dei pellegrini', *Studi in onore di Giosuè Musca*, ed. C. D. Fonseca and V. Sivo (Bari, 2000), 105–15.

Chiesa e società in Sicilia: l'età normanna, Atti del I convegno internazionale organizzato dall'arcidiocesi di Catania, 25–27 novembre 1992, ed. G. Zito (Turin, 1995).

Cioffari, G., *Storia della basilica di S. Nicola di Bari. I. L'epoca normanno-sveva* (Bari, 1984).

Cioffari, G., *et al.*, *Agiografia in Puglia. I santi tra critica storica e devozione popolare* (Bari, 1991).

Citarella, A. O., 'Patterns in medieval trade: the commerce of Amalfi before the Crusades', *Journal of Economic History* 28 (1968), 531–55.

Citerella, A. O., and Willard, H. M., *The Ninth-Century Treasure of Monte Cassino in the Context of Political and Economic Developments in South Italy*, Miscellanea Cassinese 50 (Montecassino, 1983).

Clark, R. J., 'Conrad of Querfurt and Petrarch on the location of the Vergilian underworld', *Papers of the British School at Rome* 64 (1996), 261–72.

Cohen, E., 'Roads and pilgrimage: a study in economic interaction', *SM* 21 (1980), 321–41.

Colomba, C., 'Repertorio agiografico pugliese', *Hagiographica* 16 (2009), 1–54.

Comparetti, D., *Vergil in the Middle Ages*, trans. E. F. M. Benecke (London, 1895; reprinted 1966).

Connolly, D. K., *The Maps of Matthew Paris. Medieval Journeys through Space, Time and Liturgy* (Woodbridge, 2009).

Contesting the Sacred. The Anthropology of Christian Pilgrimage, ed. J. Eade and M. J. Sallnow (London, 1991).

Costanza, S., 'Per una nuova edizione delle "Vitae Sanctorum Siculorum"', *Schede medievali* 5 (1983), 313–25.

Cowdrey, H. E. J., 'Pope Urban II's preaching of the First Crusade', *History* 55 (1970), 177–88.

———*The Age of Abbot Desiderius. Montecassino, the Papacy, and the Normans in the Eleventh and Early-Twelfth Centuries* (Oxford, 1983).

Culte et pèlerinages à Saint Michel en occident: les trois monts dédiés à l'archange, ed. P. Bouet *et al.* (Rome, 2003).

Cushing, K. G., 'Events that led to sainthood: sanctity and the reformers in the eleventh century', *Belief and Culture in the Middle Ages. Studies Presented to Henry Mayr-Harting*, ed. R. Gameson and H. Leyser (Oxford, 2001), 187–96.

Da Costa-Louillet, G., 'Saints de Sicile et d'Italie meridionale aux VIIIe, IXe et Xe siècles', *Byzantion* 29–30 (1959–60), 89–173.

Dalena, P., *Dagli itinera ai percorsi: viaggiare nel mezzogiorno medievale* (Bari, 2003).

———'Percorsi e ricoveri di pellegrini nel mezzogiorno medievale', *Tra Roma e Gerusalemme*, ed. M. Oldoni, 3 vols (Salerno, 2005), i. 227–53.

D'Angelo, E., 'San Giorgio e i normanni', *San Giorgio e il Mediterraneo*, ed. G. de' Giovanni-Centelles (Vatican City, 2004), 195–217.

———'Agiografia latina del mezzogiorno continentale d' Italia (750–1000)', *Hagiographies IV*, ed. G. Philippart, Corpus Christianorum (Turnhout, 2006), 41–134.

D'Arienzo, M., 'Il pellegrinaggio al Gargano tra XI e XVI secolo', in *Culte et pèlerinages*, ed. P. Bouet *at al.* (Rome, 2003), 219–44.

De Gaiffier, B., 'L'Hagiographie et son public au XI siècle', in his *Études critiques d'hagiographie et d'iconologie* (Brussels, 1967), 475–507.

Delehaye, H., 'La Translatio S. Mercurii Beneventum', in *Mélanges Godefroid Kurth*, 2 vols (Liège, 1908), i. 17–24.

———'Hagiographie napolitaine', *AB* 57 (1939), 5–64.

Delogu, P., *Mito di una città meridionale (Salerno, secoli VIII-XI)* (Naples, 1977).

Demus, O., *The Mosaics of Norman Sicily* (London, 1950).

De Palma, L. M., *San Corrado il Guelfo: indagine storico-agiografico* (Molfetta, 1996).

———'Santi martiri crociati? Storia e leggenda di un culto medievale', *Verso Gerusalemme: pellegrini, santuari, crociati tra X e XV secolo*, ed. F. Cardini *et al.* (Bergamo, 2000) available at www.enec.it/VersoGerusalemme/08LUIGIMICHELEDEPALMA.pdf.

Di Scipio, G.-C., 'Saint Paul and popular traditions', *Telling Tales. Medieval Narratives and the Folk Tradition*, ed. F. Canadé Sautman *et al.* (London, 1998), 189–208.

Dolbeau, F., 'Le Rôle des interprètes dans les traductions hagiographiques d'Italie du sud', *Traduction et traducteurs au moyen age*, âctes du colloque international du CNRS, 26–28 Mai 1986 (Paris, 1989), 145–62.

Dormeier, H., *Montecassino und die Laien im 11. und 12. Jahrhundert* (Stuttgart, 1979).

Drell, J., 'Cultural syncretism and ethnic identity. The Norman conquest of southern Italy and Sicily', *Journal of Medieval History* 25 (1999), 187–202.

Dvornik, F., *The Idea of Apostolicity in Byzantium and the Legend of the Apostle Andrew* (Cambridge, Mass., 1958).

Edson, E., *Mapping Time and Space. How Medieval Mapmakers Viewed Their World* (London, 1997).

Edwards, G. R., 'Purgatory: "birth" or "evolution"', *Journal of Ecclesiastical History* 34 (1985), 634–46.

Efthymiades, S., 'D'orient en occident mais étranger aux deux mondes. Messages et renseignements tirés de la vie de Saint Nicolas le Pèlerin (BHL 6223)', *Puer Apuliae*, ed. E. Cuozzo *et al.*, 2 vols (Paris, 2008), i. 207–23.

Fagnoni, A. M., 'I "Dialogi" di Desiderio nella "Chronica Monasterii Casinensis"', *SM* 34 (1993), 65–94.

Fasoli, G., 'Tre secoli di vita cittadina catanese', in her *Scritti di storia medievale* (Bologna, 1974).

Ferrante, N., *Santi italogreci in Calabria* (Reggio Calabria, 1981).

Finucane, R., *Miracles and Pilgrims. Popular Beliefs in Medieval England* (London, 1977).

Follieri, E., 'I rapporti fra Bisanzio e l'occidente nel campo dell'agiografia', *Proceedings of the XIIIth International Congress of Byzantine Studies (Oxford, 5–10 September 1966)*, ed. J. M. Hussey, D. Obolensky, S. Runciman (London, 1967), 355–62.

———'Il culto dei santi nell'Italia greca', *La chiesa greca in Italia dall'VIII al XVI secolo*, vol. 2 (Padua, 1973), 553–77.

Franchetti Pardo, V., 'Le città portuali meridionali e le crociate', *Il mezzogiorno normanno-svevo e le cruciate*, ed. G. Musca (Bari, 2002), 301–23.

Frolow, A., *La Relique de la vraie croix* (Paris, 1961).

Galatariotou, C., *The Making of a Saint. The Life, Times and Sanctification of Neophytos the Recluse* (Cambridge, 1991).

Galdi, A., 'Il santo e la città: il culto di S. Matteo a Salerno tra X e XVI secolo', *Rassegna storica salernitana* 25 (1996), 21–92.

———'La diffusione del culto del santo patrono: l'esempio di S. Matteo di Salerno', *Pellegrinaggi e itinerari*, ed. G. Vitolo (Naples, 1999), 181–91.

———*Santi, territori, potere e uomini nella Campania medievale (secc. XI-XII)* (Salerno, 2004).

———'Pellegrinaggi e santità nelle tradizioni agiografiche', *Tra Roma e Gerusalemme*, ed. M. Oldoni, 3 vols (Salerno, 2005), i. 295–311.

———'La diffusione del culto di San Pantaleone in Campania e in Puglia nei secoli xi–xv', *Pantaleone da Nicomedia: santo e taumaturgo tra oriente e occidente*, Atti del convegno, Ravello, 24–26 luglio 2004, ed. C. Caserta and M. Talalay (Naples, 2006), 57–75.

———'Troia, Montecassino e i Normanni: la traslazione di s. Eleuterio tra identità cittadina e dinamiche di potere', *Vetera Christianorum* 47 (2010), 63–83.

Gallina, M., 'Il mezzogiorno normanno-svevo visto da Bisanzio', *Il mezzogiorno normanno-svevo visto dall'Europa e dal mondo mediterraneo*, Atti delle XIII giornate normanno-sveve, Bari, 21–24 ottobre 1997, Centro di studi normanno-svevi, ed. G. Musca (Bari, 1999), 197–223.

Gameson, R., 'The early imagery of Thomas Becket', *Pilgrimage. The English Experience from Becket to Bunyan*, ed. C. Morris and P. Roberts (Cambridge, 2002), 46–89.

Gargano, G., 'La cattedrale santuario: il culto di S. Andrea ad Amalfi', *Pellegrinaggi e itinerari*, ed. G. Vitolo (Naples, 1999), 193–201.

Gargiulo, M., 'L'iconografia del Pellegrino', *Tra Roma e Gerusalemme*, ed. M. Oldoni, 3 vols (Salerno, 2005), ii. 435–87.

Garton, T., *Early Romanesque Sculpture in Apulia* (New York, 1984).

Geary, P. J., *Furta Sacra. Thefts of Relics in the Central Middle Ages* (Princeton, 1978).

———'Reflections on historiography and the holy: center and periphery', *The Making of Christian Myths in the Periphery of Latin Christendom (c. 1000–1300)*, ed. L.-B. Mortensen (Copenhagen, 2006), 323–30.

Gianfreda, G., *Il mosaico pavimentale della Basilica Cattedrale di Otranto*, 2nd edn. (Frosinone, 1970).

Glass, D. F., *Romanesque Sculpture in Campania. Patrons, Programs and Style* (University Park, PA, 1991).

———*Portals, Pilgrimage, and Crusade in Western Tuscany* (Princeton, 1997).

Golinelli, P., *Città e culto dei santi nel medioevo italiano*, new ed. (Bologna, 1996).

Good, J., *The Cult of St George in Medieval England* (Woodbridge, 2009).

Granier, T., 'Napolitains et Lombards aux VIIIe-XIe siècles. De la guerre des peuples à "la guerre des saints" en Italie du Sud', *MEFRM* 108 (1996), 403–50.

Guidoboni, E., and Ciuccarelli, C., 'First historical evidence of a significant Mt. Etna eruption in 1224', *Journal of Volcanology and Geothermal Research* 178 (2008), 693–700.

Guidoboni, E., and Ebel, J. E., *Earthquakes and Tsunamis in the Past. A Guide to Techniques in Historical Seismology* (Cambridge, 2009).

Hackel, S. ed., *The Byzantine Saint*, University of Birmingham Fourteenth Spring Symposium of Byzantine Studies (London, 1981).

Halkin, F., 'St Barthélemy de Grottaferrata. Notes critiques', *AB* 61 (1943), 202–10.

Hamilton, B., *The Latin Church in the Crusader States* (London, 1980).

Hamilton, L. I., 'Desecration and consecration in Norman Capua, 1066–1122: contesting sacred space during the Gregorian reforms', *Haskins Society Journal* 14 (2003), 137–50.

———*A Sacred City. Consecrating Churches and Reforming Society in Eleventh-Century Italy* (Manchester, 2010).

Hayden, R. M., 'Antagonistic tolerance: competitive sharing of religious sites in South Asia and the Balkans', *Current Anthropology* 43 (2002), 205–31.

Hayward, P. A., 'Translation narratives in post-conquest hagiography and English resistance to the Norman conquest', *Anglo-Norman Studies* 21 (1999), 67–93.

Head, T., *Hagiography and the Cult of Saints. The Diocese of Orleans 800–1200* (Cambridge, 1990).

———'Discontinuity and discovery in the cult of saints: Apulia from Late Antiquity to the High Middle Ages', *Hagiographica* 6 (1999), 171–211.

———'Postscript: the ambiguous bishop', *The Bishop Reformed. Studies in Episcopal Power and Culture in the Central Middle Ages*, ed. J. S. Ott and A. Trumbore Jones (Aldershot, 2007), 250–64.

Herrick, S. K., *Imagining the Sacred Past. Hagiography and Power in Early Normandy* (Cambridge, Mass., 2007).

Hiestand, R., 'S. Michele in Orsara. Un capitolo dei rapporti pugliesi – iberici nei secoli xii–xiii', *Archivio storico pugliese* 44 (1991), 67–79.

*Hilken, C., *Memory and Community in Medieval Southern Italy. The History, Chapter Book, and Necrology of Santa Maria del Gualdo Mazzocca* (Toronto, 2008).

Hofmann, H., *Die Heiligen Drei Könige: Zur Heiligenverehrung im kirchlichen, gesell-schaftlichen und politischen Leben des Mittelalters* (Bonn, 1975).

Horden, P., and Purcell, N., *The Corrupting Sea. A Study of Mediterranean History* (Oxford, 2000).

Houben, H., 'L'autore delle 'Vitae Quatuor Priorum Abbatum Cavensium'', *SM* 26 (1985), 871–9.

———*Die Abtei Venosa und das Mönchtum im normannisch-staufischen Süditalien* (Tübingen, 1995).

———'"Iuxta Stratam Peregrinorum": la canonica di S. Leonardo di Siponto (1127–1260)', *Rivista di storia della chiesa in Italia* 56 (2002), 323–48.

———*Roger II of Sicily. A Ruler between East and West*, trans. G. A. Loud and D. Milburn (Cambridge, 2002).

———'Templari e teutonici nel mezzogiorno normanno-svevo' *Il mezzogiorno normanno-svevo e le crociate*, ed. G. Musca (Bari, 2002), 251–88.

Howe, J., *Church Reform and Social Change in Eleventh-Century Italy. Dominic of Sora and his Patrons* (Philadelphia, 1997).

———'St Berardus of Marsica (d. 1130) "Model Gregorian Bishop"', *Journal of Ecclesiastical History* 58 (2007), 400–16.

Inge, J., *A Christian Theology of Place* (Aldershot, 2003).

Ivanov, S. A., *Holy Fools in Byzantium and Beyond* (Oxford, 2006).

Jacob, A., 'Le Culte de Saint Martin de Tours dans la terre d'Otrante hellénophone', *Puer Apuliae*, ed. E. Cuozzo *et al.*, 2 vols (Rome, 2008), i. 345–56.

Jasper, K. L., 'Reforming the monastic landscape: Peter Damian's design for personal and communal devotion', *Rural Space in the Middle Ages and Early Modern Age. The Spatial Turn in Premodern Studies*, ed. A. Classen (Berlin, 2012), 193–208.

Joannou, P., 'La personalità storica di Luca di Bova attraverso i suoi scritti inediti', *ASCL* 29 (1960), 179–237.

Johns, J., *Arabic Administration in Norman Sicily. The Royal Dīwān* (Cambridge, 2002).

Jones, C. W., *Saint Nicholas of Myra, Bari and Manhattan. Biography of a Legend* (Chicago, 1978).

Jotischky, A., *The Perfection of Solitude. Hermits and Monks in the Crusader States* (University Park, PA, 1995).

———'Pilgrimage, procession and ritual encounters between Christians and Muslims in the Crusader States', *Cultural Encounters during the Crusades*, ed. K. Villads Jensen, K. Salonen and H. Vogt (Copenhagen, 2013), 245–62.

Kaftal, G., *Saints in Italian Art. Iconography of the Saints in Central and South Italian Schools of Painting*, vol. 2 (Florence, 1965).

Kangas, S., 'Inimicus Dei et Sanctae Christianitatis? Saracens and their prophet in twelfth-century crusade propaganda and western travesties of Muhammad's life', *The Crusades and the Near East*, ed. C. Kostick (London, 2011), 131–60.

Kazhdan, A., 'Hagiographical notes', *Byzantion* 53 (1983), 538–58.

Keene, D., 'London from the post-Roman period to 1300', *The Cambridge Urban History of Britain, Vol. I 600–1540*, ed. D. M. Palliser (Cambridge, 2000), 187–216.

Kelly, T. F., *The Beneventan Chant* (Cambridge, 1989).

———*The Exultet in Southern Italy* (Oxford, 1996).

Kersken, N., 'God and the saints in medieval Polish historiography', *The Making of Christian Myths in the Periphery of Latin Christendom (c.1000–1300)*, ed. L.-B. Mortensen (Copenhagen, 2006), 153–94.

Klein, H. A., 'Eastern objects and western desires: relics and reliquaries between Byzantium and the west', *Dumbarton Oaks Papers* 58 (2004), 283–314.

Kleinberg, A. M., *Prophets in Their Own Country. Living Saints and the Making of Sainthood in the Later Middle Ages* (Chicago, 1997).

Kreutz, B., *Before the Normans. Southern Italy in the Ninth and Tenth Centuries* (Philadelphia, 1991).

Lapina, E., 'Demetrius of Thessaloniki: patron saint of crusaders', *Viator* 40 (2009), 93–112.

Lavezzo, K., *Angels on the Edge of the World. Geography, Literature, and English Community, 1000–1534* (Ithaca, NY, 2006).

Le Goff, J., *The Birth of Purgatory*, trans. A. Goldhammer (Aldershot, 1991).

Lentini, A., 'Sulla "passio S. Modesti" di Alberico Cassinese', *Benedictina* 6 (1952), 231–5.

Lewis, S., *The Art of Matthew Paris in the Chronica Majora* (Aldershot, 1987).

Leyser, H., *Hermits and the New Monasticism. A Study of Religious Communities in Western Europe 1000–1150* (London, 1984).

Licini, P., 'A multi-layered journey. From manuscript initial letters to encyclopaedic mappaemundi through the Benedictine semiotic traditions',

The Hereford World Map. Medieval World Maps and their Context, ed. P. A. Harvey (London, 2006), 269–92.

Limone, O., *Santi monaci e santi eremeti: alla ricerca di un modello di perfezione letteratura agiografica dell'Apulia normanna* (Galatina, 1988).

——'Italia meridionale (950–1220)', *Hagiographies II*, ed. G. Philippart, Corpus Christianorum (Turnhout, 1996), 11–60.

Loud, G. A., 'The Norman counts of Caiazzo and the abbey of Montecassino', *Monastica I. Scritti raccolti in memoria del XV centenario della nascita di San Benedetto (480–1980)*, Miscellanea Cassinese, 44 (Montecassino, 1981), pp. 199–217, (reprinted in his *Montecassino and Benevento in the Middle Ages* (Aldershot, 2000)).

——'The Gens Normannorum. Myth or reality?', *Proceedings of the Fourth Battle Conference on Norman Studies 1981*, ed. R. A. Brown (Woodbridge, 1982), 104–16 (reprinted in his *Conquerors and Churchmen in Norman Italy* (Aldershot, 1999)).

——'Norman Italy and the Holy Land', *The Horns of Hattin*, ed. B. Z. Kedar, (Jerusalem, 1992), 49–62.

——'A Lombard abbey in a Norman world: St. Sophia, Benevento, 1050–1200', *Anglo-Norman Studies* 19 (1997), 273–306 (reprinted in his *Montecassino and Benevento in the Middle Ages* (Aldershot, 2000)).

——*The Age of Robert Guiscard. Southern Italy and the Norman Conquest* (Harlow, 2000).

——'The kingdom of Sicily and the kingdom of England, 1066–1266', *History* 88 (2003), 540–67.

——'Monastic miracles in southern Italy, c.1040–1140', *Studies in Church History* 41 (2005), 109–22.

——'Monastic chronicles in the twelfth-century Abruzzi', *Anglo-Norman Studies* 27 (2005), 101–31.

——*The Latin Church in Norman Italy* (Cambridge, 2007).

Luongo, G., 'Alla ricerca del sacro. Le traslazioni dei santi in epoca altomedioevale', *Il ritorno di Paolino*, ed. A Ruggiero (Naples and Rome, 1990), 17–39.

——'Itinerari dei santi italo-greci', *Pellegrinaggi e itinerari*, ed. G. Vitolo (Naples, 1999), 39–56.

Luttrell, A., 'Gli ospedalieri nel mezzogiorno', *Il mezzogiorno normanno-svevo e le crociate*, ed. G. Musca (Bari, 2002), 289–300.

Luzzi, A., *Studi sul sinassario di Constantinopoli* (Rome, 1995).

MacEvitt, C., *The Crusades and the Christian World of the East. Rough Tolerance* (Philadelphia, 2008).

Magdalino, P., 'The Byzantine holy man in the twelfth century', *The Byzantine Saint*, ed. S. Hackel (London, 1981), 51–66.

Mallardo, D., 'L'incubazione nella cristianità medievale napoletana', *AB* 67 (1949), 465–98.

Martin, J.-M., 'Les Modèles paléochrétiens dans l'hagiographie apulienne', *Bulletin de la société nationale des antiquaires de France* (1990), 67–86.

—— *La Pouille du VI au XII siècle* (Rome, 1993).

—— 'Anthroponymie et onomastique à Bari (950–1250)', *MEFRM* 106 (1994), 683–701.

—— *Foggia nel medioevo* (Rome, 1998).

—— 'Les Normands et le culte de Saint-Michel en Italie du sud' in *Culte et pèlerinages*, ed. P. Bouet *et al.* (Rome, 2003), 341–64.

Matthew, D., *The Norman Kingdom of Sicily* (Cambridge, 1992).

Menache, S., *The Vox Dei. Communication in the Middle Ages* (Oxford, 1990).

McGuire, B. P., 'Purgatory and the communion of saints: a medieval change', *Viator* 20 (1989), 61–84.

McLaughlin, M., *Consorting with Saints. Prayer for the Dead in Early Medieval France* (Ithaca, 1994).

McNulty P., and Hamilton, B., ' "Orientale Lumen et Magistra Latinitatis": Greek influences on western monasticism (900–1100)', *Le Millénaire du Mont Athos 963–1963, études et mélanges*, 2 vols (Chevatogne, 1963), i. 181–216.

Ménager, L.-R., 'La Byzantinisation religieuse de l'Italie méridionale (IXe–XIIe siècles) et la politique monastique des Normands d'Italie', *Revue d'histoire ecclésiastique* 53 (1958), 747–74.

Messina, A., *Sicilia rupestre* (Rome, 2008).

Metcalfe, A., *Muslims and Christians in Norman Italy. Arabic Speakers and the End of Islam* (London, 2003).

—— *The Muslims of Medieval Italy* (Edinburgh, 2009).

Meyvaert, P., 'Peter the Deacon and the tomb of St Benedict: a re-examination of the Cassinese tradition', *Revue bénédictine* 65 (1955), 3–70 (reprinted in his *Benedict, Gregory, Bede and Others* (London, 1977)).

Il mezzogiorno normanno-svevo visto dall'Europa e dal mondo mediterraneo, Atti delle XIII giornate normanno-sveve Bari, 21–24 ottobre 1997, ed. G. Musca (Bari, 1999).

Il mezzogiorno normanno-svevo e le cruciate, Atti delle XIV giornate normanno-sveve, Bari, 17–20 Ottobre 2000, ed. G. Musca (Bari, 2002).

Milazzo, V., and Rizzo Nervo, F., 'Lucia tra Sicilia, Roma e Bisanzio; itinerario di un culto (IV–IX secolo), *Storia della Sicilia*, ed. S. Pricoco (Catania, 1988), 95–135.

Miller, M. C., *The Bishop's Palace. Architecture and Authority in Medieval Italy* (Ithaca, 2000).

Miller, M. C., 'New religious movements and reform', *A Companion to the Medieval World*, ed. C. Lansing and E. D. English (Oxford, 2009), 211–30.

Mola, S., 'L'iconografia della salvezza sulle strade dei pellegrini', *Tra Roma e Gerusalemme*, ed. M. Oldoni, 3 vols (Salerno, 2005), ii. 489–527.

Mollat, M., *The Poor in the Middle Ages. An Essay in Social History*, trans. A. Goldhammer (Yale, 1986).

Monti, G. M., *Le corporazioni nell'evo antico e nell'alto medio evo* (Bari, 1934).

Morris, R. 'The political saint of the eleventh century', *The Byzantine Saint*, ed. S. Hackel (London, 1981), 43–50.

—— 'The Byzantine Aristocracy and the monasteries', *The Byzantine Aristocracy, IX to XIII Centuries*, ed. M. Angold, British Archaeological Reports, International Series 221 (1984), 112–37.

——*Monks and Laymen in Byzantium, 843–1118* (Cambridge, 1995).

Murray, A. V., *The Crusader Kingdom of Jerusalem. A Dynastic History 1099–1125* (Oxford, 2000).

——'Norman settlement in the Latin kingdom of Jerusalem, 1099–1131', *Archivio normanno-svevo* 1 (2008), 61–85.

Musca, G., *L'emirato di Bari, 847–71* (Bari, 1964).

Nef, A., 'Sur les saints de la Sicile normande: à propos du martyrologe MS QQ E2 de la biblioteca comunale de Palerme', *Puer Apuliae*, ed., E. Cuozzo *et al.*, 2 vols (Rome, 2008), ii. 477–90.

Newton, F., *The Scriptorium and Library at Monte Cassino, 1058–1105* (Cambridge, 1999).

I normanni, popolo d'Europa, 1030–1200, ed. M. D'Onofrio (Rome, 1994).

Noto, V., *Santa Rosalia* (Milan, 2008).

Oldoni, M., 'Agiografia longobardo secolo ix e x: la leggenda di Trofimena', *SM* 12 (1971), 583–636.

Oldfield, P., 'St Nicholas the Pilgrim and the city of Trani between Greeks and Normans, c. 1090-c.1140', *Anglo-Norman Studies* 30 (2008), 168–81.

——'The Iberian imprint on medieval southern Italy', *History* 93 (2008), 312–27.

——*City and Community in Norman Italy* (Cambridge, 2009).

Otranto, G., *Italia meridionale e Puglia paleocristiana. Saggi storici* (Bari, 1991).

Pace, V., 'Echi della Terrasanta: Barletta e l'oriente crociato', *Tra Roma e Gerusalemme*, ed. M. Oldoni, 3 vols (Salerno, 2005), ii. 393–408.

Panarelli, F., *Dal Gargano alla Toscana: il monachesimo riformato latino dei pulsanesi (secoli xii–xiv)* (Rome, 1997).

Parks, G. B., *The English Traveller to Italy. First Volume: The Middle Ages (to 1525)* (Rome, 1954).

Pasini, C., 'Osservazioni sul dossier agiografico ed innografico di San Filippo do Agira', *Storia della Sicilia*, ed. S. Pricoco (Catania, 1988), 173–201.

Patlagean, E., 'Les Moines grecs d'Italie et l'apologie des thèses pontificales (VIIe–IXe siècles)', *SM* 5 (1964), 579–602.

Pellegrinaggi e itinerari dei santi nel mezzogiorno medievale, ed. G. Vitolo (Naples, 1999).

Pertusi, A., 'Monasteri e monaci italiani all'Athos nell'alto medioevo', *Le Millénaire du Mont Athos 963–1963, études et mélanges*, vol. 1 (Chevatogne, 1963), 217–51.

——'Rapporti tra il monachesimo italo-greco ed il monachesimo bizantino nell'alto medio evo', *La chiesa greca in Italia dall'VIII al XVI secolo*, vol. 2 (Padua, 1973), 473–520.

——'Ai confini tra religione e politica. La contesa per le reliquie di S. Nicola tra Bari, Venezia e Genova', *Quaderni medievali* 5 (1978), 6–56.

Peters-Custot, A., *Les Grecs de l'Italie méridionale post-byzantine. Une acculturation en douceur (IXe–XIVe siècles)* (Rome, 2009).

Petersen, J. M., *The Dialogues of Gregory the Great in their Late Antique Cultural Background* (Toronto, 1984).

*Petroni, G., *Della storia di Bari dagli antichi tempi sino all'anno 1856*, 2 vols (Naples, 1857–8).

Philippart, G., 'L'Hagiographie sicilienne dans le cadre de l'hagiographie de l'occident' *La Sicilia nella tarda antichità e nell'alto medioevo*, ed. R. Barcellona and S. Pricoco (Catania, 1999), 167–204.

Pioletti, A., 'Artù, Avallon, l'Etna', *Quaderni medievali* 28 (1989), 6–35.

*Pirri, P., *Il duomo di Amalfi ed il chiostro di paradiso* (Rome, 1941).

Pispisa, E., 'Il vescovo, la città e il regno', *Chiesa e società in Sicilia*, ed. G. Zito (Turin, 1995), 137–54.

Pratesi, A., 'Alcune diocesi di Puglia nell'età di Roberto il Guiscardo: Trani, Bari e Canosa tra Greci e Normanni', *Roberto Guiscardo e il suo tempo*, Atti delle prime giornate normanno-sveve, Bari, 28–29 maggio 1973 (Bari, 1991), 225–42.

Prawer, J., *Crusader Institutions* (Oxford, 1980).

Pricoco, S., 'Un esempio di agiografia regionale: la Sicilia', *Santi e demoni nell'alto medioevo occidentale (secoli V-XI)*, Settimane di studio del centro italiano di studi sull'alto medioevo 36 (Spoleto, 1989), 319–76.

Pryor, J., *Geography, Technology, and War. Studies in the Maritime History of the Mediterranean 649–1571* (Cambridge, 1988).

Puer Apuliae. Mélanges offerts à Jean-Marie Martin, ed., E. Cuozzo et al., 2 vols (Paris, 2008).

Purkis, W. J., *Crusading Spirituality in the Holy Land and Iberia c. 1095-c.1187* (Woodbridge, 2008).

Ramseyer, V., *The Transformation of a Religious Landscape. Medieval Southern Italy 850–1150* (Ithaca, NY, 2006).

——'Pastoral care as military action: the ecclesiology of Archbishop Alfanus I of Salerno (1058–85)', *The Bishop Reformed. Studies in Episcopal Power and Culture in the Central Middle Ages*, ed. J. S. Ott and A. Trumbore Jones (Aldershot, 2007), 189–208.

Rees-Jones, S., 'Cities and their saints in England, circa 1150–1300: the development of bourgeois values in the cults of Saint William of York and Saint Kenelm of Winchcombe', in *Cities, Texts and Social Networks, 400–1500. Experiences and Perceptions of Medieval Urban Space*, ed. C. Goodson *et al.* (Farnham, 2010), 193–213.

Remensnyder, A. G., *Remembering Kings Past. Monastic Foundation Legends in Medieval Southern France* (Ithaca, 1995).

Richard, J., *Les Récits de voyages et de pèlerinages*, Typologie des sources du moyen âge occidental 38 (Turnhout, 1981).

Richards, J., *Consul of God. The Life and Times of Gregory the Great* (London, 1989).

Ridyard, S. J., 'Condigna Veneratio: post-conquest attitudes to the saints of the Anglo-Saxons', *Anglo-Norman Studies* 9 (1987), 179–206.

——'Functions of a twelfth-century recluse revisited: the case of Godric of Finchale', *Belief and Culture in the Middle Ages. Studies Presented to Henry Mayr-Harting*, ed. R. Gameson and H. Leyser (Oxford, 2001), 187–96.

Runciman, S., *The Eastern Schism. A Study of the Papacy and the Eastern Chruches during the XIth and XIIth Centuries* (Oxford, 1955).

Saggi, L., *S. Angelo di Sicilia* (Rome, 1962).

San Bruno di Colonia: un eremite tra oriente e occidente, ed. P. De Leo (Catanzaro, 2004).

Sansterre, J.-M., 'Recherches sur les érémites du Mont-Cassin et l'érémitisme dans l'hagiographie cassinienne', *Hagiographica* 2 (1995), 57–92.

Scaduto, M., *Il monachesimo basiliano nella Sicilia medievale: rinascita e decadenza sec. XI-XIV* (Rome, 1947).

Scalia, G., 'La traslazione del corpo di S. Agata e il suo valore storico', *Archivio storico per la Sicilia orientale* 23–4 (1927–9), 38–128.

Schirò, G., 'Quattro inni per santi calabresi dimenticati', *ASCL* 15 (1946), 17–26.

Schmitt, J.-C., *Ghosts in the Middle Ages. The Living and the Dead in the Middle Ages*, trans. T. Lavender Fagan (Chicago, 1998).

Scorza Barcellona, F., 'Santi africani in Sicilia (e siciliani in Africa) secondo Francesco Lanzoni', *Storia della Sicilia*, ed. S. Pricoco (Catania, 1988), 37–55.

———'Note sui martiri dell'invasione saracena', *La Sicilia nella tarda antichità e nell'alto medioevo*, eds. R. Barcellona and S. Pricoco (Catania, 1999), 205–20.

Settis Frugoni, C., 'Per una lettura del mosaico pavimentale della cattedrale di Otranto', *BISIME* 80 (1968), 213–56.

Shepard, J., 'Byzantium's last Sicilian expedition: Scylitzes' testimony', *Rivista di studi bizantini e neoellenici* 14–16 (1977–9), 145–5.

———'The uses of the Franks in eleventh-century Byzantium', *Anglo-Norman Studies* 15 (1993), 275–305.

La Sicilia nella tarda antichità e nell'alto medioevo. Religione e società, Atti del convegno di studi (Catania – Palermo, 24–27 Settembre 1997)], eds. R. Barcellon and S. Pricoco (Catania, 1999).

Sigal, P.-A., 'Maladie, pèlerinage et guérison au XIIe siècle: les miracles de Saint Gibrien à Reims', *Annales: Economies, Sociétés, Civilisations* 24 (1969), 1522–39.

Spiegel, G. M., *The Past as Text. The Theory and Practice of Medieval Historiography* (Baltimore, 1999).

Stallman-Pacitti, C. J., 'The Encomium of St Pancratius of Taormina by Gregory the Pagurite', *Byzantion* 60 (1990), 334–65.

Stanton, C. D., *Norman Naval Operations in the Mediterranean* (Woodbridge, 2011).

Stelladoro, M., *Agata, la martire* (Milan, 2005).

Stopani, R., *La Via Francigena. Una strada europea nell'Italia del medioevo* (Florence, 1988).

Storia della Sicilia e tradizione agiografica nella tarda antichità, Atti del convegno di studi, Catania, 20–22 maggio 1986, ed. S. Pricoco (Catania, 1988).

*Strazzeri, M. V., 'Una traduzione dal Greco ad uso dei normanni: la vita Latina di Sant'Elia lo Speleota', *ASCL* 59 (1992), 1–108.

Takayama, H., *The Administration of the Norman Kingdom of Sicily* (New York, 1993).

Thompson, A., *Cities of God. The Religion of the Italian Communes 1125–1325* (Pennsylvania, 2005).

Tolan, J. V., *Saracens. Islam in the Medieval Imagination* (New York, 2002).

Toubert, P., *Les Structures du Latium médiéval*, 2 vols (Rome, 1973).

Tra Roma e Gerusalemme nel Medioevo. Paessagi umani ed ambientali del pellegrinaggio meridionale, ed. M. Oldoni, 3 vols (Salerno, 2005).

Travaini, L., *La monetazione nell'Italia normanna* (Rome, 1995).

Turner, V., and Turner, E., *Image and Pilgrimage in Christian Culture. Anthropological Perspectives* (New York, 1978).

Tronzo, W., *The Cultures of his Kingdom. Roger II and the Cappella Palatina in Palermo* (Princeton, 1997).

Van Herwaarden, J., 'Pilgrimages and social prestige. Some reflections on a theme', *Wallfahrt und Alltag in Mittelalter und früher Neuzeit*, ed. G. Jaritz and B. Schuh (Vienna, 1992), 27–79.

Van Houts, E., 'Rouen as another Rome in the twelfth century', *Society and Culture in Medieval Rouen, 911–1300*, ed. L. Hicks and E. Brenner (Turnhout, 2013), 101–24.

Vanni, F., 'Itinerari, motivazioni e status dei pellegrini pregiubilari. Riflessioni e ipotesi alla luce di fonti e testimonianze del e sul meridione d'Italia', *Tra Roma e Gerusalemme*, ed. M. Oldoni, 3 vols (Salerno, 2005), i. 71–156.

Vauchez, A., *La Sainteté en occident aux derniers siècles du moyen âge: d'après les procès de canonisation et les documents hagiographiques, revised edn.* (Rome, 1988).

———'A twelfth-century novelty: the lay saints of urban Italy' in his *The Laity in the Middle Ages. Religious Beliefs and Devotional Practices* (Notre Dame, Ind., 1993), 51–72.

———'Du Gargano à Compostelle: la sainte pèlerine Bona de Pise (v. 1115–1207)', *Puer Apuliae*, ed., E. Cuozzo *et al.*, 2 vols (Paris, 2008), ii. 737–43.

Vetere, B., 'Il "Liber de Apparitione" e il culto di San Michele sul Gargano nella documentazione liturgica altomedievale', *Vetera Christianorum* 18 (1981), 423–42.

———'Cattedrale, santo patrono e cives', *Salerno nel medioevo*, ed. H. Taviani-Carozzi *et al.* (Galatina, 2000), 55–95.

Villani, M., 'Il contributo dell'onomastica e della toponomastica alla storia delle devozioni', *Pellegrinaggi e itinerari*, ed. G. Vitolo (Naples, 1999), 249–66.

Vincent, N., 'The pilgrimages of the Angevin kings of England', *Pilgrimage: The English Experience from Becket to Bunyan*, ed. C. Morris and P. Roberts (Cambridge, 2010), 12–45.

Vitolo, G., 'Città e chiesa nel mezzogiorno medievale: la processione del santo patrono a Salerno (sec. XII)', *Salerno nel XII secolo. Istituzioni, società, cultura*, Atti del convegno internazionale, guigno 1999, ed. P. Delogu and P. Peduto (Salerno, 2004), 134–45.

Von Falkenhausen, V., *Untersuchungen über die byzantinische Herrschaft in Süditalien vom 9. bis ins 11. Jahrhundert* (Wiesbaden, 1967).

———'I monasteri greci dell'Italia meridionale e della Sicilia dopo l'avvento dei normanni: continuità e mutamenti', *Il passagio dal domino bizantino allo stato normanno nell'Italia meridionale*, Atti del II convegno internazionale di studi sulla civiltà rupestre medievale nel mezzogiorno d'Italia, Taranto–Mottola, 31 Ottobre-4 novembre 1973 (Taranto, 1977), 197–229.

Vuolo, A., 'Monachesimo riformato e predicazione: la "vita" di San Giovanni da Matera (sec. XII)', *SM* 27 (1986), 69–121.

———'Agiografia beneventana', *Longobardia e longobardi nell'Italia meridionale. Le istituzioni ecclesiastiche*, ed. G. Andenna and G. Picasso (Milan, 1996), 199–237.

———'Le nave dei santi', *Pellegrinaggi e itinerari*, ed. G. Vitolo (Naples, 1999), 57–66.

Walsh, C., 'The role of the Normans in the development of the cult of St Katherine', *St Katherine of Alexandria. Texts and Contexts in Western Medieval Europe*, ed. J. Jenkins and K. J. Lewis (Turnhout, 2003), 19–35.

——*The Cult of St Katherine of Alexandria in Early Medieval Europe* (Aldershot, 2007).

Walsh, D. A., 'The iconography of the bronze doors of Barisanus of Trani', *Gesta* 21 (1982), 91–106.

Walter, C., *The Warrior Saints in Byzantine Art and Tradition* (Aldershot, 2003).

Watkins, C. S., *History and the Supernatural in Medieval England* (Cambridge, 2007).

Webb, D., *Patrons and Defenders. The Saints in the Italian City States* (London, 1996).

Webber, N., *The Evolution of Norman Identity, 911–1154* (Woodbridge, 2005).

White, L. T., *Latin Monasticism in Norman Sicily* (Cambridge, Mass., 1938).

White, S. D., *Custom, Kinship, and Gifts to Saints. The Laudatio Parentum in Western France, 1050–1150* (Chapel Hill, NC, 1988).

Wickham, C., *The Inheritance of Rome. A History of Europe from 400 to 1000* (London, 2009).

Wieruszowski, H., 'Roger II of Sicily, *Rex Tyrannus*, in twelfth-century political thought', *Speculum* 38 (1963), 46–78.

Yarrow, S., *Saints and their Communities. Miracle Stories in Twelfth-Century England* (Oxford, 2006).

Index

Made in the USA
Lexington, KY
22 October 2017